Post-Soul Satire

Post-Soul Satire

Black Identity after Civil Rights

Edited by Derek C. Maus and James J. Donahue

University Press of Mississippi / Jackson

www.upress.state.ms.us

The University Press of Mississippi is a member
of the Association of American University Presses.

First printing 2014

∞

Library of Congress Cataloging-in-Publication Data

Post-Soul Satire : Black Identity After Civil Rights / edited by
Derek C. Maus, James J. Donahue.
   pages cm
  Includes bibliographical references and index.
  ISBN 978-1-61703-997-3 (hardback) — ISBN 978-1-61703-998-0
(ebook) 1. African Americans in mass media. 2. African Americans—Race identity. 3. Satire, American—History and criticism.
4. African Americans in literature. 5. African Americans in
motion pictures. 6. African Americans in popular culture. 7.
African Americans—Intellectual life. I. Maus, Derek C., editor of
compilation. II. Donahue, James J., editor of compilation.
  P94.5.A372U565 2014
  302.23089'96073—dc23   2013046022

British Library Cataloging-in-Publication Data available

Contents

ix   Acknowledgments

xi   "Mommy, What's a Post-Soul Satirist?": An Introduction
Derek C. Maus

3   Post-Black Art and the Resurrection of African American Satire
Derek Conrad Murray

22   Blackness We Can Believe In: Authentic Blackness and the Evolution of
Aaron McGruder's *The Boondocks*
Terrence T. Tucker

38   The Lower Frequencies: Hip-Hop Satire in the New Millennium
Kinohi Nishikawa

56   Knock, Knock the Hustle: Resisting Commercialism in the African American
Family Film
Thomas R. Britt

68   Dirty Pretty Things: The Racial Grotesque and Contemporary Art
Michael B. Gillespie

85   Percival Everett's *Erasure*: That Drat Aporia When Black Satire Meets
"The Pleasure of the Text"
Gillian Johns

98   Who's Afraid of Post-Soul Satire?: Touré's "Black Widow" Trilogy in
The Portable Promised Land
Bertram D. Ashe

110   Touré, Ecstatic Consumption, and *Soul City*: Satire and the Problem
of Monoculture
Linda Furgerson Selzer

125   "I Felt Like I Was Part of the Troop": Satire, Feminist Narratology, and Community
       Brandon Manning

137   Pilgrims in an Unholy Land: Satire and the Challenge of African American
       Leadership in *The Boondocks* and *The White Boy Shuffle*
       Cameron Leader-Picone

150   Dissimulating Blackness: The Degenerative Satires of Paul Beatty and
       Percival Everett
       Christian Schmidt

162   "It's a Black Thang Maybe": Satirical Blackness in Percival Everett's *Erasure* and
       Adam Mansbach's *Angry Black White Boy*
       Danielle Fuentes Morgan

175   Coal, Charcoal, and Chocolate Comedy: The Satire of John Killens and
       Mat Johnson
       Keenan Norris

189   How a Mama on the Couch Evolves into a Black Man with Watermelon:
       George C. Wolfe, Suzan-Lori Parks, and the Theatre of "Colored Contradictions"
       Jennifer Larson

201   "Slaves? With Lines?": Trickster Aesthetic and Satirical Strategies in Two Plays
       by Lynn Nottage
       Aimee Zygmonski

214   Satirizing Satire: Symbolic Violence and Subversion in Spike Lee's *Bamboozled*
       Luvena Kopp

228   Charlie Murphy: American Storyteller
       James J. Donahue

240   Embodied and Disembodied Black Satire: From Chappelle and Crockett to
       Key & Peele
       Marvin McAllister

254   Television Satire in the Black Americas: Transnational Border Crossings in
       Chappelle's Show and *The Ity and Fancy Cat Show*
       Sam Vásquez

269   Afterword: From Pilloried to Post-Soul: The Future of African American Satire
       Darryl Dickson-Carr

281   Composite Bibliography

299   Contributors

307   Index

Acknowledgments

James J. Donahue would like to thank Maryemma Graham for her early instruction in, and passion for, African American literature. He would also like to thank Kathleen Kelly, Jerry Phillips, Robert Stanton, and Robert Tilton for their instruction and encouragement over the years.

Derek C. Maus would like to thank a host of teachers, mentors, and colleagues who have nudged him down the road to personal maturity and professional competence. These include: Tandy Cobb, Matilda (James) Buchanan, Susan May, Charles Brown, Charles Lance, Janet Tucker, William Tucker, Lynda Coon, David Edwards, M. Keith Booker, Suzanne MacRae, Keneth Kinnamon, Margaret Jones Bolsterli, Christopher Putney, Madeline Levine, Julius Rowan Raper, Pam Cooper, Philip F. Gura, Richard Rust, Susan Pearsall, Marc Fusco, Shannon Wooden, Kathleen Drowne, Christopher Goodson, Jeffrey Campbell, Robert Spirko, Bryan Sinche, Jonathan D'Amore, and the utterly inimitable force of nature that is Linda Wagner-Martin.

Together, we would like to thank our SUNY Potsdam colleagues Christine Doran, Libbie Freed, Christina Knopf, Jo Luloff, Donald McNutt, Liberty Stanavage, and John Youngblood for their good cheer, movie recommendations, calming advice, and/or their steadfast dedication to therapeutic evenings of bowling during the time in which this book was assembled.

Additionally, we wish to thank Camille Alexander, Renée Ater, Brendan Beirne, Daphne Brooks, Gena Chandler, Michelle Charles, Earle Fisher, Molly Hatcher, Regina Jones, Gerald Joyner, Jeannine King, Lovalerie King, Michael Levine, Paul Mahaffey, Claudia May, Sarah Newman, Laura Quinn, Joshunda Sanders, T'ai Smith, Asali Solomon, Ken Stiggers, Doug Taylor, Dana Williams, and Katherine Zakos, for their contributions to making this volume stronger.

We also wish to thank Leila W. Salisbury, Craig Gill, Katie Keene, Mallory Little, Courtney McCreary, Steve Yates, and all of the other staff at the University Press of Mississippi for their efforts in helping to produce the final version of this book. We especially wish to thank the anonymous reader whose comments in the initial stages of composition helped us improve the volume's coherence immensely.

Finally, we wish to thank Walter Biggins, whose enthusiasm contributed to this project in countless ways and without whom its publication would not have been possible.

"Mommy, What's a Post-Soul Satirist?": An Introduction

Derek C. Maus

Author/blogger Patrice Evans—a.k.a. "The Assimilated Negro"—published an online essay in 2008 that lauded the return of Aaron McGruder's *Boondocks* television series while simultaneously lamenting the seeming lack of satire in mainstream black culture: "Why does it seem like black people are missing the boat—treating the SS Satire like a slave ship? Sometimes it feels we only get the joke if it's the lowest common denominator, otherwise we have to put on our suits and let Oprah or Tyler Perry hold our hands and make sure there's a heavy Maya Angelou level of respect. . . . Where are the black branded satirists? Maybe we don't get it. Maybe we don't care to get it. Are there no satirists because of the lack of demand? It can't be for lack of opportunity. Every week we get a new race-event begging for lampooning: Watson, Jena 6, OJ, Imus, Michael Richards, Vick . . . all present unique opportunities to make a joke that might mean a little more to someone with melanin." Evans goes on to engage in some "speculative armchair psychology," wondering openly if what he calls the "critical," "literary," and "detached" elements of satire are not barriers to African Americans' participation in this mode of cultural commentary. He concludes by arguing that black-produced satire is more necessary than ever as part of continuing processes of racial uplift and cultural self-determination: "Satire at the highest level is practical art; content that can impact a bottom line through money as well as productive criticism. When we laugh at our literacy rate, or the ridiculousness of Flavor of Love, or how we can use race-events to get us on the red carpet, we are making light, but also setting the groundwork for raising the bar. After we laugh, we can settle into the reality of making the punch line dated. Then we can look for something new to laugh at and do it all over again. But until we loosen up and stop taking ourselves so seriously on everything, I fear we won't be taken seriously about anything" ("If You Can't"). Not surprisingly, Evans's forthright article garnered considerable attention around the Internet, in the process bringing a discussion that had been going on for some time within academia to a wider audience. This collection of scholarly essays about satire in contemporary African American culture is an effort to add further depth and breadth to these existing conversations, examining both the premises that undergird Evans's claims (among others) and particular works by a wide-ranging sample of African American satirists from the past thirty years.

Our volume builds on the solid foundation laid by Darryl Dickson-Carr's *African American Satire: The Sacredly Profane Novel* (2001); Paul Beatty's edited anthology of African American humor, *Hokum* (2006); Bambi Haggins's *Laughing Mad: The Black Comic Persona in Post-Soul America* (2007); Dana Williams's edited collection of essays, *African American Humor, Irony, and Satire* (2007); and Glenda Carpio's *Laughing Fit to Kill: Black Humor in the Fictions of Slavery* (2008). Additionally, there is a substantial body of work on individual African American writers such as Langston Hughes, George Schuyler, Wallace Thurman, Ishmael Reed, and Percival Everett that takes into account the role that satire plays in their oeuvres. Somewhat dismayingly, though, the MLA International Bibliography database still, as of October 2013, generated only sixty-six results for an "all fields" keyword search combining the terms *African American* and *satire*. We believe that this dramatically underscores the need for additional work on a powerful mode of artistic expression in contemporary (African) American culture.

It is our contention that there has, in fact, been a consistent—if also under-appreciated—flow of satirical creativity by African American artists during the past three decades. Moreover, this satire has been created alongside such emergent cultural-critical discourses as "the New Black Aesthetic," "post-soul" culture, and "post-blackness" that seek to delineate the contours of "the far-reaching and multifaceted reorganization of black life that has occurred over the last couple of decades" (Taylor 625) as a younger generation of African American artists who came of age after the Civil Rights Movement has risen to prominence. Paul C. Taylor's 2007 essay, "Post Black, Old Black," skillfully surveys both the convergences and the divergences among these perspectives. For the purpose of our collection of essays, Taylor's articulation of the ludic and self-critical tendencies among this younger generation of artists—what Greg Tate called the "open[ing] up of the entire 'text of blackness' for fun and games" (*Flyboy* 200)—is a foundational premise of why their satirical work merits closer consideration: "Where soul culture insisted on the seriousness of authenticity and positive images, post-soul culture revels in the contingency and diversity of blackness, and subjects the canon of positive images to subversion and parody—and appropriation" (631).

Almost all of the satirical works discussed within the essays in this collection were produced after 1989, the year in which Trey Ellis's landmark essay, "The New Black Aesthetic," appeared in *Callaloo* and boldly announced that African American artists "just have to be natural, [they] don't necessarily have to *wear* one" (236; emphasis in original). We have introduced this boundary in order to focus our collective critical attention on artists whose work is (intentionally or unintentionally) conversant with Ellis's sense of a sea change within African American culture. At the same time, we are following the lead of Ellis, Haggins, Carpio, and Williams in examining satire not just in its usual literary confines, but also in media such as television, film, theatre, music, stand-up comedy, the visual arts, and (most recently) the Internet. The decision to thus make our volume both broader and more immediate in focus than most of the sustained work done thus far on African American satire is consciously intended to appeal to a wider, interdisciplinary audience and to stimulate a critical examination of satire as a mode of artistic discourse rather than simply a literary (sub)genre. Thus far, the discussion of African American satire has been heavily literary-critical in nature, at least regarding book-length publications. Some outstanding, albeit sporadic work has appeared that has verged on applying this lens outside literature—for example, several scholarly articles have assessed visual artists such as Kara Walker, Hank Willis Thomas, and Glenn Ligon in terms of the ironic reappropriations of slavery-related images in their work; Daphne Brooks contributed a sanguine essay titled "Burnt Sugar: Post-Soul Satire and Rock Memory" to a collection on pop music published in 2004; and some of the criticism of dramatists Suzan-Lori Parks and George C. Wolfe addresses the satirical aspects of specific performances of their plays (rather than just the texts thereof)—but no single volume has synthesized analysis across multiple media beneath the capacious critical umbrella of satire. The twenty-one scholars who have contributed to this volume all feel strongly that the time has come to rectify that situation in order to understand how and why a pervasive satirical mood has influenced African American art over the past thirty years.

The unifying thread running through the essays that comprise this book is the inherently dual-vectored nature of post-soul satire. By this, we mean that the satirical subtext embedded within individual works simultaneously transmits its ethical critique at two distinct frequencies. The first of these is aimed at "in-group" audiences—that is, at African American readers, viewers, and so on—and generally offers a Horatian (namely, a relatively mild ridicule of vices and hypocrisy) satirical commentary on follies and self-destructive habits (compare to Evans's comment about "the ridiculousness of Flavor of Love") within the African American community. Alongside this, there is usually also a more Juvenalian (namely, scornful and morally indignant mockery) satire directed at political institutions, social practices, and cultural discourses that arise outside the community and constrain, denigrate, or otherwise harm it in some way. With a few notable exceptions, such as Wallace Thurman's *The Blacker the Berry* (1929) and *The Infants of Spring* (1932), George Schuyler's *Black No More* (1931), and Langston Hughes's "Simple" stories—the latter tendency predominated in African American satire until relatively recently, when African American satirists increasingly: "provide[d] the critiques of his or her community that might otherwise be elided [in order to] push African Americans forward to improve their liminal, physical, and economic conditions" (Dickson-Carr 18). Ellis suggests a possible explanation for this shift when he argues that the artists of the New Black Aesthetic (NBA) are what he calls cultural mulattoes: "Just as a genetic mulatto is a black person of mixed parents who can often get along fine with his white grandparents, a cultural mulatto, educated by a multi-racial mix of cultures, can also navigate easily in the white world. And it is by and large this rapidly growing group of cultural mulattoes that fuels the NBA. We no longer need to deny or suppress any part of our complicated and sometimes contradictory cultural baggage to please either white people or black" (235). Twenty-two years later, Michael Eric Dyson echoes Ellis in noting the detachment from both internal and external racial expectations: "In Black communities the artist has often been burdened with what James Baldwin called the 'obligation of representation.' But now part of what it means to be black is [that] I can be true to what I believe. The reason why Black artists have the leisure not to be obsessed with what kind of Blackness is authentic or legitimate is because people who were obsessed with Blackness as legitimate or authentic paved the way" (quoted in Touré, *Who's Afraid* 29–30).

The potentially oxymoronic notion of art that is subversively respectful toward its ancestors shows up repeatedly in the theorizations of what makes contemporary African American cultural discourse distinct from that of previous periods. In his *Who's Afraid of Post-Blackness?* (2011), Touré notes that African American culture has "had bold, original thinkers who took Black identity to new places and challenged the traditional identity boundaries for decades—Prince, Basquiat, Pryor, Hendrix, Sly, Baldwin, Ellison, Miles, George Clinton, Octavia Butler, Nina Simone, Ornette Coleman, Thelonious Monk, Zora Neale Hurston, and on and on" (23). Likewise, Ellis realized that the New Black Aesthetic was not something that arose sui generis in the 1980s, but rather was built on a foundation laid by members of the very generation against which NBA artists were rebelling:

Our spiritual and often biological older brothers and sisters, those who were artistically coming of age just as the bloom of Mr. Baraka's Black Arts Movement was beginning to fade, are our constant icons. Though during the mid-seventies they were a minority of the black-arts community, branded either counter-revolutionary, too artsy or just not good propagandists, nevertheless avant-garde artists like novelists Ishmael Reed, Clarence Major, Toni Morrison, and John Edgar Wideman; George Clinton . . . [,] David Hammons[, and] . . . Richard Pryor . . . all helped forge our current aesthetic. Stripping themselves of both white envy and self-hate they produced supersophisticated black art that either expanded or exploded the old definitions of blackness, showing us as the intricate, uncategorizeable folks we had always known ourselves to be. (237)

In the process of expanding the "post-soul aesthetic" (a term coined by Nelson George in 1992), Mark Anthony Neal identified a notable swing away from "essential notions of blackness to metanarratives on blackness, without any nostalgic allegiance to the past . . . , but firmly in grasp of the existential concerns of this brave new world" (3). Neal's rejection of "nostalgic allegiance" does not preclude the possibility of acknowledging the past and the sacrifices made on behalf of future generations by artistic and political forebears; it only suggests that any debt of gratitude owed to them neither includes uncritical acceptance nor precludes pointed satirical subversion.

Touré calls these trailblazers "identity liberals" and contends that "their ranks are multiplying, maybe even exponentializing," among the younger generation of artists who produced the bulk of the work examined in this volume (*Who's Afraid* 23). Whether as an avant-garde in the 1960s and 1970s or as a cadre that "finally ha[s] the numbers to leverage this point of view" (Ellis, "New Black Aesthetic" 237) as of the late 1980s, the artists of the post-soul aesthetic are engaged in a "radical reimagining of the contemporary African-American experience, [and are] attempting to liberate contemporary interpretations of that experience from sensibilities that were formalized and institutionalized during earlier social paradigms" (M. Neal 3). Such sensibilities obviously include the dominant "white gaze" (Touré, *Who's Afraid* 29), and Ellis remains clear-eyed that "despite this current buppie artist boom, most black Americans have seldom had it worse" ("New Black Aesthetic" 239); but the post-soul generation also normalizes a strident, frequently comedic self-critical tenor that remained relatively marginal or even taboo during earlier periods such as the Harlem Renaissance or the Black Arts Movement.

Dickson-Carr notes that African American critics (including no less a luminary than W. E. B. Du Bois) have long had an "aversion to overt humor" (122), a position he considers grounded in a fundamental misunderstanding of how and why ironic forms of comedy direct their ridicule at their objects. During the late 1960s and early 1970s, this aversion was coupled with the fact that "in the case of many *black* satirists, this object could easily include the black community itself, which directly contradicts the Black Arts movement's call for racial unity" (123; emphasis in original). Given that "intragroup satire, even that which may indict the satirist, is frequently well within the bounds of fair play," Dickson-Carr observes that literary satirists from this period such as Douglas Turner Ward, William Melvin Kelley, John Oliver Killens, and Ishmael Reed often ran a difficult gauntlet between white and black critics, who viewed them as ungrateful complainers and race traitors, respectively (123–124).

In the wake of the tenuous successes of the Civil Rights Movement, though, recent generations of African American artists have more frequently and more pervasively included the reflexive vector of satire in their works. Despite the fact that few, if any, satirical works by African Americans entirely abandon the externally focused satirical vector in favor of the self-critical mode, engaging in intragroup satire risks charges of airing "house business" that presents a less-than-noble picture of the race to an audience of outsiders already disinclined to accept African Americans as truly equal partners in American society. In her essay "Aaron McGruder: Post-Racial Obama Hater?," Natalie Hopkinson notes with some frustration that a protective mentality she equates with living in a household with "elementary-age kids" persists in the African American community: "As a community, black people have house business. When you are a minority group under siege, some secrets are necessary for your own self-preservation." Hopkinson claims that the pointed criticisms of Barack Obama that appeared in the third season of McGruder's *Boondocks* are a sign that the members of the African American community are publicly "acknowledging the complex and often conflicting emotions that come with this historic milestone of having a black president" rather than simply retreating to the relative safety of a uniform and uncritical perspective. She echoes Evans's contention that African Americans should "loosen up and stop taking ourselves so seriously on everything" in order to be "taken seriously on anything" when she writes that "I'm happy that we are a step closer to eliminating this 'house business' in the black community. It's a sign that we're taking our seats at the grown-up table" (Hopkinson).[1]

The multivectored satirical discourse of recent years represents an explicit challenge to the long-standing mandate—exemplified variously by Alain Locke's "New Negro" concept from the Harlem Renaissance and by the "Black Aesthetic" articulated by Larry Neal and others involved in the Black Arts Movement—that African American artists have to use their talents for the "uplift" and empowerment of the community as a whole, in the process making sure that house business is not revealed to the wider culture. While recounting an incident in which the performance artist William Pope.L was angrily confronted by a fellow African American who believed him to be proffering a racially damaging image in depicting a black man in a seemingly subservient and degraded position (the performance was intended as a symbolic commentary on homelessness), Touré claims that the "imperative to unity is sometimes a disguised weapon that someone can use to try to enforce social control. The moment gives us two men with opposing conceptions of how to uplift the race coming unto conflict, and because one did not understand the other's method, he incorrectly judged him a race traitor" (*Who's Afraid?* 31). Adam Mansbach fictionally depicts a similar tension in his novel *Angry Black White Boy* (2005) when an African American character who has just commented sarcastically about the names black parents give to their children "felt a pang of guilt for making such jokes in front of a whiteboy, and winced as if the red-black-and-green Afropick of race pride had just flown across the room and jabbed him in the ass" (37). Post-soul satirists reject—albeit not always comfortably, as Dave Chappelle's well-documented anxiety with the success of his Comedy Central television series shows—the notion that airing house business is synonymous with being a "race traitor." Furthermore, the inroads that black artists have made in finding and developing audiences for nonliterary works have not only significantly broadened the potential avenues for satirical expression, but have also (as the list of missed opportunities enumerated in the quote from Evans above suggests) expanded the field of ready objects of African American satire. Post-soul satire, thus, widens both its rhetorical and its formal scope to comment critically not only upon the oppressive political, economic, and social forces that still encircle African American culture in the late twentieth and early twenty-first centuries, but also upon the multitude of ways in which African Americans have misused their hard-won freedoms and thereby hindered their own ascendance to equality.

In one of the short essays he contributes as the editor of *Hokum: An Anthology of African-American Humor*, Paul Beatty makes a number of forthright humorous comparisons that illustrate the latter tendency, claiming that when he was growing up in the 1960s, "being black . . . was like growing up in East Germany. The sloganeering. The uplifting songs. No electricity. No long-distance phone service. The insufferable, hopelessly vague daily admonishments to 'grow up and be somebody'" (105). He suggests that the "What Not to Be list" provided by the "almighty irrefutable Führer of the furor the Reverend Jesse Jackson" specified the following: "Don't be no nigger. Don't be no junkie. Don't be talkin' about my mama.

xviii   Derek C. Maus

And, first and foremost, don't be no fool" (105–106). This last admonition—which he claims was enforced through "numerous beatings, detentions, and dunce-capped public self-criticisms"—is especially damning for Beatty, since he "was an inveterate fool, and a wry one at that" in a society that allowed "no room for wryness" (106). However, Beatty joins Ellis, George, and others in noting that "in the mid-eighties . . . the fool—along with segregation, pornography, child molesters, and unabashed corporate greed—received a quasi-reprieve," allowing "the trickster's public histrionics . . . to clear enough head space to allow for some wry, American, backstage blackness" (106).[2]

Such a position is rife with literal and metaphorical peril—the company that Beatty's "fool" keeps in "quasi-reprieve" in the passage above is, after all, questionable at best—and, as such, it is hardly surprising that many of the artists and works discussed within this collection of essays have met with a lukewarm or even hostile reception by their audiences both inside and outside the African American community. Satirists have historically not been the most popular artists of their time, and the intertwined recent tendencies towards commodifying and simplifying the arts and the media have not changed that situation for the better. To discuss satire effectively requires extensive discussion of the cultural and historical discourses in which it is embedded, since those discourses are most often the "targets" of the satire itself, even when they are embodied within recognizable individuals. In his introduction to a 2007 issue of *African American Review* devoted entirely to discussion of the post-soul aesthetic, Bertram D. Ashe articulates the "core issues" of this aesthetic as "the peculiar pains, pleasures, and problems of race in the post–Civil Rights Movement United States; the use of nontraditionally black cultural influences in their work; and the resultant exploration of the boundaries of blackness." Ashe asserts that "these issues will remain as long as there are discrete cultural categories such as 'black' and 'white' and as long as there are Americans who live their lives believing separate and distinct cultural practices can be assigned to each. For there, in the unstable, wobbly interstices of those two categories, is where the post-soul aesthetic lives" ("Theorizing" 611). George Clinton's spoken-word lyrics to the 1970 song, "Mommy, What's a Funkadelic?," express the parameters of those "interstices" eloquently:

> *I recall when I left a little town in North Carolina, I tried to escape this music.*
> *I said it was for the old country folks. I went to New York. Got slick.*
> *Got my hair made. I was cool, I was cool.*
> *But I had no groove, no groove, no groove, no groove, no groove.*
> *I had no groove. But here it comes! But now, fly on, baby.* (Funkadelic)

Formulated nearly two decades later, the post-soul aesthetic tries also to strike a balance between the overly "slick" and "cool" new perspective and anything associated with the "old country folks." Balance between these two is necessary in order to avoid losing the "groove" that defines not only Funkadelic's music (which the title of the band's 1978 album suggests will unite *One Nation Under a Groove*) but also post-soul art within a more expansive, yet still distinct black identity. Benji Cooper, the narrator of Colson Whitehead's *Sag Harbor* (2009), symbolizes this new identity as he describes his relationship to an old "movie palace" in his upper Manhattan neighborhood: "The Olympia had a new marquee of hot-pink neon and new seats with red upholstery, but was still beset by a few gremlins. . . . The curtains always bugged me, apart from the obvious way they bothered everyone else. The curtains were just wrong in there, considering the dingy exploitation fare we had paid to see, the slasher flicks, the low-budget pyrotechnics of time-traveling Terminators. It was a sentimental relic of the time when people came to the Olympia for the stage spectacles of a kinder, classier age, and had to place in our lives. As a former twin, I liked things separate. You are there, me over here. Be nostalgic for the old days, but do it over there on your own time. Right here is the way things are now." (17–18) These last two sentences not only encapsulate the perspective of this quintessentially post-soul bildungsroman, but also of "cultural mulattoes" like Benji (and Whitehead) in general.

To describe the overarching "cultural work" performed by these artists residing in the "unstable, wobbly interstices" between extant racial categories, Ashe coins the term *blaxploration*, which he defines as follows: "These artists and texts trouble blackness, they worry blackness; they stir it up, touch it, feel it out, and hold it up for examination in ways that depart significantly from previous—and necessary—preoccupations with struggling for political freedom, or with an attempt to establish and sustain a coherent black identity. Still, from my vantage point, this 'troubling' of blackness by post-soul writers is ultimately done in service to black people" (614). We would argue that the addition of this "troubling of blackness . . . in service to black people" to the more traditional African American satirical practice of deriding external forces of discrimination and subjugation is the primary defining characteristic of post-soul satire, inasmuch as satire's primary function—especially in its quintessentially postmodern subversive strain—is to destabilize and ultimately to undermine morally or ethically suspect behaviors and/or beliefs wherever they are found. The essays within this collection all work to discern how the wonderfully diverse markers, structures, tones, and rhythms of post-soul satirical discourse achieve both their internally and externally focused effects within a broad range of works across several media.

Our book opens with a quintet of essays that collectively establish the critical discourses of blaxploration that are applicable across the selection of primary texts that the remainder of the collection examines. Derek Conrad Murray undertakes a critical survey of a number of the most prominent contemporary visual artists whose satirical work engages with the *post-black* designation coined by the curator of the Studio Museum in Harlem, Thelma Golden, and the artist Glenn Ligon for a show titled *Freestyle* in 2001. Although far from universally accepted by either critics or the artists labeled by it, this term has helped delineate a generational shift in subject matter, style, and rhetoric within the visual arts that parallels similar developments in other creative media. Terrence T. Tucker picks up this thread by examining the ways in which both the comic strip and the televised forms of McGruder's *Boondocks* use "comic rage" to undermine existing notions of race in American culture, especially the idea of a monolithic and authentic blackness. Kinohi Nishikawa's essay about the recent development of what he calls "hip-hop satirists" expands the grounds of this discussion into the realm of contemporary music. The artists he analyzes go beyond the strident critiques of the "socially conscious" rappers of the past and instead engage in a metacommentary that questions and destabilizes the racialized assumptions that have come to pervade the multibillion-dollar hip-hop industry. Thomas R. Britt shifts the critical focus on this satirical metadiscourse into the realm of Hollywood, looking specifically at the ways in which three films—none of which achieved critical or commercial success—satirized the "self-destroying commercial forces of modern mainstream entertainment," specifically their pernicious influence on African American culture. Finally, Michael B. Gillespie provides the coda for this opening section by explicating the use of what he calls the "racial grotesque" as a satirical technique in recent works of art from several media. He argues that the racial grotesque is a means of understanding how contemporary artists are recontextualizing material objects associated with the racist legacy of slavery and using them to tell new stories that uncouple African Americans from a past that inherently diminishes their humanity.

The next seven essays function together as a discussion that centers around three of the most significant post-soul literary lions: Paul Beatty, Percival Everett, and Touré. Each of these writers has produced influential works of fictional satire while also offering extensive commentary in other settings on the major themes that appear in those fictions. As such, their writings serve as a valuable point of departure for critical comparisons with a wide range of other literary and nonliterary artists. Moreover, Beatty, Everett, Touré, and all of the other writers with whom their work is being compared in this section, directly and indirectly engage with the critical discourses enumerated in the opening quintet; this subsequent septet, then, solidifies the conceptual affinities between satirical modes of expression found in nonliterary media and those present in the more traditional literary realm.

Gillian Johns starts things off by analyzing Everett's *Erasure* (2001) as a novel that cautions against disengaged reading, particularly of satirical texts, in order to avoid falling into interpretive habits that severely constrain the critical potential of such texts. Bertram D. Ashe and Linda Furgerson Selzer follow this with a pair of essays that examine fictional works by Touré through the lens of his nonfictional writing. Ashe compares the "satirical tension between a black vernacular-inspired traditional blackness and an expansive, non-traditional blackness" in Touré's *The Portable Promised Land* (2002) with his critique of black essentialism in *Who's Afraid of Post-Blackness?*, arguing that the latter is less compelling precisely because it lacks the former's tension. Selzer argues that Touré's novel *Soul City* (2009) simultaneously offers celebration and satirical criticism of what she calls "ecstatic consumption" of hip-hop culture as a process of creating and maintaining a black communal identity. Brandon Manning next offers a rejoinder to what he calls the androcentric tendency of post-soul satires such as *Erasure* and Ellis's *Platitudes* (1988). He develops a feminist narratological lens and applies it to ZZ Packer's short story "Brownies." He asserts that such an approach reveals a satirical rhetoric that seeks to build a communal and positive relationship between author and reader rather than simply uniting the two in marginalizing the "target" of the satire, a process that Manning claims has often unfairly demonized African American women.

The final three essays in this section pivot around Beatty and Everett and the ways in which their works satirize a host of stale discourses about blackness and its representation. Cameron Leader-Picone begins by comparing the ways in which both Beatty's *The White Boy Shuffle* (1996) and McGruder's *Boondocks* satirically undermine the notion that the contemporary African American community is diminished by a seeming lack of heroic leaders in the mold of Dr. Martin Luther King Jr. Christian Schmidt follows up by analyzing Beatty's *Slumberland* and two novels by Everett as metafictional parodies that satirize not only clichéd tropes of blackness in the African American literary canon but also the very presumption that blackness can (or should) be definitively represented. Lastly, Danielle Fuentes Morgan compares *Erasure* with Adam Mansbach's *Angry Black White Boy* as exemplary post-soul novels that illustrate the manner in which racialization has become "so pervasive that it persists even in the absence of signifiers," particularly those pertaining to authorship and/or agency.

Although the next four essays do not share any primary texts in common, they intertwine critically and thematically in providing an interdisciplinary analysis of the historical recalibration of collective and individual black identity that Ellis, George, Golden, Ligon, and others have articulated over the past twenty-five years. Keenan Norris begins by comparing two satirical depictions of Harlem—John Killens's *The Cotillion* (1968) and Mat Johnson's *Hunting in Harlem* (2003)—regarding the way the former valorizes the very Afrocentric ideology that the latter deems insufficient for living in the era of the New Black Aesthetic. Jennifer Larson similarly focuses on this generational shift in values, discussing satirical dramatic works by George C. Wolfe and Suzan-Lori Parks in the context of their quintessentially post-soul calls to embrace a more inclusive, possibly even self-contradictory notion of black identity. Remaining in the realm of drama, Aimee Zygmonski looks at how Lynn Nottage's plays, *Fabulation* (2004) and *By the Way, Meet Vera Stark* (2011), utilize characters who function as quasi-folkloric "trickster" figures in broadly satirizing racial stereotypes and the processes by which they are perpetuated. Luvena Kopp moves the discussion into the realm of film once again, using sociologist Pierre Bourdieu's concept of "symbolic violence" to analyze Spike Lee's *Bamboozled* (2000). She reads the film as a satire that targets not just overtly racist cultural practices like minstrelsy but also more subtly insidious forms of discrimination like corporate misappropriation of black artistry that are obscured and perpetuated by the supposedly post-racial "color blindness" of contemporary American society.

The final section of our volume takes a close critical look at perhaps the best-known post-soul satirist, Dave Chappelle. His *Chappelle's Show* television program achieved unprecedented ratings for the Comedy Central network during its brief run, and the DVD sales for the series set records. Chappelle has cited his discomfort with the fact that many of the characters he created for the show became iconic figures in their own right as one of the reasons he suddenly departed the program in the midst of filming its third season ("Chappelle's Story"). Although Evans seems to feel that few artists stepped into the void created by Chappelle's departure, the closing trio of essays both offers interpretations of Chappelle's satire on its own and examines how it relates to a number of more recent black satirists on television. James J. Donahue starts this section by examining two of Chappelle's best-known skits, a pair of parodic-satiric recreations of encounters that Chappelle's co-star, Charlie Murphy, had with Rick James and Prince. Donahue claims that these skits participate in the long-standing literary tradition of the "tall tale" to offer a broad satirical commentary on targets both within and outside the African American community. Marvin McAllister picks up by comparing Chappelle with three more recent television comedians: Affion Crockett, Jordan Peele, and Keegan-Michael Key. McAllister argues that each of these men has produced relatively simplistic and mean-spirited work that "abdicate[s] the core responsibilities of satire" by relying overly on "low" physical comedy. He also notes, however, that each has produced what he calls "disembodied" satires that not only convey more substantive social commentary but even repair some of the damage of their own "embodied" satirical miscues. Sam Vásquez concludes this section with a comparative analysis of *Chappelle's Show* and the popular Jamaican television series *Ity and Fancy Cat*, arguing that "although both programs usefully explore racism as being indebted to long-established, institutional paradigms," the latter ultimately offers a more inclusive model of communal identity for its audience as an antidote. Her analysis offers a valuable stimulus to future research in demonstrating the value of hemispheric and transnational critical perspectives on satire in general and black satire in particular.

The collection closes with an afterword by one of the godparents of the critical study of African American satire, Darryl Dickson-Carr. His essay not only offers a snapshot of the current state of African American satire and the criticism thereof, but also muses philosophically on some of the directions in which both might develop in coming years. It is our hope that his thoughts in this regard serve to punctuate the myriad approaches taken by the other contributors, all of which raise provocative questions for which we hope our readers will be motivated to formulate answers. In the meantime, this book offers what we hope is a reassuring and resounding answer to Patrice Evans's question, "Where are all the black branded satirists?" Whether there are enough of them (or enough women among them, or enough political diversity among them, or enough thematic diversity among them, or . . .) is another question altogether, one that will have to wait for the next wave of readers, writers, and critics. But now—as George Clinton and Mark Anthony Neal might say in two-part harmony—fly on, soul babies!

Notes

1. Percival Everett likewise espouses comic satire as a means of stimulating self-analysis: "Humor is an interesting thing. It's hard to do, but it allows you certain strategic advantages. If you can get someone laughing, then you can make them feel like shit a lot more easily" (quoted in Shavers 48).

2. Beatty fictionally revisits the metaphor of a de-racializing trickster subverting a rigidly authoritative discourse like that of East Germany in his novel *Slumberland*, which was published in 2008, two years after *Hokum*.

Post-Soul Satire

Post-Black Art and the Resurrection of African American Satire

Derek Conrad Murray

A proliferation of the prefix "post-" has come to mark oppositional artistic practices. New categories of art, first labeled *postmodern* (in reaction to modernist standards of art) and *postcolonial* (that is to say, proceeding from the colonial experience), emerged as a means of capturing an ethos in art, culture, and scholarship.

In the early 1990s Kwame Anthony Appiah, building upon the theorization of Fredric Jameson and others, unpacked the "post" of postmodernism and the "post" of postcolonialism as in fact divergent. Appiah argued that postcoloniality suggested something more than merely "after" the colonial; it pointed toward a new brand of scholarship and cultural production connected to an imaginary that exists between the colonizer and the colonized. More specifically, he described the inhabitants of this imaginary as "a comprador intelligentsia: a relatively small, Western-style, Western-trained group of writers and thinkers, who mediate the trade in cultural commodities of world capitalism at the periphery" (Appiah 348). These entities, he argued, are distinct from the home culture they purport to represent, savvy about the commodification of that same culture, yet operating from the margins of Western centers as emissaries for colonized locales. In effect they are neither colonizer nor colonized, but a third something birthed from the encounter and nurtured by global capitalist enterprise. "Perhaps," Appiah explained, "the predicament of the postcolonial intellectual is simply that as intellectuals—a category instituted in black Africa by colonialism—we are, indeed, always at the risk of becoming otherness machines, with the manufacture of alterity as our principal role" (356).

The "post" of postmodernism, on the other hand, constituted a space-clearing gesture (Appiah 346) that was consistent with the multiple modernities springing up globally, making voice and place for those formerly underrepresented or erased. Needless to say, this was inextricably tied to the coming of advanced capitalism: "To sell oneself and one's products as art in the market-place," Appiah wrote, "one must, above all, clear a space in which one is distinguished from other producers and products—and one does this by the construction and the marking of differences" (356). The fluid definition of "post," the profitable marking of otherness within the context of global capitalism, and the making of a space for oneself—these all come to bear upon more recent terminologies in vogue, particularly *post-black* as a marker of emergent generations of cultural producers whose works significantly depart from their forebears'. It refers to a time "after" Black Power but is indeed fraught and embroiled in a complicated relationship to the notion of liberation. Do post-black artists manufacture packaged notions of otherness for the sake of market success? Are so-called post-black visual artists merely, as Appiah described in relation to the postcolonial, under the constant threat of becoming "otherness machines" that churn out marketable alterity?

The unpacking of the term *post-black* and the deployment of satire as a key delineating strategy of this emerging group of artists is the subject of my investigation. An important component of satire is that it brashly surpasses the comfort zone, challenging every audience. Post-blackness does not deal with the problem of racism by merely making external critiques of the dominant culture's bigotry; it also looks inward and critiques the black community's own complicity with normative standards that cut across race, gender, and sexuality.

The term *post-black* emerged in a casual conversation between artist Glenn Ligon and curator Thelma Golden in regard to the latter's *Freestyle* exhibition, held at the Studio Museum in Harlem in 2001. Since finding its way rather inauspiciously into the art world's consciousness, it has produced a discourse all its own and is hotly debated to this day, inspiring journalists and cultural critics outside of the visual arts to ponder the term's larger social impacts. Journalist and author Touré's recent book, *Who's Afraid of Post-Blackness: What It Means to Be Black Now* (2011), follows Ytasha L. Womack and Derek T. Dingle's *Post Black: How a New Generation Is Redefining African American Identity* (2010). Both texts have taken on the wildly unpopular challenge of redefining black identity beyond essentialism, self-ghettoization, and compulsory racial politics. The result has been the reemergence of a divisive intracultural debate about post-racialism and the policing of *proper* blackness by what Touré calls America's "self-appointed identity cops" within the African American community.[1] Touré's book has received great attention, garnering stellar reviews in the *New York Times* and the *New York Review of Books*.

Post-blackness resonates because it articulates the frustrations of young African American artists (the post–civil rights generation) around notions of identity and belongingness that they perceived to be stifling, reductive, and exclusionary. For many, blackness is a nationalist cultural politics that produced a set of values and visual expressions overly concerned with recovering black male dignity by advocating for traditionally heterosexual archetypes of patriarchal strength, domination, and virility. Post-blackness can also be understood as issuing from a general attitude of ambivalence toward compulsory solidarity, insularity, and intracommunity demands to maintain a sense of racial pride. It could also be said that there is a broad rejection of the generational passing down of racial trauma and the expectation that the post–civil rights contingent will carry the torch of survivorship and anti-racist politics. The elusiveness of post-blackness makes it difficult to fully define, and certainly not all African American artists grouped under this banner can easily be encapsulated by it. It is more of an ethos than a dictum; nevertheless it continues to define a generation of artists, many of whom seek to escape the limitations imposed by race.

The prevailing criticism of the post-black ethos is that its artists are enthusiastic participants in the market and gleefully indulge the glittery spoils of success at the expense of social engagement. Post-black visual art, exemplified by the work of Kehinde Wiley, Mickalene Thomas, Layla Ali, Iona Rozeal Brown, Kori Newkirk—and more recently by Kalup Linzy and Rashaad Newsome—has fully embraced the extreme marketability of black corporeality (Murray and Murray, "On Art" 88–93). Wiley's oeuvre exemplifies this approach, which could best be defined as an unabashed embrace of market demand for the visual signifiers of blackness. This is not asserted to demean the work of these individuals; quite the opposite is true. African American artists produce their work in an enduring climate of racial hostility and dismissiveness and in conditions where the very notion of black artistic achievement is continually called into question. My interest issues from the absence of overt political engagement in the work of many young black artists, as well as disengagement with the troubling realities of contemporary black life. Often, the works deceptively seem to present a series of cleverly constructed visual quips that use the black body to create readily saleable objects. Post-blackness speaks to a desire for creative freedom and a need to liberate oneself from the often-suffocating nature of racial polemics. It simultaneously articulates a departure from a heteronormative definition of blackness that was often restricting and negating (as with the Civil Rights and Black Power Movement representations). African American art in the 1980s and 1990s was politically oppositional vis-à-vis the dominant white, patriarchal culture and concerned with the effects of intolerance on black subjecthood. These concerns have been largely abandoned and have given way to an aesthetic that appears very similar to former expressions, only drained of didactic political or historical content. Nevertheless, if one were to characterize post-blackness as a type of collective consciousness, the satirical and often contradictory engagement with the signifiers of black-ness renders it strange, unknowable, and open to the process of significa-tion: a queering of blackness, so to speak.

But the term seems to also convey the psychic dualities, the "two-ness" that W. E. B. Du Bois speaks about in his notion of "double consciousness." Thelma Golden described post-blackness in contradictory terms: as a type of cognitive dissonance, whereby emergent African American artists produce work about blackness but simultaneously seek to transcend the limitations often imposed by race. In his catalog essay for *30 Americans* (2008–2012), an exhibition to which I will return, curator Franklin Sirmans discussed Golden's now infamous *Freestyle* show, pondering its impact as an inspira-tion for *30 Americans* and questioning the efficacy of black-themed exhibi-tions: "Considering that Thelma Golden's 2001 exhibition 'Freestyle'—one of the inspirations for this exhibition—posited the fact that a show of black artists could in fact be post-black in subject matter, this presentation also questions the term and wantonly throws it into flux" (Sirmans 40). While acknowledging it as a contested term, Sirmans apparently sees post-black-ness as a potential departure from the limiting lens through which we regu-larly consume and contemplate black cultural production. However, he does not see it as a rejection of the visual and political rhetorics of black identity among the artists and scholars who define the genre. In short, black-themed exhibitions are no longer implicitly shorthand for discussions about race, as contradictory and perplexing as that may seem. Post-blackness opens up the possibility for a type of apolitical play (with the visual signifiers of black identity) that is not engaged with race discourse per se, but rather with the cultural currency and visual force of black bodies in American society. But what is most striking about the current generation is that its work marks a departure from the black avant-garde of the late 1960s and 1970s, a gen-eration of artists whose production was self-consciously *about* race. Artists such as Robert Colescott, Betye Saar, and David Hammons mark a time when black visual producers were reconsidering the work of art as a concep-tual and often political tool and by extension broadened our understanding of how race and representation function as social constructs (Sirmans 41).

This trajectory continued on through the 1980s and 1990s, when iden-tity politics reigned supreme in the art world. Golden's *Freestyle* exhibition introduced twenty-eight emerging black artists who sought to redefine the genre of African American art, stripping it of its oppositional politics, its didacticism, and its essentialisms while simultaneously refusing to abandon the black body as a representational tool. The show marked what Kobena

Mercer would call a "rupture and re-articulation of black identity" in which the relations of race, class, and culture are remixed ("Black Art" 250). The post-black generation that emerged became a beacon for a type of post–civil rights privilege, and its work was largely void of the social antagonisms and racial polemics that had come to define black art up to that point.

What strikes me as more urgent, however, is that post-blackness represents a crisis in black artistic production that issues from a desire to be liberated from racial polemics, nostalgia, and belongingness while trying to negotiate voracious market demand for the black body. This represents a conundrum of sorts. African American artists born in the 1970s and later are particularly impacted by this existential crisis, because many have shed communal bonds and comforts of membership by not conforming to "heritage" representations that foreground cultural preservation, even though commercial interest in the visualization of blackness is more fervent than ever. But what happens when an African American artist no longer sees the critical potential of the black body—or has become disinterested in the political and polemical importance of its imaging—a cultural climate that demands its persistent visualization? Is what one sees on the walls of galleries and museums across the U.S. conceptually clever and visually rich depictions of abject blackness that are ultimately empty signifiers? At what point did the black body officially become a fetish object? Greg Tate ponders this phenomenon in regard to the so-called dominant culture's ongoing lust for all things black: "What has always struck Black observers of this phenomenon isn't just the irony of white America fiending for Blackness when it was once debated whether Africans even had souls. It's also the way they have always tried to erase the Black presence from whatever Black thing they took a shine to" (Tate, "Introduction" 2).

Tate's interest in white desire to consume the Other (as image) while simultaneously rejecting its presence—or historical burden—is actually quite meaningful when endeavoring to understand both the aesthetics and the reception of recent forms of black art. Given the tenuous state of race relations in America, one would be led to believe that the souls of black folk are as embattled today as they were in 1903, when W. E. B. Du Bois first crafted those epochal words. I want to place emphasis on the notion of "soullessness" as a descriptor for the rather hollow use of the racialized body in post-black aesthetics. Tate suggests that white viewers want the body, but not the burden, and what we now see are commoditized images of an emptied ethnic subjectivity, bereft of dialogic intent. Many of these works depict an aesthetic of ennui and disavowal (in regards to the politics of blackness) or they endeavor to broaden an investigation into the mechanisms of intolerance and violence that are universal or to explore crosscultural hybridization. I contend that it is not that these works lack politics, in fact, but that the focus of their politics has broken from the past.

It may be hard to imagine a black art that is ambivalent in its engagement with racial politics. Is it even possible? The black-themed exhibition was once the staging ground for racial sermonizing, despite the works' ultimate status as commodity objects. In addition to *Freestyle*, the Whitney Museum's 1994 *Black Male: Representations of Masculinity in Contemporary American Art*, the Studio Museum in Harlem's 2006 *Frequency* (both curated by Thelma Golden), and the Contemporary Arts Museum Houston's 2005 *Double Consciousness: Black Conceptual Art since 1970* (curated by Valerie Cassel Oliver) are each exemplars of major exhibitions dedicated to redefining our relationship to what historian Darby English has termed "black representational space" (27). Each of these exhibitions explored the intricacies of black identity and its attendant politics and ideologies to various degrees, but since the 1993 Whitney Biennial exhibition ushered in a sense of legitimacy around identity politics in art discourse, there has been a broad shifting away from serious racial conversation toward an embrace of what could be termed a satirical turn in black art production. Curated by Elisabeth Sussman, John G. Hanhardt, Thelma Golden, and Lisa Phillips, the 1993 Biennial was one of the most politically aggressive, controversial, and altogether hated exhibitions in American history because of its engagement with issues related to identity and difference. Prior to the 1993 edition of the Biennial, the Whitney Museum had come under scrutiny for its lack of diversity—particularly the dearth of women and ethnic minority artists included in its collections and major exhibitions. The 1993 installment made explicit reference to race, class, gender, sexuality, the postcolonial condition, imperialism, AIDS, and poverty—concerns that had not traditionally been a significant part of the critical lexicon of contemporary art. The art world establishment responded with virulent condemnation, dismissing the exhibition as a bastion of political correctness. Leading art critic Robert Hughes characterized the biennial as "A Fiesta of Whining," deriding the exhibition and its organizers for abandoning art in favor of superficial musings on oppression and victimization (R. Hughes 68–69). Needless to say, there was a shift in attitude after the critical response to the Biennial. The subject of difference remained fertile ground for art making and was a continued presence in exhibitions. However, it became clear that while racialized identity could be made visible and put on display for our consideration, it could also have a sense of play, of humor, and ultimately give us aesthetic pleasure. *Freestyle* dared to foreground black art while leaving aside the requisite identity politics and black rage. *Freestyle* was witty and fun, even upbeat. It was filled with formally inventive works that seemed to reposition African American art above and beyond the stoicism we as viewers had come to expect. These were aesthetics of privilege and entitlement, though for many, post-blackness suggests the end of African American art as a peripheral subgenre, one defined by a limited set of political concerns. Furthermore, it signals a new conceptual and aesthetic openness, a free play where racial fetishism is a virtue and satire reigns supreme.

The *30 Americans* exhibition was a landmark display of African American art because, like *Freestyle*, it defied the American art establishment to reconsider the traditional manner in which racial categorization informs what is on display. The Rubell family, which dedicated its remarkable collection of African American art to the exhibition, insisted that the show be titled "30 Americans" rather than "African Americans" or "Black Americans" because "nationality is a statement of fact, while racial identity is a question each artist answers in his or her own way, or not at all" (Rubell 7). *30 Americans* presented the opportunity to contemplate the evolution of black art from the 1960s to the present and made visible the shift from self-conscious political resistance to post-postmodern meditations on blackness as an imago of enduring cultural fascination. The roster included elder statespeople such as Robert Colescott, Barkley L. Hendricks, Jean-Michel Basquiat, Carrie Mae Weems, Lorna Simpson, Renée Green, Kerry James Marshall, Glenn Ligon, and William Pope.L alongside such post-black mainstays as Mark Bradford, Iona Rozeal Brown, Rashid Johnson, Kalup Linzy, Kara Walker, and Kehinde Wiley. *30 Americans* additionally created the opportunity to reflect upon a history of art making in which individuality and creative freedom have grated against ethnic allegiances and the political concerns of race.

The issue of satire holds great significance to the post-black era, because it very well may be the most apt descriptor for a set of aesthetic and conceptual strategies that have proven elusive for many critics and historians. Satire has not always proven to be a popular strategy for black visual artists. Furthermore, the conceptual strategies of African American literary satire vary greatly from artist to artist and from generation to generation. African American art viewers have not always taken kindly to harshly ironical engagements with the history and present-day realities of black life. This fact was evidenced in the response to the 1993 Whitney Biennial exhibition's didactic racial polemics. Considerable risk is involved, since in order for cultural producers to employ satire, African American life must be held up to an unflattering light, if not also made subject to ridicule through rigorous self-criticism. As a conceptual strategy, satirical works often indict African American complicity with the system that exploits and marginalizes them while simultaneously critiquing the dominant culture's attitudes towards the Other.

There has been no shortage of controversies and volatile debates when satire has emerged in African American art, with perhaps the most notorious example being the dispute that ensued between artists Betye Saar and Kara Walker in the wake of the latter being awarded the prestigious MacArthur "Genius" Fellowship in 1997. Saar began a campaign to protest Walker's imagery, which she felt peddled the most egregious racial stereotypes. The elder generation of African American artists has generally remained sharply critical of Walker's satirical engagement with the history of slavery, a conceptual approach that lampoons the way historical memory becomes a means both to create and to police essentialist narratives of the past. The late painter Robert Colescott—known for his satirical play on stereotypes, sexuality, the construction of history, and the melodramas of race—has always been at the center of controversy and criticism, but it is Walker whose visual (and at times written) embrace of satire has invited the greatest scrutiny and even condemnation. Saar, who came to prominence for her conceptual assemblages that resurrected nineteenth-century racist caricatures, was accused of being a hypocrite for her critiques of Walker. While both artists essentially play with historical representations of racism, stereotypes, and caricatures, Saar's work is perhaps less satirical, if not entirely devoid of satirical engagement, whereas Walker's cutout tableaux (that image antebellum bacchanalian scenes of violence and depravity) are meant to expose not only the absurdity of slavery but also the manner in which it is remembered. According to Saar, though, Walker utilizes the black body as a foil, making it into a joke that is meant to diminish and mock the often-tragic but also noble history of African Americans: "I felt the work of Kara Walker was sort of revolting and negative and a form of betrayal to the slaves, particularly women and children; that it was basically for the amusement and the investment of the white art establishment" ("The Freedom You Will Take").

This debate rests on the fault line between an externalized critique of white racism and an internalized and decidedly more Foucauldian exploration of power and its abuses, one that is not afraid to direct a potentially unflattering and self-critical lens toward one's own culture. For example, Saar's mixed-media assemblage, *The Liberation of Aunt Jemima* (1972), is—despite its somewhat whimsical-sounding title—actually a serious critical engagement with racist imagery created by whites. It looks outward, casting a harsh light on a history of segregation, debasement, and ridicule even as it employs humor and irony. Its aim is to shame the dominant culture and force it to reflect on its own lack of humanity, but I wouldn't characterize it as satirical, despite the fact that her work strategically employs humor and wit for the purposes of social commentary. Saar's Aunt Jemima seems, at least of the surface, to employ satire in its whimsical flipping of a racial stereotype (a symbol of debasement) into an emblem of uplift and resistance. Nevertheless, the focal points of Saar's critique are the historical sins of white America and not the African American community's collusion with the system that mistreats it. The unspeakable is absent in Saar: that holistic and cyclical critical engagement with the messiness of culture that is not afraid to employ self-criticality. Saar's iconic artwork is perhaps too soothing and affirming of African American viewers' sensibilities for it to be truly satirical. Walker's cutout installations, on the other hand, emerge from an ethos where black culture is neither held aloft nor perceived to be beyond critique. The shaming is there, but the focus of her indignation is broader and takes aim at the simplistic dichotomy of black/white power dynamics. It's important to note, however, that Walker's work is not devoid of political critique—quite the contrary, in fact. The artist creates a fictive counterworld where everyone is implicated in the absurdity of race, but her production is also a recurring meditation on the cyclical nature of racism: the twisted desires, follies, and abuses that define its interactions. In short, her work is no less a biting form of social criticism than Saar's, despite the fact that the elder artist characterizes Walker's post-black aesthetic as an art of self-loathing, a very public form of self-flagellation that panders to the white art establishment.

It has often been stated that the post-black artist is no longer interested in the inherent and uncritical maintenance and preservation of a sense of dignity around African American culture and history. For better or for worse, post-black artists are not afraid to lampoon their own culture, and it is in this shifting attitude (troubling or not) that satire becomes foregrounded. Walker has always been accused by the older generation of having a cavalier, mocking, and disrespectful attitude towards her own history, and part of the backlash has been directed toward the self-loathing the artist articulates in regard to her own identity. On several notable occasions, Walker has spoken openly about her ambivalence towards her African American identity and has articulated a kind of passive complicity with the incestuous and sadomasochistic mechanisms of American racism. In a 1996 interview with New York art critic Jerry Saltz, Walker notoriously stated that "All black people in America want to be slaves a little bit" (Cotter E36). Walker has made other inflammatory statements over the years; comments seemingly designed to poke fun at certain black folks, particularly those who, in their essentialist attitudes, wield black victimization as a form of cultural currency.

Like Walker, the Austin, Texas-based painter Michael Ray Charles has been accused of disrespecting his own as a result of his now-infamous satirical paintings that lampoon the absurdity of American racism. Charles's painterly engagement with racial stereotypes gained notoriety for their appropriation of advertising aesthetics, combined with the polemical comparison he often makes between minstrel images of the past and contemporary mass-media representations of African American celebrities and athletes. However, it is the satirical element in Charles's oeuvre that rubs many African Americans the wrong way, because it dares to take aim at black people and challenges their complicity in the system that oppresses them. In this regard, Charles's satirical approach is perceived to be a threat simply because the "wrong" parties are being satirized. For example, Charles's 1999 mixed media painting (*Forever Free*) *Tommy Hilnigguh* depicts a mock Tommy Hilfiger logo, an explicit reference to the popular clothing designer. In Charles's painting, the patriotic red, white, and blue colors of the traditional logo have been replaced by red, black, and green, rendering it more reminiscent of the Black Nationalist flag. The words "Tommy Hilnigguh" are painted in gold, and at the center of the composition is a minstrel-like image of a man in blackface, with full toothy grin and bulging eyes. Charles's logo is a hybrid satirical creation, meant to evoke the American designer's exploitation of black urban culture, but also to censure the black community's uncritical consumption of Hilfiger's waspy designs. The aspirational attainment of the American Dream, so conspicuously constructed and marketed by the Hilfiger line, has always been about the fetishishization of whiteness. However, Charles's logo is also eerily similar to the now defunct clothing line Cross Colors (Clothing Without Prejudice), which opportunistically used a similar Afrocentric-infused design in its marketing strategy. The Tommy Hilnigguh piece is aggressively satirical because it indicts African America's uncritical embrace of capitalism as much as it does the commodity culture that seeks to exploit the dreams and aspirations of black inner-city youth. Ultimately, Walker and Charles produce work that is politically incorrect, iconoclastic, and often offensive to the point of being perceived as causing injury to the African American community (Dickson-Carr 5). One of the potential consequences of Charles's aesthetic strategy is that he may be perceived as one of Appiah's aforementioned "otherness machines" that churns out essential difference. In this case he assumes the role of repeatedly manufacturing the iconography of Afrocentrism as a means of both critiquing the pernicious embrace of consumerism by some African Americans while creating objects to be consumed in the art market.

Film director Spike Lee was influenced to such a degree by Charles's work that he enlisted Charles as a consultant on his 2000 film, *Bamboozled*. Lee's satirical film told the tale of disgruntled, Harvard-educated television executive Pierre Delacroix (Damon Wayans) who creates a modern-day minstrel show with disastrous effects. In this case, the "otherness machine" busied himself with the production of detrimental media images of black stereotypes, examples of visual culture that, while lucrative, set into motion destructive and ultimately lethal results. The fact that *Bamboozled* was not well received by African Americans is part of the reason why it is perhaps effective satire (or at the very least a poignant and necessary self-critical intervention), a fact that highlights what has become a volatile rift between pre- and post–civil rights generations. Lee has always been an outspoken critic of American racism (often to his own detriment), and his cinematic works have consistently advocated for black uplift, despite Hollywood's resistance to creating diverse and complex content for African Americans. It is noteworthy, however, that Lee's self-described satire did not successfully find a black audience beyond the intelligentsia. Critics expressed confusion at, and even revulsion for, both the story and the characters, forcing Lee into a defensive posture where he repeatedly had to justify his use of satire as a polemical tool.

Bamboozled entered into an existing debate in the visual arts around the resurrection of racist imagery, a discussion that was outlined by art historian Michael D. Harris in his 2006 book, *Colored Pictures: Race and Visual Representation*. In response to Walker's stated ambivalence toward the history of slavery, Harris suggests that the artist has "locked herself into the racial discourse she is attempting to subvert. By identifying with slavery, she seems to trivialize it, and this has alienated her from preceding generations who have profound memories of racial violence and oppression and therefore a deep empathy for the crushing and violent consequences of slavery" (M. Harris 216). Harris was sharply critical of Charles and Walker specifically, but the ensuing debates among black scholars and artists nevertheless paved the way for the rise of post-blackness.

In the wake of the Studio Museum in Harlem's *Freestyle* exhibition, there was a palpable sense that black art (and its discourses) had shifted formally, conceptually, and intellectually. However, this change was also evidenced by the greater presence of women artists, whose engagement with the intersection of race and feminist representational politics produced striking results. Painter and photographer Mickalene Thomas is one of the most celebrated of Thelma Golden's roster of post-black artists. Her spectacularly colorful and decorative images explore the representation of African American women, taking on such themes as femininity, celebrity, sexuality, and power while simultaneously sending up the kitschy Blaxploitation aesthetics of 1970s black visual culture. The artist's mixed-media painting, *Hotter Than July* (2005), depicts a reclining black female nude in seductive mode: breasts partially exposed and miniskirt hiked up. The figure stares into the distance wantonly, with that slightly detached and glazed-over expression common in soft-core pornographic images found in men's magazines. Painted flatly in dull brown, with no rendering to articulate form and shape, Thomas chooses a decidedly graphic approach when imaging the black body. The flatness situates her work within a history of African American figurative painting from William H. Johnson to Kerry James Marshall, though Thomas's paintings image women exclusively and satirically embrace many of the stylistic tropes common to popular representations of women. In its déclassé mise-en-scène, the scene itself most aptly recalls a still image from a Blaxploitation film, and the figure (whose mouth seems frozen in the act of speaking) has an uncanny resemblance to actress Pam Grier. The background, painted in muted yellow ochre and purple, has the tacky cheapness of a 1970s porn set, while the pose is pure Orientalist fetishism. The only articulated figurative elements (clothing, eye makeup, and the figure's Afro) are rendered in colorful rhinestones. They convey a type of kitchy regalness, while the background is rendered primarily in flat acrylic washes with occasional decorative flourishes in muted rhinestone.

Conceptually, *Hotter Than July* employs a combustible, albeit satirical, mixture of intellectual references, from feminist critiques of European modernism, critical race discourse on Blaxploitation aesthetics, to Orientalism; but Thomas's work is perhaps most concerned with the representation of African American women. Her images are critical of the exploitation and commoditization of black female bodies by the dominant culture, but there is something disturbingly urgent about the intracultural dialogue she engages around the way black people image themselves. It's important to remember that Thomas is a woman imaging other women, which positions her within a lineage of feminist representational strategies, whereby women (as image makers) aggressively claim agency and control over the female body in an oppositional act of self-representation. Works such as this one are not concerned with chastising the objectifying manner in which men look at women; rather, they are more explicitly concerned with the black female gaze (empowered female looking). *Hotter Than July* queers the black female body by taking on many of the stylistic tropes of heteronormative sex images and rearticulating them through a distinctly queer-feminist desiring lens. The queering, however, is also a means to render the black body strange, to give it a signifying potential that allows the possibility for new meanings to be constructed. In *Hotter Than July*, the black female form is elevated above and beyond the object status typically assigned to the types of visual forms it references. Thomas endeavors to present a new black female subjectivity that (at its most effective) is both defiant and playful, even as it directs a critical lens on the culture that has all too often neglected or objectified the bodies of African American women.

Included in the *30 Americans* exhibition, Thomas's work reflects the shift in black art from didactic political narrative to post-black satire, particularly with regard to her rearticulation of fetishistic representations of black women. Her images critique American media culture's debasement of black women while simultaneously taking aim at misogyny within the black community, particularly in the male-dominated Black Power era of the 1970s. The rise of satire in post-black visual art—particularly in the creative production of black women—is notable when considering the history of satire.[2] As Darryl Dickson-Carr has noted, satire has tended to be most associated with and dominated by men. He notes that in the literary tradition, "certain types of sexism have dogged satirists—and women have often been dismissed as sexual objects, decried as ideological femme fatales, and assigned a hefty part of the blame for the demise of civilized discourse in at least a few African-American satires" (Dickson-Carr 5). Satirical wit is one of the primary and most incendiary characteristics of post-black art created by women because it not only approaches the subject of racism, but also the enduring problem of black chauvinism.

The sexual and gender politics implicit within post-black aesthetics have not yet been fully unpacked. Many of the most prominent post-black artists are women and gay men, whose diverse products utilize the black body (and the visual culture of blackness) as *image*—not in an overtly political manner, but rather as an ontological imago of mythical resplendence. Considering the "post-" of post-black in relation to the work of African American women artists poses a series of interesting questions. Their artworks often straddle the fault line between feminist consciousness and racial allegiances and express an uneasy relation to both. What results is a lessened commitment to what Amelia Jones calls the performative female body that is common in earlier forms of feminist art (29). Specifically, these black female artists appear less interested in the viewer/viewed matrix that has become a lynchpin of women's oppositional aesthetics. Much of their work is unapologetically formal—almost aggressively so—and is perhaps more motivated by the pleasures of the visual (which could be read as "masculinist" or "universal" in the sense of universal formalism) than by an engagement with the abuses of the patriarchy. Nevertheless, the gesture to radically colonize the formal could be read as stridently feminist. The irony in Thomas's painting, for example, has a dual function: to expose the hypocrisies of racial fetishism and to liberate the work from identity politics that have become outdated.

A question that often emerges is whether or not these cultural workers are disconnected from mainstream feminism and estranged from dominant understandings of blackness. In some instances, the post-black production of these women appears to constitute a radical rethinking of feminism, one that reconsiders the notion of feminist agency as an act of creativity. Thomas's *Sista Sista Lady Blue, From Odalisque* (2007), for example, is reminiscent of 1970s soft-core pornographic imagery, Blaxploitation, and modernist masterworks such as Edouard Manet's *A Bar at the Folies-Bergère*, and it positions the black female body somewhere between racial fetishism and feminist transgression. The color photograph depicts an interior den space filled with competing patterns of wood paneling, plants, art, wallpaper, densely decorated furniture, throw pillows, carpeting, and animal prints. A dominant figure, a woman with a red dress and knee-high black-heeled boots, reclines in a love seat. Her large black Afro frames an attentive, commanding look aimed directly at the viewer. Behind her and to the right stands a tall, wood-framed mirror that reflects the image of a second woman in a partially unbuttoned dress. She is taking a drag off her cigarette. There is a triangulation of gazes between the photographer at the moment of capture (whose perspective becomes that of the viewer), the foreground subject's look, and the reflected subject's secondary gaze. This complicated configuration of looks suggests, just as Manet's *Bar* indicates a bourgeois male spectator, that the presumed viewer is the second woman, a black woman at that. Thomas's playful visualization of black female spectatorship encourages the viewer to pleasurably occupy Otherness while disidentifying at the same time. In a sense, the viewers give in to the commodity spectacle of difference while simultaneously having both their desires and revulsions indicted. This push/pull of pleasure and guilt resonates in her work, denying the viewer a chance to sit comfortably with the artist's imaginings.

In Thomas's paintings, the charade of beauty is in violent struggle with the complexities of identity. However, it becomes apparent that both the formal and the political represent dueling expressions of identity politics, each performing an essentialist masquerade while remaining concealed under their respective veils. In keeping with that sentiment, Thomas's representations of the black female imago are not just symbols for objectification; they are also reminders that the content/form opposition represents irrecoverably fundamentalist positions in the visual arts. Among the discursive powers of Thomas's art is its facility for making social subjectivity for the viewer to turn the gaze upon itself. The artist is all too aware of how recognition interpenetrates viewership when the signifiers of race are visualized. The black female body as presented in *Sista Sista* is an intentional marker of cultural difference, and a mode of representing Otherness. Unhinged from the overbearing burden of race discourse, her ornately rendered black bodies become concentrated objects for consumerist consumption as well as painfully uncomfortable meditations on their visual presentation. They hover in the realm of the uncanny, the familiar made strange, especially in these instances where their subject position effectively displaces the viewer's.

Kehinde Wiley is perhaps the best-known and most successful post-black artist. Also exhibited in *30 Americans*, Wiley's paintings are some of the most unapologetically satirical in subject matter and tone while at the same time elevating the formal over the political. In contrast to Thomas's work, Wiley's now-iconic *Passing/Posing, Three Graces* (2005), depicts three African American men dressed in what would typically be described as hip-hop or urban attire. The painting is emblematic of Wiley's signature style of melding the masculine pose of classical Western art with the African American male body. The odd pairing of two ideologically determined fictions—one considered high culture, the other considered low—creates a clever visual pun that speaks to the desirability of the black body as a commodity fetish in the era of hypercapitalism. Wiley's work is often characterized as postpolitical in its formalist engagement with the history of Western painting; however, the satirical queering of hip-hop culture's masculinist pose sheds a critical light on the performance and maintenance of gender norms. Additionally, his *Three Graces* utilizes the black male not in the service of making a metacommentary on the plight of the urban underclass, but rather as a glorious fantasy or as a phantasmagoric and brandable good to be exchanged in the global marketplace. The politics embedded in Wiley's satire (like that of many of his post-black contemporaries) are perhaps more focused on the aggressiveness of a rapacious capitalism that renders us all commodities to be exchanged and fetishized.

The commodity aspect of the black body's usage in post-black art could not have been possible had it not been for the successes of hip-hop, a cultural movement that fully exploited the economic potential of black male objectification. The success of Wiley's work marks a decisive break from the self-conscious seriousness and stoicism of black art during the heyday of identity-based art in the 1980s and 1990s. Wiley's conceptual raison d'être is intentionally disconnected from the burden to represent blackness as something to be revered or respected or as a symbol for racial solidarity, resistance, and oppositional politics. His paintings are also effective in their ability to dislodge the African American male from the now-mythical backdrop of urban blight, violence, and social discrimination. The vision of manhood on display is not symbolic of defiance, but is rather a black masculinity that is divinely market-ready in its tragic resplendence. Project onto it as you wish, it will absorb all: revulsion, condemnation, lust, and martyrdom, or merely the indignity of commodity fetishism. Greg Tate has called Wiley the quintessential urban fetishist due to his uncanny ability for melding "racial profits with racial progress" ("Wherein" 12). One of the primary critiques of art produced by so-called post-black artists is that their production fetishizes and exploits the Other in a capitalistic and ethnographic form of authorship. However, in Wiley's satirical work, economic profits and social advancement seem to hold precedence over racial progress. But whether or not today's post-black fetishist (the commodity fetish / ethnographer / author / capitalist) is socially engaged does not elide the fact that the black body—so gleefully offered up in the marketplace—is now often presented as nothing more than a commodity symbol (Murray and Murray, "Uneasy" *passim*). Essentially, you get the body and not the content. It becomes merely an empty fetish, the soulless object of projection that is bereft of rhetorical force. Meaning is brought to it, and pleasure is derived from the superficiality of its beauty. However, it does not speak; it is spoken to.

This complex engagement with representation is yet more fraught. Within the black arts community, there is a lingering sentiment that racism demands that African American artists and intellectuals focus only on black culture in their production. That mandate is contrasted by the enduring presence of an intracultural obligation that places a similar restriction on them. The result is a sociocultural and economic climate where a contingent of African American elites is charged with presiding over blackness as gatekeepers. These elites are thus said to be restricted to a racially specific and limited playing field where blackness is their product, despite their indifference (and at times disregard) toward its histories, political mandates, aesthetics, and present-day realities. Thus, a dual pressure is exerted by the commercial interests of the art world, as well as by the African American community, for black artists to continually manufacture their own differences and become the "otherness machines" of which Appiah forewarned.

The art of Glenn Ligon is crucial to this discussion because, as an originator of the term *post-black*, his production truly exemplifies the basic qualities of the genre, particularly the satirical turn. Prominently featured in the *30 Americans* exhibition, Ligon's *Untitled (Malcolm X)* (2008), for example, is one of the artist's more literal works, consisting of a screen-printed and painted image of Malcolm X that is itself reproduced from an Afrocentric coloring book from the 1970s. The bodiless head speaks to the ubiquitously commodified representation of the political icon in mass culture. Malcolm X's image has become almost like a logo, a ready-to-sell emblem for racial pride and uplift. Ligon re-purposes the image as a fraught and potent symbol for a type of ethnic authenticity that negates sexual difference. In a sense, the artist reduces Malcolm X's image as a visual signifier of a certain kind of blackness and then defaces it, a gesture that signifies both its malleability and its inability to fully encapsulate the complexity of the African American experience. Reminiscent of an individual portrait, the disembodied head is presented as a coloring-book outline on a white background but is adorned in brightly colored hues of blue over the eyelids, with magenta reddening the cheeks and lips in a manner that suggests poorly applied and even clownish makeup. While the image reads clearly as though colored in by a child, within the contemporary art context the iconic Malcolm X appears intentionally queered "and becomes an exploration of childhood memory, ideology, and nebulous issues of identity formation mediated through the aesthetic" (S. Murray 88).

A series of letter-sized silkscreen reproductions of report cards from Ligon's fifth-through-seventh-grade education accompanied an earlier iteration of the Malcolm X painting when it was exhibited at New York's D'Amelio Terras Gallery in 2003. Each report card consists of testimonials from Ligon's teachers recounting the particularities of his behavior. Many of these end-of-year reports advanced rather cruel observations of the young artist's disposition: "He likes to dominate in his relationships with the boys (he has nothing to do with the girls other than insulting them)." Others are more troubling in their judgmental tone: "Glenn has a good knowledge of slavery and black history, but finds standard social studies uninteresting and, as yet has developed no social conscience. He tends to be politically apathetic about being black, which is a shame." It is telling that the teacher would question young Glenn's attitude towards black identity, "suggesting that there is a right and a wrong way to respond to one's African American identity" (S. Murray 88). Ultimately, the critical underpinnings of Ligon's *Untitled (Malcolm X)* "seem to orbit tentatively around more fundamental issues of queer shame, ambivalence toward blackness, and an underlying defensiveness about identity that ultimately remain untapped. This is unfortunate, since those very notions may provide an infinitely more nuanced disruption of monolithic notions of blackness" (S. Murray 89). The work's brilliance is connected to the artist's willingness to mine the roots of his ambivalence toward blackness, an attitude that ultimately led to the formation of post-blackness, which has in the meantime become a generation-defining ethos.

Another defining work by Ligon is *Hands* (1996), a large silkscreen on unstretched canvas. *Hands* is a critically forceful exploration into the controversial Million Man March that took place in Washington in 1995. Ligon's artistic response to the March was in keeping with widespread skepticism and condemnation of the gathering, which urged African American men to convene on the National Mall as a gesture of atonement and anti-racist activism and as a rededication to the cause of uplifting the African American family. The conglomeration of activists and political leaders at the helm of the March asked that women stay home in support of the effort. In response, many notable scholars, cultural commentators, and public intellectuals decried the event as being rooted in bigotry and exclusion. Presented in stark black and white, Ligon's work consists of a media-based image from the March that depicts black hands as they reach towards the sky in a gesture of collective celebration, and more importantly in a call to action. Ligon's satirical *Hands* expresses a critical indifference toward the March, characterizing it as a misguided attempt at collective black male catharsis. Ligon configures the event as a negation of both black female and black queer identities, and therefore as a mass expression of willful intolerance. While Ligon's artwork deals with the crucial issues of homophobia and misogyny in the African American community, it does so potentially at the expense of those sincerely endeavoring to confront the scourge of American racism. There is little argument that the Million Man March's key organizer, Louis Farrakhan, is a polarizing figure and that his agendas issue from a fundamentalist perspective that advocates for racial, ethnic, and religious divisiveness and regressively patriarchal heteronormative values. Nevertheless, criticisms of Ligon's post-black satire claim that, despite its shortcomings, the March still sincerely attempted to speak to the legacy and persistent presence of racial hatred in the U.S. It was that legacy that drew massive crowds to the nation's capital on October 16, 1995. Ligon's work clearly speaks to a groundswell of shifting attitudes toward black cultural values that are not afraid to expose the intolerances deeply embedded within the African American community.

The politics of blackness is intertwined in this history, and its visual signifiers contain cultural meanings that perhaps should not be disparaged or demeaned—despite their ideological limitations—but that does not diminish the importance and urgency of Ligon's critique. The artist's unflinching ability to critique not just the dominant culture's intolerances but also the bigotries deeply embedded with the African American community is one of Ligon's great strengths. It is certainly a risky endeavor to satirize black folks while in the act of collective resistance and uplift. *Hands* is both iconoclastic and offensive on profoundly political levels, but it also employs humor (and perhaps a bit of ridicule) to make an important statement about intolerances lurking largely unseen within an iconic political movement. On the other hand, Ligon's piece is conceptually diffuse and obfuscating without the presence of didactic materials to guide the viewer. Those who experienced the March may consume Ligon's artwork uncritically and without the slightest hint that the artist is making a critique of the black community. In fact, *Hands* appears (at first read) to uncritically commemorate the event, a quality that potentially renders its satire even more caustic and biting. The satire in Ligon's artwork does not always lie on the surface in the form of an overtly placed visual pun or aesthetic contradiction. On the contrary, works like *Hands* are more opaque; they lure the viewer into a queer-activist critique that seeks to satirically expose the absurdity of intolerant attitudes within a community historically besieged by racism.

Ultimately, the rise of female, gay, and lesbian artists as legitimate African American creative voices is essential to the development of black art. That much is true. Their work resonates with present-day cultural imperatives to finally bring an end to gender inequity and legalized homophobia. But are we to believe that those imperatives simultaneously signal that the battle against racism has been won? In that regard, post-racial and post-black are not the same thing, and I would venture to say that few African American artists believe that racism in American society is a thing of the past. Darryl Dickson-Carr suggests that satire always "manages to fascinate, infuriate, and delight us to the extent that it transgresses boundaries of taste, propriety, decorum, and the current status quo" (1). Both celebrated and reviled, post-black art manages to embody all of these characteristics while it simultaneously manages to give us pleasure and make us rethink the ideological boundaries we prescribed to our identities.

Notes

1. Orlando Patterson's review of *Who's Afraid of Post-Blackness?* in the September 22, 2011, issue of the *New York Times* noted Touré's critical stance toward black essentialism and class warfare.

2. See also Brandon Manning's article in this collection, pp. 125–36.

Blackness We Can Believe In: Authentic Blackness and the Evolution of Aaron McGruder's *The Boondocks*

Terrence T. Tucker

We live in an age of comedy. More specifically, we find ourselves in a moment when perhaps humor has become, for many, the primary lens through which we approach the world and how many of our impressions of political issues and figures are formed. Younger generations receive their news sometimes exclusively from shows that parody the news as part of their larger cultural critique. In an increasingly divisive era, humor has often acted as a weapon to reveal the absurdity of ideological dogmas, hypocrisy and pop cultural / media failures. The critiques leveled at contemporary media and culture have made *The Daily Show* and *The Colbert Report* runaway hits. Simultaneously, *Countdown with Keith Olberman* and *The Rachel Maddow Show* are characterized by an anger-fueled examination that specializes in pointing at the danger of extremist positions. What becomes clear, however, is that underneath the absurdist tone of such shows—and less comedic examples in Fox's *The O'Reilly Factor* and *Hannity*—is a deep anger and frustration that has permeated the last half century of our sociopolitical lives. Yet whether it was the conservative counterrevolution of the 1970s and 1980s or the fury of liberals at the seeming abandonment of progressive ideas, what has been consistent is that these voices of humor and fury are virtually all white. Voices of black rage are almost completely marginalized, while black humor is often labeled as mere entertainment that can be easily dismissed. The latter is particularly important because the tradition of black humor has always contained critiques of white America and racism. The promotion of a color-blind or post-racial America has led many to see critiques of racism as unproductive and has sought to rob black expressions of humor of their critical voice. In response, African American expressive culture has developed a strain of humor I refer to as comic rage, which frequently and aggressively explores the wide-ranging impact of institutional racism in post-integration American culture.

For Aaron McGruder, the use of comic rage opens his creative possibilities, particularly in his use of satire and parody. The election of President Barack Obama has, in the minds of many, ushered in a post-racial era, an era defined by the belief that the country has transcended race because of the millions of whites who voted for Obama. Obama's discussion of race was minimal because he—perhaps due to his mixed heritage—was able to speak to both sides of the color divide; many believe (or wish to believe) that we can eliminate racial oppression not by actually talking about race, but by gaining an inherent understanding of each other. Most importantly, however, the post-racial suggests that the promise of the Civil Rights Movement has been fulfilled, the implication of which claims racial harmony and marginalizes voices that openly critique white supremacy or actively engage racially sensitive topics. So while African American comedies and sitcoms have maintained a presence over the last few decades, they rarely provide the social and/or political commentary that we see in the previously mentioned cable shows. Starting with Asheru's opening rap about being "the stone that the builder refused," the animated television version of McGruder's comic strip, *The Boondocks*, and establishes itself as a work that sits boldly outside the mainstream and actively engages in resistance by challenging fundamental assumptions about race, particularly blackness.

Beginning as a syndicated newspaper strip in 1999 and expanding to an animated television series in 2005, *The Boondocks* uses comic rage to openly challenge the post–civil rights mainstream belief in a "color-blind" society and currently sits at a vital place in American pop cultural and African American literary / cultural thought. Like the work of novelist Ishmael Reed and comics Richard Pryor and Chris Rock, it wears its rage on its proverbial sleeve and, by rejecting the concept of an idealized past to which we must return, commits itself to dismantling racist structures and hierarchies that have endured. *The Boondocks* sits alongside neither stereotypical representations of blackness nor similarly narrow counterrepresentations. Both assume an essentialized blackness that excludes complex and nuanced images; both remain dependent on markers of power and identity that reinforce white supremacist hegemony. As such, *The Boondocks* revels in critiquing both sides of the color line.

Moreover, *The Boondocks* expands ideas of blackness and angrily ridicules white ideas of racial harmony and African Americans who unquestioningly adopt mainstream ideas of race. This essay argues that McGruder's work comically employs overt expressions of black rage as a way to ignite our racial discourse at a moment when many find such expressions divisive and discouraging in the face of the multi-ethnic, multi-racial coalition President Obama was able to forge. Also, McGruder's fusion of militancy and humor, the hallmarks of comic rage, highlights the presence of white supremacist hegemony in the rhetoric of the post-racial while using both comedy's ability to realign the lens through which the mainstream situates racial discourse and militancy's overt rage to avoid being considered apolitical entertainment. As a result, *The Boondocks* has become one of the most significant works of comic rage by deploying parodic satire to assail contemporary America's silencing of racial discourse in the midst of an African America that possesses a myriad of voices, ideologies, and experiences. In particular, McGruder's use of satire takes aim at both sides of the color line for their attempts to sustain a limited concept of authentic blackness, one that ignores the continuing structural inequalities; the reconfiguration of white supremacy and privilege; and the failure of some in black America to take personal responsibility for the adoption of distorted, narrow visions of what it means to be black in twenty-first-century America.

McGruder's work interrogates the contradictions and tensions within African America, most notably through the ten-year-old Huey Freeman and his eight-year-old brother Riley. Huey's "radical scholar" contrasts Riley who is, according to McGruder himself, "shortsighted, ignorant, and concerned only with instant gratification" and who follows his guiding principle "to stick to his thug life ambitions in the name of 'keepin' it real'" (Kang 139). In the foreword to Fredrik Stromberg's *Black Images in the Comics* (2003), Charles Johnson notes that while we can see in American comic art "risible yet demeaning (and often dangerous) images of *all* racial Others," one cannot forget that "since the European Age of Exploration, when whites first encountered and entered into sustained relations with Africans, the Negro has been the very special object of the white man's deepest—and perhaps primordial—fears and fantasies" (Johnson 10; emphasis in original). As a result, the images of blacks seen in comics are reflective of the constructions of blackness that have existed for centuries; according to Johnson, the African American was "seldom conceived as fully human, or culturally and intellectually equal, and was granted by whites superiority in but one area— the physical" (Johnson 10). *The Boondocks* becomes crucial, then, because of its unyielding focus on African American perspectives, however varied, and the ways in which those perspectives reflect on the impact of white supremacist capitalist hegemony.

In both of its incarnations, *The Boondocks* centers on the two brothers who grew from their urban Chicago upbringing to the fictional, almost wholly white suburb of Woodcrest. The strips and episodes pit the brothers against each other or in relation to their white neighbors as McGruder examines how contemporary, particularly conflicting ideas of blackness operate and adjust to whites in a post–civil rights context. The presence of Robert Freeman ("Granddad" to Huey and Riley), their parental guardian who moves them out the suburbs, provides a glimpse into a civil rights–era perspective and at times highlights the tensions between generations of African Americans. Oliver Wang notes that McGruder's comic strip "leaps backwards over the politically stale black humor of the 1980s and 1990s. Compared to both Bill Cosby's bourgeois idolatry and Eddie Murphy's self-loathing caricatures of black life, *The Boondocks* shares more in common with the radical black comics of the 1970s, exemplified by Richard Pryor's, Paul Mooney's, and Dick Gregory's embrace of political commentary as well as incisive, humorous celebrations of blackness" (Wang 3). I would extend this lineage forward to comics like Chris Rock and Dave Chappelle, both of whom McGruder has credited with providing a space on television where his style of humor might find an audience. That McGruder's protagonist is named for the famous Black Panther, Huey Newton—a fact that is made known in the initial episode—adds to the confrontational tone of *The Boondocks*.

The presence of the Freemans in the suburbs provides McGruder the opportunity to address issues of class in addition to issues of race, particularly in his critique of middle-class, assimilationist (read: sellout) African Americans as well as whites. What Wang sees as groundbreaking about *The Boondocks* "is the strip's explicit hip-hop attitude. Even the strip's cultural hijacking of newspapers resembles hip-hop's use of the music industry to package and distribute nuggets of black political thought" (3–4). While hip-hop's political critiques have often been choked away by hypermaterialism and misogyny, *The Boondocks* embodies the aggression and bravado of hip-hop in its confrontation with a number of cultural and national inequities. *The Boondocks* emerges, and is indeed fostered, in a time when the satirical and the sarcastic have become the primary mode of critique in popular culture, whether in *The Daily Show*, *The Simpsons*, *Family Guy*, or *Doonesbury*. Although *Doonesbury* has been, by his own admission, an influential comic strip for him, McGruder has also argued that "[creator Garry] Trudeau can get away with things but I can't say the word 'pimp'" (*All the Rage* 161). McGruder's comment reveals the discomfort many have with African American satire generally and comic rage specifically. Like *The Boondocks*, *Doonesbury* has in some newspapers been moved from the comics page altogether and placed on the editorial page.

The implications for McGruder's strip, however, are very different. For example, although *Doonesbury* has similarly been the source of controversy because of its tendency to be overtly political, this has not changed the reality that, as Michael Moore points out in his foreword to McGruder's first collection of strips, *A Right to Be Hostile*, "the comics pages seem to be one of the last vestiges of the belief that white faces are just . . . well, you know

. . . so much more happy and friendly and funny!" (Moore 7). By contrast, pointed critiques that these works produce, particularly through parody and fury, are viewed with suspicion and fear because they rarely fit within the desire for black expressive culture as solely a vehicle for white entertainment. Indeed, the strip gained national attention soon after 9/11. McGruder began addressing the terrorist attacks on September 24, 2001—less than two weeks after 9/11—and was almost immediately pulled by the *New York Daily News*. Many of the 250 newspapers in which *The Boondocks* appeared either pulled the comic strip or moved it to the editorial pages, as the *Dallas Morning News* did. The latter act is significant here because of the intertwined presumptions that the comics pages are an apolitical site, one that must be devoid of overt critique, and that satire normatively promotes a return to hegemonic ideas of ethics, morality, and/or ideology.

McGruder's work subscribes to J. Martin Favor's contention in *Authentic Blackness* (1999) that "one cannot view racial authenticity as an either-or-proposition; writers continually struggle to negotiate the folk-bourgeoisie boundary in an effort to produce art that demonstrates the complexity of 'race' as a marker of identity" (14). In refusing to minimize the importance of the Freemans' blackness to their own identity, *The Boondocks* resists mainstream calls for color blindness or the post-racial in favor of a multitude of characters that reflects the diversity in thought, class, and gender within the African American community. For example, a major theme throughout the comic strip has been Huey's frequent disagreements with his biracial friend and neighbor Jazmine. Jazmine's optimism and naiveté contrast with Huey's suspicious, overly pessimistic nature. Jazmine frequently disagrees with Huey's political critiques, when she catches them at all. Instead, she relies on an uncritical acceptance of messages she receives from any figures or institutions of authority, which McGruder wickedly exploits. Seen from the outside as the embodiment of integration and of a post-racial society, McGruder's strips and episodes situate Jazmine squarely within the tradition of the tragic mulatta figure. In fact, Jazmine internalizes white hegemonic ideologies so thoroughly that when Huey compliments her on her Afro, Jazmine denies she has one, only suggesting that her hair is "frizzy." In the comic strip, Jazmine frequently complains about the curliness of her hair, wishing instead that it would be straight. When her parents are unable to console her, Huey encourages them to emphasize the specifics and beauty of her ethnic background. Yet in a family that does not overtly discuss race, markers of blackness are consistently treated with fear and dread. The privileges of both class and light skin that Jazmine enjoys are ones that she and her parents attempt to protect through an embrace of color blindness. McGruder's satirical assaults on America's attempts to avoid conversations about race—or to embrace blackness—include holding up Jazmine's internalized privilege to ridicule and critique. So in the television episode "A Huey Freeman Christmas," Jazmine gives a Christmas sermon in which she conflates Jesus Christ with Santa Claus, imploring her congregation to "Praise Santa," and exposes the deification of Santa Claus with that of Christ. Here, McGruder uses the seemingly innocent mistake by a child to construct a commentary on the appropriation of Christmas's spirit of selflessness and hope by mainstream culture's embrace of capitalist, materialist excess. Through her friendships with Huey and Riley, Jazmine often stands in a middle space between a decolonized mind and black bourgeois princess.

McGruder's three post–9/11 comic strip collections—*A Right to Be Hostile* (2003), *Public Enemy #2* (2005), and *All the Rage* (2007)—not only reveal an escalating embrace of comic rage, but signal a broadening of the scope of his rage to include the larger national and cultural concerns. Disappearing from the comic strip in 2001, Jazmine returns in 2004 claiming to have remained in her house because of her fear of terrorists. At a certain point, however, she attempts to turn herself in to federal authorities because she is told that being afraid is unpatriotic. Here McGruder uses absurdity to expose the culture of fear generated in the immediate years after 9/11 and the mixed, often contradictory messages that Americans received. Living in a society that uses the fear of terrorist attack to silence any dissent and labels any demonstration of fear or perceived weakness (read: nuanced critique) as unpatriotic has emotionally paralyzed Jazmine. In the episode "A Date with the Health Inspector," Jazmine's response to her father's arrest—in a clear instance of racial profiling—is to ask, "Was he kidnapped by terrorists?" Thus, her all-encompassing fear of terrorists cloaks the police, immigration, and antiterror policies that frequently target people of color. Jazmine's desire to be color-blind ignores the larger forces that shape both the world around her and her own personal responses and experiences. Similarly, the country's racial discourse has pursued a colorless universalism at the expense of a distinctly African American perspective. The by-product of such a pursuit has been the suppression and paralysis of expressions of black rage, particularly rage that manifests itself in the critique of white supremacy. Like McGruder's works, those voices are usually described as "angry" and "divisive" even as the voices of white male rage increase their presence in mainstream popular culture, whether on cable news shows or on talk radio. *The Boondocks* differs from its contemporaries because its construction—a mix of hip-hop culture, Japanese anime, contemporary parody, and unapologetic black rage—eschews charges that its critiques are outdated with the emergence of new black leadership embodied by political leaders like

Barack Obama, Deval Patrick, and Cory Booker. Most importantly, however, the post-racial suggests that the promise of the Civil Rights Movement has been fulfilled.

The critiques and protests often launched by stalwarts of the Civil Rights Movement have fallen increasingly on deaf ears, not because their claims are illegitimate, but because they have not accounted for the shifting landscape that they helped initiate, a shift that questions tactics and rhetoric of the old guard because they have not changed with the society that surrounds them. It is the absence of this shift that has fueled many conservative arguments that African Americans now only embrace a culture of victimization. Favor asks us to consider that "positing too-concrete bonds between authenticity, culture, color, and class risks reliance on a vision of identity so dependent on marginality as its legitimizing feature that it can never effectively deconstruct the center, which, in turn, may hold the margins to be inauthentic" (9). Beneath those bonds is a desire to maintain the hierarchy of white supremacy that benefits whites and like-minded African Americans or to avoid the uncomfortable, volatile conversation about race. *The Boondocks* refuses to shy away from the conversation, but as the opening rap suggests, it stands proudly on the margins of the mainstream racial narratives. Indeed, McGruder's work attempts to use its marginalized status to launch satirical broadsides at subjects that might be considered taboo in white and black communities while also seeking to "dismantle those margins without wholly erasing" the difference that McGruder's work celebrates.

However, McGruder's work sidesteps the pitfalls of his elders because of two very important facts. The first is that McGruder does comically what the late August Wilson did dramatically, which is to say he constantly engages in a process of self-examination in order to determine which cultural traditions and behaviors should be kept and which ones should be thrown away. So in one episode of the television show titled "The Itis," Huey rails against his grandfather's refusal to cook anything healthy in place of more and more pork. McGruder, of course, suggests here that African Americans' use of as many parts of the pig as possible was once necessary because that was all which was available during slavery and segregation, but that this could now be altered because of greater access to healthier foods. The second reason that McGruder avoids the fate of others who critique white supremacy is that he is part of a generation of African Americans who grew up in predominantly white neighborhoods. Referred to as "cultural mulattoes" by author Trey Ellis in 1989, artists from those neighborhoods not only witnessed how white supremacy was realigned after the Civil Rights Movement, but many also wrestled with the question of authenticity because their experience was different from that of African Americans who grew up in predominantly African American neighborhoods.

One of the central elements in the work of cultural mulattoes is the use of parody, whether in the work of Keenan Ivory Wayans, Robert Townsend, or even Dave Chappelle. The use of the parodic makes their work and critiques at once palatable and challenging to white audiences. Although McGruder's tone is harsher than his contemporaries', his willingness to critique both sides of the color line gives his work, in the minds of many, credibility because he demands that everyone take responsibility. He moves away from a monolithic reading of African Americans, despite his very pointed critiques of them, and moves toward what Favor suggests is a "shift in the goals of African American literary production, a re-placement of emphasis that signifies difference rather than sameness among African Americans" (11). In the second episode of the first season, titled "The Trial of Robert Kelly," R. Kelly is placed on trial for child molestation and child pornography, which pits Huey and Riley against each other as they argue about Kelly's guilt or innocence. The two are representative of the larger debate within the African American community about Kelly, who infamously made a video in which he had sex with and urinated on an underage girl. Arriving at the trial, Huey and Riley encounter two groups in front of the courthouse. The first group, which Huey supports, is made up of older civil rights activists and academics who critique Kelly for the problematic images of race, gender, and sexuality he promotes. The second group, with which Riley proudly associates himself, is filled with unnamed African Americans barbequing and listening to R&B, and who staunchly support Kelly simply, as one woman notes, "Cause he good!" When a fight between the two breaks out, replete with chicken wings and karate, McGruder's parody of both groups' failure to provide more nuanced discourse becomes clear.

During Kelly's trial, Jazmine's father, the African American district attorney Tom Dubois, makes a clear and evidenced-based case, including a video that makes it absurdly obvious that Kelly is the culprit. Yet R. Kelly's attorney upends the trial by turning the focus toward the relative authenticity of Kelly and Tom, whose last name is a clear reference to noted African American intellectual and activist W. E. B. Du Bois. Kelly's attorney uses Tom's white wife and Jazmine to suggest that, while Kelly can be readily identified on the video, it also proves that "at least we know he's attracted to black women" ("The Trial of Robert Kelly"). McGruder caps off the lawyer's attempts to appeal to the tribalism of the all-black jury by having Kelly actually break into song. Here, then, the episode questions the ways in which ideas of authentic blackness are exploited both within and outside the African American community to benefit certain individuals and behaviors, while excluding others based on arbitrary and often unstable criteria.

McGruder's work establishes a consistent, complex set of images within his conception of blackness, an act that rebuts one of the fundamental tenets of white supremacy: that African Americans are monolithic, tribal, and uncritical. Not only do Huey and Riley represent a generational shift from their grandfather, but all three of the Freemans stand in stark contrast to Tom. Tom is consistent with a portrait of the African American elite whose authenticity is called into question because they often side with whites ideologically, particularly in refusing to acknowledge the continued by-products of racial oppression in contemporary America. Favor claims that the primary objection of critics of the African American middle class is that "the desire for wealth, it seems, often makes one 'less black,' or at least a less authentic representative of racial identity. Separated in terms of class from these critics' notion of folk, the black middle class cannot express the 'authentic' African-American experience" (13). Viewed through Favor's argument, McGruder's depiction of Tom is problematic because he is often ridiculed for being disconnected from the more "authentic" Huey and Riley. This misses the point. It is not the pursuit or the possession of wealth that creates intraracial tensions in African America. It is the adoption of specific ideological and political positions by the African American middle class, ones that benefit them individually and ignore systemic oppression that is frequently in conflict with collective uplift. A self-proclaimed liberal, Tom's promotion of ideas of the color blind often requires the adoption of white ideology—indeed whiteness itself—as normative. Thus, while Huey constantly plots to overthrow the government for its exploitation of African Americans, one series of strips finds Tom kidnapping Ralph Nader because he believes that Nader cost Gore the election in 2000 and fears that Nader's candidacy would result in Bush's reelection in 2004. Surprised by Huey's hesitation, Tom contends that Huey "would support decisive revolutionary action." Huey responds by pointing out that instead of taking action against the "power structure," Tom has "accosted a consumer advocate" (McGruder, *All the Rage* 143). The strip questions the construction of Nader as the reason Gore lost in order to avoid the more controversial reality of systematic voter disenfranchisement. As Huey later suggests, "All I'm saying is you Democrats are worried about Nader stealing some votes, and you need to be worried about Bush stealing the whole election outright" (McGruder, *All the Rage* 144). However, the kidnapping of Nader reveals Tom's disconnect from the black lower and underclass he has attempted to escape in Woodcrest. The arrival of the Freemans places him face to face with African Americans who both erode his uniqueness in the neighborhood and whose behavior may reflect poorly on him as the "good black."

Yet instead of making the Dubois family the sellout foils to the Freemans' righteous authenticity, McGruder satirizes the inconsistencies in both families in order to critique the pervasive impact of white hegemonic forces across multiple boundaries. *The Boondocks* collapses the discourse that makes authentic blackness class based, leaving its most incisive comic critiques for the parody of mainstream culture's often open, unyielding, and uncritical hostility to African Americans generally and African American culture and experience particularly. Through the outrageous, vulgar, and self-hating figure of Uncle Ruckus, however, McGruder takes the concept of the Uncle Tom to its hilariously enraged extreme. Although a figure that first appeared in the television episodes—where his praise of white Jesus, his open lust for white women, and his disdain for blacks he doesn't necessarily consider human are unmistakable—Ruckus has quickly become one of the most recognizable, controversial characters in *The Boondocks* treasury.

Grotesquely overweight, with an outsized eye reminiscent of Edgar Allan Poe's "The Tell-Tale Heart" or a character from the blackface minstrel tradition, Uncle Ruckus possesses a hatred of blackness running so deep that he claims to not be African American at all, despite having dark brown skin. He claims to suffer from revitiligo, a fictional disease that allegedly turns the skin darker and is the opposite of what the late Michael Jackson had. Because of this, Ruckus often refers to Jackson as a "lucky bastard" because he became lighter. In the episode "The Passion of Reverend Ruckus," Ruckus meets Ronald Reagan in what he initially thinks is heaven but what is actually, according to Reagan, "White Heaven." Replicating the racial hierarchy of the secular world in the divine space of heaven, Reagan feels free to confess openly to Ruckus that Jesus is white and that "God doesn't really have that much of a problem with racism. He doesn't remember slavery, except in February" ("The Passion of Reverend Ruckus"). Reagan then offers to turn Ruckus white if he will spread the "good news" of White Jesus. While this encounter appears to Ruckus as a dream and is a seeming reaction to the inoperable tumor on his back, Ruckus becomes a wildly famous televangelist—to the horror of Granddad and Tom—with memorable phrases like "Praise White Jesus!" and a white audience undergoing a cathartic celebration of its white privilege. McGruder wraps these threads up neatly in its clear play on Mel Gibson's wildly popular film, *The Passion of the Christ* (2004)—in which Christ is white and which many have argued unfairly characterizes Jews—and the image of Ronald Reagan, virtually deified after his death and frequently thought of as one of the greatest presidents of all time.

Yet McGruder's Ronald Reagan informs, "White Heaven is for decent, good, God-fearing Christians who just happen to, well, hate everyone and everything relating to black people. That means no Muhammad Ali, no hip-hop music and no fucking Jesse Jackson" ("The Passion of Reverend Ruckus"). His presidency is celebrated as reestablishing American credibility and power after many inside and outside the United States began to question its standing because of Vietnam, Watergate, and the Civil Rights / Black Power Movements. McGruder, however, casts a radically different narrative. Reagan's presidency recovered white middle-class ideology and values as the desirable standard through which to judge one's authentic American-ness in contrast to the tumultuous period of the 1960s and 1970s. In his mind, Reagan oversees the reassertion of white power and privilege through the emergence of a conservative counterrevolution based on white rage, the erosion of the gains of the Civil Rights Movement, and the stark urban decay that socially and economically marginalized the working- and underclass African American. As he takes Ruckus on a tour of White Heaven, Reagan ticks off a frightening list of accomplishments that many African Americans, particularly in their support of and excitement over Jesse Jackson's two presidential campaigns, often see as Reagan's true legacy: "Personally, I hate black people, Ruckus. That's why I did everything I could to make their lives miserable. Crack? Me. AIDS? Me. Reaganomics . . . come on, I'm in the name" ("The Passion of Reverend Ruckus"). Reagan's confession acts as a comic critique of the gulf between Reagan's public persona and the impact of his policies, a gulf that recalls Reagan's days as an actor whose honesty in White Heaven evokes a humor rooted in rage connected with the recognition of not only the policies' impact on black lives but the coded language that cast African Americans in parodies as extreme as the one that Reagan constructed of himself. Reagan then offers to turn Ruckus white if he will spread the "good news" of White Jesus.

While Ruckus is eventually struck by lightning and cured of his cancer at the end of the episode, his continued presence in the series and eventual presence in the comic strip demonstrate that he has become an effective lens through which we can view black self-hatred and the internalizing of certain white supremacist hegemonic messages. Ruckus's encounter with Reagan acts as metaphorical birthing, one that mirrors the emergence of black conservatives in the 1980s who were influenced by the Reagan mythos. An amalgamation of black conservative figures from Supreme Court Justice Clarence Thomas to commentators Armstrong Williams and Larry Elder appear in "Passion" as Armstrong Elder and praise Ruckus's work. Elder is a hero to Ruckus, if for no other reason than Elder's marriage to a white woman, and the two men receive a sizable amount of comic invective from McGruder. Yet it is not their conservativism that The Boondocks finds offensive. It is their uncritical adoption of white hegemonic ideologies of a newly color-blind America without flaw that accompanies constructions of post–civil rights African American embracing of a culture of victimhood. While the show satirically reveals the moments of crisis that occur when the

Dubois family is confronted by the presence of race, figures like Elder and Ruckus tie themselves into proverbial knots in order to avoid acknowledging the impact of racial oppression and structural inequalities.

One of the second season's most controversial episodes, indeed one of two that were banned from appearing, is "The Uncle Ruckus Reality Show," which imagines BET airing a reality show centered on Uncle Ruckus as he struggles with test results that confirm his ethnic identity. In addition to McGruder's continued assault on BET for its narrow, destructive images of African Americans, the episode reveals the impact of constructions of race on Ruckus. Claiming at the beginning of the episode that he had thirty-two jobs when he still believed he was white, Ruckus quits all of them once he is "black" and believes that, in order to make money, he will "probably have to start selling crack. Or rapping. Or rapping about selling crack" ("The Uncle Ruckus Reality Show"). Ruckus's depression is so complete that BET's villainous executives have to force doctors to lie about the results of his test, which had initially found him not simply black, but 102 percent black. The show not only unleashes an unabashed criticism at BET, but it reveals the investment American national and ideological identity has in racial categorization and performance.

Part of the investment in categorization casts whites as innocent and allows "justified" expressions of rage and violence. By contrast, the Freemans frequently embody a significant portion of African America that rarely takes the narratives constructed by the (white) mainstream at face value and relies on perspectives rooted in their cultural traditions and continued exposure to racist experiences. Thus, McGruder's work, and African American humor generally, exposes how African American experiences with racism have impacted their critical viewing of American identity and ideology. For example, polls continually showed that African Americans were the most skeptical of the nation's construction of America as completely innocent in the War on Terror and, eventually, of arguments for the invasion of Iraq. Similarly, while other forms of media were slow to cast a critical eye on the nation's problematic responses post-9/11, *The Boondocks* pursues media and national responses with dogged intensity and unyielding irony. McGruder broadened his satirical critiques to consider white supremacy through the prism of terrorism, faux patriotism, and fear. For instance, Huey calls the FBI terrorist hotline to report someone who he claims helped the terrorists. That person turns out to be, in one strip, Ronald Reagan and, in another, George W. Bush. Of the latter Huey originally issues an edict to the FBI: "Make sure you bring nightsticks," a cutting reference to the police brutality directed at African Americans in both the Civil Rights Movement and with Rodney King in 1991. His editors wanted the strip changed, and the strip that was printed replaced nightsticks with "the really tight handcuffs" (McGruder, *All the Rage* 143). That he became a target for the rhetorical strategy of labeling dissenters or critics as unpatriotic only fueled his explicit rage. Indeed, the rampant, uncritical patriotism provided McGruder with an extended story arc and multiple opportunities for the expressions of comic rage that, if you will, animated his strip and opened the door for multiple instances for the parodying and satirizing of national and cultural hypocrisy. While many African Americans pointed out that America had been engaged in a centuries-long reign of terror on African America that ranged from slavery to Reconstruction to police brutality, *The Boondocks* succeeded in its open critique of the push toward invading Iraq because of the presence of its satiric fury.

Part of his open critique eventually resulted in the 2005 launch of the animated version of *The Boondocks* on the cable station Cartoon Network. As part of its [*adult swim*] block, which contains adult-themed cartoons, McGruder was free to be bolder and even more controversial—thematically and rhetorically—in his critiques. Thus, in his review of the first season's DVD collection, David Swerdlick soundly points out that "*The Boondocks* airs dirty laundry within the larger black community, but does so with wit, and without letting society as a whole off the hook for falling off the wagon when it comes racism" (para. 1). It is the controversial episode "Return of the King" that became the lightning rod for the first season and the manifestation for the show's willingness to "air dirty laundry" on both sides of the color line.[1] Imagining that Martin Luther King Jr. survived his assassination in 1968, the episode follows King after he awakes from a thirty-two-year coma. After witnessing an African America that has spiraled downward into lewdness, nihilism, and disarray, King explodes at a rally he calls in order to establish an independent black political party. While Huey watches from the side of the stage, King furiously proclaims, "WILL YOU IGNORANT NIGGAS *PLEASE* SHUT THE HELL UP?!" He launches into a speech that simultaneously questions ("This is it?! This is what I took all those ass whoopings for?!") and accuses ("But lo and behold, some four decades later, what have I found but a bunch of triflin', shiftless, good-for-nothing niggers!") ("The Return of the King"). King's frustration leads him to move to Canada where he dies at ninety-one, the same day Oprah is elected president as the result of an African American populace whose rage is transformed by King's speech into mass political action. The selection of Oprah, however, undercuts the potentially transformative nature of her election because Oprah, like Obama, is considered a post-racial figure that dismisses the more uncomfortable institutional, cultural critiques that King frequently made.

The King episode drew immediate criticism from Al Sharpton, who objected to King's use of the "n-word" and accused Cartoon Network of "desecrating black leaders" ("Sharpton Criticizes" para. 2). Unfortunately, Sharpton misses the episode's willingness to express frustration at certain destructive elements that many—even Sharpton himself—see within the African American community. More importantly, Sharpton also misses, as does Swerdlick, McGruder's critique of America's appropriation of the image of King and his use of nonviolence as a way to ignore contemporary and radical critiques of white supremacy. So not only is King not able to vote in the 2000 election because of a "voting irregularity," a clear reference to the significant number of African Americans who were disenfranchised during that election, but he is vilified for maintaining his commitment to nonviolence even after 9/11. As a guest on Bill Maher's former ABC show *Politically Incorrect*—itself a casualty of post-9/11 censoring—King encourages the nation to "turn the other cheek" as he encouraged African Americans to do during the Civil Rights Movement. King is immediately cast as unpatriotic and marginalized by mainstream society. Here, McGruder uses King to parody and indict the post-9/11 atmosphere that attempted to silence critical voices—including McGruder's own—that questioned the attacks on Islam, the use of violence, and policy decisions from torture to the Patriot Act. Moreover, the hostility shown toward King recalls his waning popularity because of his criticism of American involvement in Vietnam and reveals a double standard that rejects radical, violent forms of resistance by African Americans while American military engagement is often uncritically celebrated.

In situating McGruder as "Cosby's Younger, Hipper Son," Swerdlick asserts that "McGruder has jettisoned the family-friendly, 'best foot forward' approach that characterized Cosby's career. . . . In a certain sense, with the TV incarnation of *The Boondocks*, McGruder bailed Bill Cosby out by using comedy to mount a guerilla campaign on black issues where Cosby's frontal assault has stalled for lack of street cred, pathos, and humor" (Swerdlick para. 10). The collective act of self-determination that McGruder provides differs from Cosby's critiques. Cosby's demands to return to hard work and personal responsibility are not only mean-spirited, but they resonate with core tenets of American mythology and ideals that often ignore the institutional factors that hinder certain groups from advancing collectively. Moreover, *The Boondocks* frequently points out that those ideals are rarely ever the cause of success in the first place. From the pilot episode, the show makes clear that Riley's older, white friend and neighbor Ed Wuncler III remains protected by the power and money of his grandfather. His advancement is predicated on a legacy of exploitation, particularly of those of color. In the episode entitled "Let's Nab Oprah," Ed and Gin Rummy—voiced by

Samuel L. Jackson and Charlie Murphy, respectively, in a stunning act of signifying on blackface minstrelsy—take Riley along as they rob a bank. The use of Jackson and Murphy becomes important because it ridicules whites whose fascination with and appropriation of African American culture leads them to "act black" while sustaining the privileges and benefits of whiteness. Their use is intentional because both actors have been consistently associated with black "cool," with Jackson linked to the 1970s emergence of black "cool" through Quentin Tarantino's films *Pulp Fiction* (1994) and *Jackie Brown* (1997) and his starring role in the remake of *Shaft* (2000). By contrast, Charlie Murphy's association with *Chappelle's Show* (2003–2006), and especially his memorable stories about Rick James and Prince,[2] have provided a comic "cool" counterpoint to Jackson that, while laced with fear of black violence, has eclipsed his previous claim to fame, being Eddie Murphy's brother. When the police show up to Ed's house after the bank robbery, Ed demands to know why they suspect him. Revealing the wallet he dropped at the scene, the squirming police officers let Ed go, profusely apologizing for inconveniencing him. When Ed and Gin initially fail to kidnap Oprah, mistakenly taking Maya Angelou instead, they gain access to Harpo Studios when Huey distracts the guards in his attempt to stop Riley from participating. In the green room they find Bill Cosby mumbling and ranting incomprehensibly to himself. Although Ed and Gin eventually kidnap Cosby, they soon return him because, as the voice of Huey proclaims, Cosby was "too annoying." Thus, the episode rejects Cosby as a spokesperson and ideological father in part because, as Swerdlick notes, "Cosby has unintentionally stepped on his own message by leaving out the key ingredient of humor that enabled him to become a black spokesman in the first place" (par. 12). *The Boondocks* ridicules Cosby not only because of his failure to recognize the institutional factors at work in African Americans' lives, but also because of the absence of a comic lens that helps frame his critique or satirize the absurdity to which he bares witness.

Mainstream sentiment toward the possibility of post-racial America threatens to censor—if not erase—voices that critique the inconsistencies or hypocrisies in America's racial narrative. In an interview, McGruder contends that humor is an effective way to mine the explosive terrain of race: "it allows people to sort of let their guard down—and rethink some issues. Certainly, it's been done effectively by stand-up comics. I mean Chris Rock and Richard Pryor, you know, have—have addressed race in a—I think in a very effective way" (*All the Rage* 135). McGruder's reference to Pryor and Rock situates his work within the tradition of African American humor that moves beyond traditional forms to enact expressions of comic rage. In Pryor's work this emerges in a sketch in which a slave celebrates

America's Bicentennial by giving thanks for all the horrors enacted upon African Americans. In Rock, it is the challenge he launches against black and white responses to the first O. J. Simpson trial as a way to disrupt the racial polarization that characterized the case. In a post–civil rights context, that dichotomy situates those who claim to act in favor of color blindness against those for whom race is preeminent and intractable. Works of comic rage realign this debate by taking on the fundamental assumptions upon which the initial dichotomy is formed. Put more simply, *The Boondocks* looks at representations of blackness both alongside and independent of its relationship to whiteness.

The key element of *The Boondocks* in its comic assault is its unfettered focus on challenging and expanding ideas of blackness. McGruder's concern does not emerge from an attempt to initiate feelings of universality but is instead motivated by a desire to celebrate a dynamic blackness. While the discourse of authentic blackness has at times been a constructive way to explore the oftentimes patriarchal, homophobic, and regional biases that accompany some calls for racial solidarity, its more recent moments consider behaviors and characteristics that appeal to whites and minimize difference in support of ideas of the post-racial. The controversy that has surrounded McGruder has made the strip and the show, as McGruder argues, "better, more honest, and more truthful than a lot of what's in the newspapers today" and, with a tongue-in-cheek embodiment of black nationalist bravado, the strip became "a daily foot in the ass of The Man, and I think that's what Huey would want" (*Right to Be Hostile* 10). *The Boondocks* celebrates difference by exploring which aspects of African American cultural traditions are constructive and which ones are destructive. It becomes blackness we can believe in, one that takes its historical status as the abjected race and transforms it—through the mix of African and European traditions—into what Ralph Ellison once called "the embodiment of American democratic ideals," particularly through their ability to critique; their constant, if sometimes ineffective, negotiation with minority voices within the community; and their belief in collective uplift.

Notes

1. See also Marvin McAllister's article in this collection, pp. 240–53.
2. See also James J. Donahue's article in this collection, pp. 228–39.

The Lower Frequencies: Hip-Hop Satire in the New Millennium

Kinohi Nishikawa

In 2000 Paul Gilroy launched a scathing critique of popular culture, and particularly the global branding of hip-hop, in his provocatively titled book, *Against Race*.[1] Gilroy argued that throughout the 1990s, hip-hop had forsworn the struggle for social justice in its blind pursuit of commercial success. In his estimation, that pursuit had irrevocably transformed the variegated intercultures of hip-hop into a depoliticized, corporate-controlled package whose purchase on racial authenticity ironically made it appear to be "the very *blackest* culture" (181; emphasis in original). The consequences of this massively monetized sleight of hand were dire, according to Gilroy. Passing itself off as the very essence of blackness, commercial hip-hop kowtowed to market forces that would only countenance iterations of "revolutionary conservatism, misogyny, and stylized tales of sexual excess" among black artists (178). In fact, hip-hop had been so consumed by the branding and commodification of African American pathology, Gilroy said, that the music now stood alongside fascist propaganda as the most pernicious forms of race-essentialist oppression in the twentieth century. In suggesting we conceptually orient our thinking "against race," then, Gilroy was in many ways encouraging us to move beyond hip-hop's mainstream success.

In the time since Gilroy's critique was published, a surprising number of hip-hop artists have come to echo key points in his analysis. They have done so not by lamenting the music's ostensible decline but by fashioning innovative work that aims to deconstruct the corporate logic propelling the genre's mass appeal: commodifying racial authenticity. If, following Gilroy, mainstream hip-hop has succumbed to the reifying conditions of the market for racial essentialism, these artists have emerged with the intention of performing hip-hop against itself, of reanimating the music in a way that challenges the coherence of race as such. While underground activist rappers have been the most prominent artists to be linked to such a transformation in hip-hop,[2] less recognized has been the work of what this essay will refer to as "hip-hop satirists": rappers who lampoon, ironize, and otherwise point up the folly of society's hegemonic understanding of rap. Unlike the high-minded, dead-serious music of "socially conscious" artists, hip-hop satirists have taken refuge in the comic mode as a means of undoing authenticity's hold on African American culture. Their efforts have led to the development of a growing, if still inchoate, field of hip-hop satire: a subgenre that advances the funniest, and often most profound, critique of rap's investment in "keeping it real."

That oft-repeated phrase has become the butt of hip-hop satirists' jokes despite its presumption to speak for the marginal and oppressed. On the one hand, according to hip-hop scholar Tricia Rose, the positive motivation behind "keeping it real" asks rappers to draw from their experiences to create music that bears witness to "truths about poor black urban life that many people want to shove under the rug" (134). Whereas the news media, politicians, and middle-class Americans routinely ignore actually existing racial and class inequalities, hip-hop ideally could give first-person narrative voice to those who live them out every day. The flip side, however, is that the commercial market for rap has promoted only specific aspects of that life—to wit, "drug dealing, hustling, gang-banging, hoes and pimping" (135)—as touchstones of authentic black experience. And on this count, Rose has argued, hip-hop's corporate backers have in "keeping it real" a ready-made defense to manufacture what sells: the basest, most prurient iterations of violence, criminality, and sexual objectification among African American performers. The phrase thus papers over a dubious marketing strategy that would turn "voyeuristic fantasies about black people as pimps, hustlers, and gang-bangers" into street-level accounts of "ultimate realness" (141–142, 137).

This essay will contend that hip-hop satire offers a withering but no less humorous assessment of commercial hip-hop's fetishization of racial authenticity. Its argument will orbit around three acts—two emcees, Mighty Casey and Childish Gambino, and a group, Little Brother—that have contributed to the subgenre's rise in the new millennium. Taken together, these acts advance what might be called hip-hop's post-real imaginary: an arena of discourse whereby hard men, fast women, and the cycle of exploitation in which they participate are satirized through the lens of a rigorous anti-essentialism. And despite their apparent differences in age, background, and geographic origin, the artists examined here share a conception of the post-real as an aesthetic and material riposte to commercial hip-hop. Aesthetically, Mighty Casey, Little Brother, and Childish Gambino venture lyrical wordplay (especially in rhyme and metaphor) and performative styles (vis-à-vis sampling and flow) that suggestively curtail commercial rap's declarative, first-person masculine voice. But equally important, these hip-hop satirists are encouraged to take risks in their art because they have relied on independent record labels and, more recently, on digital media to fly under the corporate radar and get their music to listeners. Insofar as the post-real has never been commercially popular, then, this essay will maintain that, at its core, hip-hop satire is aesthetically and materially predetermined to be a musical subgenre, operating exclusively on the lower frequencies of black cultural life.

To begin, we turn to Boston native Mighty Casey, who released his first and only studio album, *Original Rudebwoy*, in 2003. The son of a black Jamaican father and a white South African mother, he was born Casey Gane-McCalla, grew up in nearby Cambridge, Massachusetts, graduated from high school in 1994, and went on to take studio production classes at Columbia University in New York. Upon graduating from college in 1998, Gane-McCalla gained an underground following as Mighty Casey with vinyl and extended play, or EP, recordings that promoted his satirical acumen. One single in particular, "White Girls," became so popular that he adapted it into a music video that began airing regularly on Black Entertainment Television (BET) on the late-night show *BET: Uncut* in 2002. The single's cult success drew attention to Mighty Casey's album, which was distributed exclusively by the small, independent label Busted Lip Records. Both artist and label achieved a degree of crossover success in 2004, when "White Girls" played during the end credits for the Wayans brothers' film, *White Chicks* (Mighty Casey, "Bio").

A self-described humorist, Mighty Casey was one of the first rappers to satirize the contradictions in commercial hip-hop's valorization of racial authenticity. In "White Girls" and "Black Rapping School," in particular, he parodies the image of urban black masculinity that became well-nigh synonymous with the genre in the 1990s. The former pokes fun at the rapper's desire for white women in such a way as to point up his color consciousness, while the latter underscores hip-hop's unnatural relation to the street by having a record executive instruct a student on how to become a "real" emcee. In both tracks, Mighty Casey's choppy, almost labored, flow evokes an image of the untutored, amateur rapper as the ironic obverse to mainstream hip-hop's cool, self-possessed male voices.

"White Girls" is musically laid on the foundation of a widely recognizable source: Melle Mel's 1983 track "White Lines (Don't Do It)," a classic of old school hip-hop. But where Melle Mel cautions against drug use ("white lines" referring to cocaine), the emcee in Mighty Casey's single revels in his addiction to white women. The song's hook goes, "White girls (Suzy, Jen, and Karen) / Goin' through my mind (Sarah, Jess, and Julie too) / White girls (Judy, Beth, and Sharon) / Help me unwind (The more I see the more I do) / Don't tell Minister Farrakhan (That's right) / He don't wanna know what's goin' on (OK) / 'Cause white girls won't go away." Mighty Casey's plodding delivery of these lines nicely reflects the speaker's dreamlike state, wherein generically "white" names tiptoe around his conscious realization that pro-black nationalists such as Louis Farrakhan would frown upon his predilections. Yet it is precisely the Nation of Islam leader's fundamentalist stance toward race—widely cited in nationalist rap of the 1990s[3]—that Mighty Casey is interested in debunking here. For if race essentialism demands a certain fidelity to the notion of a "pure" blackness, his very mixed-race background makes Mighty Casey a suspect, "not black enough" rapper. The speaker quickly dismisses such ideology with rhymed couplets in the first verse: "What up, baby girl, how ya doin', is you single? / Have you ever messed with a light-skinned Mandingo?" and "I can give a damn what all my friends say to me / You and me, baby, can start makin' up for slavery." With these lines, the speaker at once embodies gender and racial stereotypes (that is, the black buck) and undoes their social legibility. Indeed, the male voice comes across not as a self-possessed lothario but as an opportunist with skin color always on his mind.

So it is that "White Girls" satirizes hip-hop's masculine ethos with a figure whose predilections are objectifying but ridiculous. The rapper's obsession with white women is drawn out to such a degree that we cannot help but laugh at the false idol he has created out of his virility. The second verse, for example, names a host of white celebrities whom the speaker claims to have bedded. Two lines read, "Gwyneth Paltrow's always sayin' I be makin' her laugh / She gave me head 'cause if I hit it, I break her in half." The clear incongruity the speaker develops between Paltrow's sweet demeanor and the baseness of his (fantasized) sexual act has the effect of casting the latter as compensatory overkill. The same might be said of the following lines: "And I got Alyssa Milano hittin' high notes like sopranos / When we all up in my bedroom makin' some mulattoes." In this instance, however, the idea of compensation is explicitly linked to a dubious act of integration-by-miscegenation, which Mighty Casey highlights by emphasizing internal and end rhymes: "Milano," "sopranos," and "mulattoes." The very next couplet, near the end of the song, summarizes the folly of the speaker's color consciousness as a kind of satirical obverse to racial authenticity: "I really don't think there's a girl that I missed / I used to like Mariah 'til I learned she was mixed." With the rapper's unswerving preference for white women running up against the complex racial background of songstress Mariah Carey, we arrive at Mighty Casey's finest in-joke about what happens when his own impure blackness is projected onto the opposite sex.

Like "White Girls," "Black Rapping School" presents an unreliable speaker to convey Mighty Casey's critique of commercial hip-hop. The song's title refers to Robert Townsend's 1987 film, *Hollywood Shuffle*, which featured a daydream sequence, "Black Acting School," that skewered the motion picture industry's limiting African American roles in Hollywood to that of "a butler or a slave." Adapting Townsend's vision to the record industry, Mighty Casey's droning, repetitive hook simply says, "Black Rapping School (Just do the hip-hop shuffle)." And indeed, we soon find that the voice behind the drone is the school's master teacher, a profits-first executive who reveals what it takes to succeed as a corporate-sponsored black emcee. The speaker begins his pitch with, "Do you wanna be a rap star? Live large and push a phat car? / Get some ice, a Rollie, and a Jaguar? / (It's yours!) But only for the video shoot / 'Cause we just wanna make people think you got loot." Taking aim at rap's fetishization of so-called "bling," Mighty Casey's lyrics position the executive as offering the promise of riches, only to withdraw that promise with the frank acknowledgment that bling is an illusion that sells records. As the verse continues, what proves to be just as illusory is the "gangsta" persona around which much of commercial rap's investment in "living large" orbits: "First things first, nigga, learn your limitation / Why be yourself, go be a Jigga imitation (Hov!) / We don't need creativity or originality / Just an R&B gangsta with a thug mentality." The speaker cites the extraordinary success of Jay-Z ("Jigga" being one of his aliases) as the model on which the tutee must base his own act. The use of the word "nigga," in this context, is strategic, for its rhyming with "Jigga" renders the hip-hop star complicit in the reduction of hip-hop's ethos to "a thug mentality." As the mouthpiece for Mighty Casey's satirical critique, the executive cannot help but point up the fiction of "keeping it real," to reveal not only its constructedness but its status as a shameless marketing gimmick.

For that reason, Mighty Casey's labored flow over a relatively simplistic beat is not incidental to the aesthetics of "Black Rapping School." Rather, it is the very reflection of commercial hip-hop's clunky, obtuse effort to transform rap into prepackaged goods. In one couplet, the speaker stumbles through, "This ain't rap for the art, so don't try and be smart / Just play your part and rap for the chart." The hard internal and external rhymes here are pronounced; they do not lend themselves to smooth utterance. The second line's first word ("Just"), moreover, is unduly drawn out by Mighty Casey in order to make the rhythmic sequence exact. But the choppy flow is very much part of the act: it is the post-real kernel of a performance that recoils on itself, that turns hip-hop satire's gaze back on the speaker's advice. "Trade in your soul for a chain and a throwback," he counsels the young charge, "But once you sell your soul it can't grow back." "Black Rapping

School" trades on such wisdom, and it is to Mighty Casey's credit that he manipulates ostensible weaknesses—to wit, repetitive phrases and clumsy rhymes—into indices of his speaker's suspect motives.

Despite his undoubted talent, which made hip-hop satire precisely consonant with the low production value of his songs, Mighty Casey found little success after the release of his album. Aiming to buttress his groundswell of support, in 2005 he adapted "Black Rapping School" into a music video that, unsurprisingly, was rather critical of the record industry. The move proved to be a step too far for the fledgling rapper, and in his words the video was "censored" by both BET and Music Television, or MTV (Mighty Casey "Bio"). Mighty Casey has since retreated from the music scene, though as Casey Gane-McCalla he has continued to pillory commercial hip-hop in other media. His most notable projects have been two underground film parodies—*6 Brothaz in a Cadillac* (2006) and *Monkey Gang: The Mockumentary* (2011)—and a Web comedy show titled "Thats Whatsup." If Mighty Casey's trailblazing work ultimately ran up against the corporate media's dictate to "keep it real," Gane-McCalla has remained a hip-hop satirist in the digital age, using alternative media to echo Chris Rock's sarcastic gloss on the phrase as "keep it real dumb."[4]

Like Mighty Casey, the North Carolina rap group Little Brother had flourished in the hip-hop underground before its satirical acumen was lauded by mainstream critics and fans alike. And having released its major studio work at the same time as Mighty Casey, Little Brother, too, experienced corporate resistance to its recordings. The group began in 2001 as an offshoot of the Durham hip-hop collective, The Justus League. Its three members had known each other since 1998, when they were students at the city's historically black North Carolina Central University. Emcees Phonte (born Phonte Coleman) and Big Pooh (born Thomas Jones) rapped the lyrics, while deejay and producer 9th Wonder (born Pat Douthit) provided the group's innovative and infectious beats. Unlike Mighty Casey, this group oriented its music around technically superb production values, and Little Brother soon garnered a loyal following at its live shows. After certain of their tracks exploded on the Internet, Little Brother secured a recording contract with Oakland-based independent label ABB Records. The group's debut studio album, *The Listening*, appeared in 2003, and with its rave reviews in tow, Little Brother and ABB subsequently teamed up with industry behemoth Atlantic Records to bring out a second album, *The Minstrel Show*, in 2005 (Huey).

For its time, Little Brother was at the forefront of promoting a distinctly southern alternative to the dominant East Coast-West Coast axis along which commercial hip-hop had defined itself in the 1990s. But in addition to offering a different way of listening to the music, thanks in large part to the talents of 9th Wonder, the group also conceptualized hip-hop satire as the organizing principle behind its inevitable branding by record labels in the form of its studio albums. The eighteen tracks of *The Listening*, for example, are framed as a full day's programming at the fictional "WJLR," or "Justus League Radio." While not every track in the album is of a satirical bent, the media frame itself subtly calls our attention to the racial logic of the "urban" radio market. This frame device is deployed to more powerful effect in Little Brother's masterwork *The Minstrel Show*, whose seventeen tracks are interlaced with programming for the fictional "UBN," or "U Black Niggas Network." In UBN's name, Little Brother risks a wink at underground hip-hop fans who would have sneered at the group's signing with Atlantic. But that wink bespeaks a self-consciousness about "selling out" that inflects Little Brother's entire musical output. The album's frame narrative thus positions the group's otherwise deeply personal songs as meta-reflective of the terms of black cultural representation.

UBN references the now-defunct broadcast television network, United Paramount Network (UPN), which in the late 1990s and early 2000s was known to feature a critical mass of African American–oriented sitcoms, including *Moesha*, *Malcolm & Eddie*, and *The Parkers*. In calling its network "U Black Niggas," Little Brother no doubt lampoons the watered-down version of black life displayed on these mostly forgettable shows. But the album's overarching concept extends well beyond an isolated critique of UPN. Indeed, its very title gestures to Spike Lee's 2000 film *Bamboozled* as inspiring a broader critique of race in commercial popular culture. For it is on UBN, the initial track makes clear, that *The Minstrel Show* program airs with Little Brother as its main act. Here the reference to nineteenth-century blackface spectacles is performed with a straight face, as YahZarah's melodic theme song and white host Chris Hardwick's welcome betray no sign of parodic intent. And that, on a deeper level of meaning, is the ironic point: just as Lee's television executive Pierre Delacroix (Damon Wayans) is bamboozled to find America hungry for a twenty-first-century minstrel show, so are we left to wonder how much of our own tastes and desires are bound up with Little Brother's openly fetishistic frame narrative.

Intriguingly, despite the fact that the album is structured throughout by its UBN frame, most of the actual songs are performed sincerely, with comic elements embedded in microunits of lyric, not in the rappers' voices as such. Unlike Mighty Casey, then, Big Pooh and Phonte do not typically assume the personae they aim to critique.[5] Instead, the emcees speak openly about their struggles to make it in hip-hop, the idea of "selling out" emerging as one of their greatest fears. It thus takes a keen ear for detail to hear how the music contests the album's invocation of "the biggest colored show on earth." The track "Not Enough," for example, follows Little Brother's move from the underground to the mainstream with lines that venture a critical view of the record industry. Phonte raps, "It's history in the makin' / When I write it's for all of NC, call me the State Pen / And now I'm makin' my name for those who hate that I'm / Stakin' my claim just like Nationwide." With the accompaniment of a string-instrumental sample from Teddy Pendergrass's track, "Easy, Easy, Got to Take It Easy" (1977), Phonte negotiates local roots in North Carolina with a clever pun ("the State Pen," or rhyme creator) as well as the travails of commercial rap with a supremely executed enjambment ("I'm / Stakin'") that ends in a comic analogy ("like Nationwide" [the insurance company]). To be sure, such wordplay is a touchstone of hip-hop writ large, and its citation in "Not Enough" does not itself constitute a satirical critique. But these lines do operate on a satirical register if we recall the frame narrative of *The Minstrel Show*, which in reality would deny space for calling out "those who hate" Phonte's revealing the truth of his experience.

The interplay between lyrics and frame in *The Minstrel Show* thus brings to the fore post-real iterations of blackness that are, paradoxically, grounded in Little Brother's personal experiences. The group's suggestion is that if conventional minstrel shows did much to erase the humanity behind the mask (that is, face paint), UBN's version will do precisely the opposite even while highlighting the potential for the group's message to be drowned out by the corporate media. That aim is further illuminated in "Say It Again," a song that begins with a male voice posing as a female "correspondent" for *The Minstrel Show* as he sits down with the group over some "Sean Don," the street moniker for the champagne Moët and Chandon. The genderbending introduction signals Little Brother's ambitious effort to combine a smooth, melodic riff from Five Special's "Do Something Special (For Your Lady)" (1980) with hard-nosed observations on the current state of hip-hop. Around the falsetto phrase, "Make you wanna say, 'Ah!' When it's good," Phonte and Big Pooh rap, respectively:

I'm comin' out with a bang
Straight Tay [Phonte], Pooh, and 9th with no middle man
Everybody at the label askin', "Will it bang?"
I say chill, just take a Percocet or Ritalin
Now let my people sing
[1line ellipses #]
And my fingers start crampin' up
Pose ampin' up, I'm standin', what
Y'all niggas ain't man enough, chill

Agitatin' like dandruff
I ain't talkin' all tough, but the people keep sayin'

Phonte and Pooh make their way through these lines by drawing out aural rhymes that, on paper, seem impossible: for example, "bang" with "Ritalin" (the last syllable pronounced "lane") and "sing" (pronounced "sang"); or "crampin' up" with "standin', what" (as in a mock surprise, "What?") and "dandruff" (pronounced with three syllables). While such stereotypically masculine bravura recalls classic rap boasts, what distinguishes this song from others is how 9th Wonder ends these verses on the key phrase, "When it's good." That musical touch not only softens the force of the emcees' boasts ("bang," "ain't man enough") but also ventriloquizes the satisfaction of the group's primary audience: "the" or "my people." It is a combination that underscores how crafty *The Minstrel Show* can be in ironic counterpoint, a microstrategy of autobiographical revelation that works with and against the album's edifice of commercial blackface.

Having established a high point in aesthetic achievement for hip-hop satire, *The Minstrel Show* also turned out to be Little Brother's last major work as a three-person group. The album seemed ill-fated even before it was released. As early reviews were being published, Joshua Ratcliffe, editor-in-chief of the industry magazine *The Source*, resigned from his position, allegedly in protest over the album's rating demotion by the company's higher-ups. The presumed reason for the demotion was that Little Brother's satirical romp could in no way be seen on equal terms with hip-hop's more commercial acts (V. Walker). Around the same time, the group's music video for the single "Lovin' It" was denied airplay by BET for allegedly being "too intelligent" for its hip-hop-oriented audience. The music video was especially notable for poking fun at both commercial and underground rap, with respective "gangsta" and "backpacker" labels being cast aside in the narrative (Chery).[6] Yet despite Little Brother's walking a fine line between indie and mainstream acceptance, *The Minstrel Show* was a commercial failure. Two years later, not only did 9th Wonder leave the group to pursue other projects, but the reorganized duo also parted ways with Atlantic over the company's lack of artistic development support (Kayser). Although Little Brother released two more albums, in 2007 and 2010, neither approached the creative peak of its earlier recordings.

By the late 2000s it had become abundantly clear that hip-hop satirists had no real place to cultivate their art through traditional media channels. Indeed, as physical record sales plummeted with the rise of digital media, it became even less feasible to craft post-real iterations of blackness in commercial rap. Hip-hop satirists have responded to these changes by disseminating their work through the very medium that has otherwise ravaged the industry: the Internet. In particular, the precipitous rise of emcee Childish Gambino is symptomatic of how a critical mass of online buzz may propel an unsigned artist to mass-media attention. He experienced this after independently producing three studio albums, an EP, and two mixtapes, and then releasing all of them as free downloads between 2008 and 2011. In fact, it was not until 2011's *Camp* that he worked with a label at all, in this case Glassnote Records. The stage name of actor, writer, stand-up comedian, and deejay Donald Glover, Childish Gambino tapped into a more expansive and diverse listenership for hip-hop satire than had previous artists. Not only did the Internet expand the audience for his music, it also raised the stakes on how intelligent and funny listeners expected his work to be. Indeed, as the avatar of hip-hop satire in the digital age, Childish Gambino has had to exert considerable talent in order to stay around for even this long.

About ten years younger than the other artists discussed here, Glover took up the microphone as a student at New York University for a reason that echoes the motivation behind all hip-hop satire: the need to fashion an alternative voice in rap that would reflect, by comic insight or ironic contrast, his own tastes and experiences rather than "hip-hop's boilerplate subject matter: babes, bullets, bling" (C. Lee). The acclaimed album *Culdesac* (2010) does just that in a way that underscores Childish Gambino's dexterity as a vehicle for satirical critique. For in Glover's hands the rapper alternates between performing the object of critique (as we see in Mighty Casey) and deploying the autobiographical self to contest the regime of commodified stereotypes (as we see in Little Brother). "Put It in My Video," a track familiar with the objectification of so-called video vixens, exemplifies the former, while the personal testimonials we find in "The Last" illustrate the latter.

Driven by an up-tempo beat around which an electric sitar riff from The Stylistics' "You Are My Everything" (1971) curls, "Put It in My Video" features the rapper in full braggadocio mode as he puffs up his own "swagger." The song's hook makes good on his demonstrated machismo by listing the types of "girls" he wants to put in his music video: "light-skinned girls," "dark-skinned girls," "thick girls," "thin girls," "smarty art chicks," "dumb hoes," "smooth girls," and "nerd girls." The indiscriminate references to females of all types of shades, backgrounds, and sizes have a double valence: they at once buy into the fantasy of sexual objectification flaunted in commercial hip-hop's video vixens and undercut the racially authentic coordinates of that fantasy. Descriptors in the vein of "thin," "smarty art," and "nerd" are nonexistent in "keeping it real" discourse for the very reason that they lie beyond the scope of the corporate media's construction of urban black life. The anti-essentialist core of Childish Gambino's otherwise bluster-filled performance is revealed more clearly in two key lines in the first verse: "So now I'm in the club tellin' strippers they should back it up / I wanna hang with Lil Wayne, I just hope that I'm black enough." Here the rapper conjures an apparent contradiction between vixen fetishization ("tellin' strippers they should back it up") and racial anxiety ("I just hope that I'm black enough"). Because he admits to not being as readily "black" as the infamously hard-core emcee Lil Wayne, Childish Gambino qualifies his sexual prowess as either lacking or illegible in hip-hop circles.

To the extent that the macho persona of "Put It in My Video" is shown to be self-reflexive about its constructedness, it constitutes a post-real riposte to commercial rap's exploitation of black and brown female bodies in the music video industry.[7] For where the conventional male hip-hop persona is presumed to be promiscuous, unfeeling, and interested in only a certain type of woman, Childish Gambino embodies sexual appetite to such an extreme that one cannot help but laugh at its absurdity. Observing people at the club, he raps: "It's funny how these niggas all treat me like we best friends / I wanna fuck these small girls, minus "SM" / Meaning that I fuck all girls, that is wordplay / Catch me on my iPhone doin' what the birds say." Lodged in a rhyme scheme that gestures to other nodes of thought (posers who treat him as "best friends" and sending "tweets" over Twitter, the social media website) is a superb joke about Childish Gambino's sexual proclivities. Once more he casts himself as a kind of voracious consumer of "small girls." But the word "small" is uttered, we realize, only in the service of a subtraction game that would transform its complete phrasing into "all girls." It may be a cheap joke, but it is one that subordinates the rapper's sexual ego to his propensity for "wordplay," mentioned here in a redundant and thus satirical fashion. And although the joke by no means dispenses with sexual objectification, it does denaturalize the link commercial hip-hop draws between it and black masculinity, for there is nothing transparent or unconstructed about the rapper's excessive speech.

A significant component of Childish Gambino's performance of reflexivity is his own nasally, stereotypically "educated" voice. On this point, Glover does not conceal his middle-class roots in Stone Mountain, Georgia, a predominantly black suburb of Atlanta, through an affected "street" or "thug" persona. Instead, Childish Gambino's rapping style bears traces of Glover's own background and experiences, congealed into a heady gumbo of interracial musical and cultural influences and grounded in a bold rejection of the hood as his everyday reality. The song "The Last" makes use of hip-hop satire's microstrategy of autobiographical revelation to set Childish Gambino's signature style in relief against the implied backdrop of commodified racial authenticity. His voice occasionally coming across as a whine over the cool, electro-pop beat, Childish Gambino confesses, "Other rappers try and go and get over / You want that hood shit best to go and call Hova / I was a good kid, backpack on my shoulder / 98 test score in my *ThunderCat* folder." In these rhymed couplets, the speaker first cites his familiarity with the black vernacular tradition, linking a certain "coming up from the hood" narrative with the idea of "getting over," or surviving and prevailing over the conditions of one's oppression. Yet Childish Gambino calls that narrative "shit," implying that the way "Hova," or Jay-Z, has rendered it a cliché in commercial hip-hop does not account for his own youth. Rather, he "was a good kid" growing up, academically minded and drawn more to underground hip-hop (a double meaning succinctly captured in the word *backpacker*). We might even call him a nerd, safely removed from the streets, as the references to a "98" score and the cartoon series *ThunderCats* suggest.

For all that, the speaker relates his fair share of uncertainty and confusion about never quite fitting in. African American kids keep their distance, he says, "'Cause I talk too white and I got a dad who's there," while among white friends, he continues, "I'm wishin' I was someone else always." Far removed from the stuff of commercial hip-hop, these concerns are relayed sincerely, without parodic intent. "Leave the joke raps aside," Childish Gambino tells us. Yet considering the degree to which the genre of confessional rap has been winnowed down by the record industry to prop up only those artists whose back stories legitimate its marketing of "keeping it real," Childish Gambino's reflections do tap into a satirical register of some consequence. Indeed, "The Last" recuperates frank and even vulnerable confessional rap for the nonhood set, including those who, like the man behind Childish Gambino's stage persona, grew up black, middle class, and highly conversant with suburban American popular culture. In the song's finest example of the post-real's autobiographical impulse, the rapper looks back on his early career, a moment when "nobody was jockin' my style / 'Cause I had a high voice, they called me faggot 8 Mile." Rather than shirk the homophobic reference to white rapper Eminem (who starred in his own autobiographical film *8 Mile* [2002]), Childish Gambino embraces the label through the nasally twinge of his voice, drawing out the end rhymes in the couplet. That drive to push the boundaries of what is acceptable in hip-hop is, we soon learn, a product of the advice and encouragement he received from an unlikely figure: Glover's real-life mentor and costar, comedy writer Tina Fey. That a white woman of a "nerdy" disposition is figured as Childish Gambino's true source of inspiration—Fey, he notes, "Taught me everything that is good comes from honesty"—does the work of freeing up experience as a category for self-definition in hip-hop. Not only does it concretize the rapper's truth as divergent from, say, Hova's; it also legitimates that truth as a subject for the music. Thus, the satirical point in citing Fey here is that "keeping it real" discourse would normally not countenance such a gesture, which is precisely why its hold on the music need be undone.

Outside of his rap persona, Donald Glover has extended his embodiment of the post-real to other media through his burgeoning writing, acting, and stand-up comedy career. Tina Fey helped bring Glover on board NBC's media satire sitcom *30 Rock* as a writer and cameo actor early on. But it has been his turn as student Troy Barnes on the network's show *Community* that has allowed Glover to don the post-real in more visible ways. In an episode from the first season, for example, Troy, a former star high school quarterback, mulls over playing for his college's struggling football team. In one scene, Troy discusses the possibility with fellow Greendale Community College student Jeff Winger (Joel McHale). Their conversation begins with Jeff reflecting on his personal failures, on what might have been had he not been suspended from practicing law:

> JEFF: I'm locked out of my old kingdom. You're not. You see what I'm saying?
> TROY: You're saying I can be a lawyer.
> JEFF: I'm saying you're a football player. It's in your blood!
> TROY: That's racist.
> JEFF: Your soul!
> TROY: That's racist.
> JEFF: Your eyes?
> TROY: That's gay?
> JEFF: That's homophobic.
> TROY: That's black.
> JEFF: That's racist!
> TROY: Damn.

The particular brilliance of this exchange rests in showing us how racial authenticity cuts both ways. Troy, on the one hand, rightly calls Jeff out for ascribing only physical traits such as athleticism and brawn to blackness. But as the dialogue develops, we find Troy defending his own determination of essential blackness, unduly linking an anti-gay ethos to his racial being. That Glover offers "That's gay?" as a question rather than as a clear statement is significant: it signals to us Troy's hesitant embrace of an ethos with which he may not readily identify. It is only when he "falls back" on racial authenticity—"That's black"—that we see the folly of his choice. So it is that Jeff is put in the ironic position of articulating the scene's post-real punchline to a black man: "That's racist!" Having been called out himself, Troy can only voice a disheartened but self-knowing "Damn," which, considering Glover's comic oeuvre, comes off as a fitting Gambino-esque deconstruction of his character.

In the new millennium, artists such as Mighty Casey, Little Brother, and Childish Gambino have risked commercial failure and mainstream obscurity to promote a body of work that would challenge the terms by which hip-hop has achieved global popularity. At stake for these artists is the recognition that blackness may be embodied and performed differently, outside of what consumers have been conditioned to expect from rappers. In cultivating their art around this theme, hip-hop satirists have turned their outsider status relative to the record industry's marketing norms into a privileged standpoint from which they can issue critical insight into how and why the music is packaged in the way that it is. Indeed, it is precisely because hip-hop satirists have been restricted to the margins of commercial popular culture that their musical innovations and modes of self-critique are readily interpreted by their niche fan base as necessary and trenchant, ear-catching yet thoughtful. Commercial artists may engage some elements of satirical discourse in their work, but hip-hop satirists, as an emergent cohort in post-2000, digital age music culture, would seem to demand a more synoptic, perhaps even retrospective, understanding of the market for racial authenticity. We may shed light on this final point by dwelling on an act that fits both descriptions.

Hip-hop satire's marginal status has proven to be a site of creative agency for new and up-and-coming acts since the turn of the millennium. But for at least one older, more established group, the subgenre has served as a refuge from the very commercial sphere it once occupied. Made up of a trio of Long Island, New York, natives—Posdnuos (born Kelvin Mercer), Dave (born David Jude Jolicoeur), and Maseo (born Vincent Mason)—De La Soul is widely recognized not only as one of hip-hop's most innovative collective voices but also as the undisputed progenitor of satirical rap since its breakout success in the late 1980s and early 1990s. What sets De La Soul apart from the other artists taken up in this essay is that its music was in fact commercially popular for a time. Attached to the Tommy Boy Records label, the trio's landmark album *3 Feet High and Rising* (1989) not only advanced humorous wordplay, genre-bending samples (from work by artists ranging from Johnny Cash to Hall & Oates), and the original frame narrative device (in this case a game show) but also was highly critical of the contemporary taste for gangsta rap. While the album may be best remembered for its hit single "Me Myself and I," *3 Feet High and Rising* as a whole laid the ground for a commercial hip-hop that refused to abide by the code of the street, that gave voice to the urban middle-class black experience, and that depicted male adolescent struggles not as the building blocks for violent, vengeful fantasies but as the stuff of humdrum everyday experience.

However, De La Soul discovered very quickly that its brand of satirical rap could not find an enduring place in commercial popular culture. The group's sophomore album, *De La Soul Is Dead* (1991), which was even more critical of the record industry's efforts to promote thug and gangsta types, did not fare well commercially, despite garnering rave reviews. Over the next two decades, while the group continued to push the boundaries of what hip-hop could be—making particular inroads in the development of jazz hip-hop, for example—each subsequent album release saw a steady decline in sales.[8] Even so, De La Soul remained faithful to its signature blend of witty lyricism and musical innovation; the group did not change so much as it ran up against the brute fact that genre-critical satire was simply not commercially viable in the long run. The trio became "alternative" only after the fact of its initial mainstream success.

All of which is why De La Soul's 2012 album, *First Serve*, is a welcome addition to the subgenre of hip-hop satire. In many respects, the group that first gave satire a try in the commercial sphere has finally found its place among hip-hop satirists' postmillennial audience niche. The album, which was independently produced and distributed by De La Soul's new label, Duck Down Music, entails a heady mixture of self-mockery and sincere understanding. *First Serve*, like *The Minstrel Show*, is structured around a frame narrative that constitutes a meta-reflection on the terms of black cultural representation. The story follows the fictional hip-hop group First Serve as it navigates the highs and lows of mass media success in the late 1990s. With its sixteen tracks bookended by "Opening Credits" and "Ending Credits," the album unfolds like a film or radio play, one that, from today's point of view, nostalgically plots the all-too-familiar coordinates of a rap group's rise and fall during hip-hop's crossover heyday. But in taking up First Serve's duo as their alter egos, Posdnuos (as Jacob "Pop Life" Barrow) and Dave (as Deen Witter) lend a parodic edge to their narrative. For as much as we are meant to empathize with the characters' struggle to make it big (say, in the early track "Pushin' Aside, Pushin' Along"), we are also given insight into the way the industry changes people (not necessarily for the better) when the group enjoys its peak level of fame. Recalling the personae embodied by Mighty Casey and Childish Gambino, Jacob and Deen become cartoonish stereotypes when they sign with the corporate label Goon Time Records. Nested between two interlude skits poking fun at Goon Time's multimedia enterprise is the track "Must B the Music." Although the radio deejay at the beginning of the track puffs up the single by telling us it is in "heavy rotation," it is actually First Serve's most ridiculous song. In trading nonsense lyrics that contain ungainly internal rhymes—from boasts about street life ("Been there, done that, murder, gun rap") to advice on women ("Don't dare ignore 'em, lie 'em, bore 'em")—over a staccato beat, Jacob and Deen emerge in the middle of the album as parodies of the kind of hard men Goon Time wants to employ. As with Mighty Casey's labored flow and Childish Gambino's nasally twang, De La Soul's bluster-filled performance of Jacob and Deen render them cardboard cutouts of racial authenticity. Posdnuos and Dave in effect give voice to the flatness of character that Goon Time foists onto the duo's act.

Despite selling out to the corporate media and then running out the clock on their fifteen minutes of fame, Jacob and Deen reconnect in—of all places—France to start their act from scratch. The final third of *First Serve* testifies most clearly to De La Soul's real-life transatlantic collaboration with French deejays Chokolate and Khalid on the album. From the jazzy, bossa nova–propelled sound of "Pop Life" (which features dialogue in French and English) to the infectious electropop dance beat of "Move 'Em In, Move 'Em Out," the French production team contributes a distinct European flavor to the final arc of the narrative. Rapping over this highly experimental sound-scape, Jacob and Deen, we slowly realize, have been sonically granted the new beginning in hip-hop—post-Goon Time and hence post-real—they crave. Ironically, this very worldly turn in First Serve's fortunes has the effect of returning the group to its hip-hop roots; that is, rapping for the love of the art and for the sake of aesthetic innovation.

Insofar as the entire concept behind *First Serve* was a product of this unusual Franco-American collaboration,[9] we might aver that De La Soul's 2012 turn to hip-hop satire has shown how the subgenre remains absolutely dependent on alternative modes of cultural production and distribution. For while it may be the case that there had once been some room for De La Soul's satirical elements to appear in commercial rap, that window of opportunity was closed when racial authenticity became synonymous with the music. Thereafter, the group had to rely on riskier, less defined, but continuously experimental forms of hip-hop creation that commercial popular culture ultimately could not accept. Thus, in the same way that De La Soul became "alternative" after the fact, the group's resonance with hip-hop satire crystallized for critics and fans only when the idea of the post-real in hip-hop became virtually unmarketable on a wide scale. In what could be construed as a feedback loop (rather than a direct genealogy) of influence, De La Soul, although a tacit inspiration for all of the artists under consideration in this essay, joined their ranks as hip-hop satirists after the fact, when its music could no longer be identified with mainstream acceptance or widespread popularity.

Ralph Ellison's 1952 novel, *Invisible Man*, concludes with the oft-quoted sentence: "Who knows but that, on the lower frequencies, I speak for you?" Nested in an aside, the evocative phrase "lower frequencies" gestures toward the literal voice and the figurative subconscious from which the narrator's question is issued. The phrase's sonic valence is especially notable, given that the narrator has just asked to be heard ("What else but try to tell you what was really happening") in the face of not being seen ("when your eyes were looking through?"). And yet the possibility that his voice should speak for others—that is, resonate with their experiences—"frightens" the narrator (439). For if it does, it means his invisibility is not a singular condition but rather a general symptom of black social life in America. In a similar vein, hip-hop satirists have crafted their voice strictly on the lower frequencies of cultural production so as to counter what the corporate media validates and thereby "sees" as racially authentic. And despite their fringe, underground, and more or less independent status, these satirists, like Ellison's narrator, broach the idea that many others identify with the marginal experiences of which they speak. So it is that if Mighty Casey, Little Brother, Childish Gambino, and the looped return of De La Soul do speak for us, it is a sign not only of how pervasive invisibility-by-stereotype continues to be in our culture, but also of where possibilities for post-real imaginings lie.

Notes

1. The chapter in which Gilroy advanced his critique had been originally published in a 1994 special issue on the "Black Public Sphere" in the journal *Public Culture*. But the monograph in which the revised version was deployed outlined a far more consequential thrust to Gilroy's argument: that hip-hop commercialism bore a striking resemblance to race-based fascism. It is in *Against Race*, then, that Gilroy made abundantly clear his desire to consign hip-hop's presumed essentialism to the dustbin of history.

2. On the institutional and aesthetic formations of politically oriented, underground hip-hop, see Anthony Kwame Harrison's and Marcyliena Morgan's ethnographies of the scenes in San Francisco and Los Angeles, respectively.

3. Charise L. Cheney cites Farrakhan, the leader of the Nation of Islam, as a key source of inspiration for a number of acts, including Public Enemy, Ice Cube, Kam, Paris, Brand Nubian, X-Clan, and Poor Righteous Teachers. Farrakhan's idolization by this generation of rappers yielded references to all white people as "devils" (Cheney 135) and figurations of an eschatology in which a presumptive "race war" distinguished "between the god(s) and the devil(s), or between black men and white" (145).

4. Gane-McCalla interned for *The Chris Rock Show* in 1998. Rock's quip was made in his wildly popular Home Box Office comedy special, *Bring the Pain*, in 1996.

5. The lone exception to this is a song titled "Cheatin'," in which Phonte, crooning as his alter ego, Percy Miracles, offers a parody of R. Kelly-inspired R&B songs about love and betrayal.

6. "Backpacker" is a sometimes derogatory term applied to an avowed underground hip-hop fan or purist. Because of his antipathy toward commercial rap, the purist is said to carry his bootlegs, mixtapes, and other noncommercial media around in his backpack.

7. On the alternate valorization and exploitation of video vixens in hip-hop culture, see Sharpley-Whiting and Fitts.

8. The group remained active even during its commercial decline. Most importantly, its collaboration with alternative British rock, dub, and trip-hop band Gorillaz yielded the hit single "Feel Good Inc." (2005), for which De La Soul earned its only Grammy to date.

9. The production and collaboration history behind *First Serve* is most accurately captured in "SFR Live Concerts," a television interview with the artists: Posdnuos and Dave from De La Soul and the deejays Chokolate and Khalid. SFR stands for Société Française de Radiotéléphonie and is a major French telecommunications company.

Knock, Knock the Hustle: Resisting Commercialism in the African American Family Film

Thomas R. Britt

For black entertainers, it is almost impossible to ignore the role of commerce in the social politics of crossing over. Whereas crossing over in early cinema usually involved avenues of race passing or putting up with blackface, advancements such as access to funding and control of image production were the means that allowed early filmmakers and actors to work toward more honest representations of race on screen. Writing for the online *Separate Cinema Archive*, Dr. Barbara Tepa Lupack provides a succinct history of cinematic "portraits of black family life." She highlights the persistent stronghold of old racial formulas that threatened to return whenever certain positive developments (such as those by the Lincoln Motion Picture Company and Oscar Micheaux) met financial difficulty: "The noteworthy advances ... were arrested and the burgeoning black film industry halted by a number of unfortunate events, including underfinancing, high production costs, and the Depression" (Lupack).

This cycle, depressing as it may be, arguably bolstered the proliferation of black comedy, which is a form that has been historically able to confront such hardships and downturns with manipulations of language and performance that subtly subvert, even when spoken from within a constraining institution. In the introduction to *Laughing Mad: The Black Comic Persona in Post-Soul America* (2007), Bambi Haggins writes, "Black comedy, in its literal and literary construction, has always overtly *and* covertly explored the trials, tribulations, and triumphs of African American communities" (2; emphasis in original). Yet despite the fact that black comedy represents a progression of representation in its embrace of the total black experience, there persists the possibility of misrepresentation and dilution when the quest for mainstream acceptance requires a compromise of vision. Haggins points out the "Byzantine task faced by the African American comic: to be funny, accessible, and topical while retaining his or her *authentic* black voice" (4; emphasis in original).

Given these historical and artistic / literary contexts, it makes sense that many of the best satires about race target the very way in which entertainment media subsume racial identity into existing forms and constructs. There exists the question of how large a sacrifice of identity is required or acceptable in pursuit of commercial crossover from minority appreciation to mainstream appeal. Haggins seems especially interested in post-soul black comics' self-awareness as mediated/mediating individuals who play roles within a commercial / capitalist entertainment industry that is always calculating its appeal to mainstream tastes. In *Great Satan's Rage: American Negativity and Rap/Metal in the Age of Supercapitalism* (2008), Scott Wilson defines the conflicts that arise within supercapitalist enterprise as "neither a mode of transcendence nor a mode of immanence, but a mode of excess that is paradoxically essential. It is its excess-essence: the essence that is one continuous process of becoming-absence in wasteful expenditure" (68). Black entertainers such as Christopher Wallace (namely, The Notorious B.I.G. / Biggie Smalls) and Tupac Shakur dramatically exemplify the self-defeating nature of that enterprise, but to a different degree so do such black comics as Richard Pryor and Dave Chappelle.

Chappelle's stated reasons for leaving his remarkably successful Comedy Central television series included being increasingly conscience stricken over the minstrelsy of the material and its reception within popular culture. To paraphrase his comments, his profitable and influential presence in the culture was manifesting a personal absence of integrity and confusion of identity. Flash-forward to 2012, and his prolonged absence from the spotlight suggests that he still doesn't trust his present ability to control the valuable brand he became. One could detect a certain Faustian quality within the lives of entertainers drawn to riches and fame at the expense of their bodies and souls. Rap beefs, for instance, are beset with victory on one side and cultural or bodily extinguishment on the other. In the still-enigmatic case of Biggie versus Tupac, there are no victors, only victims. Many decades since Julius Hudson articulated the "hustling ethic," corporate entertainment advocates aggressively for the "mode of excess" and simultaneously tries to minimize the ample evidence of self-negation.

The following essay explores an unlikely source of solutions for this paradox inherent in popular film, television, and music: family-friendly comedies such as Louis C.K.'s *Pootie Tang* (2001), Lance Rivera's *The Perfect Holiday* (2007), and Erik White's *Lottery Ticket* (2010) that are created by

and/or star African Americans satirize and dare to challenge the supercapitalist value system that permeates what is generally and generically known
as "black entertainment."

All three of these films were critical and commercial failures, and not one
of them is high art. Yet what these movies offer, all too rare in commercial
cinema, is a commendable attempt at resisting the self-destroying commercial forces of modern mainstream entertainment. Additionally, the presence
in these films of figures such as Chris Rock, Queen Latifah, Charlie Murphy, Bow Wow, Ice Cube, and T-Pain contributes verisimilitude in the sense
that all of these individuals are now, or have been previously been, cogs
in the very machine that the films try to upend. Perhaps the widespread
lack of support for these films by both critics and audiences suggests confusion over this very satirical element: the sight of recognizable stars in films
that advocate for the pleasures of ordinary low- and middle-income life, as
opposed to comparatively unattainable wealth and stardom.

Whatever their shortcomings, *Pootie Tang*, *Perfect Holiday*, and *Lottery
Ticket* are all films that deserve a deeper critical reading for the messages
they offer to their target audiences (specifically the black community, but also
a more universal one). These are films unafraid to knock the hustle and to
affirm that there's more to both life and entertainment than amassing and dis-
playing wealth. Employing satire at the PG and PG-13 ratings levels, the films
also fulfill an important function in shaping the critical thinking skills and
cultural agency of impressionable young people and offering survival strategies amidst the dominant commercial programming that surrounds them.

Each of these films ostensibly fits within a recognizable dramatic film
subgenre. In *Pootie Tang*, the eponymous protagonist (played by Lance
Crouther) is a comically unintelligible folk hero from the inner city. His
nonsensical way of speaking (originally developed on HBO's *The Chris Rock
Show*) takes pidgin / jive / hip-hop slang to its limits, beyond cool. He's the
center of this would-be Blaxploitation film. *Perfect Holiday* uses a plot as
well as narrative beats familiar from any number of Christmas movies in
telling the story of single mother Nancy Taylor (Gabrielle Union) and her
three children, all of whom desire affection and attention during the holiday
season, which is understood as a time when wishes are granted and dreams
come true. *Lottery Ticket* concerns Kevin (Bow Wow), a young man from
the projects, who buys a winning lottery ticket and tries to stay alive over
a long weekend so he can cash it in. The urban, poverty-stricken milieu
and the life-and-death stakes of the movie have much in common with the
'hood films that became popular products of Hollywood during the 1990s.

Despite this categorization, these films possess formal qualities that set
them apart from the largely uncritical and often melodramatic bodies of

work that preceded them. These tweaks and twists vary in magnitude, but their function is consistent with the fundamental definition of satire offered in Leonard Feinberg's valuable *Introduction to Satire* (1967): "a playfully critical distortion of the familiar" (19). Though each film deploys a distinct rhetorical strategy, they all place the comically verbal, and indeed the "voice" itself, at the forefront of their satirical targeting. This privileging of the voice seems to be a part of the satirical tradition that Darryl Dickson-Carr describes in *African American Satire: The Sacredly Profane Novel* (2001). He writes, "The contemporary African American satirist . . . draws upon the inherent complexity of the voices that are part and parcel of black existence for material, reducing those voices to their most ludicrous level to confront them ironically" (168).

One ancient device heavily represented in this approach is the use of a Greek chorus of sorts. Within the contemporary black film tradition, perhaps Spike Lee most memorably used such a chorus in his *Do the Right Thing* (1989). In his review of the film, critic James Berardinelli compared Samuel L. Jackson's radio DJ character to a Greek chorus, and several writers have used the same term in discussing the deceptively passive presence of the film's three Corner Men, whose commentary runs parallel to the simmering events of the plot.

Perfect Holiday's chorus is made up of Mrs. Christmas (Latifah) and Bah Humbug (Terrence Howard), characters familiar to Christmas stories that in this case adopt various disguises to remain "hidden" from the characters within the narrative. They step outside of the action to address the audience. At first, their function is to provide exposition. Yet over the course of the film, the polarity they establish (when taken as a linked character pair) comes to represent the range of responses to Christmas cheer that exists within the plot and by extension the viewer's reaction to the sentiment of the film itself. Contrasting her selfless giving against his selfish greed, Mrs. Christmas and Bah Humbug are the magically realistic "spiritual" forces of the material story world. Hence, they provide both the narrative framework and the moral critique. In one telling instance, they pose as homeless people, testing the charity of passersby.

In *Lottery Ticket*, the chorus is likewise consistent with the film's generic classification. The characters here are Malik (Vince Green), Tasha (Leslie Jones), Deangelo (Malieek Straughter), and Ray-Ray (Jason Weaver), and they sit around the Fillmore Housing project, commenting on the action that surrounds them. This quartet is vital to the film's satiric plotting, as they "comment rather than narrate, criticize rather than recite" (Feinberg 226). As in *Perfect Holiday*, their collective commentary establishes choices that will eventually become available to the central character, such as how to spend lottery winnings: on a Bugatti or a helicopter? Kevin's friend Benny (Brandon T. Jackson) and love interest Stacie (Naturi Naughton) will later continue this commentary by helping him consider less self-serving options. The Fillmore Housing chorus is like a younger generation of Lee's Corner Men, but they do become involved when push comes to shove. Of the four, Deangelo is Kevin's most active protector, comically using a water pistol in an attempt to ward off avenging "super-thug" Lorenzo (Gbenga Akinnagbe). Volunteering as Kevin's entourage, they defend him from the opportunism of the community and are rewarded as partners in his wealth.

Pootie Tang, by far the most formally self-reflexive film of the three under discussion, has nearly as many commentators as it does main characters. The film is framed as an interview of Pootie being conducted by Bob Costas (playing himself). Whereas a talk-show format would normally cut to a concise preview of a star's upcoming film and then back to the present interview, the entire feature running time of *Pootie Tang* ensues before cutting back to Costas at approximately the seventy-minute mark. He says, "That is the longest damn movie clip I've ever seen!" Another formal oddity is that Costas actually appears within the feature-length clip that he himself is concurrently hosting, also in an interview scenario but across from another interviewee (Wanda Sykes's character, "Biggie Shorty"), who asks him, "Haven't you been watching the movie?" It's the kind of film-within-a-film duality one might expect from David Lynch, yet here it exists within a Blaxploitation sendup.

Aside from the title character, Costas, and Biggie Shorty, the film's foremost narrator is Trucky (J. B. Smoove), Pootie's best friend. He comments on the story from the outside (providing hyperbolic exposition about Pootie's exploits) and from within. In one particularly absurd moment, Trucky delivers onscreen narration of Pootie's thought process from merely feet away, saying, "It hurts Pootie to kill a man, but he knows he's got to do it. But it hurts him so bad—to right those wrongs." Another scene finds the outer and inner commentaries merging, with Trucky's voice directly predicting / preceding every subsequent line of spoken dialogue, in many cases word for word. This rhetorical exaggeration is one of the film's most brilliant satirical strategies: none of what Pootie says makes sense to our ears, so Trucky says everything twice over, as if to compensate. Lacey (Mario Joyner), another sidekick, similarly repeats everything that JB (Rock) says, much to JB's frustration. These two and an out-of-control radio DJ (also played by Rock) round out the characters that collectively form the *Pootie Tang* chorus.

In addition to lending satirical exaggeration and excessive articulation of plot and character details, these choruses of commenters are in keeping with several features of what Gladstone L. Yearwood defines as "black cultural expression" borne from a "cultural basis for signifying in the black tradition" (138). At one point or another, each chorus makes "use of rhetorical devices that privilege vernacular forms such as playing the dozens, testifying or rapping" (138). Although these three works come from different spaces within the Hollywood film spectrum, they share and exhibit a rich "cultural tradition" of interactivity between spectator, commenter, and commented upon: "In the viewing encounter, the black cultural tradition functions like a framing device that provides basic parameters for filmic narration and the activity of the viewer. There is an inherent expectation based on the protocol of call-response in the African American tradition. In black cultural expression, the audience exists in a dialectical relationship. . . . The filmmaker creates his or her performance (the film) with a space present for the viewer" (141). While this specific sort of interactivity injects black culture into Hollywood products, the films also turn a satirical eye toward the messages embedded in the form of black entertainment. In this sense, the films achieve satire through parody in the mode Geoff King describes in *Film Comedy*: "Parody, aimed at formal or aesthetic conventions, can have satirical impact" (108–109). All three films play upon (and indeed "playfully distort") viewers' recognition of hip-hop and rap video aesthetics. As the earliest of the three films under discussion, *Pootie Tang* owes the most direct debt to music videos that were popular in the half-decade preceding the film's production. Stylistic elements on display include flashy clothes, quick cuts, fish-eye lenses, and frontal lighting, all popularized by Hype Williams, P. Diddy, and Bad Boy Records, among others. In *Pootie Tang*, their function is to punctuate the narrative with mediated expressions of the folk hero's achievements. As Trucky says in his introduction to the character, Pootie is a "big time celebrity, ass-kicking crime-fighter, and role-model to the children." Each of these character traits is illustrated in the film, but only the "big time celebrity" is presented in a fashion indistinguishable from its real-life stylistic counterpart. That is to say, the crime-fighting and role-modeling are carried out in absurd, highly exaggerated, and comic versions of the fight sequence format and public service announcement format, respectively. This heightening of other media formats calls attention to the fact that the mid- to late 1990s, hip-hop video is already a form so exaggerated that it could hardly be topped. Furthermore, the vanity and material excesses of the videos run counter to the anti-corporate messaging of the film as a whole, an essential incongruity to which I'll return shortly.

Perfect Holiday updates these music video references for the Jay-Z era. Nancy, a divorced mother of three, is at odds with her children's father, a music mogul named J-Jizzy (Charlie Murphy). Although he is basically an absentee dad, his brand (J-Jizzy Enterprises) appears everywhere, from posters, to a clothing line, to a ubiquitous music video in which he dances for the camera as golden dollar signs rain around him. J-Jizzy is a buffoonish product of hip-hop culture, surrounded by yes-men and sexy women. His foil in the movie is an aspiring songwriter / part-time Santa Claus named Benjamin (Morris Chestnut), whose fate intervenes with both Nancy and J-Jizzy in a complicated love triangle. The effects on Nancy's children are mixed, as the young daughter is delighted to see her mother find love through (and with) Santa Claus himself, while oldest son John-John (Malik Hammon) is loyal to his father, wearing "Jizzy Gear" and mimicking his father's dance moves in front of (and, crucially, separated by) the television screen.

Although *Lottery Ticket* doesn't contain any sort of intrafilm music video, its critique of the associated commercial culture is present in the form of a spending spree montage set to a rap song ("Million Bucks," by Maino and featuring Swizz Beatz). The lyrics of the song ("I think I might give away a million bucks") and the narrative purpose of the montage are ostensibly advocating generosity, giving back to the hood, and so on. However, the overriding value of both is wanton squandering. Unaccustomed to having money, Kevin blows his one-hundred-thousand-dollar loan from neighborhood lender Sweet Tee (Keith David). He and his entourage indulge in a Hummer limousine ride; drink champagne; and buy jewelry, watches, and every shoe in Foot Locker (Kevin's former workplace). Their excessive spending is set to lyrics:

> Man I'm a introduce to you a new dance
> It's called the money dance
> You pull the money out your pocket like this
> You put your hands in the air like this
> And you simply just um
> Bounce throw it all around
> (Throw) throw it all around
> (Throw) throw it all around
> (Throw) throw it all around

Literally a list of instructions for "making it rain," Swizz Beatz's verse soundtracks the kind of behavior all too celebrated in rap videos, which then fails to reveal the bankrupting consequences of wastefulness.

Via the inclusion of these supercapitalist music videos / montages, *Pootie Tang, Perfect Holiday,* and *Lottery Ticket* offer refreshingly subversive messages about greed. Yes, the films borrow and occasionally rely upon the visual aesthetics of hip-hop and rap, but they do so in order to comment on the various dead-end philosophies that such music often carries. Three classic examples are P. Diddy's "It's All About the Benjamins" (1997); Jermaine Dupri's "Money Ain't a Thang," (1998), which featured then-rising star Jay-Z; and 50 Cent's debut album, *Get Rich or Die Tryin'* (2003). Diddy and Dupri envision wealth so vast that it literally surrounds them, opulence becoming the norm; 50 Cent's ethos is even more hardcore, implying that a life without riches is not worth living.

To review the central dramatic action of the films being considered here is to find characters at a crossroads of either buying into these dominant attitudes or rejecting them in favor of a different set of values. Mark A. Reid's definition of "black family film" is relevant to the choices available to the characters in *Pootie Tang*, *Perfect Holiday*, and *Lottery Ticket*, films that "share narrative elements with other types of family films that dramatize issues concerning class mobility, social integration, and the effects of abandoning ethnic traditions and beliefs" (35).

In this aspect, too, *Pootie Tang* is somewhat of an exception to the kinds of films Reid analyzes, insofar as *Pootie Tang* is not "mediated by a child or teenager's point of view" (Reid 35). Yet the stakes of Pootie's actions involve the future direction of kids that look up to him, so one could say the film is (to quote the late Ol' Dirty Bastard) "for the children." In fact, as silly as the film often is, the urban landscape of *Pootie Tang* would be quite harsh for youngsters. Marked by concrete, graffiti, litter, drug dealers, and hookers, the inner city that Pootie patrols is not objectively different from the mean streets of most 1990s 'hood films. But Pootie's presence and his totally free agency minimize the threats. He's the necessary buffer protecting kids from those mean streets. His public service announcements warn children against cigarettes, fast food, and malt liquor, all products sold and promoted by the film's villainous institution (LecterCorp) and its CEO, Dick Lecter (Robert Vaughan). Lecter acknowledges Pootie's influence and attempts to lure him as a spokesman for "Tasty Heavy Pork Chunks," a disgusting cereal product for kids. Lecter's "right hand man" Frank (Dave Attell) at one point says to a reluctant Pootie, "To you they're children; to me, they're dollar signs." Pootie smacks Frank in the mouth with his magic belt and dances for the camera / spectator. These acts of resistance / performance continue until Lecter uses his wife, Ireenie (Jennifer Coolidge), to seduce Pootie, take his powerful belt, and steal the rights to his image and likeness. Thus begins the hero's struggle to reclaim his good name.

From the film's beginning, Pootie is a celebrity and also appears unconcerned with earning money, so his is not a story of class mobility. However, his status as an inner-city celebrity makes him vulnerable for exploitation by the corporate world. Although the film sidesteps making too direct a statement about the corporate masters' exploitation of Pootie's racial difference, there is an embedded "fish-out-of-water" quality that aligns with a cinematic tradition Haggins describes: "The outsider's struggle to survive and thrive in a foreign, possibly hostile, world has always provided grist for the film comedy mill. . . . This comic staple functions differently, however, when a black comic is placed at the center of the insider/outsider paradigm. In such cases black stars are situated in cinematic milieus cut off from other representations of blackness, or even from other black characters, thereby placing them in the dubious position of representing the race" (99). LecterCorp's isolation of Pootie and appropriation of his unique language ("Sa da tay" and "Wa-da-tah" are two popular favorites) is a prescient precursor to Dave Chappelle's loss of language, as his own catchphrases were drained of all satiric intent when peddled by Comedy Central and regurgitated by heckling fans. One of the film's more subversive touches is to have Pootie's restoration of dignity occur completely beyond the city. The movie segues into a Western genre film, with Biggie Shorty providing sexual succor before sending the hero to her farmhouse to heal, or in her words, to "find himself, blah, blah, blah." By the end of the Western section, Pootie engages in a duel with another of the film's villains before making his triumphant return to the city.

Although *Perfect Holiday* doesn't use 'hood imagery and/or genre shifts to position the characters, nor does it utilize a fish-out-of-water narrative tradition (excepting Benjamin's lower economic status), the film does defy expectations for what the characters hope to gain from the Christmas season. When Mrs. Christmas introduces Nancy, she says, "Over on the fancy side of town lives Nancy Taylor. She's nice, too. As far as money goes, she doesn't have a worry in the world. . . . Better watch out girl. Santa's coming to town." This introduction suggests that Nancy isn't lacking money, but she's in need of something that Santa is going to provide. One twist to the familiar narrative is that Santa himself is lacking and desirous of his own dreams coming true. Benjamin wants nothing more than to make a living as a songwriter. As he composes, he wears a t-shirt that reads, "Man on Top of His Hustle." After Nancy's daughter relays to Santa / Benjamin her mother's wish to receive a compliment, Benjamin and Nancy begin their sweet relationship.

The complicating commercial force in *Perfect Holiday* is J-Jizzy himself. His influence on the culture means that Benjamin must beg him to listen to a composition and possibly launch his career. J-Jizzy's financial support of his kids means that Nancy must grin and bear the charade he self-servingly performs about loving his family. One scene that unites multiple negative layers of J-Jizzy's personality and power is his brief visit to Nancy's house. He drops off his child support payment in an envelope and chides Nancy for all the "paper" he gets from her. Considering that his own life is a brazen, nonstop paper chase, it's highly hypocritical for him to judge her for accepting what's rightfully hers. That the children are the audience for this insult makes his behavior particularly inappropriate. Mrs. Christmas closes the film with an affirmation of Nancy's choice to live apart from her moneymaking ex. Assessing Nancy, Benjamin, and the fulfilled children, she declares, "The best Christmas present is a happy family, all wrapped up together."

Set entirely within the projects and involving characters whose potential for social mobility seems limited, *Lottery Ticket* has the most to say about the lure of money as well as its corrupting force. At the beginning of the film, we hear a reporter announce the $370 million lottery prize that will be awarded just before the Fourth of July, and she delivers a pun: "Independence is all about the money." Of course, this has a few meanings for the residents of Fillmore Housing, for whom those winnings could spell their ticket out of the 'hood. There's a bit of *Charlie and the Chocolate Factory* in the telling of *Lottery Ticket*, as a modest young man like Kevin has little means to corner the market on playing numbers. What's more, he defends his decision not to play the lottery by saying it is "designed to keep poor people poor by selling them false dreams." However, as righteous as he tries to be, the power of commercialism draws him in. For instance, the film renders his weakness for expensive shoes in a theatrical fashion: the lights flicker and the camera swoops as Kevin stares at, and lists the statistics of a rare, five-thousand-dollar pair of Nike Air Force 1s.

Keeping his reluctantly purchased winning ticket a secret proves to be an impossible challenge, and for Kevin's neighbors, the potential to get some money from their newly rich friend seems to drive them literally wild. They chase him in a stampede through the housing project, threatening his safety. By the end of the film, his life and limbs will be threatened by the thug Lorenzo and the deadly benefactor Sweet Tee. Money yields anything but independence for Kevin, whose dreams of one day leaving Fillmore and starting his tennis shoe line turn into a darkly comic nightmare of survival.

Kevin's personal economic rise and fall forms a cycle that Benny articulates in the film's funniest and most insightful moment of satire. After helping Kevin escape the rush of neighbors, Benny produces (out of absolutely nowhere, as if in a cartoon) a map of the Underground Railroad. Though no one ever explicitly says Kevin is a slave to his circumstances, the visual and narrative comparison makes the point. Benny gestures to the map and says, "This is what we call the Underground Railroad. Many slaves have used this to escape. We can escape, Kevin. We can get out the 'hood." His inspirational speech hits all the right notes. He fantasizes about finding the North Star and writing Negro spirituals detailing the experience. But then, as if he cannot help himself, he inflates the journey into a profit-making venture, suggesting that they turn these (imagined) spirituals into a mix tape and make money. This is a very clever, excellently acted scene that reinforces how deeply ingrained is the drive to hustle and become rich. With this in mind, Kevin's money might be just as psychically "enslaving" as his prior lower-class status.

A later exchange between Kevin and Benny treats more seriously the pivotal position in which Kevin finds himself: to be young, black, and with a lot of money. Burned by the opportunism of those around him, Kevin withdraws, saying to Benny, "Money don't change you, it changes people around you." When it becomes clear that Kevin suspects even Benny of trying to rob him, Benny explodes with a melodramatic monologue that outlines the effects of living a lower-class lifestyle, of being on the outside of economic potential and looking inward: "I'm sick of worrying about WIC cards. . . . I can't eat. I'm broke, nigga. I'm broke. And you've got the power to change that."

These are two young men, but their discussion about how to best consider and use economic capital is miles ahead of the limited self-awareness of young black males who populated the 'hood films of the 1990s. In "The New Ghetto Aesthetic," Jacquie Jones writes with disappointment of *New Jack City* (1991), which she calls a "propaganda film" that "suggests that the problem with communities plagued by drugs and crime is that the residents are either dealers, users, or complicit bystanders—all unwilling or unable to help themselves" (43). Jones says *Boyz N the Hood* (1991) "depicts with cinematic fluency the senseless self-destruction of young black men" (44). *Lottery Ticket* is not content to see its characters get stuck in a cycle of complacency, arrested development, or self-destruction. By the film's end, a wealthy Kevin (aided by Benny and other friends) creates a park for Fillmore, pursues his shoe business, and creates a foundation to support businesses and scholarships.

In her largely negative assessment of films adhering to "the new ghetto aesthetic," Jones asks a question about black films as products of Hollywood: "Is the goal of black filmmakers, ultimately, to be included, integrated into the existing protocol of mainstream cinema? Or is it to transform the language of mainstream cinema, to force it to acknowledge the plurality of American culture?" (40–41). I would answer that question by suggesting that in the decades following the 'hood film explosion, some of the most successful transformation is occurring in the African American family film. *Pootie Tang, Perfect Holiday*, and *Lottery Ticket* are not anti-capitalist works, inundated as they are with product placements and acknowledgements of material comforts. However, the films' parodic and satirical views of black entertainment's get-rich / get-famous imperatives create a plurality of alternative sources of happiness and fulfillment. To poke fun at the life-and-death stakes entertainers assign to their commercial potential is a good first step toward realizing that compared to the bonds of family, friends, and community, money "ain't a thang."

Dirty Pretty Things: The Racial Grotesque and Contemporary Art[1]

Michael B. Gillespie

In her *Laughing Fit to Kill: Black Humor in the Fictions of Slavery* (2008), Glenda Carpio questions whether a possibility exists for contemporary art to untether stereotypes from their fetishistic moorings, even as she remains wary that such work risks ultimately reinforcing the lure of stereotypicality: "As the prominence of stereotype-derived art in the late-twentieth and early-twenty-first centuries attests, the idea of forever cleansing the American psyche of its racial fetishes may be not only a futile project but one that might fuel the power of the fetish all the more by making it taboo and therefore seductive" (22). The dilemma she articulates serves as a foundation for this essay, which examines some of the ways in which contemporary artists have courted this risk by redirecting the conventional iconography of racist caricature. In the process of doing so, these artists demonstrate a tactful and purposeful ambivalence[2] akin to Carpio's about the continued use of stereotypicality in contemporary art and respond to Ralph Ellison's mordant observation that "perhaps the object of the stereotype is not so much to crush the Negro as to console the white man" ("Twentieth" 41). This essay will consider how contemporary creative practices expose and contest this crushing / consoling intention of anti-black iconography.

My analysis is driven by a consideration of re-accentuation in the context of art, race, and historiography. In his essay "Discourse in the Novel," Mikhail Bakhtin stated that "every age re-accentuates in its own way the works of its immediate past. . . . Thanks to the intentional potential embedded in them, such works have proved capable of uncovering in each era and against ever new dialogizing backgrounds ever new aspects of meaning; their semantic content literally continues to grow, to further create out of itself" ("Discourse" 421). By focusing on work that contends with history and craft, I emphasize the ways in which the artistic technique / rhetoric of the racial grotesque compels new and timely encounters with the persistently abhorrent American hegemonies focused around race, nation, and citizenship. This kind of work is always timely in the sense that the racial grotesque is never simply the anachronistic revival of a dead phenomenon, but rather a creative practice attendant to the continued impact of racialization and white supremacy. Bakhtin's writings are extremely valuable in understanding how the racial grotesque derives new meaning from old ideas. In *Rabelais and His World*, he considers the "carnivalesque" and "grotesque realism" in the work of François Rabelais, addressing the "material bodily principle" of medieval folk culture and detailing how the grotesque body along with all manner of precious bodily fluids and orifices performatively disturb and shock social hierarchies. As Bakhtin notes, "The essential principle of grotesque realism is degradation, that is, the lowering of all that is high, spiritual, ideal, abstract; it is a transfer to the material level, to the sphere of earth and body in indissoluble form." (*Rabelais* 19).

It is the indissoluble quality of this degradation and the irreconcilable tension of grotesque realism that I explore in William Villalongo's *The Centaur's Kiss* (2005), Jabari Anderson's *The Gullah Sci-Fi Mysteries* (2007–2009), Travis Somerville's *Well Division* (2009), James Hannaham's "Napkin Ring" (2010), and Pierre Bennu's *Black Moses Barbie* (2011). This diverse cluster of work contains a "Mammy" relic, an Underground Railroad doll, an African centaur, a modern staging of drinking fountains from the era of Jim Crow segregation laws, and comic book covers featuring intergalactic black vernacular beings. Paying especial attention to their critical materiality, I examine how these works stage the racial grotesque through a recontextualization of historical, often iconic instances of anti-black visual culture. The racial grotesque in the American historical context almost invariably evokes a fundamental paradox of black slavery, namely the antinomy between human and nonhuman, person and property.[3] In doing so, the racial grotesque protests the manner in which stereotyping iconography contributes to the fixed rendering of a person as a thing. As Leonard Cassuto proposes, "To view people as nonhuman is an open invitation to the most fundamental and enduring category problems" (11). Therefore, the epistemological power of the racial grotesque arises directly in opposition to extant white supremacist discourses concerning visual representation and (non)personhood.[4]

The artistic works examined in this essay each employ the racial grotesque as both a parodic and satirical critique of such racialized visuality, trafficking in the familiar affective economies of anti-black visual culture and white supremacy.[5] As Ian Baucom notes in context of a diasporic philosophy of history, "For no matter how strenuously we might forget what was begun, or wish to call an end to it, what-has-been is, cannot be undone, cannot cease to alter all the future-presents that flow out of it" (330). In this way, this cluster of work rhetorically mobilizes and parodically reinscribes especially notorious aspects of American history through visual artifacts, all the while remaining attentive to the affective impact that the past has on the present and the future.

The visual historiography of these works thrives on the ceaseless quality of history and also a sense of what Sianne Ngai calls its "reanimation." In *Ugly Feelings* (2005), Ngai suggests through her analysis of three distinct figurations of animation that "racial stereotypes and clichés, cultural images that are perversely both dead and alive, can be critically countered not just by making the images *more* 'dead' (say, by attempting to stop their circulation), but also, though in more equivocal fashion, by *reanimating* them" (124; emphasis in original).The parodic-satiric aspect of these works reanimates the iconography and material relics of anti-black visual culture, thereby wrestling with issues of national identity, race, mythology, pop culture, and cultural memory in the key of the racial grotesque.

James Hannaham explained his involvement with the *Significant Objects* project, which solicits writers to compose a text for an object, as follows: "*Significant Objects* is a project that Joshua Glenn and Rob Walker have been doing for a while, where he asks writers to respond to photos of objects in the form of letters, so he makes some of the work easy for you. He asked me to select an object from a number of photographs. I don't remember what the other ones were, but the napkin ring spoke to me. And since my muse is a daredevil who likes touchy race/sexuality issues, bad taste, and awkwardness, I could not resist choosing her" ("Re: Question"). These objects have little to no inherent value, but their post-textualized auction on eBay results in a measurable increase in both their significance and their monetary worth. The project thus comments on a doubled sense of value: value as an affective measure and value as quantifiable commercial worth. It illustrates how the narrativization of something deemed worthless imparts a subjective value that impacts the objective value. The shift from immaterial to material, the supplementarity of sentimental and commercial worth, remains a fascinating feature of this ongoing project. In the case of Hannaham's "Napkin Ring" (2010), the meanings of value and objecthood resonate significantly with the idea of the racial grotesque.

Identified as "Ms. Bethuna," the object in question is a wooden napkin ring shaped in the form of a "Mammy" caricature with a hole bored through the lower regions of the base. Hannaham's accompanying text is a largely noncomic parody of the form of a legal notice of intent to sue for damages resulting from "fraud, discrimination in hiring, forced labor, and sexual assault" ("Napkin Ring"). Ostensibly drafted by "Ms. Minerva Lee Battle," Ms. Bethuna's legal representative, and addressed to "Mr. R.S. Pennyback" of "Shady Acres Estate," the letter describes the physical and mental abuse endured by Ms. Bethuna at the hands of the Shady Acres Estate proprietors since her birth (September 14, 1855). Citing a sworn deposition, the notice catalogs Ms. Bethuna's labor during her tenure at Shady Acres Estate: "Yourself and the previous proprietors of "Shady Acres" . . . required my client to operate as a culinary, housekeeping, gardening, landscaping, and childcare professional. During the ensuing one hundred and fifty-five (155) years, my client prepared an estimated 168,987 meals, including 121 Christmas and 107 Thanksgiving dinners, made 15 beds a total of 56,206 times, dusted 18 rooms over the course of her life, and nursed a total of 54 children, 33 of whom were not her own—including yourself—and the balance of whom were the issue of herself and various proprietors and associates of "Shady Acres" (Hannaham, "Napkin Ring"). This letter also notes that, although the exploitation of Ms. Bethuna's labor was not punishable by Alabama law at the time of her birth, Ms. Bethuna was never notified of the change in her legal status upon the abolition of slavery. As a result, the lawsuit claims that Ms. Bethuna was a victim of a conspiracy that violated her inalienable rights: "The owners of 'Shady Acres' conspired to conceal the change in her legal status indefinitely, thereby preventing her from discovering and curtailing the criminal activity of 'Shady Acres' to the extent that this required keeping her from acquiring any skill in the reading and writing of the English language, and prohibiting contact with any persons, organizations, news outlets, or other publications which may have informed her of the change in her legal status." In addition to being subjected to slavery by another name, Ms. Bethuna "suffered frequent and unrelenting physical and sexual abuse, culminating in the removal of a circular portion of her lower abdomen." The letter closes with a demand for unpaid back wages and compensation for benefits and legal fees. Most importantly, Ms. Battle requests that in light of the hole bored through Ms. Bethuna that "the abdominal subdivision in question be returned to Ms. Bethuna's possession and repaired to the extent that medical science may accomplish such a reparation" (Hannaham, "Napkin Ring").

In the case of "Napkin Ring," the epistolary conceit resembles an absurdist memoir of slavery or of servitude under Jim Crow segregation. In Hannaham's recontextualized creation, Ms. Bethuna becomes both a material object and what Robin Bernstein calls a "scriptive thing." Such an object is like the script of a play in that it "broadly structures a performance while allowing for agency and unleashing original, live variations that may not be individually predictable. Items of material culture *script* in much the same sense that literary texts *mean*: neither a thing nor a poem (for example) is conscious or agential, but a thing can invite behaviors that its maker did and did not envision, and a poem may produce meanings that include and exceed a poet's intention. To describe elements of material culture as 'scripting' action is not to suggest that things possess agency or that people lack it, but instead to propose that agency emerges through constant engagement with the stuff of our lives" (Bernstein 12; emphasis in original). Ms. Bethuna takes on such an agency through Hannaham's text as her critical materiality focuses around the experience of an abused tool within the legacy of slavery. His reanimation of this napkin ring pivots on its iconographic reference to Mammy, the caricature of the undesirable nurturer of the plantation household and, later, of the black domestic servant. The linking of the slave and the collectible grotesquely associates the inhuman utilization of slave labor and the comparatively innocent domestic function of memorabilia like the napkin ring. As Eden Osucha notes of the proliferation of anti-black iconography in the emerging mass culture of the twentieth century, "Postbellum commodity racism tendered more figurative correspondences between the look of the commodity and its content or function" (81). Hannaham's incarnation of the napkin ring affectively disrupts the Mammy figure's sanitized, nostalgic recollection of servitude by foregrounding the inherent association with the systemic violence of white supremacy.

Amid the cheeky disorder of people made indistinguishable from tableware, Ms. Bethuna's presentation as a vessel of the racial grotesque amplifies its "ontological residue." As Bill Brown argues in the context of Spike Lee's *Bamboozled* (2000), anti-black collectibles affectively generate the history and the conditional possibility of slavery: "Even as we point to a certain moment in a certain place when and where it is no longer possible for a person to be a slave (to be someone's property, to be . . . a thing), we nonetheless find, in the post-history of that moment, residues of precisely that possibility—in other words, an ongoing record of the ontological effects of slavery" (B. Brown 182). In this case, the ontological residue of the napkin ring bespeaks a century and a half of economic exploitation and sexual violence.

As a response to this residue, "Napkin Ring" invokes a two-part rhetoric of reparation. In Ms. Bethuna's case, reparation means the literal repair of the hole in her belly, but also a figurative reparation in the form of monetary compensation for her years of involuntary labor. As Salamishah Tillet notes, the contemporary reparation discourse "argues that material restitution is a belated redress for the legacy of economic disenfranchisement and functions as a pre-condition for racial democracy" (137). Ms. Bethuna's legal suit compels this sense of material compensation explicitly, but "Napkin Ring" also implies a need for an additional form of compensation that Tillet calls "mnemonic restitution." Tillet formulates this term as a "challenge [to] the purposeful and 'polite' national amnesia around slavery, as well as those practices of racism that uphold the civic estrangement of all blacks, natu- ralized, or native born, that live in the United States" (137). Thus, "Napkin Ring" contests the historical erasure necessary for the continued trafficking in the history of slavery evidenced by memorabilia and collectibles such as "Napkin Ring." The legal call to atone for services rendered and citizenship denied insists on an act of unsanitized memory and Hannaham's parodic- satiric use of the racial grotesque in regard to the Mammy figure brings the nature and scope of such debt into stark relief.

Pierre Bennu's *Black Moses Barbie* (2011) is a series of three video shorts featuring a doll version of Harriet Tubman that was originally posted on the Internet over the course of nine months in 2011. Each short is formally structured as a parody of a toy commercial, a fact announced by Tubman's first line of dialogue ("Hey kids, looking for freedom?") and driven home by the typically rapid "fine print" voice-over at the end (for example, "Black Moses Barbie comes with a higher sense of purpose"). The series follows the abolitionist adventures of Harriet Tubman carrying out her duties as a con- ductor on the Underground Railroad. The plot of the first two shorts of the series follows Black Moses Barbie aiding the escape to freedom of Runaway Ken and Runaway Christie with slave catchers in hot pursuit. The final short features Black Moses Barbie, Runaway Billy Dee Williams, and Abolitionist John Brown.

The series transcends the typical commercial and normative functions of doll culture—especially that of the iconic, best-selling Barbie doll—as these faux advertisements feature a black doll embedded within an act of resistance to the unsavory historicity of slavery. This rebellious slave doll becomes a disobedient "performing object" in Bennu's films.[6] This disobe- dience is a categorical paradox about race (after all, slaves are by definition intended not to be disobedient) that marks the series as an enactment of the racial grotesque. The performing objects narrativized by *Black Moses Bar- bie* channel the personhood / objecthood slippages that have characterized doll play since the nineteenth century. As Robin Bernstein argues, "The cul- tural effort to objectify and later reobjectify African Americans found rich potential in doll play and doll literature, because all stories about sentient dolls reorganize the boundary between human and thing" (17). Accordingly, the affective intensity of *Black Moses Barbie* resides in the tension between human and thing, between history and fantasy.

Rather than Barbie's traditional (normatively white) adventures in acces- sorized lifestyles, careers, and leisure, *Black Moses Barbie* tactically rebrands the cherished Barbie by explicitly historicizing the narrative of play within the context of nineteenth-century slavery. This act does more than simply alter Barbie's skin color, something Mattel had already done by introducing Barbie's African American friend Christie in 1968 and a black version of Barbie in 1980; instead, it renders the idea of race in terms more constitutive than incidental. As Anne duCille notes, the actual black Barbie doll represents a racialization of Barbie culture that provided a broader potential identification, but this identification always remained limited by the demands of a commercial market: "Questions about the ties between multiculturalism and capitalism are by all means larger than Barbie. But given the doll's status as an American icon, interrogating Barbie may facilitate an analysis of the commodity culture of which she is both part and product. What makes such an interrogation difficult, however, is the fact that Barbie simultaneously performs several disparate, often contradictory operations. On the one hand, ethnic Barbie dolls seem to color in the whitewashed spaces of my childhood. They give little colored girls toys to play with that look like them. On the other hand, this seeming act of racializing the dolls is accomplished by a contrapuntal action of erasure. In other words, Mattel is only able to racialize its dolls by blurring the sharp edges of the very difference that the corporation produces and profits from" (42–43). Bearing in mind that a black Barbie must be a profitable exercise for the toy industry, duCille highlights the way doll culture represents a collusion between socialization and commercial consumption as she recognizes the extent to which the black Barbie must be a difference mediated by historical erasure.

The historiographic premise of *Black Moses Barbie* entails the commemoration of a black cultural heroine, a black shero. In doing so, the series amplifies the innocuous utility of doll play with an object's struggle to become liberated. Bennu states that he "chose Barbie dolls and other children's toys because [he] wanted the piece to comment on marketing, gender projection and training, and the ways that boys and girls are encouraged to look up to very different 'heroes' and play out very different stories" ("Re: Question"). By introducing the possibilities for alternative narratives of heroism and identification, *Black Moses Barbie* tacitly contests how ownership and use inform doll culture. The historical specificity of Bennu's version of Barbie bypasses the earlier black Barbie iterations that were simultaneously distinctive (albeit only in terms of superficial ethnic characteristics) and essentially indistinguishable from (or implicitly subsidiary to, as was the case with Christie) their normatively white counterpart. As performing objects in genre-parodies of both slave narratives and toy commercials, the *Black Moses Barbie* dolls are rebellious counterfeits.

Furthermore, the series touches upon the shortfalls of the black doll—specifically, the black version of an iconic white doll—as a reconcilable vessel of a kind of simplified multiculturalism in which nuanced differences in categories of cultural being are sacrificed for the greater goal of stable commonality and "tolerance."[7] The real-world commercial possibilities of Bennu's performing objects are clearly scuttled by the ugly historical context in which their existence is inextricably embedded. Unlike Mattel's Christie or black Barbie, Black Moses Barbie is very aware of the racialized implications of her identity, as demonstrated by her killing of multiple "pattyrollers" (that is, slave catchers) over the course of the three shorts. However, Bennu's act of reanimating both the story of Harriet Tubman and the cynically insubstantial rebranding of Barbie for black consumers creatively refigures issues of personhood, reification, and commodity fetishism through a dialogical framing of slavery and doll culture. Escape to freedom in this context means escape from complicity with forms of whiteness that efface black difference by means of apolitical fantasies of consumer citizenship. *Black Moses Barbie* satirically contaminates the market with the proposition of seditious instruction.

A section of Richard Pryor's comic performance in Mel Stuart's documentary *Wattstax* (1973) illustrates how *Black Moses Barbie*'s satirical force results from giving voice to a person hitherto presumed a mute thing because of white supremacy and anti-black racism. Pryor jokes, "When they [white folks] found out niggers could talk, other than 'doh wah ho,' they got scared to death." The comic approximation of African speech ("doh wah ho") marks the joke as commentary on the legacy of slavery. As Pryor continues by acting out a brief exchange between a white man and a black man, his joke illustrates not only that whites still associate modern-day blacks with African slaves—human commodities perceived as speechless—but also that their fear results in explicit silencing even when blacks do speak: "You know, like, one day, some whitey said 'Nigger, talk!' 'Well, motherfucker, I been wanting to tell you something!'" The white man abruptly responds by saying "I beg your pardon!" thus shutting down the conversation and punctuating Pryor's sardonic humor. Imparting speech to Black Moses Barbie echoes the consequential substance of Pryor's joke and proposes a new radical sense of the doll's value in much the same way that the letter of intent to sue from Hannaham's "Napkin Ring" embodies the speech act of a commodity. Such moments convey a subjective agency that in context of the historicity of slavery shatters the anti-black presumption that the slave is a laboring object incapable of substantive utterance rather than a person. Satirically undermining the commodified slave artistically stages Fred Moten's critique of Marx's hypothetical consideration of a speaking commodity that comments on its own use-value and exchange-value. As Moten proposes, "The truth about the value of the commodity is tied precisely to the impossibility of its speaking, for if the commodity could speak it would have intrinsic value, it would be infused with a certain spirit, a certain value given not from the outside, and would, therefore, contradict the thesis on value—that it is not intrinsic—that Marx assigns it" (13). *Black Moses Barbie*'s parodic evocation of "a certain spirit, a certain value" demonstrates the discomforting, provocative, and creative capacity of the racial grotesque to disrupt commercial flows and reanimate history with the heroic play of freedom dreams.[8]

William Villalongo's *The Centaur's Kiss* (2005) features a statuette of a white man mounted atop an African male centaur sculpture that is holding a decapitated African female's head. The rider possesses the generic quality of a curio that one would expect to find in the gift shop if Epcot opened a "Confederacy Land" exhibit. Clad in dress grays, the ceramic rider is General Robert E. Lee, the commander of the Confederate army. The statuette's resemblance to Lee remains somewhat superficial, however, due to the limited production values of mass-produced collectibles, ensuring that its historical relation to the Civil War remains a dull smear of nostalgia rather than a refined sign.

As a work of art, Lee's mount does not conform to the genre conventions of either kitschy military commemoratives or classical equestrian statuary. Adorned with rhinestones and velour in a manner that gives it the bearing of a prince or tribal elder, the African centaur is an amalgamation of different styles and pieces. Beyond the slight tilt of his head and neck as a result of the pull of his rider's reins, he pays no meaningful attention to the figure on his back, though their relative situations and the reins in the rider's hands do strongly suggest the compulsory nature of their relationship. In this instance, the juxtaposition of the rider and mount compels the viewer to give more attention to the latter. The centaur's figural liminality (part human and part horse) functions in many cultures and mythologies— most familiarly, the Greek tradition that lends the creature its name—as metaphor for the division of barbarism and civility, even as it also appears as a wise and noble figure associated with magic and fantasy.[9] In the context of *The Centaur's Kiss*, however, the centaur deftly evokes a more disruptive sense of liminality and alchemy. Much as in the cases of *Black Moses Barbie* and "Napkin Ring," the parodic depiction of iconic cultural artifacts refers back to the history of slavery, and Villalongo uses its inescapable contextual dread for satirical purposes.

The sculpture has a profoundly incongruous and yet compatible quality. One of the reasons for this stems from the piece's conjoining of two mythologies, Greek and American, that historically characterize the ideal of the antebellum American South but also resonate with the vision of the "New South" that arose during Reconstruction. As Houston Baker notes in the context of American literature, the design of this ideal was most evident in popular form through the Plantation Tradition: "the Plantation Tradition consists of white American literary works which project a southern ideal based on a somewhat ad hoc model of the enlightened Greek city-state. In order to achieve the tradition's fictively projected ideal, southern society must be divided into discrete classes with white masters at the helm, black slaves in the galley, and all voyagers aware of the boundaries and duties of their respective positions. Shored up by Walter Scott's romantic chivalry, the plantation prospect produced literary narratives that represent kind masters, gracious manor houses, chastely elegant southern belles, and obediently happy dark servants who are given to a life of mindless labor and petty hijinks" (130). In this way, *The Centaur's Kiss* evinces the collusion between mythology and a historiography that allows for an ennobling, tragic vision of the demise of the anti-black, slave-owning American South.

The unmistakably African centaur shatters any attempt at a harmonious parallelism between the Greek city-state and the Confederacy. The African centaur introduces a transvaluative dose of black cultural nationalism into this white mythology and, in doing so, celebrates blackness as a valuable mode of cultural expression.[10] In the context of the sculpture, the African centaur functions as an indelible sign of blackness that undoes the selective claims to humanity associated with the values of the Confederacy for which Lee fought. He is not riding a Greek steed despite its Greek name any more than the foundation of the American South was anything other than superficially Hellenic. The regal detail of the African centaur represents the imagining of an alternate modality of blackness than that of the subservient African slave who served, literally and figuratively, as the beast of burden upon whom the planter class rode to prosperity and power. As Villalongo states, the racial grotesque reanimates the classical and neoclassical understanding of (African) American civilization in historical and mythological terms:

> Subversive visual constructions . . . make us question our own notions, stereotypes and visual orientation with regards to race or racial and gendered images. We like to employ Du Bois's "double consciousness" as a signal of racial sensitivity and a sophisticated understanding of the psychology within the politics of identity. As a visual artist, I think it's important to make visible this psychology. What does it LOOK like to see oneself as double or any exponential or mutation? There will surely be monsters that reflect the great visual

nightmares of the past or at the very least our irrational fears, depravities and desires. In this way, I suppose the racial grotesque pushes against the grain of how we are taught to look at histories in our Western civilization classes trading in one mythology or creative narrative for another and with a sense of humor. ("Re: Question")

The double iterative of the African centaur, the human/nonhuman paradox, imparts an excess that is satirically recuperated by fashioning the steed as more complex, more noble, more distinct, and ultimately more valuable that the mass-produced rider (the ostensibly "valuable" figure in the original historical context) upon his back.

In this way, the content of black cultural resistance attributable to the aesthetics of the regal African suggests a parodic-satirical adaptation of the classical and neoclassical mythological form. The piece demonstrates its phantasmagoric ploy of shock and reanimation with a significant gesture of tenderness. After all, the piece does not feature a mere beast of the lower stratum sniffing at a bone. The African centaur's downcast look upon the African woman's head in its hand is a sentient and emotionally complex expression, a sign of consciousness. Perhaps this look is an arrested sorrow song or just the recollection of the taste of a kiss. Conjoining two narratives of cultural history, the piece resplendently illustrates the nonreciprocity of Lee and the African as the former represents a sentimental revisionist ploy and the latter a fantastical abstraction of a tragedy.

Travis Somerville's "Dedicated to the proposition . . ." gallery show of 2009 featured a large selection of the artist's work (including drawings, paintings, installation pieces, and sculpture). Derived from Abraham Lincoln's 1863 Gettysburg Address, the show's title deliberately engages with that famous speech's invocation of the nation's egalitarian ideals during splintered times. The exhibit invokes the cultural memory and historical significance of Lincoln's speech while also gesturing satirically toward a kind of historiographic mutiny.

The work in the exhibit demonstrates a scripting of American history that forgoes a synchronic causality. Instead, Somerville's work intermingles visual and verbal references to the discrete relics and the semiotics of the Civil War, Reconstruction, Jim Crow, the Civil Rights Movement, and the Age of Obama. In doing so, the exhibit parodies a categorical crisis of racialization as a historical and cultural discourse. Rather than depicting a grotesque individual body, Somerville's work mobilizes a visual and material (re)scripting of a history of the scarred and battered American body politic. As such, his work profoundly resonates with the disorientating and destabilizing effects of the racial grotesque. Somerville himself points out that his work complicates the sense of a collective memory about how race has shaped the political, historical, cultural, and social contours of America: "As I attempt to navigate the terrain between autobiography, history, and art, all sorts of collisions take place. It is these interesting moments and the inconsistencies that inform them that I try to capture in my work" (Thomas 10).

One work from the gallery show that is most emblematic of this collision is *Well Division* (2009). *Well Division* features a row of seven working drinking fountains against the gallery wall that are conjoined by a single copper pipe. A refrigerated metal fountain with a Confederate flag on its foundation sits at the center of the row, with three smaller identical porcelain fountains on either side. Each fountain has a small sign hanging above it; from left to right they read MUSLIM, ASIAN, NATIVE AMERICAN, WHITE, BLACK, PACIFIC ISLANDER, and LATINO. The coupling of the signs and the water fountain evokes an iconic aspect of both material and visual culture from the Jim Crow era, specifically reminding viewers of the racialization of space that characterized the power of segregation. As Elizabeth Abel points out, the visual culture of Jim Crow was particularly dependent on the use of plaques and signs that spatially demarcated racial segregation, as evidenced in the seminal photographs from the civil rights visual archive of signs indicating "WHITE" and "COLORED" drinking fountains.[11] As Abel points out, "By looking at disturbing words, tacked to the walls of another time and place, as neither alien to our gaze nor as threatening to absorb it, but as reflecting one of our concerns, we may elicit the relation between Jim Crow signs and the more enigmatic signs of our times" (xx). Although the occasion proffered by *Well Division* represents an amplification of Jim Crow's order of things, the installation does not function as a mere model of a historical past that has been duly archived and fixed in time and place. Rather, the piece suggests something of the way that the history of the Civil Rights Movement remains incomplete, if not what Russel Reising would term a "closural" failure.[12] This is because the signs are not the sole iconography in play that references the white supremacist taxonomy of being. Except for the WHITE fountain, the basin of each fountain contains a painting that acts as a material expression of the histories of exploitation and/or a hateful visual rhetoric that corresponds to the respectively identified group. Thus, the sink paintings include a suicide bomber's vest (MUSLIM), a fortune cookie and railroad tracks (ASIAN), a Jack Daniels bottle with an eagle's feather (NATIVE AMERICAN), a blackface minstrel (BLACK), an atomic mushroom cloud (PACIFIC ISLANDER), and an "immigrant crossing" caution sign (LATINO).

The categories that Somerville uses in his piece are based on the 2000 census and make imminent projections of the shifting cultural, ethnic, and generally emerging nonwhite clusters of nonwhite difference. Despite the fact that not all of these categories correspond directly to a racial formation, they are deployed with a future census in mind and by implication (due to the centrality and uniqueness of the WHITE fountain) from the perspective of an individual complicit with white hegemonies of privilege. These categories are deliberately distended senses of nonwhite categories of being. Each category becomes delimited by a stereotype, a fixing figuration that disavows citizenship, humanity, and self-defining agency. *Well Division* presciently exhibits an age of the new Jim Crow, the way white supremacy operates on a spectrum that is grotesquely expanded beyond strictly black and white boundaries.[13] Significantly for the satirical undertones of the piece, the flanking arrangement of these formations of nonwhite difference cumulatively hint at a future in which the ratio of six basins to one will grow and eventually constitute a demographic majority, a united coalition of more linked "basins" (that is, nonwhite identities) to come.

Well Division corresponds to what Abel identifies as the inherent inadequacy of the segregationist signs to master the deeply dynamic nature of the social: "Signs that attempted to write race on social space were also mediated by the spatial dynamics that invited and exceeded their efforts at control" (6). In this way, the public spectacle of power and racialization at work in the exhibition space with the working fountains willfully invites more than a choice of how best to satiate one's thirst. The piece's distinctive alienation effect insists that its viewers / participants question issues of complicity, consent, and privilege.[14] The piece satirizes both the historical triumphalism of the Civil Rights Movement's successes in undoing segregation and the premature neoliberal declaration of a post-racial society in the wake of Barack Obama's election victory and subsequent reelection as president of the United States. While seemingly mere relics, Somerville's fountains are chronotopic or spatiotemporal forms that are acutely current.

Dawolu Jabari Anderson's *Gullah Sci-Fi Mysteries* (2007–2009) is series of poster-sized paintings designed as individual comic book covers.[15] Rather than reproducing Roy Lichtenstein's "Pop Art" isolation of a single frame with an evocative thought or speech bubble, the *Gullah Sci-Fi Mysteries* series engenders a sense of narrativity at the level of the comic cover.[16] With a dog-eared patina, these covers convey the worn intimacy of old tales that were once regularly revisited while also attempting to breathe new life into them: "The function of a comic book cover is to encapsulate the most striking components of a narrative into a one-page composition. Covers are often loaded with ambiguity and will play on what that imagery may possibly suggest. I sample imagery that I find to have a kind of condescending nostalgia transmitted through a one-dimensional narrative. I sample them and then refurbish these images. At the same time it resuscitates that image and gives them a new significance. But I am gratified by reversing colonialism by removing the creators and taking ownership of the culture" (Anderson, "Re: Question"). His process of resuscitation seeks to dissolve proprietary cultural claims to the significance of the images and characters he depicts: "Like an oral tradition, comic books imply shared authorship, and require audience assistance in visualizing a 'text.' The fact that Anderson's comics are only covers can be understood as a sendup of the limited dimensionality of stereotypes, but they can also be read as prompts to be completed by the viewer" (Mueller 182). In this way, Anderson's canvases incite the viewer to sequentially arrange the covers and assemble an idiosyncratic narrative arc that reanimates the vernacular tradition, subverting various authoritarian discourses in the process.

Set on and around a southern plantation, Anderson's series of covers enlists a cast that includes such anti-black figures of the antebellum South as Mammy, Remus, and Rastus. The covers also feature alligator-humanoids, a golem made of grits, John Henry, a Kool-Aid beast, Seminoles, and Madame Ethiopia. Madame Ethiopia, or Emereciana, is an extraterrestrial time traveler from the Bandung Dimension of Saturn. Anderson's Bandung not only shares a name with the Indonesian city that hosted the Afro-Asian Conference in 1955, but also shares that event's spirit of solidarity, expanding its scope from global resistance to European colonialism and subjugation outward to a galactic scale. Madame Ethiopia endows Mammy, Remus, and Rastus with a cosmic energy that acutely transforms these symbols of dutiful domesticity, diminished intellect, and simple folksiness into super-powered beings. Transmogrified from less-than-human to more-than-human, Mammy becomes Mam-E once her cosmic broom is activated by the frequency of her voice. When the Saturn Ring is placed on his finger, Remus has the power to use his storytelling to induce mind control and also wields a tar baby, a receptacle for his psychic power that induces the feeling of being fathomlessly stuck in tar. Rastus psionically fashions shapes from the very cream of wheat his image was used to sell for decades. Each of the figures still visually triggers their respective iconographic precedent. Mam-E is still apron-clad and wears a gingham shirt with a handkerchief atop her head, but her buxomness is now more muscular than corpulent. Remus appears as raggedy-clad as his Joel Chandler Harris forebear, but in Anderson's work he more closely resembles The Hulk than the typical "old Uncle" storyteller figure. Anderson's science-fictional mutation of the kindly old narrator calls for the destruction of the plantation rather than offering "Zip-a-Dee-Doo-Dah"-style platitudes.

These tales are bannered as "mysteries" authored by the slave descendants of the Sea Islands and provide an alternate serialization of the Plantation Tradition. By linking the Motherland and the Mothership and staging black diasporic history and science fiction, the series conceptually alludes to Afrofuturism. As an interpretative and creative strategy, Afrofuturism reimagines the history of the African diaspora with particular attention to the ideas of abduction, alienation, and technology.[17] The abstraction of blackness as otherworldly and alien, a central aspect of white rationalizations that slavery was essentially a trade in nonhumans, is literally and figuratively reanimated through an Afrofuturist lens in Anderson's work. As Kodwo Eshun notes, "Afrofuturism uses extraterrestriality as a hyperbolic trope to explore the historical terms, the everyday implications of forcibly imposed dislocation, and the constitution of Black Atlantic subjectivities: from slave to negro to coloured to evolué to black to African to African American" (298–299). Anderson orchestrates the racial grotesque as a parodic struggle between primitivism and modernity in the form of galactic vernacular beings.

As Adilifu Nama points out, black superheroes signify more than merely the standard struggle of good versus evil because they also "symbolize American racial morality and ethics" (4). Anderson's heroes exhibit a further complication of this signifying on race and justice.[18] For example, Mam-E is often featured in the series as defending the plantation *against* her fellow cosmic beings. In this way, Mam-E echoes her progeny, Aunt Jemima, whose commercially romanticized story of life as a slave involved saving her plantation master with a pancake recipe.[19] Nevertheless, the series circulates among different temporalities (past and future) and spaces (Africa, North America, and The Milky Way) as Anderson's canvases depict an epic struggle whose disorienting and satirical comedy renders these figures of black dispossession as uncanny.

The futurist blues of the *Gullah Sci-Fi Mysteries* series is emblematic of the ways in which all of the works discussed in this essay deal with acts of what Kobena Mercer calls disremembering: "When artists seek out the disremembered past, the aim of such truth-seeking is not to bring the narrative of history to an end, but to work through the memories of trauma in order to symbolize it and hence separate oneself from the unbearable emotional weight that is the only trace of its ever having occurred at all" ("Keith Piper" 166). The critical wit of each work compels distinct truths that ultimately demonstrate a sense of the severing that Mercer mentions. The utility of a napkin ring, the role-playing of dolls, antinostalgic sculpture, Jim Crow relics, and the Afrofuturist vernacular collectively testify to the power of the racial grotesque to make strange our understanding of race and history in satirically productive ways. The works discussed here are blunt, perhaps even rude, and riveting acts of satire that bear witness to and attempt to redress the everyday amnesia of America regarding its history of race and its white supremacist tendencies.

Notes

1. I wish to thank James Hannaham, Pierre Bennu, William Villalongo, Travis Somerville, and Jabari Anderson for sharing their thoughts about their work. Also, thanks to The Kitchen, The Ben Maltz Gallery at Otis College of Art and Design, The Catharine Clark Gallery, and Meg Shiffler at the San Francisco Arts Commission. I wish to thank Derek C. Maus and James J. Donahue for their invaluable editorial suggestions. I owe special thanks to Bill Condee, Nicole Fleetwood, Chip Linscott, and Paula Massood. This essay is dedicated to the memory of Ossie Lee "Bo" Williams (1950–2012) and Mary Elizabeth Gillespie (1935–2012).

2. In *Playing in the Dark*, Toni Morrison identifies my sense of redirection as a critical act: "Studies in American Africanism, in my view, should be investigations of the way in which nonwhite, Africanist presence and personae have been constructed—invented —in the United States, and of the literary uses this fabricated presence has served. . . . My project is an effort to avert the critical gaze from the racial object to the racial subject; from the described and imagined to the describers and imaginers; from the serving to the served" (90–91). My analysis in terms of ambivalence and irreconcilability is informed by Kobena Mercer's work on the racial grotesque. In "Tropes of the Grotesque in the Black Avant-Garde," Mercer orchestrates Bakhtin's use for inquires of race from the perspective of art history in a way that values multiplicity over finite claims. As he states in his closing comments, "The disruption of consensual definitions of identity and difference does not replace one order of 'truth' with another but fundamentally questions the relations of 'race' and representation from which the social construction of 'reality' is negotiated as a struggle over signs and meanings" (Mercer, "Tropes" 157).

3. See Stephen Best, *The Fugitive's Properties: Law and the Poetics of Possession*. Chicago: University of Chicago Press, 2010.

4. For more on the racial grotesque, see Gillespie, "Reckless Eyeballing."

5. As Sara Ahmed notes in her conceptualization of emotions in terms of an economy or structure of exchange and transaction, "Affect does not reside in an object or sign, but is an effect of the circulation between objects and signs (=the accumulation of affective value). Signs increase in affective value as an effect of the movement between signs: the more signs circulate, the more affective they become" (45).

6. As Frank Proschan explains, "performing object" refers to "material images of humans, animals, or spirits that are created, displayed, or manipulated in narrative or dramatic performance" (4).

7. As Vijay Prashad contends, "Multiculturalism tends toward a static view of history, with cultures already forged and with people enjoined to respect and tolerate each cultural world" (53).

8. Mark Anthony Neal insightfully comments on the "Black Moses Barbie" series with particular reference to the controversy surrounding the developed but never released "slave action figures" for Quentin Tarantino's *Django Unchained (2012)*. See Neal, "Bennu Unchained."

9. See Padgett, "Horse Men."

10. See Glaude, "Introduction."

11. For example, the photographs of Elliot Erwitt and Danny Lyon. See Berger, "For All the World to See."

12. "By thus reifying closural moments, traditional narrative theory has unnecessarily constructed endings as the embedded and fully coherent essence of the narrative act, which given the numerous energies and agendas driving toward some perfectly revelatory, demystifying closural epiphany, can only be imagined as fully sufficient as both origin and telos of narrativity" (Reising 8)

13. For an important sense of *new* Jim Crow with an emphasis on America as carceral state, see Alexander, "New Jim Crow."

14. "Somerville's works imply that it may not be useful to moralize whether a stereotype is good or bad, but rather to confront the regime of representation that such images produce" (Post Brothers 60).

15. Anderson also produced two earlier series of covers that mined the tropes of D. W. Griffith's white supremacist fantasy, *The Birth of A Nation* (1915), and the Black Panther Party for their subject matter. The most recent comic covers series featured the character "James Evans" (John Amos) from the television show *Good Times* (1974–1979) as a superhero.

16. See Cassel, "Splat."

17. See Nelson, "Introduction"; White et al., "Afrotech."

18. Adilifu Nama considers the value of the black superhero of comics as a distinctive figuration of race, visual representation, and cultural history. As he notes, the figure of the black superhero deviates from the white/normative standard of the comic book hero because the introduction of blackness into the equation alters the general perception of what constitutes just measures: "As fantastic, imaginary, and speculative as superheroes are, once they engage real social events that clearly resonate as oppressive and unjust their actions or inactions become a source of moral scrutiny because the superhero archetype is steeped in affirming a division between right and wrong" (96).

19. See Witt, "Black Hunger" (21–53).

Percival Everett's *Erasure*: That Drat Aporia When Black Satire Meets "The Pleasure of the Text"

Gillian Johns

Percival Everett's essay "Signing to the Blind" contains a pyrotechnic display of his quite paradoxical attitude toward his readers. He delineates the situation that he and his fellow contemporary African American authors face as follows: "Simply put, our readers are white. Black people do not buy books. We are at the economic mercy of a market which seeks to affirm its beliefs about African-Americans. An army of liberal book-readers marches into stores and feeds on fad and trend and reads, but not too deeply, and so does to our work what the movies seek to do. I do not believe that the works we produce need to be any different; the failing is not in what we show but in how it is seen. And it is not just white readers, but African-American readers as well who seek to fit our stories to an existent model. It is not seeing with "white" eyes, it is seeing with "American" eyes, with brainwashed, automatic, comfortable, and "safe" perceptions of reality" (10). In his mind's eye, Everett here figures an existent public who reads (even avidly) with an instrumental racialized frame, one perhaps reliant on what Robert Stepto has called unarticulated pre-textual "race rituals."[1] What is especially intriguing to me is that although Everett displays a prescient sense that a long tradition and history can impact the current reception of African American writing, his stance seems hopeless, even nihilistic: why write at all, given such contempt for actually existing readers, let alone labor at complex levels of cognition? Yet I want to argue in this essay that Everett's hyperbolic complaint in fact points to an aporia in some black writing that also suggests something about the rhetorical limits of satire as a viable mode for conceptual change. In particular, exploration of the complex implied dynamics of reading in the 2001 novel *Erasure* offers a glimpse at such an aporia, which is especially notable in this satire of satire (or parodic satire) when considered alongside the novel's play with Roland Barthes's work on readerly and writerly texts.[2]

The term *aporia*, from the Greek "impassible path," has been used in literary criticism to denote an "insoluble conflict between rhetoric and thought" or the "lacuna between what a text means to say and what it is constrained to mean" (Cuddon 55). Christopher Norris defines aporias as "blindspots or moments of self-contradiction where a text involuntarily betrays the tension between rhetoric and logic" (Norris 19). Scholars of satire have similarly oscillated between describing it as a mode that is primarily rhetorical (playful and game-like, or competitive, extravagant, and even absurd) or morally corrective (conservative and yet reliant on impersonal logical, analytical, cognitive work from implied readers).[3] I parse these strains to suggest that if, at the literary-critical level of conception, satire conjoins pleasure and moral / ethical cognition in a reader's "wandering viewpoint,"[4] this pairing does not necessarily describe the implied dynamics of the intended (or historical) readers of black texts. In other words, the presupposition is that pleasure neatly fits with critical praxis—that is, while I enjoy the ride, I am simultaneously self-conscious and self-critical and, indeed, anticipate the prospect of multiple layers of irony—but this dynamic seems to self-contradict in some satirical black writing. To wit, there are striking moments near the ends of both George Schuyler's *Black No More* (1931) and Zora Neale Hurston's *Moses, Man of the Mountain* (1939) when a black-identified reader might become conscious of discomfort in his or her practice of reading. In *Black No More*, we think Schuyler is satirizing racism, and our superiority to such an ideology leads us to disavow two racist white characters who, it turns out, have their own black ancestors, so we're ready for them to get their just desserts; but then we find ourselves virtually located in an imaginary lynch mob that is the express agent of our justifiable revenge. In *Moses, Man of the Mountain*, Hurston's (ever-trifling) Hebrews are dissatisfied with Moses's efforts to lead them to value self-reliance and courage, and we are primed for a display of the authentic African "powers" of his "right hand" to punish them. Instead, he enters the tabernacle and simply lies down—he "faced the angry Princes and Elders for a full minute in silence then fell on his face in the door" (Hurston, *Moses* 258)—so we might register that we, too, have been seduced by the rhetorical promise of black "powers" rather than their substance. These satirical moments, then, have engaged us in narrative pleasures that somehow turn us into lynchers and magical thinkers. They undermine confidence that our "black" desires are morally innocent and nonviolent or that our cultural commitments are mature and modern.

I present these ironized scenes of reading because they remind us that the habits, beliefs, and expectations of hypothetical readers are woven into the pre-fabric of our literary texts, even if they are "unreliable" and "distrustful," as Stepto claimed (*From Behind* 198); that they lack "mental bravery," as

Sterling Brown wrote in 1930 (46); or if such readers must develop "self-crit-icism," as Alain Locke asserted in 1950 (391). Hence, critical practice since the 1980s has often begun with Henry Louis Gates Jr.'s prescient insight that structural irony is at the root of black writing, given the ubiquity of a Western racial discourse that has marked blacks as illiterate, unreasoning, and absent.[5] Yet many of Gates's contemporaries saw autobiographical dis-course as foundational to the tradition in such way that it privileged—along with an abstracted black subject—eccentric rhetorical dynamics between author and reader. As just one example, John Sekora argues that the slave narrative was charged with re-presentation of black lives in the service of a nation-defining white imagination. Sekora begins with this premise: "The journey back in the study of black American life has of course always led to the narratives, long recognized . . . as chronologically and psychologi-cally the ground upon which later black writing is based." (482) Yet he also notes that the historical readers of such narratives—which featured simpli-fied, "nearly anonymous" black lives drawn to appeal to the senses through "facticity," "concrete detail," and "undifferentiated sameness of existence" (497)—were extraordinarily unreliable and remote. He recalls, "Wendell Phillips had said that the unconcern and insensibility of white northerners should never be under-estimated" (502). He thereby infers a critical prob-lem for the black voice: "The beginnings and endings of slaves' lives are thus institutionally bound. . . . The slave is witness in a double sense: eye-witness to a system that must be exposed, and witness called before aboli-tionist judges and jurors to reply to specific questions—no more, no less," since such "white sponsors compel a black author to approve, to authorize white institutional power" (502).

For Sekora, the slave narrative is primarily defined by the interests of its intended readers, so it does not privilege the complex self or subject we expect to encounter in autobiography. Rather, "the meaning, relation, and wholeness of the story are given before the narrative begins; they are imposed rather than chosen" (509). He concludes, in stark contrast to Gates's writer-centered argument highlighted above, that "one might say that the genre as a whole is defined by a suppression of the personal slave voice. For most sponsors, by stipulation, defined the slave as primitive and then proceeded to use the narratives to address other white people. . . . The *voice* of the narratives is a white voice. For Methodists or abolitionists to express their dominance, the slave must remain silent. . . . The slave is the primitive other whose silence allows white sponsors to describe the grace, the beauty of their own civilized voices" (510; emphasis in original). What is especially relevant about this in terms of the argument I am making here is the discursive *promise* of pleasure without risk or personal engagement.

A reader in this mode can enjoy and/or scold the black speaker-writer but is not himself or herself held to judgment or comparison. Such a racialized rhetorical relationship never breaks the chain of signifiers that sticks only to the black subject on display. Yet, miraculously, it is in such a reader's very *dis*engagement and *dis*interest from this subject that his or her superiority is confirmed! It does not necessarily follow, then, that because black writing is structurally ironic, its reading is ironized; and hence the surprise or ambivalence we might experience when a Hurston or Schuyler ask us to join their hostility to the very reading practices they have invited.[6] But in Roland Barthes's terms, the "classic"[7] black autotext would thus seem to mark an anticipated opportunity to experience the "readerly" pleasure of self-confirmation rather than the "writerly" work of co-producing the work. In *The Pleasure of the Text* (1975), Barthes traces different types of pleasure, but common to them is that his imagined reader consumes a text that does not threaten to rewrite his/her subjectivity. Barthes writes, "Text of pleasure: the text that contents, fills, grants euphoria; the text that comes from culture and does not break with it, is linked to a *comfortable* practice of reading" (14; emphasis in original).The "writerly" text of "bliss," on the other hand "imposes a state of loss, the text that discomforts (perhaps to the point of a certain boredom), unsettles the reader's historical, cultural, psychological assumptions, the consistency of his tastes, values, memories, brings to a crisis his relation with language" (14).

What does all this have to do with African American satire and, more specifically, Everett? Surely, if satire does not demand as much cognitive work as a "writerly" reading—which Barthes claims would "make the reader no longer a consumer, but a producer of the text and its user, between its owner and its customer, between its author and its reader" (S/Z 4)—it requires more alertness than the comfort and easy affirmation that Barthes ascribes to "readerly" pleasure. Frederick Kiley and J. M. Shuttleworth write that satire "is a deliberately controlled kind of literature" demanding apt critical reading since "satirists are notorious for setting traps for readers; the reader must always be alert, objective, and alive to the satire, lest he himself become an unwitting victim . . . [for] the satirist wants his reader to remain detached enough to grasp the entire range of the satire, to keep his balance, to see clearly once again what he may have lost sight of" (5). But if the cool, distant *logical*—and uncannily *not* self-critical—reading of black satire can merge with the *rhetorical* pleasure of reading the "straight" black text, we face the "blindspot" of an aporia. And this contradiction brings me to Everett's *Erasure*, which I argue presents a cautionary tale of the potential persistence of this strange racialized reading that offers ready psychic luxuries. If Everett is right that African American readers, even into the twenty-first century, can "read white"—that is, as spectators safely remote from black pain, contradiction, and excess—the very occasion of the black autotext may be enough to *promise* the pleasure that Barthes suggests can take the form of a compartmentalizing "drift,"[8] now distanced from the moral and conceptual burdens associated with slavery. What's more, it seems that for Everett—as in the case of the abolitionists?—the stories we "know" to be "black" are already available in our minds when we prepare to read. And the remarks of his highlighted above place him in a literary-critical line of concern that has, since the Harlem Renaissance, called for more astute reading. Everett writes at the end of "Signing to the Blind" that "we have no audience. At least, no audience that reads with political empowerment. And so our work becomes a matter worse than preaching to the choir. It is more like we are standing in the dark signing furiously to the blind" (11). In doing so, he echoes Sterling Brown's lament in "Our Literary Audience" that "without great audiences we cannot have great literature" (61).

In *Erasure*, the story that drives the serious and theoretically minded African American author-protagonist (Thelonious "Monk" Ellison) to fury is *We's Lives in the Ghetto*, a tale of the transcendent rise of a black woman from poverty to Afrocentric creativity; his parodic and satirical response is *My Pafology* (later, *Fuck*), an updated version of Richard Wright's *Native Son* (1940) with references to Ralph Ellison's *Invisible Man* (1952) as befits Monk's last name. Despite his mocking original intention, his book is mistaken for an unsatirical narrative and wins the fictionalized National Book Award, eventually compelling Monk to step into the "black" shoes of Bigger Thomas / Richard Wright to receive his award and attendant publicity. We might stop here and register only Everett's satire of the general public's uncritical embrace of "classic" black stories, especially given his complaint about "signing to the blind" (see below). But this is too easy; it is Monk's (not Everett's) work that wins the prize, and Monk's novella comprises only 70 pages of the otherwise 265-page, first-person autotext that Monk presents—and that we read—as his diary. Hence the novel as a whole encloses a plurality of discourses that imply metacommentary on its embedded stories, satire and parody, and (mis)readings. Indeed, when Monk delivers an academic paper in chapter 2 called "F/V: Placing the Experimental Novel," the novel explicitly announces its dialogue with Barthes's *S/Z*, which schematized five "codes" or cognitive tracks for reading Balzac's *Sarrasine*: hermeneutic, proairetic, semic, symbolic, and referential (HER, ACT, SEM, SYM, REF, respectively).

But a shift occurs when Monk, who in fact is not so very self-critical as he might like to think, tries to read Roland Barthes to *his* reader. He repeats verbatim the provocative first sentence of *S/Z* and then presents his own queries and gloss: "There are said to be certain buddhists whose ascetic practices enable them to see a whole landscape in a bean.* There are 'certain' buddhists, even two might be enough, and we are not to read the majority of buddhists or common, usual buddhists. Is it the pejorative 'certain' as in, 'There are certain people in this room who are not welcome?' Or perhaps, 'certain' means to say that those buddhists are assured, without doubt, steadfast in the beliefs. Before we enter the first sentence fully we are trapped by our first puzzle (HER, certainty)" (Everett, *Erasure* 14–15). Monk nicely registers the implicit ambiguity of Barthes's initial utterance here, but *Erasure*'s structural irony pairs this good reading with his lack of self-reflexivity within the same conceptual context. Just before he delivers his paper to the *Nouveau Roman* Society, he records his contempt for this academic circle by writing about one of its members, specifically a woman named Linda Mallory, with whom he has a sexual past: "Linda had . . . fallen into a circle of *innovative* writers who had survived the sixties by publishing each others' stories in their periodicals and each others' books collectively, thus amassing publications, so achieving tenure at their various universities, and establishing a semblance of credibility in the so-called real world. Sadly, these people made up a good portion of the membership of the *Nouveau Roman* Society. They all hated me. For a couple of reasons: One was that I had published and had moderate success with a realistic novel some years earlier, and two, I made no secret, in print or radio interviews, what I thought of their work. Finally, however, I was hated because the French, whom they so adored, seemed to hold my work in high regard" (Everett, *Erasure* 11; emphases in original). This passage betrays questionable elements of Monk's character; surely, self-absorption and undeveloped empathy must underpin such biting sarcasm. If we fail to register the implicit unreliability of the speaker-reader-writer here, however, Everett later presents Monk's CV, which reveals that he has published twice in *Frigid Noir*, a journal edited by Davis Gimbel, a member of the *Nouveau Roman* Society for whom Monk reserves his greatest contempt, musing that Gimbel "hadn't understood a word" of Monk's presentation at the conference (*Erasure* 18, 56–57).

In the opening paragraph of the book, Everett's author-narrator Monk states that his "journal" is "a private affair," but (in the first of many nods to *Invisible Man*) he imagines it becoming public in posterity. Since he wants to prepare for the event, he leads us—and himself—to think of him as multifaceted in precisely five ways, thereby implicitly beginning the dialogue with *S/Z* that is made explicit a chapter later: "My name is Thelonious Ellison. And I am a writer of fiction. This admission pains me only at the thought of my story being found and read, as I have always been severely put off by any story which had as its main character a writer. So, I will claim to be something else, if not instead, then in addition, and that shall be a son, a brother, a fisherman, an art lover, a woodworker. If for no other reason, I choose this last, callous-building occupation because of the shame it caused my mother, who for years called my pickup truck a station wagon. I am Thelonious Ellison. Call me Monk" (Everett, *Erasure* 1). Being "a son, a brother, a fisherman, an art lover, a woodworker" is perhaps not so theoretically compelling as Barthes's five codes, but the text thereby gently invites us—both black and white—to register these various grooves without necessarily having recourse to the readerly pleasures of thematic unity, closure, or synthesis. As his own author, Monk in fact does commence to offer starkly different types of speech acts—such as anecdotes about fishing and woodworking; memories of his father who committed suicide seven years before; awkward encounters with his sister, brother, and peers; and even historical voices discussing art—without integrating them like Barthes does in *S/Z*. For example, there is this rather dull journal-like record: "There are times when fishing that I feel like a real detective. I study the water, the lay of the land, seine the streambottom and look at the larvae of aquatic insects. I watch, look for hatches and terrestrial activity. I select my fly, one I've tied at streamside, plucking a couple of fibers from my sweater to mix with the dubbing to get just the right color. I present the fly while hiding behind a rock or in tall grass and wait patiently. Then there are times when I wrap pocket lint around a hook, splash it into the water while standing on a fat boulder. Both methods have worked and failed. It's all up to the trout" (Everett, *Erasure* 42–43). Then, when the more "readerly" text (attributed to Monk's obviously parodic nom de plume, Stagg R. Leigh) of the seventy-page embedded novella about the aspiring criminal Van Go Jenkins appears, even though it is simultaneously hilarious, repulsive, and violent, we can "rest" with this second, "classic" underclass black autotext that "makes sense" in its singular, familiar subject: Van Go's abjection. Indeed, Monk himself offers the simpler track for readers of his "journal" when the "story" of the reception of his parody of *Native Son* henceforth consumes his attention and serves as a distraction from the dissolution of his own upper-middle-class family. For example, we follow Monk's surprise at the money he makes from *Fuck*, his conversations with his agent and editor, a complicated visit he makes to an Oprah-like television talk show, and his arguments with the judges for the book prize.

Everett's satire reaches for more than a critique of such stories on their own terms; it bitingly extends to readers (and, moreover, writers like Monk) who would compartmentalize them and believe themselves above suspicion regarding their invention, display, and consumption. That is, if we have been duped into Monk's "readerly" approach to *Fuck*, his own "blindspots" allow us to miss the irony that the "ghetto" tale featuring a black male "other" who rapes women rolls off the tongue of the self-professed highly educated, thoughtful writer who has the interesting hobbies of fishing and woodworking and who has never felt comfortable with black English. Furthermore, we might miss the possibly interconnected characteristics of brute misogyny, (ethically) lazy ambition, and blinding narcissism in the diarist of *Erasure*, a man who (resentfully?) leaves his professorship to take up the burden of caring for his elderly mother (and his family's long-term, and also elderly, unmarried female servant) when his sister is murdered.

Monk pens the shockingly violent opening dream sequence of *Fuck* easily in "a little over a week" (Everett, *Erasure* 156) immediately after learning that his mother, suffering from worsening Alzheimer's disease, has little money to care for her expenses and that his earnings as an adjunct professor will not solve these financial problems:

> Mama look at me and Tardreece and she call us "human slough." That how it all start up. "Human slough," she say, "You lil' muthafuckas ain't nuffin but human slough." I looks at her and I'm wonderin what "slough" means and I don't like the look on her face and so I . . . walk across the kitchen and grab a big knife from the counter. She say, "And what you gone do wif that, human slough?" And I stab Mama. I put the knife in her stomach and pull it out red and she look at me like to say why you stab me? And I stab Mama again. Blood be all on the floor and on the table, drip drip drippin down her legs and my baby sister starts screamin and I says, "Why you be screaming, Baby Girl?" And she looks at me and she say it because I be stabbing on Mama. I look at my hands and they all covered wif blood and I realize I don't know what goin on. So, I stab Mama again. I stab her cause I scared. I stab Mama cause I love her. I stab Mama cause I hate her. Cause I love her. Cause I hate her. Cause I ain't got no daddy. (67)

I quote this passage at length to capture its "streaming" quality in contrast to the controlled, urbanely witty speech acts of Monk's journal. But surely, even a slightly critical or "writerly" reading can imagine a man in Monk's position having—and, since the pleasing anonymity of abjected "blackness" allows it, writing—a fantasy about destroying his mother. Recall that he records hostility toward his mother in the first paragraph of his journal when he writes that he will include his vocation of woodworking to embarrass her: "If for no other reason, I choose this last, callous-building occupation because of the shame it caused my mother, who for years called my pickup truck a station wagon" (Everett, *Erasure* 1). Monk's own narrative, though, avoids making any direct connections between the grotesques contained in his parodic text and the details of his ostensibly autobiographical narrative.

Monk, who would (quite ambitiously) read Roland Barthes to his readers, thereby gives up any similar effort toward a "writerly" reading of his own book in a standout passage that captures what I have called the psychic luxury occasioned by the "classic" black text. "I considered everything that was not good about the novel I was about to publish, that I submitted for the very reason it was not good, but now that fact was killing me. It was a parody, certainly, but so easy had it been to construct that I found it difficult to take seriously even as that. The work bored and had as its only virtue brevity. There was no playing with compositional or even paginal space. In fact, the work inhabited no space artistically that I could find intelligible. For all the surface concern with the spatial and otherwise dislocation of Van Go, there was nothing in the writing that self-consciously threw it back at me. Then I caught the way I was thinking and realized the saddest thing of all, that I was thinking myself into a funk about idiotic and pretentious bullshit to avoid the real accusation staring me in the face. I was a sell-out" (Everett, *Erasure* 161). Monk fails to explore a potentially cogent—and what Sterling Brown called "mentally brave"—insight into the identity between his own sensibility and his readerly text; instead, he retreats to admission of the already obvious fact of selling out. (The first thing we learn about *Fuck*, after it leaves his desk, is that it wins a six-hundred-thousand-dollar advance from Random House [Everett, *Erasure* 136].) But one can wonder just why he can write such a book—"so easy had it been to construct"—if he is so "distant" from the subject, and this question, I would venture, is precisely where "writerly" meaning might begin. And yet it would require multiple tracks of truly critical reading. Roger J. Kreuz and Richard M. Roberts help describe such complexity when they write, "Is it possible for a satire to also be a parody? The answer is yes, but now the reader must keep in mind at least three simultaneous representations: a representation of the events in the text itself, a representation of how the events in the text imitate the original work, and a representation of how the events in the text have implications both beyond the text and beyond the original work" (104).

Even Everett's satire of Monk's parodic intent, then, is a reductive secondary endpoint for interpretation. By my reading, Monk indeed turns out to recall Sekora's claim that "the unconcern and insensibility" of readers of near-anonymous black autobiographical subjects "should never be underestimated." He is not very reliable or likable. But we learn at about the novel's midpoint that like his father, a man who lived a noble life of service, Monk is also suicidal. At the National Gallery one morning, thinking about art that is "worth more than money," he muses: "I stopped at a late Rothko, the feathery working of the brush, the dark colors, the white edges and I thought of death, my own death, my making my own death. . . . My self-murder would not be an act of rage and despair, but of only despair and my artistic sensibility could not stand that. Throughout my teens and twenties I had killed myself many times, even made some of the preparations, stopping always at the writing of the note. I knew that I could manage nothing more than a perfunctory scribble and I didn't want to see that, have my silly romantic notions shattered by a lack of imagination" (Everett, *Erasure* 139). This psychic epicenter may move us to reconsider Monk more sympathetically, and if we thus pursue the parodic satire, as Kreuz and Roberts suggest, "beyond the text and beyond the original work," the discursive assembly leads not to (what I have called) an *abstraction* of Monk's (most black?) subjectivity but rather to the surrounding socio- and psycho-dynamics that seem to have a hand in the production of both his identity and his impasse. *Erasure*, from this broader viewpoint, abounds with efforts to construct meaning; interspersed amid crossed out (implicitly erased in the text by the signs "XXX") anecdotes and conversations, we find stunted "story ideas" in italics. Consider this paradigmatic example:

> *Story idea. A woman gives birth to an egg. She goes in for a normal delivery and what comes out is an egg, a six-pound-three-ounce egg. The doctors don't know what to do, so they slap a diaper on it and stick it in an incubator. Nothing happens. The egg is given to the mother to hold. She falls in love with the egg, calls it her baby. The woman takes the egg home, names it, bathes it, worries about it. . . . Her husband leaves. Her friends don't come over. She talks to the egg, tells her she loves it. The egg cracks . . ."* (Everett, *Erasure* 19)

The recurrence of such incongruous miniature "texts" indicates that their author—presumably Monk—is having a writerly crisis, which of course he is since his last novel (before *Fuck*) had been rejected by seven publishers.

But what is especially compelling here is that such false ideational starts are congruent with the multigenerational life of Monk's family, and in the light of the larger fictional world in which their ideals would seek meaning, our very impulse to praise or blame—an impulse that satire invites—seems perverse. There is something appallingly unsatisfactory and yet perhaps moving about the costs and results of his family's notions of service. Monk writes, "I grew up an Ellison. I had Ellison looks. I had an Ellison way of speaking, showed Ellison promise, would have Ellison success. People I met on the street when I was a child would tell me that they had been delivered by my grandfather, that I looked like my father and his brother. Father's older brother had also been a physician until he died at fifty. When very young I enjoyed being an Ellison, liked belonging to something larger than myself. As a teenager, I resented my family name and identification. Then I didn't care. Then the world didn't care. Washington got bigger and all the people my grand-father had delivered died" (Everett, *Erasure* 151). Monk's father, who dedicated his life to medicine like his own father, shot himself after having several heart attacks, and he remained for many years in love with a woman who was not his wife since his sense of duty bound him to his legal family. His mother spent her adult life nurturing a family whose relations are painfully stilted. His brother is losing his bearing after coming out as gay way too late, and his sister, who remained aloof from the population she served at a women's health-care clinic, has been murdered for her service to their needs. Moreover, although Monk is a spoiled favorite son, his relatively aimless critical-creative intelligence was cultivated by his father throughout Monk's childhood during moments of leisure (for example, while catching crabs together or during dinner conversations) or, suggestively, as a pleasurable antidote to the dry life of a race man's service and routine. Trying to make sense of his present, Monk writes of the village to which he moves his declining mother, "Columbia, Maryland was noted as a planned city right up to the time that its population exceeded its plan . . . and its original plan worked against it" (180). Such an arguably immobilizing historical insight merges with Monk's repeated (even essentialist) professions that he has always been awkward or lacking a felicitous, socially recognized pattern of action. Such thinking explains his existentialist gamble on "possibility"—as *Ralph* Ellison would say—and his willingness to acknowledge his pseudonymous identity as Stagg R. Leigh. He would rather face public approval or destruction than continue to seek a higher useful art in isolation.

Another aporia emerges in *Erasure*, then, that points to constraints in meaning making that would upliftingly conjoin race, identity, and service in Monk's big world of readers lacking articulate shared ideals and goals. Everett's work presents a fascinating, multilayered meditation on the (pleasurable) reading and misreading that black satire can permit in their absence. The implication, though, is that Everett must not be as cynical or hopeless about future readings and readers as we might think if he would make the effort to ironize the hubris of implied writers and readers and thereby promote their reconstruction. In fact, in a 2004 interview with Rone Shavers, Everett remarks that satire marks only one cognitive access point to his fiction: "I'm making fun of satire as well as satirizing social policies. I mean, I shouldn't even say this, but I write about satire." He furthermore notes, "I'm interested in all sorts of things, and form is one of them. I don't think meaning exists without form, and certainly form does not exist without meaning. Meaning and story come first. Story is the most important part of fiction. Without it, what's the point? If all you care about is form, become a critic" (Shavers 48). Indeed, if the "critical" reading praxis invited by satire is notably rationalist, arguably frigid, and yet also able to merge with the distanced, diagnostic "abolitionist" reading of narratives featuring abject black subjectivity, the ideologically based aporia that constricts (logical) meaning and (rhetorical) identification asks us to stretch—in the writerly spirit—a little further.

Notes

1. Stepto questioned the "adequacies of the 'social models' for reader-response literary analysis, especially since they do not seem to be, in Du Bois's terms, 'frank and fair' about the American 'race rituals' which invariably affect American acts of reading" (198–199). It is perhaps noteworthy that he has republished this essay in *A Home Elsewhere: Reading African American Classics in the Age of Obama* (2010).

2. My initial impetus for this project was the incongruity that struck me when students in my course on black literary humor and irony confessed that the best (or most pleasurable) aspect of *Erasure* was its updated, parodic version of Richard Wright's *Native Son* (1940).

3. For contemporary discussions of satire's rhetorical and logical "play with moral ideas" see Griffin (71–94) or Frank Palmeri's introduction to *Satire in Narrative* (1990), in which he notes that since satire "puts clichés, outmoded forms, and one-sided views to the test, narrative satire takes shape as an unresolved dialogue between opposed and parodied philosophical alternatives. . . . Yet the dialogue between these two positions remains unresolved, concluding as it does with a formulation entirely different from the other two: the need to cultivate our own garden" (3).

4. I borrow this term from Wolfgang Iser's analysis of a reader's temporal process of "grasping a text" when reading narrative (Iser 109).

5. Gates makes this argument throughout his introduction to *"Race," Writing, and Difference* (1986). But the following passage captures the centralization of irony: "Ironically, Anglo-African writing arose as a response to allegations of its absence. Black people responded to these profoundly serious allegations about their 'nature' as directly as they could: they wrote books, poetry . . . [and] autobiographical 'deliverance' narratives were the most common. . . . The narrated, descriptive "eye" was put into service as a literary form to posit both the individual "I" of the black author as well as the collective "I" of the race" (11).

6. An example of this kind of confused or surprised reader response can be found in Deborah E. McDowell's apt description of Hurston's collective reader in her foreword to the 1991 republication of *Moses*: "Satire, which literally means 'a dish filled with mixed fruits,' envelops and defines *Moses, Man of the Mountain*, a mode perhaps appropriate to a novel which insists that the fruits of everyone's loins are 'mixed.' The reader is occasionally bewildered and frustrated by this mix in that every attempt to penetrate to some essential, extractable political position or source is concealed behind the mélange of humor, conjure stories, folktales, and braided historical narratives, and is ultimately thwarted. The novel's

elusiveness, though, is partly explained by the repressive climate in which it was published" (McDowell xvi).

7. The context for my use of the term *classic* is from Barthes's discussion in *S/Z*, in which he writes, "Opposite the writerly text, then, is its countervalue, its negative, reactive value: what can be read, but not written: the *readerly*. We call any readerly text a classic text" (4; emphasis in original). More provocatively, in the context of thinking about Everett's satire, he argues in *S/Z* that irony and parody are "classical," thus always readerly: "Employed in behalf of a subject that puts its imaginary elements at the distance it pretends to take with regard to the language of others, thereby making itself even more securely a subject of the discourse, parody, or irony at work, is always *classic* language. What could a parody be that did not advertise itself as such?" (45).

8. Barthes writes in *The Pleasure of the Text*, "My pleasure can very well take the form of a drift. *Drifting* occurs whenever *I do not respect the whole*, and, whenever, by dint of seeming driven about by language's illusions, seductions, and intimidations, like a cork on the waves, I remain motionless, pivoting on the *intractable* bliss that binds me to the text (to the world). Drifting occurs whenever social language, the sociolect, *fails me* (as we say: *my courage fails me*). Thus, another name for drifting would be: *the Intractable* or perhaps even: Stupidity" (18–19; emphases in the original).

Who's Afraid of Post-Soul Satire?: Touré's "Black Widow" Trilogy in *The Portable Promised Land*

Bertram D. Ashe

Two scenes, from two books published nearly a decade apart. First, a non-fictional depiction of an episode that occurred sometime during Touré's junior year (1991–1992) at Emory University:

> It was around 2:30 a.m. and the party at the Black House was winding down. The music was off and the last twenty people at the party were seconds away from filing out the door. . . . I had a momentary and not-very-heated argument with another student about it being unfair that again the janitorial work was being dumped in the laps of the Black House residents. And then the linebacker-sized Black man from Alabama, who wasn't even in the conversation, who spoke so rarely in public I wasn't sure what his voice sounded like before then, silenced the room by loudly and angrily saying, "Shut up, Touré! You ain't Black!"
>
> I felt as though time had stopped and I was falling through space. I couldn't hear a thing as all the sound around me suddenly died. I felt the skin melting off my skull as if I was beginning to evaporate from the heat of the embarrassment. I felt like a machete was slicing through my mind. I was miniscule, deflated, worthless, nothing. (Touré, *Who's Afraid* 95–96)

Next, a clearly fictionalized treatment of that same incident:

> It happened one night at a school dance. Though there were very few Black students at Riverdale Country Day School, there was constant conflict between the scholarship kids and the non-scholarship ones, a worded and wordless ongoing debate about who is Black and what Blackness means. This was a battle for territory, for the right to define truth, and it was fought viciously. This night the battle reached a fever pitch when the DJ spun from a Snoop Dogg jam into

a Digable Planets record, and the dance floor's constituency turned over completely. Then Johnfkennedy Jackson, one of the scholarship boys, stepped into the dancing circle, and with the entire class looking on, he screamed, "Them Digable Faggots ain't Black and," turning to Isis, cocking the gun that was his mouth, "neither is you. *You ain't Black!*"

"It was," the nurse said, "for a fifteen-year-old, devastating." (Touré, *Portable* 191–192; emphasis in original)

Touré was around twenty years old when this incident happened, so from initial confrontation to fictional version to nonfictional representation, this singular, key moment from Touré's youth may well have informed his entire adult life.[1] The first quotation is from the fourth chapter of *Who's Afraid of Post-Blackness?: What It Means to Be Black Now* (hereafter, *WAPB?*), in a chapter unsurprisingly titled, "'Shut Up, Touré! You Ain't Black!'" The second quotation is from the last few pages of what I'm calling the "Black Widow" Trilogy, three consecutive stories in Touré's *The Portable Promised Land* (hereafter, *PPL*).

The first story, "You Are Who You Kill: The Black Widow Story, Part One," narrated by a journalist, acquaints the reader with Isis Jackson, also known as "The Black Widow": "six foot one with tight cornrows and curves for days . . . a dominating sexual presence" (Touré, *PPL*, 156); on her refrigerator are "acceptance letters from Stanford, Yale, and Spelman" (162); her mother is a "one-time Black Panther [who] now runs a school in Ghana" (160); and her politics and music are all about revolution. The second story, "Young, Black, and Unstoppable, or Death of a Zeitgeist Jockey: The Black Widow Prequel and Sequel," focuses on the Lucid brothers; the twins Sugar Dice; and the narrator, J-Love. In the first paragraph the narrator says, "We were young, Black and unstoppable. But it was all built on lies" (169). J-Love reveals that Isis Jackson "was not the daughter of a Black Panther and was not told about Nat Turner as a bedtime story. She was a Park Avenue penthouse princess finished by Chapin. Her dad was a big lawyer and her mom a failed actress. The whole Black Widow persona started on a dare after drama class" (169). The other important revelation is that the twins are white and passing for black. The journalist returns to narrate the comparatively brief third story, "Once an Oreo, Always an Oreo: *The Black Widow Finale*," in which The Black Widow is long gone and Isis Jackson is committed to the "George B. and Dr. Meika T. Kinkaid Center for Racialized Psychopathology at the University of California at Los Angeles . . . the nation's only race disorders clinic" (188), where she finally commits suicide.

Although the "Black Widow" Trilogy and *PPL* were published nine years and two months before *WAPB?*, both books are about race and blackness, and both books mount credible arguments that African Americans need to move "from exhaustive Blackness to expansive Blackness" (Dyson xvii), as Michael Eric Dyson writes in his foreword to *WAPB?*. But the chief difference between the two books is their method of discussing blackness. Along with artist Glenn Ligon, art curator Thelma Golden coined the term *post-black*, and she could well have had *PPL* in mind when she argued that "'post-black' was shorthand for a discourse that could fill volumes." Golden continues, noting that "for me, to approach a conversation about 'black art,' ultimately meant embracing and rejecting the notion of such a thing at the very same time. . . . It was a clarifying term that had ideological and chronological dimensions and repercussions" (14). For Golden, then, "post-black" was largely about black "discourse," ways to "approach a conversation" explicitly about black art. *PPL*, Touré's first book, seemed to fit those post-black "ideological and chronological dimensions" because the satirical tension between a black vernacular-inspired traditional blackness and an expansive, nontraditional blackness seemed to emanate from nearly every page.

But *WAPB?*, conversely, seems stuck in an observational dead-end. Instead of the intense, sometimes-explosive artistic tension created by exploring differing notions of traditional and nontraditional blackness, Touré responds to the reality that some African Americans consider some black cultural practices more "black" than others by refusing to accept that such a reality exists. Instead of embracing that tension as he does in *PPL*, Touré spends most of *Who's Afraid* flailing against the mere existence of black cultural norms rather than profitably examining the artists who, pushing back against those perceived norms, take a post-soul aesthetic (PSA)[2] approach to their art and lives. Indeed, Golden may well have anticipated this problem with Touré's book. Near the end of chapter 1, Touré writes, "When I described my initial thoughts about this book to Golden—and asked if she felt I could apply her meme about Black artists to all Black people—it felt like I was asking her if I could take her magnificent, ultra-rare, expensive car for a drive on the highway. In essence, she said she wouldn't drive it on the highway but I could, if I dared" (16). Alas, the process of applying a black artistic concept to black people at large, in the end, simply did not fit; it might be said that Touré crashed Golden's "car."

Another important difference is that Touré's satirical stance in his stories allows for credible, culturally valid PSA exploration. It is tempting to suggest that *PPL* is more exploratory because it is fictional satire, but in fact, nonfiction satire is also a worthwhile way to examine the various modes of blackness, demonstrated most recently in Baratunde Thurston's incisive, razor-sharp *How to Be Black* (2012). My purpose here is to compare Touré's

satirical "Black Widow" Trilogy in *PPL* to his discussion of black essentialism in *WAPB?* by foregrounding his employment of the black vernacular
tradition—both verbal and performative—as a way to deeply engage differing aspects of blackness.

For satirical purposes, readers must believe that The Black Widow is or
could be real, a truly authentic rapper and hip-hop personality. Touré's voice
is convincing, the events are vividly described (The Black Widow "pimp-
stride[s], whipping each leg ahead with a small, bold snap from her little
waist" [*PPL*, 157]), and the verbs Touré uses are colorful: she "cleaned niggas'
apartments" (159) (meaning stole from them), and "almost sneering at the
audience" onstage, she "rips through 'I Feel Naked Without My Gun' (the
chorus: 'Tits and ass and swole-up clit / I may as well be without my clip / it's
what it's gon be when my guns spit')" (165). Although Queen Latifah, during her early days as a rapper, likely personified the strident, swashbuckling,
larger-than-life female rappers of the past, the recent emergence of Nicki
Minaj would, I think, help contemporary readers of the Trilogy "believe"
that The Black Widow might well exist. Minaj possesses a vivid and distinct fashion and stylistic sensibility, a striking physical presence based on
her shape and her carriage, and perhaps most importantly, "She is as much
actor as musician, hopscotching among genres and personas more easily
than most of her rivals," writes Brent Staples in the *New York Times* (SR10).
Since readers of the Trilogy are aware of the real-life existence of such rappers as Queen Latifah, Lil' Kim, Missy Elliott, and Nicki Minaj, Touré's
satirical drive is maintained; as absurd as this first story is, it remains quasi-
believable, such that readers may well later question their initial belief in the
actuality of The Black Widow when the ruse is ultimately revealed.

Touré is playing with his readers' notions of reality. If his narration in
that first story is effective enough, readers might well wonder if somehow
The Black Widow does, indeed, truly exist. A projection of "reality" is a
satirist's core effect. Perhaps not surprisingly, some of the standout novels
of the post-soul aesthetic are satirical: Trey Ellis's *Platitudes* (1988), Darius
James's *Negrophobia: An Urban Parable* (1993), Paul Beatty's *The White Boy
Shuffle* (1996), Percival Everett's *Erasure* (2001), and Mat Johnson's *Hunting
In Harlem* (2003). These texts use satire's double-voiced nature to explore
blackness, an action I have previously referred to as "blaxploration" (Ashe,
"Theorizing" 614–615). Blackness, in Touré's Trilogy, is fluid, malleable, and
ill-defined, even as it is portrayed through solid, culturally familiar personas. Touré's "reality," then, allows his satire to work: it is the distortion, and
the reader's recognition of that distortion, that allows for the satirical message to have the possibility of arrival. As Dustin Griffin writes in *Satire: A
Critical Reintroduction*, "A work of satire . . . seeks to persuade an audience

that something or someone [in this case, restrictive blackness] is reprehensible or ridiculous; unlike pure rhetoric, it engages in exaggeration and some sort of fiction. But satire does not forsake the 'real world' entirely. Its victims come from that world, and it is this fact (together with a darker or sharper tone) that separates satire from pure comedy" (1).

The fluidity of the realities in the "Black Widow" Trilogy mirrors the fluidity of the post-soul aesthetic. As I put it in my essay "Theorizing the Post-Soul Aesthetic: An Introduction," "the core issues that PSA artists address—the peculiar pains, pleasures, and problems of race in the post–Civil Rights Movement United States; the use of nontraditionally black cultural influences in their work; and the resultant exploration of the boundaries of blackness—will remain as long as there are discrete cultural categories such as "black" or "white" and as long as there are Americans who live their lives believing separate and distinct cultural practices can be assigned to each. For there, in the unstable, wobbly interstices of those two categories, is where the post-soul aesthetic lives" (Ashe 611). Touré's fiction seems to embrace an "unstable, wobbly" American racial reality. But his nonfiction book seems intent on stabilizing African Americans' racial reality. The best examples of black racial fluidity in the Trilogy come from "Cornbread" and "Louis M. Armstrong." These two men's racial ideas seem ideologically at odds with each other but, tellingly, neither character seems to be figured by Touré as "right" or "wrong" in terms of their divergent conceptions of blackness.

"I always told you white boys you look Black," says Cornbread to the Lucid brothers on the day of their graduation from Cricket Academy. "'Race is fluid,' Cornbread said. 'And y'all already live in an epidermal-racial no-man's land. I'm just sayin you should take advantage'" (Touré, PPL 173). The Lucid brothers "talked Blackness" with Cornbread that night and on into the next day, and Cornbread moved to Manhattan with them to stay the summer. "'Listen, race isn't essentially about color,' he said. 'It's about rhythm. The way you speak, walk, eat, think—it's all tied to a sense of rhythm. If y'all can just start moving to a different philosophy of time then y'all will come off like niggas'" (173). J-Love narrates that the twins "spent months studying" blackness, including "voice, . . . movement, . . . clothes[,] . . . how to wear a hat [,] . . . how to be nonchalant, . . . how to play brer-rabbit tricks, . . . [and] how to magnetize women" by studying men from Richard Pryor and Rakim to Miles Davis, Huey Newton, and Clyde Frazier. They even studied "Bryant Gumbel, Blair Underwood, and Grant Hill" for "how not to be" (174). After a while, narrates J-Love, "Blackness began to emanate" from the twins. Finally, Cornbread drove them "out to Bed-Stuy, to a little hole-in-the-wall club called Coffee. A place that white men couldn't get into even if they had badges. He sent us to the door by ourselves. The two linebackers blocking it looked us up and down and stepped aside. We were in the club" (174).

This section is maximally blaxplorative, as the implied question *What is black?* floats above, around, and underneath the entire passage. The indeterminate skin of the Lucid brothers allows them passage into blackness, but it is blackness that is unmoored from black childhoods; or black relatives; or black history; or beyond a scant few months, a lived black experience. Touré's characters and their actions are provocative in the best post-soul aesthetic fashion here, as Cornbread, Sugar Dice, and J-Love—and their hip-hop colleague, The Black Widow—interrogate and upend all sorts of traditionally black assumptions about what makes black people, well, black.

Contrast Cornbread's conception of blackness with the inmate J-Love meets in jail, a man who introduces himself as "Louis Motherfucking Armstrong!" (Touré, *PPL* 181). The two inmates are in separate cells, too far away to see each other. Armstrong has previously seen J-Love on television, and he asks, "I been lookin close at ya on that TV and I know ya say ya Black, but I been lookin at ya. What is you? . . . Cuz Black ain't in a man's face. I got white cousins darker than you and Black cousins lighter. Black don't register on the eyes" (181–182). At this point, Cornbread's and Armstrong's racialized points of view seem virtually identical. But when J-Love asks what he means, Armstrong's essentialist response diverges sharply from Cornbread's race theory: "Black is sweaty slow-grinding in a dark basement while Marvin Gaye sings I want you. Getting spanked on your thighs with a switch from a tree in the backyard. Combin your Afro til all the naps get out. Slidin your hand up a Black woman's big, round, firm, tender ass. Playin the dozens. Smokin Newports. Bootleg whiskey, double dutch, and spades. Hittin a quick crossover dribble as you come down the lane, stutter-steppin, and goin up for a nasty dunk right in someone's mug. Flippin a cane to the beat as you cool down 125th street. Lettin the word *nigga* just flow off ya lips. Bending the King's English til it's inside out. Stayin sane in a world constructed to make you insane" (182). As Lucid was being led away, Armstrong calls out, "Lucid! Is you Black?" J-Love hears the call, and then narrates his own nonresponse: "And I really didn't know what to say" (182).

Touré offers, here, two related but distinctly different conceptions of blackness, one educational, the other experiential. Cornbread offers the twins models of performative black behavior in order to "come off like niggas" (Touré, *PPL* 173); Armstrong, on the other hand, tests J-Love by asking about a range of experiences that come from a black childhood (getting spankings, jumping rope); from black adolescence and/or young adulthood ("slow-grinding in a dark basement," "the dozens," the "quick crossover dribble"); from, perhaps, black middle age (drinking whiskey, playing cards); or even, maybe, from advanced age ("Flippin a cane" as one walks down a Harlem avenue). Many of these are experiences the Lucid brothers have not had and cannot go back in time to attain. Touré, in his fiction, seems to be subtly asking questions about and probing the efficacy of the borders of blackness, questions that he summarily squashes with his one-note, restrictive views about black culture in *WAPB?*: "I have been told, explicitly and implicitly, that there are borders to Blackness, and that sometimes I had strayed beyond them. Am I the fish that swam away from the school or did the school become as big as the ocean—so big you can't swim away from it? If Blackness is, like the ocean, too high to get over and too low to get under, then how could any Black person ever not be Black?" (17).

My own readers would be forgiven if, after reading the foregoing quotation, they shook their heads in wonder at my introducing this quotation as "restrictive." After all, doesn't Touré argue the exact opposite? Nevertheless, I'm suggesting that his conception of blackness as merely skin-deep-and-no-more denies a set of black cultural experiences that form traditional blackness. Even oceans, no matter how big, no matter how wide, have borders. So, too, do cultures. And even though cultural borders are necessarily—and often thrillingly—hazy and diffuse and impossible to concretely pin down, that doesn't mean the people who inhabit those cultures believe such borders aren't there. The term *traditional* refers to the set of experiences and types of behaviors that Louis M. Armstrong rhapsodizes about above. And what Touré argues in *WAPB?* is that there are no recognizable borders. His fiction, on the other hand, argues that there *are* "borders," there *is* traditional, familiar black behavior; but it also argues that blacks who possess a PSA or a post-black perspective retain their blackness when they transgress those black boundaries.[3] That latter stance acknowledges traditional black behavior but refuses to be bound by it. But to suggest that there are no boundaries at all is to implicitly dismiss the very cultural norms that both Cornbread, with his behavioral pedagogy, and Armstrong, with his experiential insistence, espouse as they each relate racial concepts to the Lucid brothers.

But there's more. Touré created the Cornbread character, and although we don't know much about him, what we do know is telling: he possesses an expansive knowledge about blackness, and he also insists that "race is fluid" (*PPL* 173). Those are important, but what seems equally important are the linguistic codes he uses to verbally express those ideas. In the process of discussing Cornbread's lexical habits, I'd like to talk about the protagonists of two other stories in *PPL*, "How Babe Ruth Saved My Life" and "The Playground of the Ecstatically Blasé." If Cornbread's liberal use of "y'all" and his dropping of "g's" at the end of gerunds suggest that he represents a more traditional black persona at Cricket Academy (even if his thinking about race is decidedly nontraditional), the presumably black, unnamed narrator of "Babe Ruth" offers a decidedly different set of linguistic markers. This narrator, along with the protagonist of "Ecstatically Blasé," uses colloquial, conversational words that are more associated with a non-black California dialect than traditional black speakers. The words—*totally, like*, and a peculiarly deployed present-tense *this*—are, of course, sometimes used by young black suburban speakers, but in the main, according to Mary Buckholz and her fellow authors of "Hella Nor Cal or Totally So Cal?," the words *like* and *totally*, in specific, "often co-occurred with the social labels *Valley Girl* and/ or *surfer* (or variants thereof), the two groups most associated" with the terms (345; emphases in original).

In "Babe Ruth," the narrator says this: "They'll get their lawyer father to sue me and my whole family, or they'll come into my room in the middle of the night and pour hot jelly all over me. I was totally not worried" (Touré, *PPL* 127). This same character uses a colloquial "this" in a sentence from the next page: "Even when the Sox won game five and were one game from the title I still had this supernatural calm" (128). Further, contrast Cornbread's lexical usage with the protagonist, again, presumably black, of "Ecstatically Blasé," who spins out sentences like these: "It was the worst block in the world for a restaurant. It was *this* small cobblestone block and there was *like* no parking and everything else on the block was a brownstone, so there was no reason to go to that block except to go home or to Jamais" (83; emphases added). In both "Babe Ruth" and "Ecstatically Blasé," Touré uses linguistic gestures that are far more often aligned with white, middle-class speakers than traditionally black speakers. In both these stories, Touré insists, in a pointed PSA manner, that black speakers are varied and are not restricted to using "y'all" all the time, even as he employs more traditionally black narrators and speech-acts in other stories in the collection, such as "A Hot Time at the Church of Kentucky Fried Souls and the Spectacular Final Sunday Sermon of the Right Revren Daddy Love" or "The Sad, Sweet Story of Sugar Lips Shinehot, the Man with the Portable Promised Land." By varying the linguistic nature of his black speakers from story to story and scene to scene, Touré drives home his point about black bodies—and black speech—necessarily transcending traditional black boundaries.

But when it's time to have a crucial character, in this case Cornbread, assume a culturally authoritative position in order to teach his Black Cultural Summer School class to the Lucid brothers, Touré, intentionally or not, employs just the sort of traditional speaking codes of which someone like Louis M. Armstrong would likely recognize and approve! Much of Cornbread's cultural, pedagogical authority derives from his perceived black authenticity, and much of that authenticity, in turn, is based on how he expresses himself verbally, the traditional aspects of his speech. Much the same could be said of Louis M. Armstrong. (Imagine how those two important scenes would have played out with Cornbread—even his name screams "traditional," ditto for "Louis Motherfucking Armstrong!"—instead using the middle-class, "suburban" verbal codes and references used by the protagonists of "Babe Ruth" and "Ecstatically Blasé." It is difficult to imagine, but not impossible, and such a gesture would have added yet another layer to Touré's satirical gloss on black essentialism.)

Perhaps the reason Touré employs a traditional black voice with Cornbread and a traditional black voice and character with Armstrong is because, unlike his assertions in *WAPB?*, there are, indeed, black performative cultural norms, and in both scenes he demonstrates them. Touré playfully employs those norms—otherwise known as the black vernacular tradition—in nearly all of the stories in *PPL*. As Henry Louis Gates Jr. suggests in *The Signifying Monkey* (1988), most "black writers, both explicitly and implicitly, turn to the vernacular in various formal ways to inform their creation of written fictions. . . . Whereas black writers most certainly revise texts in the Western tradition, they often seek to do so 'authentically,' with a black difference, a compelling sense of difference based on the black vernacular" (xxii). This is especially the case when a black writer such as Touré revises another black writer, Ralph Ellison.

It is, perhaps, not surprising that Touré chooses to signify on Ellison. The latter's preoccupation with the varieties of the black vernacular tradition dominate *Invisible Man* (1952). The novel has, at its core, an expansive improvisational aspect and vivid, animated black speech-acts (sermons, speeches, and monologues, combined with crackling call-and-response exchanges ranging from street conversations and street performances to scenes taking place in, say, the office of a college president). Touré was likely attracted to the novel's range of black representations as well. The title character is, after all, a college junior who drops out of a southern school and moves north; in that sense, Touré's connection with the narrator is experientially explicit. But further, the authentic, black vernacular speakers in the novel range from the school's president, Dr. Bledsoe, whose elevated speech can also employ the most blunt street language, to Jim Trueblood, a sharecropper who tells a long and fascinating tale about a cold night, economic difficulties, and the surprising results of the two.

Touré, in his trilogy, signifies on *Invisible Man* repeatedly. There are references to the Battle Royale scene ("The blows were coming too quick to block. It was pain like I'd never known, intense and blinding. My blindfold fell off and I opened my working eye a slit" [*PPL* 185]) as well as to Louis

Armstrong's appearance in Ellison's prologue ("Way off I could hear sing-ing," writes Touré, "from someone with soul in his throat. . . . *'What did I do? . . . To be so Black and blue'''* [181; emphases in orginal]). But perhaps the most telling reference to *Invisible Man* concerns the insane asylum inmates who visit the Golden Day. Early in Ellison's novel, racial truths are expressed through the words of a mentally unbalanced man called "the vet," who says to the narrator and Mr. Norton, "Poor stumblers, neither of you can see the other. To you he's a mark on the scorecard of your achievement, a thing and not a man; a child, or even less—a black amorphous thing. And you, for all your power, are not a man to him, but a God, a force," and then the vet ends the scene abruptly by shouting at the college boy and the multimillionaire, "I'm sick of both of you pitiful obscenities! Get out before I do you both the favor of bashing in your heads!" (95).

Touré revises the scene, placing his version at "the Kink" at UCLA (*PPL*, 188). As in Ellison's novel, a nominally mentally unbalanced man speaks, and readers are left to decide whether these are the words of an insane man or a racial truth that transcends the scene, reflecting a larger, racial-ized perspective. The journalist narrator has visited the Kink to see what has happened to Isis Jackson, formerly The Black Widow. He finds her at lunch, they exchange a few words, and "Just then, a Black man a few feet away leapt up from his chair, hot dog in hand, flapping his arms, screaming at no one in particular, 'I ain't Black!! You ain't Black!!' Three linebacker-sized staff members rushed in and tackled him hard. They stuffed him into a straitjacket and carted him off as he screamed, 'No one is Black! We all are!' In the commotion Isis walked off to her room" and eventually took her own life (190–191).

The inmate's words do more than merely echo Ellison's "vet," however. On the surface of the story, these assertions are merely the absurd rantings of a mentally ill man. But they actually anticipate the governing perspective of *WAPB?*: "We are in a post-Black era," writes Touré a decade later, "where the number of ways of being black is infinite. Where the possibilities for an authentic Black identity are boundless. Where what it means to be black has grown so staggeringly broad, so unpredictable, so diffuse that Blackness itself is undefinable" (*WAPB?* 20). Such pronouncements lack the nuance, the sense of exploration, the post-soul idea that what black artists do, as I suggested in my earlier article, is to "trouble" blackness: they "worry black-ness, they stir it up, touch it, feel it out, and hold it up for examination in ways that depart significantly from previous—and necessary—preoccupa-tions with struggling for political freedom, or with an attempt to establish and sustain a coherent black identity" (Ashe, "Theorizing" 614). The sat-ire Touré deploys in his collection of stories is the perfect vehicle for such an exploration. In *Problems of Dostoevsky's Poetics* (1984), Mikhail Bakhtin writes that the most important characteristics of the genre of the Menippean satirists are "bold and unrestrained use of the fantastic and adventure ... [,] the creation of *extraordinary situations* for the provoking and testing of a philosophical idea, a discourse, a *truth* ... as a mode for searching after truth, provoking it, and most important *testing* it" (114; emphases in original). It seems clear that using satire to execute blaxploration in *PPL* offered a clear advantage over his polemical commentary on blackness in *WAPB?*.

Touré's writerly choices are his own, and the wonderful stories we're left with are what they are. But we also have the complexities of the varieties of blackness Touré expresses in the satirical *PPL*, post-soul aesthetic complications that leave the reader with a sense of the depth and breadth of issues that attend to those who would approach the world—both the black world and the non-black world—from a PSA perspective. Perhaps Touré would have done well to pay heed to the sort of nuance expressed by Gates, who is quoted in *WAPB?*: "'We want to think Blackness was a unified thing you could hold in your hand,' Gates says, 'but it was always like holding water in your hand. There was a core, like there still is a core—you could go to any Black church and feel at home. When you go to the barbershop, you know, it's like a warm bath, it's nice. There is a core, a recognizable Black culture, but out of that core it's splintered and fragmented and it goes off in ten thousand different directions" (11–12). I couldn't possibly agree more. "Blackness" does, indeed, splinter and fragment in the "Black Widow" Trilogy of *PPL*, an excellent example, ultimately, of spacious, expressive blackness that nevertheless expands and enlarges far beyond any expectation. Cornbread, I have no doubt, would be proud.[4]

Notes

1. In *Who's Afraid of Post-Blackness?*, Touré writes this of the incident: "It was the most humiliating moment of my life but also one of the best moments of my life, because it forced me to take a searingly painful look inside and figure out exactly what it means to be Black. It led to a liberating epiphany and being at peace with who I am. That moment started me inching down the mental road that would lead to this book. The world had before that told me I wasn't black, or wasn't their vision of Black, but subtly, never that bluntly. It was for me a sort of nigga wake-up call" (75). Later in the book he adds that the "you're not Black ... accusation can cut to the core of a person. It can hurt so deeply it can change lives" (154–155).

2. For more about the "post-soul aesthetic"—a term essentially interchangeable with "post-blackness"—see M. A. Neal; George; and Ashe, "Theorizing the Post-Soul Aesthetic." Foundational PSA texts include Ellis, "The New Black Aesthetic"; Tate, *Flyboy in the Buttermilk*; L. Jones; and Golden.

3. In his *African American Satire: The Sacredly Profane Novel* (2001), Darryl Dickson-Carr notes that black satire, especially recent examples thereof, often uses an "'unstable' irony" that makes it "nearly impossible to decide if [the author] possesses an unambivalent view of the target of his or her irony." Dickson-Carr argues that black satire confronts the reader with "ironies that are stable within a number of African American discursive communal contexts but only if the reader has a substantial degree of knowledge about black diasporic cultural customs and social histories. On the other hand, some recent novels, such as Paul Beatty's *The White Boy Shuffle* (1996) or Darius James's *Negrophobia* (1993), seem to defy even those stabilities, revealing a marked ambivalence toward numerous phenomena in African American culture" (Dickson-Carr 25). Dickson-Carr's book was published the year before *The Portable Promised Land*, but Touré's fiction—and his satirical stance—echoes Beatty's and James's such that the above statement might well be written about Touré's collection of stories as well.

4. My daughter, Jordan Sioban (Elaiyne) Ashe, raised in a household in which the words "post-soul aesthetic" were as common as any others, once declared that Touré's *The Portable Promised Land* and *Soul City* (2004) were among her favorite books. This essay is lovingly and affectionately dedicated to her on the occasion of her college graduation.

Touré, Ecstatic Consumption, and *Soul City*: Satire and the Problem of Monoculture

Linda Furgerson Selzer

Touré is one of a generation of black writers born in the 1970s that grew up contemporaneously with the emergence of New Media, his work as a journalist, television commentator, radio host, cultural critic, and fiction writer seems to provide a model of the intellectual entrepreneurship both enabled and evoked by a rapidly changing public sphere. Similar to the way that New Media blurs old boundaries, Touré's image has appeared across a variety of media: he has hosted a show on MTV (in a shirt emblazoned with a picture of Jimi Hendrix), appeared on MSNBC as cultural critic (in a three-piece suit), and starred in the television show *I'll Do Anything Once!* (in the make-up and costume of a rodeo clown). Before turning to publishing fiction with *The Portable Promised Land* (2002) and *Soul City* (2009), Touré was a successful journalist who wrote frequently on hip-hop culture in outlets such as *Rolling Stone*, the *Village Voice*, the *New Yorker*, and the *New York Times*. The publication of *Who's Afraid of Post-Blackness?: What it Means to Be Black Now* (2011) and his subsequent tour of college campuses to discuss that book's ideas solidified Touré's status as an emerging black public intellectual. If his enthusiastic media crossing is one reflection of the increased interpenetration of Old and New Media that is restructuring authorship at the beginning of the twenty-first century, it is also an invitation to read Touré's fiction from the perspective provided by his other creative endeavors, and especially from the point of view expressed in his cultural criticism. Such a strategy helps to define a particular conceptual tension energizing the social satire in *Soul City*, a tension created by the opposition between the expansive push of artistic experimentation and the unifying pull of monocultural consumption.

In a 2011 essay published in *Salon* titled "Why I Miss the Monoculture," Touré expresses a fear that popular culture's modes of consumption have become so diversified that they are in danger of being "Balkanized."

Consumed by individuals on iPods rather than experienced face-to-face in neighborhood settings or enjoyed en masse through the consumption of pop media, music loses its ability to evoke the shared responses that help to create communal identities. As Touré argues: "The epic, collective roar . . . just doesn't happen today. Those Moments made you part of a large tribe linked by sounds that spoke to who you are or who you wanted to be. Today there's no Moments, just moments. They're smaller, less intense, shorter in duration and shared by fewer people. The Balkanization of pop culture, the overthrow of the monopoly on distribution, and the fracturing of the collective attention into a million pieces has made it impossible for us to coalesce around one album en masse. We no longer live in a monoculture" ("Why I Miss"). Touré's critique points to the velocity of change in a public sphere that has become increasingly structured by new technologies, even as those technologies themselves continue to evolve rapidly.[1]

Ironically, his nostalgia for a so-called lost monoculture does not refer to some longing for the passing of a separate black public sphere or the fading of a more stable Old Media environment. Rather, it is the passing of MTV as a culturally dominant musical outlet with a "monopoly on distribution" that Touré mourns. While one might expect such a monopoly to be viewed with suspicion, one far removed from, say, the early days of hip-hop when DJs like Kool Herc began to broadcast music through oversized boomboxes at parties in the Bronx, Touré looks back at the heyday of MTV as a cohesive force uniting listeners into a monoculture or a community of musical consumers. As Touré clarifies, "Back when MTV played videos, it functioned like a televised boombox. It was the central way for many people to experience music they loved" ("Why I Miss"). A media crossing format that has only been in existence since 1981 (when Touré himself turned ten), MTV's period of shaping the cultural identity of a generation, he suggests, is already past. Eerily echoing an earlier generation's concern about the passing of a separate black sphere (believed by some to be an unforeseen result of greater integration), Touré's analysis seems to replace bonds forged by social marginality with ties created by shared consumption. At the same time, his emphasis on the importance of a monoculture may also strike some as inconsistent with his implicit endorsement of "post-Blackness," or his sometimes stated view that "we are in a post-Black era, which means simply that the definitions and boundaries of Blackness are expanding in forty million directions—or really, into infinity" (*Who's Afraid* 12). As I will argue, lying at the heart of Touré's satire in *Soul City* is a similar tension between an insistence on the need for the consumption of shared cultural forms and on the recognition of the importance—and perhaps the necessity—of diversifying those forms.

Never Drank the Kool-Aid (2006), Touré's collection of writings on hip-hop, helps to delineate more precisely the cohesive force he attributes to monocultural consumption. Two essays from the collection, "I Live in the Hiphop Nation" and "It Was a Beautiful World," are especially salient for the insight they provide into the particular nature of Touré's understanding of community and the forces, both external and internal, that threaten its survival. At one point in "It Was a Beautiful World," Touré cogently describes a particular "Moment" that links participants through sound:

> One night during that summer I go to Nell's. The place is packed. Everyone looks like they're getting dollars and gulping deep from the cup of life. Then the DJ spins into "Who Shot Ya" and you couldn't have told me we weren't in Utopia. As Big rhymes, "I can hear sweat trick-uh-lin down ya cheek / Ya hearbeat sound like Sasquatch feet / Thunderin / Shay-kin the concrete," a brother in the middle of the room starts doing pull-ups on a waterpipe hanging from the ceiling. Then another does some pull-ups. Then a third, and as he strains through his fourth pull-up, the pipe breaks! Water rains down! The pull-up men rejoice, dancing in the downpour like kids in the stream of a fire hydrant . . . Although it's raining on the dance floor, everyone is moving with abandon, shaking and bouncing amidst the water and chaos. ("It Was" 16)

I quote this passage at some length because it captures so precisely the experiential quality of what I call "ecstatic consumption," those shared moments of musical intensity that for Touré make you "part of a large tribe" ("Why I Miss"). Positioned as an alternative to mainstream spaces, the club provides a utopian interval, a "Moment," where "the pull-up men" can display their physical prowess and simultaneously recapture the spontaneity of children. The combination of musical enjoyment, physical exertion, and celebratory downpour creates a singular experience with a unifying effect: outside the club, life may be bare, but inside the club it is overflowing. In his *Salon* essay, Touré identifies community as the result of such shared moments of ecstatic consumption, whether they are experienced firsthand at jam parties or through mass outlets like MTV.

"I Live in the Hiphop Nation," another essay in *Never Drank the Kool-Aid*, is significant for the manner in which it draws upon musical consumption to delineate a generational version of black cultural nationalism (anticipating the narrator's realization in *Soul City* that "how you party is very political" [12]).[2] Touré expands on the trope of nation in the essay's title to describe "Hiphop Nation" as a territory with its "own language, culture and history" ("I Live" 333), and to evoke its founding "fathers" and "pioneers" (333, 334).[3] Even as he recognizes that some of these pioneers are multicultural, Touré emphasizes the fact that "this world was built to worship urban black maleness," an identity denigrated by the nation at large (334). As he elaborates, "America is still white enough that we know how much we need a Blackened oasis" (337). Touré's lionizing of MTV's monoculture in *Salon* becomes more understandable in light of his argument here that when hip-hop was in danger of dying out, mass media embraced the form, saving it from extinction: "Now our music was broadcast on primetime MTV and our political views, via Chuck D and KRS-One, were heard on CNN and Nightline. Hiphop, like jazz and rock and roll before it, had become the defining force of a generation. It was not going to die" (338). Even if, as a site of ecstatic consumption, MTV could not provide the familiarity of neighborhood parties or the physical intimacy of clubs like Nell's, Touré asserts that the format still had the power to create among its listeners a "collective roar."

It is important to note that Touré's description of such ecstatic moments is tinged with nostalgia. Indeed, the actual subject of "It Was a Wonderful World" is not the jubilant moment at Nell's, but rather the internal threat to the Hiphop Nation posed by the music's complicity in a culture of violence. Although Touré doesn't recognize this threat when he is participating in the moment of communal euphoria at Nell's, it is present nonetheless, implicit in the lyrics of the song—"Who Shot Ya?" by The Notorious B.I.G., also known as Biggie Smalls—to which the men dance. The lyrics not only address the titular question regarding a shooting, but also describe what appears to be a later shooting yet to take place (in which the rapper's persona places his gun in a victim's mouth).[4] Touré pens his essay in 1999, after the March 9, 1997 drive-by shooting during which Biggie Smalls was killed. The piece is written in the form of a letter to his nephew, Sakeem, to explain why Touré threw out his hip-hop CDs rather than passing the collection on to a younger relative. In the letter, the ecstatic moment at Nell's both precedes and provides a context for Touré's later visit to interview Biggie, "the man responsible for a summer's worth of joy" ("It Was"16). Touré finds the hip-hop superstar sitting in the hallway of his building, "gripping a gat," because, as Biggie explains, a "Nigga could be coming to blow my head off" (17). The essay's focus, then, is not on the seemingly utopian moment at Nell's, but on the dystopian features of hip-hop culture. As Touré writes to Sakeem, "Stay and live in this Hiphop Nation if you want, but I won't. I can see now that murders and killings come with the beats and the rhymes" (15). If Touré's generation is often labeled "post-soul," he is positioned here more precisely as "post-Hiphop," suggesting the speed with which popular culture forms—and the identifications they inspire—cohere, collapse, and reconstitute in the contemporary public sphere. In any case, both "It Was a Wonderful World" and "Why I Miss the Monoculture" mourn ecstatic moments, now lost.

In *Soul City*, Touré will offer a more complicated analysis of the potential—and the potential dangers—of ecstatic consumption through a narrative shaped by dual designs: the desire to give full imaginative play to the idea that communal and personal identity can be effectively rooted in ecstatic consumption and the desire as well to satirize ecstatic consumption's more deleterious and even dangerous excesses.[5] The epigraph to *Soul City*, a quotation from Oscar Wilde, declares that "a map of the world that does not include Utopia is not worth even glancing at." Indicating the desire to explore at some length the positive dimensions of a society built on shared consumption, the epigraph introduces an imagined community where even the political structure is based upon musical consumption. Soul City's mayor, Emperor Jones, serves as "DJ for the town" (13), whose official responsibility is to select the music that maintains the town's style and character. The turntable in the mayor's mansion connects to a system of speakers throughout the city's sidewalks, providing a shared musical experience for all the city's inhabitants. While such a system might seem to intimate monopolistic (or imperial) control, this is not the narrative's intent. Instead, Emperor Jones's character is designed to satirize racist white discourse such as that found in Eugene O'Neill's 1920 play, *Emperor Jones*. In the play, Emperor Jones's self-loathing leads him to tyrannize other blacks, and his corrupt rule seems designed to confirm the stereotypical belief that black people are not capable of governing themselves. Drawing instead on the neighborhood musical tradition of the DJ as a culture hero, Touré's Emperor Jones celebrates black culture and enhances the stability of the community. By providing a central outlet for musical consumption (similar to the positive role that Touré's *Salon* article approvingly ascribes to neighborhood boom boxes and the "televised boombox" of MTV), Emperor Jones helps Soul City to cohere as a monocultural community based on shared musical consumption. Touré signifies on O'Neill, then, to make clear that Soul City stands in ideological opposition to stereotypical white discourse about the black community, as Soul City's geographical location in the novel is opposed to the primarily white city beyond its borders, a society whose attitudes toward black people disturbingly echo those expressed in O'Neill's play.

The initial stability of Soul City, however, is put at risk by an upcoming election for a new mayor. Emperor Jones's term has ended, and he is to be replaced by a candidate from the Jazz Party, Hiphop Nation, or Soul Music Party. Because Soul City's sense of identity depends upon shared musical consumption, any change in leadership has the potential to lead to "all sorts of catastrophes" (*Soul City* 14). As Emperor Jones explains, "You may think [the election] is about music, but it's not. It's about character. The character of this very city" (15). The threat posed by a change in leadership is heightened by the fact that Emperor Jones plays "a balanced playlist with a variety of sounds," while the other party candidates have "neither the vision nor the ears to get beyond their party's narrow platform" (13). If at the outset of the novel Soul City seems to have achieved a balance between a monopoly on musical distribution (through the mayor's speaker system) and a diversity of musical consumption (through Emperor's Jones's commitment to a varied playlist), the upcoming election that threatens this balance suggests the ease with which affiliations based on the consumption of popular culture can be disrupted.

Emperor Jones clarifies the relationship between identity and ecstatic consumption when he impresses upon the folk of Soul City the importance of the upcoming election. Quoting his grandmother's adage, "sound'll shape ya!," he elaborates on her meaning: "what she meant was music is just like food! You are what you eat, and what you hear makes you what you are. On Monday, when you go to the polls, don't think about what you want to hear, think of who you want to be" (*Soul City* 15). The mayor's equation of food, music, and character traces an economy of consumption that is in fact generative of personal as well as communal identity in the novel. While the communal character of the town is created by the people's shared consumption of the mayor's playlist, personal character is given expression through the unusual cars driven by Soul City's residents, each complete with a jukebox that includes all the music ever created by a single artist. There is a Billiemobile (a car that plays all Billie Holiday songs), Steviemobile, Milesmobile, Jamesbrownmoile, JayZmobile, and even a Beatlesmobile and a Sinatramobile. Somewhat similar to the way that Touré allows for the recognition of a few white musical performers as pioneers in "I Live in the Hiphop Nation," Soul City's vehicles make some allowance for racial diversity among performers while maintaining a predominantly African American distinctiveness. More important, by playing the music of artistic geniuses whose work has achieved iconic stature, the cars provide a shorthand means for citizens to brand one's personal identity; one's car becomes "a sonic temple, a rolling emblem of you" (*Soul City* 22). Once again, at the beginning of the novel it appears that Soul City has found a way to balance the needs of shared consumption (the mayor's playlist) with those of individual expression (the cars people choose to drive). Over the course of the novel, however, such iconic identifications as those captured by the city's fantastic automobiles will come under increasing satiric pressure.

As Soul City's remarkable automobiles suggest, play with iconicity is in fact extremely important to the satiric technique of *Soul City*. The geography, culture, and characters of the city are developed through a heavily deployed (even overdetermined) strategy of iconic representation. The important role that iconic representation plays in the genre of satire in general has long been recognized. As Northrop Frye points out, the genre operates in part by the "imposing of oversimplified ideals" or interpretations on a more complex reality (231). Or, as Darryl Dickson-Carr observes, satire "virtually demands reliance upon some generalizations" (206). For example, characters in satiric works are commonly types rather than complexly realized individuals. What is important to Touré's practice of satire in *Soul City*, however, is that because the operation of iconicity depends upon both shared social meanings and a reduction in the complexity of available meanings, there is an inherent duality to iconic representation that can be manipulated for various purposes. In part, iconic representations function by eliciting shared emotions among a people, which is to say that such representations have an affective charge that can unite. On the other hand, iconic representations involve a reduction of complexity that excludes.[6] Iconicity, then, can both carry shared social meaning and erase individualized attributes. The novel's reliance on iconic representation thus lends itself to the expression of the desire both to celebrate and to satirize the ecstatic consumption of black cultural forms. Over the course of *Soul City*, Touré exploits the duality of iconic representation to achieve different narratological and conceptual effects.

One notable effect is the reversing of white people's negative stereotyping of black culture through the text's multiplication of iconic representations of African American life from the perspective of an insider in love with the culture. The novel introduces Soul City to readers largely through the reactions of a newcomer to the city: black journalist Cadillac Jackson, whose perspective establishes an appreciative alternative to the white gaze. With a name that serves as a parodic recoding of one cliché of black consumerism, Cadillac clearly delights in Soul City's everyday aesthetics, from the barber who clips "with the arrogance of a famous painter wielding his brush" to the street sweeper who sweeps "with a theatricality that transformed his duty into modern dance" (*Soul City* 6). By focusing on Cadillac's response to the epiphenomena of black culture, the narrative asks readers to share in his joyful consumption of stylized black cultural forms. Away from the critical glance of the predominantly white population of The City, iconic features of black culture are proudly displayed and happily consumed. For example, the town's central landmark, its "Eiffel Tower," is a "one-hundred-foot-tall, black steel, black-fist Afro Pick" (11). The city streets bear names such as Cool Street, Nappy Lane, Cornbread Boulevard, and Honeypot Hill. Soul City also sponsors a museum dedicated to iconic African American culture, "The Museum of African-American Aesthetics (MoAAA)" (81), which includes a "multimedia tribute to the Black male strut, the Afro, the ultratheatrical shoe shine, and the hand greeting, from hi-fives to lo-fives, including fist pounds, tight clasps, and finger snaps" (83–84). Parodying New York's City's MOMA (Museum of Modern Art), and presumably, the high-brow artistic traditions that the famous New York museum represents, Touré's narrative can be seen to function somewhat like a Museum of African American Aesthetics itself, as it collects a wide variety of popular representations of African American life and invites viewers, from Cadillac's perspective, to enjoy the self-consciously exaggerated display.[7]

Importantly, the novel's celebration of Soul City's iconic style is developed specifically against a satire of white cultural consumption. In *Imagined Communities* (1983), Benedict Anderson argues that "all communities larger than primordial villages of face-to-face contact (and perhaps even these) are imagined. . . . Communities are to be distinguished by the style in which they are imagined" (6). In *Soul City*, the style of the majority black community is clearly juxtaposed against that of a minority white community living in Soul City. The dominant style of the black community becomes unmistakable in a scene where Cadillac first meets Mahogany, the young woman he becomes attracted to shortly after arriving in the city. Mahogany works as a DJ at the Biscuit Shop, the novel's emblematic site of gustatory and communal consumption. When she begins to play a Prince number, the Biscuit Shop's patrons suddenly "screa[m] as one and launc[h] into dancing so intense that the room was just this side of a riot" (*Soul City* 11). Reminiscent of the "Moment" of musical enjoyment described in Touré's essay "Why I Miss the Monoculture," the moment in the Biscuit Shop clearly defines the style of Soul City in terms of ecstatic consumption. White culture, on the other hand, is satirized in the novel specifically for lacking a sense of ecstatic consumption. For example, at one point Cadillac and Mahogany visit the Honky Tonk, a restaurant that plays "all white music, all the time" (*Soul City* 71). Upon entering the establishment, Cadillac hears an "average white band . . . urging some white boy to play that funky music" (71–72). The song selection ("Play that Funky Music") is here positioned as an uninspiring effort to appropriate black culture (or funk) by an "average" white band ("Play that Funky Music" was originally released in 1976 by the all-white band Wild Cherry). Not surprisingly, rather than the enthusiastic patronage of the Biscuit Shop, the Honky Tonk has a hard time attracting even a "meager" crowd. Another white restaurant visited by Cadillac, named Lolita, is also opposed to the sensual and social gratifications of the Biscuit Shop. Established by a white man named Humbert Humbert, Lolita is designed to satirize an alienated white aesthetic style, as is suggested by the fact that all its waitresses and waiters must perform the identities of characters from novels. Although a few characters from black-authored works are included in the restaurant's roles, the overwhelming focus is on characters from iconic white works, including a cynical Holden Caulfield, the "oblivious" Harry Potter (*Soul City* 24), and the harried Lolita herself. While the Biscuit Shop features a DJ who brings the customers together in spontaneous dance, Lolita offers its patrons "twenty-four large screen televisions" tuned to "the twenty-four hour news stations" (26). As real people play fictional characters while multiple TVs project other realities, a pervasive atmosphere of "intellectual vertigo" is created at Lolita (26), a locale marked not by ecstatic consumption but by estrangement.

As the previous analysis demonstrates, one feature of Touré's narrative is the celebration of the euphoric consumption of black cultural forms, especially as those forms are understood in opposition to certain satirized (or parodied) instances of white cultural production and consumption. But the narrative's dual design also takes ecstatic consumption as a target of satire. Touré's unfolding criticism of black consumption takes three primary forms. First, the continuing danger to Soul City posed by white racist discourse is emphasized through the machinations of the character John Jiggaboo and the consumption of the unusual product he sells, Jiggaboo Shampoo. Second, the excesses to which ecstatic consumption itself can lead are satirized through the community's use of the drug Bliss. Third, in a complex passage that reflects self-consciously upon the operation of iconicity, the novel introduces a character called the JimiMan who raises serious questions about the limitations to individual freedom posed by a monoculture of consumption. As these elements of the narrative will suggest, the precarious balance that Soul City seems to have achieved at the beginning of the novel between shared consumption and individual expression is in fact continually in danger of being upset by both external and internal threats.

The novel levies some of its harshest satire on the figure of John Jiggaboo and the destructive ideology of black inferiority that he threatens to introduce into Soul City. In a complication of the novel's election plot, Jiggaboo, whose hair products had previously been banned from the city by Emperor Jones, uses the election to seek revenge by ingratiating himself with the new mayor, Cool Spreadlove, in order to sell his product. Although a black man himself, Jiggaboo—as his name implies—represents the intrusion into Soul City of white stereotypical understandings of blackness. Believing that deep down all blacks *want* to be white, the schemer threatens to pervert the joyful consumption of black cultural forms upon which Soul City is based. Having originally made a fortune in films playing a "semi-retarded, tap-dancing side kick" who constantly has to be rescued by the film's white star (*Soul City* 39), Jiggaboo has more recently built an empire selling Jiggaboo

Shampoo. Known for producing "good hair," the shampoo works by "seeping down into your brain and eroding your pride" (38). In a device somewhat reminiscent of the quasi-scientific satire of George S. Schuyler's *Black No More* (1931), the secret ingredient in Jiggaboo Shampoo turns out to be microscopic cells from the cloned brain of Stepin Fetchit, and with each shampoo, users rub Stepin Fetchit's subservient attitude into their scalps.[8] The shampoo bottle itself, which bears multiple stereotypes of black people, reflects in miniature Touré's broad, overdetermined play with iconicity: the container portrays an image of a slave with exaggerated features in the act of eating a watermelon as Aunt Jemima stands behind him shampooing his hair. In addition, a cartoon on every bottle chronicles the adventures of the incompetent "SuperNigger" (a character created by Richard Pryor), "who always succeeded in screwing up whatever mission he set out to accomplish, tacitly proving the supremacy of the white superheroes" (37). Through such hypberbolic images, Touré satirizes an entire history of negative stereotyping of black people.

But the narrative also satirizes the degree to which black people (even "super" ones) continue to consume or to internalize white racial discourse. After all, it is culturally induced anxiety over their hair that leads many of the citizens of Soul City to become addicted to Jiggaboo Shampoo, revealing the degree to which they have already internalized white standards of beauty. The menace posed by an encroaching white style is brought to a moment of crisis in the novel when Cool Spreadlove (one of the shampoo's early converts) gives Jiggaboo access to the mayor's mansion, where he threatens the entire city by attempting to broadcast a Barry Manilow record over the mayor's speaker system. Manilow's iconic status as a producer of uninspiring white pop-rock standards is buttressed by the fact that an actual radio station—KBIG in L.A.—ran a promotion in 1994 trying to attract listeners by advertising the fact that the station would *not* play Manilow records (Lait). Apparently agreeing with KBIG's assessment, Touré here humorously suggests that blasting a Barry Manilow song through the mayor's sound system would be more deleterious to the community of Soul City than the use of Jiggaboo Shampoo. As HueyNewton Payne (the town's resident "bad man" and protector) observes before he pushes Jiggaboo out of a window to order to save the city, "a moment of Manilow could ruin Soul City forever" (*Soul City* 142).[9] Through his play with iconicity in the representation of Jiggaboo (and Manilow), Touré's election plot satirizes the dangers presented by the social circulation of racial codes in a manner that recalls the satiric techniques of both Ralph Ellison and Ishmael Reed. In *Invisible Man*, Ellison satirizes the operation of a racial code so pervasive that white people's understanding of black identity renders the narrator virtually invisible. Reed's novels characteristically deploy hyperbolic characterizations in an attempt to break the social spell of racial coding by making racist assumptions clearly visible. Through the exaggerated characterization of Jiggaboo and the eagerness with which the people of Soul City consume his shampoo, Touré similarly satirizes the social circulation of racist discourse and the degree to which black people unwittingly or willingly participate in its consumption.

In addition to the attractions of Jiggaboo Shampoo, addiction also threatens the community of Soul City in another form—one that more clearly satirizes the excesses of ecstatic consumption itself—through the popularity of the drug Bliss. To a community built on ecstatic consumption, the temptation of a drug that "exponentialized your ability to hear" is clear (*Soul City* 31). As Mahogany's friend Precious Negro explains, Bliss has the ability to take you "*inside* the music"; it's like "LSD for your ears" (31; emphasis in original). Bliss, as its name implies, suggests the danger of carrying ecstatic consumption to the extreme. Opposed to collective and participatory moments of consumption, Bliss lends itself to being consumed clandestinely and makes users lethargic: "you put your body in a coma and you just lay there, can't move, can't talk" (31). With overuse, users' ears fall off, reducing their ability to hear. Most important, rather than leading to a collective experience that links the individual to others, Bliss takes the user inside, on "a journey into [the] subconscious" (42). As Cadillac personally discovers, Bliss also carries the risk of a bad trip. When he journeys into his own subconscious via Bliss, Cadillac disturbingly finds it already peopled with the stereotypical figures of the white imaginary, including an oversized Aunt Jemima, who in this case is naked and sexually aggressive. In addition to evoking the surrealist transformations of a bad trip, the conversion of Aunt Jemima's maternal associations into sexually aggressive ones parodies white discourse about nurturing mammies. At the same time Cadillac's bizarre, nightmarish hallucination of the "mammy as rapist" reveals a psychological truth by expressing the underlying threat to black people posed by all racist representation. Emphasizing the limits of ecstatic consumption taken as an end in itself, Bliss also underscores the danger of passively consuming pre-established social meanings and points to the importance of producing social meanings as well as consuming them.

A related danger inherent in basing one's identity on the shared consumption of iconic cultural forms is brought home forcefully in the novel through the experience of the "JimiMan," a resident of Soul City born with the "soul of Jimi Hendrix" (*Soul City* 77). The best guitar player in town, JimiMan not surprisingly drives a Hendrixmobile, a car that "defined him for the city and for himself" (78). JimiMan's growing dissatisfaction over his identification with Hendrix allows the narrative to focus self-reflectively on the operation of iconicity, drawing attention to the danger of defining oneself through any preexisting models, no matter how accomplished or admired: "While Jimi was kissing the sky JimiMan was stuck on the ground, channeling someone else while longing for freedom. He loved Jimi. There was no one else in history he'd rather have had inside him, but it was his twenty-first birthday and what he really wanted was to be himself. But Jimi had consumed him so completely he didn't know who he was" (78). The JimiMan, then, reflects the danger of being consumed by what one consumes. As in the case of Bliss, the problem is in part the imbibing of so much of a good thing that one does not have access to a wider diversity of experience. But the JimiMan also suggests that the reliance in Soul City on an association with past iconic figures for the expression of contemporary identity can lead to alienation akin to that experienced by the workers in Lolita who are forced to perform their iconic fictional roles.

The JimiMan's particular situation, moreover, resonates forcefully with that of post-soul generation members aware of the iconic achievements of those who came before them but who seek to forge their own, separate identities. In a moment of rebellion, JimiMan sets his Hendrixmobile afire. By doing so, he challenges the supposed balance maintained in Soul City between communal and personal expression, revealing an inherent tension between shared social meanings and the individual's desire for freedom of expression.[10] Through the JimiMan's experience the novel also speaks to an important issue raised in *Who's Afraid of Post-Blackness?*, which defines post-blackness as distinct from popular conceptions of the post-racial. For Touré, the term *post-racial* conveys the meaning of living in a society where "race doesn't exist anymore." He finds this position untenable, partly because it fails to acknowledge that black people continue to confront racism. By using the term *post-blackness*, Touré instead wants to emphasize "the complexity of modern Black identity" that is "rooted in but not constrained by Blackness" (*Who's Afraid* 256). The desire to recognize black identity as rooted in black culture (and therefore to retain the ability to celebrate one's connections to a larger black culture) but also to see black culture as not constrained by any particular definition of blackness (and therefore to reserve the ability to critique its forms) is also a fitting description of *Soul City*'s dual narrative design. As the JimiMan illustrates, sharing a monoculture can both generate communal bonds and limit individual freedom, setting in place the need for a cultural process in which the individual's affiliations and disaffiliations must be continually renegotiated. After his car goes up in flames, JimiMan plays his guitar in a new way, "His fingers danc[ing] over the guitar with the thrill of touching a lover for the first time. He wasn't playing a song, wasn't confining himself to a structure, he was just playing, improvising, exploring his guitar and himself . . . he was playing the autobiography of someone just being born" (*Soul City* 79). Significantly, it is only by freeing himself from Hendrix's iconic style—while simultaneously drawing upon the African American tradition of musical improvisation that inspired Hendrix himself—that JimiMan moves beyond the pleasures of ecstatic consumption to those of ecstatic production.

In his essays "Why I Miss the Monoculture," "It Was a Beautiful World," and "I Live in the Hiphop Nation" and in his novel *Soul City*, Touré speaks to a manner in which ecstatic moments of musical consumption forge communal identifications. Such identifications, he fears, are threatened by the conditions operating in a new public sphere where changing formats for the distribution and consumption of music (and other cultural forms) seem to be moving away from monocultural to individualized consumption. It is arguable whether Touré is correct in his fears about the loss of a monoculture or whether popular culture was always too unstable a ground to serve as a foundation for lasting communal affiliations. It is perhaps precisely because Touré is a member of the post-soul generation whose public sphere has been marked by rapid change—by changing popular media formats and by increased media crossing—that he at times looks back nostalgically to the seemingly more settled joys of a disappearing monoculture. In any case, the desire for a shared community of ecstatic consumption—inflected as it may be with Utopian impulses—plays a significant role in *Soul City*, a novel designed in part to celebrate the euphoric consumption of black cultural forms (especially as read in opposition to a satirized white cultural consumption). Yet Cadillac Jackson comes to appreciate that although Soul City is "amazing," it is "not Utopia" (*Soul City* 80). Recognizing that immersion in a monoculture can limit individual freedom and artistic experimentation, Touré pointedly satirizes the danger inherent in monocultural identifications. *Soul City's* dual satiric design, therefore, prompts reflection upon the operation of iconicity itself, on the importance of shared meanings to the creation of communal and personal identity and upon the limitations such preexisting meanings impose. A significant contribution to the African American satiric tradition, *Soul City* embodies a twenty-first-century generation's desire to create new forms of identity "rooted in but not constrained by Blackness."

Notes

1. See also Kinohi Nishikawa's article in this collection, pp. 38–55.

2. I should point out that the relationship between the stances taken in his essays and Touré's own opinions is complicated by his description of his voice in the essays as assuming a "posture meant to portray an emotion" (*Never Drank* 7). Such a disclaimer warns readers against associating the views expressed in his essays too closely with Touré's own and suggests that the opinions expressed in different essays may involve the development of personas.

3. The evocation of "nation" in the essay's title and the self-conscious reference to older forms of cultural nationalism—dismissively referred to as "jingoistic" (Touré, "I Live" 333)—positions Touré's community as both part of, and different from, earlier iterations of cultural nationalism. Touré is clearly having fun expanding the metaphor of nation, yet his equation of the threat of hip-hop's extinction to the Holocaust of the Jewish people may strike readers as overwrought.

4. Some believe "Who Shot Ya?" played a role in the East-West hip-hop rivalry and judge the song to be a diss track aimed at taunting Tupac Shakur, who had been shot and wounded on November 30, 1994. Biggie Smalls denied the connection, arguing that he composed the song for an earlier project, from which it had been dropped as too violent. Others find the timing of the release (two months after Shakur's shooting) suspicious. Shakur was killed on November 7, 1996. Smalls was shot and killed on March 9, 1997.

5. See also Thomas R. Britt's article in this collection, pp. 56–57

6. It is important to note in this regard that iconic representation is important historically to racist stereotyping, which also reduces complex individuals to preexisting types.

7. This display continues a cataloguing that Touré began seven years earlier in *The Portable Promised Land*, especially in the chapters titled "The African American Aesthetics Hall of Fame, or 101 Elements of Blackness (Things That'll Make You Say: *Yes! That There's Some Really Black Shit!*)" and "We Words: *My Favorite Things*" (95–104, 133–141).

8. Stepin Fetchit was a character who embodied white stereotypes of the foolish, slow-witted, lazy black man. The character was played by actor Lincoln Perry in the early to mid-twentieth century.

9. As with so many other characters in the novel, Touré gives the protector of Soul City an iconic name. Such names serve multiple purposes in the narrative, as does the author's play with iconicity more broadly. At times, names are used to parody white representations; at other times, to quickly characterize figures by presenting them as examples of an exaggerated type or ideology. Wordplay with names also serves as a source of humor in the novel (as in the case of the name "Precious Negro").

10. Although it is beyond the scope of this analysis, I should mention that in addition to the election plot, the novel's marriage plot also explores the tension between the monoculture and individual freedom. Cadillac wants to marry Mahogany, but the townspeople disapprove of her marriage to an outsider. Mahogany belongs to a venerable Soul City family with the gift of flight, and it is believed that her children will lose the ability to fly if she marries outside the community. Moreover, the welfare of the entire community is at stake; the birth of a first-born child unable to fly will signal, tradition has it, the beginning

of the end for Soul City. Diversity in the form of marriage to an outsider, then, is seen as a threat to Soul City. Somewhat like the JimiMan's rejection of iconic expectations, Mahogany objects to being the "town's talisman" (Touré, *Soul City* 122). She does marry Cadillac, and their child does fly (if due to divine intervention). The marriage plot thus suggests that Soul City will be able both to accommodate difference and to retain its own distinctive magic.

"I Felt Like I Was Part of the Troop": Satire, Feminist Narratology, and Community

Brandon Manning

Scholars have long considered African American satire a repository for androcentric perspectives that largely exclude themes and issues pertaining to black women's subjectivity. Indeed, African American satire often uses black women and their experiences as fodder for both the humor and the vitriol of their works. For example, Ishmael Reed has been taken to task by a number of feminist critics and writers for, among other things, his depiction of the character of Tremonisha Smarts (usually interpreted as a parody of Alice Walker, Reed's longtime nemesis) in his novel *Reckless Eyeballing* (1986). Although Kathryn Hume does not indict Reed as thoroughly as many other critics, she does note that "Reed is so bent on reestablishing black manhood that he can picture it only in conjunction with a differentiated and (many would say) subordinated black womanhood" (511). Kimberly Nichele Brown identifies Trey Ellis's satirical novel *Platitudes* (1988) as "follow[ing] in Reed's footsteps by offering his own satiric portrayal of Walker (and, by extension, other established black female writers) . . . with his characterization of Isshee Ayam." Brown allows that "Ellis seems to be more sympathetic to black women writers than is Reed," but adds that neither is "engaging in any meaningful dialogue with black feminists about sexism within the black community, while simultaneously insinuating that the texts of black women like Walker are therapeutic experiments designed to allow women to vent their sexual frustrations" (K. N. Brown 3).

However, shortly after the turn of the millennium, ZZ Packer issued a brief but potentially groundbreaking rejoinder to the androcentric narrative conventions of contemporary African American satire. Packer's investment in creating a sense of community serves as a refreshing counternarrative to black male satirists' relatively exclusionary gendered voices, one that promises confirmation of Darryl Dickson-Carr's suspicion "that when the satirical novel asserts its place in twenty-first-century African American literary traditions, women will be at the forefront of the new movement. With luck, this will yield the benefit of forcing the old political directions of African American communities—and African American satire itself—to take fresh, new turns into more inclusive examinations of those same communities and their individual members (207).

This chapter analyzes the importance of community in contemporary African American satire by using a black feminist narratology to underscore some of the salient differences in the ways male and female authors have traditionally engaged their readers' solidarity. Part of this project is geared toward understanding what a black feminist narratology looks like and how it would benefit the field of narratology more generally. This project goes on to apply black feminist narratology to Packer's short story, "Brownies," as a representative example of the way contemporary African American women writers engage in wide-ranging community building in the midst of a text that still performs the satirical function of ethical and moral critique.

In her introduction to *Ambiguous Discourse: Feminist Narratology and British Women Writers* (1996), Kathy Mezei understands "the essence of Feminist narratology" as "the context of how stories are told, by whom, and for whom" ("Introduction" 1). She goes on to historicize the field of feminist narratology, touching on myriad issues ranging from feminism and theory to formalism and the science of narratology. Her introduction strongly suggests that extant feminist narratology has been hamstrung by a very limited understanding of feminism. Apparently trapped in the second wave, feminist narratology (at least as Mezei articulated it) had yet to recognize and consider how race and gender both, as socially constructed as they may be, can simultaneously constitute unique ways of understanding "how stories are told, by whom, and for whom." Perhaps tellingly in this regard, the scholars in the very collection of essays that Mezei is prefacing almost exclusively chose to examine white British women writers such as Virginia Woolf and Jane Austen. Even the seminal essay "Toward a Feminist Narratology," in which Susan Lanser created a space for feminist narratology as a way to engage "women's language" and the concept of weak narrativity, understands the written performance of gender as a race-less construct.

More recently, though, Lanser has found space to include more complex identity formations using Kimberle Crenshaw's concept of intersectionality, or the "various ways in which race and gender intersect in shaping structural, political, and representational" realities for people living on the margin (Crenshaw 1244). In "Are We There Yet? The Intersection Future of Feminist Narratology," Lanser speaks to many of the concerns articulated above as well as addressing the ways that both feminism and narratology have grown since her initial essay in 1986. Lanser also acknowledges Ruth

Page's criticism that "Toward a Feminist Narratology" reaffirms the gender binary by suggesting that men innately write one way while women write in another and by not seeing the act of writing as a performance of gender unto itself. "Are We There Yet?" enlivens and enriches feminist narratology and suggests a host of new directions. Lanser proposes that narratology should function as a tool for understanding the intersections of and interconnections among race, class, gender, and sexuality.

The initial omission around issues pertaining to race could have happened for a number of reasons during this late-twentieth-century moment. Manifestos like Barbara Christian's "The Race for Theory" and Joyce A. Joyce's "The Black Canon: Reconstructing Black American Literary Criticism" both speak to black women scholars' reservations about structuralism and poststructuralism as theoretical sites of erasure concerning the problems of black women. Scholars such as Deborah McDowell and bell hooks embraced and defended more traditional notions of theory, and Christian's essay denounces their approaches, stating that "people of color have always theorized—but in forms quite different from the Western form of abstract logic. And I am inclined to say that our theorizing (and I intentionally use the verb rather than the noun) is often in narrative forms, in the stories we create, in riddles and proverbs, in the play with language, since dynamic rather than fixed ideas seem more to our liking" (52). If theorizing did happen on the narrative level and Christian's laments about the decentering of authors by egocentric scholars are accurate, then why have there not been more black women and people of color taking up narratology as a theoretical framework to analyze African American literature and that of other subaltern groups? While the discussion of potential answers to this question should take place in venues that can dedicate the necessary room to a robust and nuanced response, this essay seeks, as Lanser writes, "[to offer] the questions that [feminist narratology] does not yet seem to have addressed" (454).

Central to both black feminist criticism and feminist narratology are the issues of visibility / legibility and the creation of communities. In 1977, The Combahee River Collective published a statement that best demonstrates black women's need to help each other out. In this statement the collective writes, "We realize that the only people who care enough about us to work consistently for our liberation are us. Our politics evolve from a healthy love for ourselves, our sisters and our community which allows us to continue our struggle and work" (9). Similarly, in "Toward a Feminist Narratology," Lanser's interest in "theory that would define and describe *tone* in narrative" and later the ideas of public versus private narration all speak to the creation and communication of a discursive female community. Lanser writes that "communication, understanding, being understood, becomes not only the objective of the narration but the act that can transform (some aspect of) the narrated world" (467; emphasis in original). Both Lanser's articulation of the objective of narration in feminist narratology and The Combahee River Collective statement—a narrative in its own right that articulates the goals, direction, and solidarity of black feminism—speak to the transformative power of being visible and being heard.

A black feminist narratology should take elements of both narrative theory and black feminist criticism and forge new ways of understanding texts for, by, and about black women. This would prove especially fertile ground from both a black feminist and a narrative perspective because of stereotypical narratives about black women. Often read as complacent, angry, and ignorant (compare to Reed's depiction of Tremonisha Smarts), the narratives created around black women's subjectivities are themselves relevant and warrant a narratological approach in attempting to understand their construction, dissemination, and continuation. Furthermore, it is potentially quite valuable to examine how black women writers resist, rewrite, or undermine these stereotypes through the tone they adopt in their works. Just as black feminist criticism is not only concerned with black female–authored texts, so too should black feminist narratology look at other texts to engage in wide-ranging revisionist work similar to what Toni Morrison does in her monograph *Playing in the Dark: Whiteness and the Literary Imagination* (1993). While the possibilities seem endless for this new mode of intellectual excavation, I will limit myself here to a brief exploration of some of the ways that a black feminist narratology affects the way we read satire.

In *Gendered Interventions: Narrative Discourse in the Victorian Novel* (1989), Robyn R. Warhol picks up where Lanser leaves off, speaking of the importance of using a feminist narratology to understand the relationship between authors and their readership in terms of community. Warhol lays out the ways that authors either embrace their readership or distance themselves from them by either explicitly identifying the reader as the narratee (that is, the character to whom the narrator is telling the story) or points out that the narrative is intended for someone else. She suggests that women writers of the nineteenth century were prone to centering the reader within their work (in other words, making them a part of a community that includes the narrator), whereas male authors were more prone to distance themselves by creating narratees within the text who ruptured the storytelling process. While Warhol is very specific in outlining the gendered implications of female authors' tendency to build narrative communities with their readers more often than their male counterparts, I am interested here more in the ways that this paradigm shifts somewhat when applied to the gendered narrative dimensions of satire.

Satirists' decisions to embrace and/or to distance themselves narratively from various portions of their readership both differs from and overlaps significantly with Warhol's ruminations on the subject. Instead of the narrator complicating or obscuring the intended audience of a particular narrative by addressing a narratee who is separate from the reader, satirists often distance themselves from particular readers through the scope and nature of their moral and ethical commentary. In contemporary African American satire, satirists narratively both embrace and distance the text from specific sets of readers by delineating the ways that particular narratees / readers are morally or ethically suspect within the author's social commentary. In other words, the way Warhol understands the choice of writers either to create a reader-centered community or to distance themselves from their readers is similar to the way what I will call a "narratee-community" is established in satire. Although such a community is not always explicitly delineated, the inherent Bakhtinian "double-voicing" of satirical texts determines which groups are privileged and which are censured in its moral / ethical calculus, thereby also establishing who is invited into and who is excluded from the narratee-community.

In satires written by African American men, the scope has generally been very limited in regard to who the fictive narratee is and how that relates to the sense of community that is established between author and reader. As Brown's and Hume's comments above suggest, African American male satirists such as Reed and Ellis have not necessarily always included women centrally in their narratee-communities, placing them instead into the category of those made the object or target of their satire, a position inherently outside the author-reader solidarity. Many of the communities created in these male-authored texts are severely limited in terms of class and gender because their authors define their narratee-community primarily as relatively affluent and educated black men who share the values and characteristics of their narrators. For instance, in the 2001 novel *Erasure*, Percival Everett patronizes both black families from lower socioeconomic strata and women with some of the satirical gestures he makes through his protagonist. There is an early moment in the novel where Monk, Everett's protagonist and narrator, is waiting in the lobby of his sister's clinic and is having a conversation with a young woman who is sitting next to him. Upon hearing that he is a professor of literature, she begins to speak to him about African American literature that she has read. After their short conversation Monk thinks, "I felt an inch tall because I had expected this young woman with the blue fingernails to be a certain way, to be slow and stupid, but she was neither, I was the stupid one" (21). Just pages later, though, Monk's sister explains that the names of the children of the young woman with whom

Monk was speaking are "Mystery" and "Fantasy," respectively, after their different fathers (26). Everett includes this tidbit to ameliorate Monk's earlier feeling of remorse for assuming the young woman was ignorant. Furthermore, the perceived guilt behind the idiocy of the children's names is made to rest solely on the young woman. The fact that the children's names are Mystery and Fantasy is in no way a critique on the missing fathers; instead, the mentioning of these names serves as a critique of the black woman's assumed promiscuity and class status. Monk notes that "I make shit up for a living and I couldn't have come up with that [the children's names]," and he furthermore distances himself not only from the young woman but most of humanity when he adds, "Sometimes, I feel like I'm so removed from everything, like I don't even know how to talk to people" (26). Thus, while Everett does not distance the narrative from the reader through Warhol's traditionalist understanding of the narratee, the narratee-community that this text is intended for (as well as the types of people excluded from that community by being the target of its satire) manifests itself through a series of negations that would distance the narrative (and the narrator) from some, if not most, of its readers.

Similarly, in *Platitudes*, Ellis seems to evoke Baldwin's short story, "Going to Meet the Man," when his protagonist, Dewayne, fails to reach a full erection at the end of the novel. Instead of thinking about the violent sexual acts that he performs on others (as is the case with Baldwin's sheriff), he finishes writing a work of fiction in which he is able to do something he cannot yet do in real life, namely to convince his fellow writer and soon-to-be lover, Isshee, to amend her negative attitudes about black men. Dewayne's success in being able fictionally to change Isshee's mind as to what constitutes blackness, and more importantly black masculinity, leaves him excited and ready to go wake Isshee whose real-life presence seems almost exclusively at that moment intended for his sexual gratification: "Now that it [his erection] presses the underside of his desk, he will go wake Isshee" (Ellis, *Platitudes* 183). In the novel's last scene, Brown claims that this moment serves to reassure male readers that "her dubious depiction of black men as villains [in her own writing] is the result of her own failed relationships rather than a realistic critique of sexism" (K. N. Brown 3). As such, the masculinely gendered nature of the novel's narratee-community is made explicit.

While couching these gendered differences within the realm of narratology may be new to African American satire, there is nothing new in claiming that satire, as a form, is predominantly masculinist in its scope. Most contemporary scholars on satire have spoken to the presence of androcentricism within different historical and regional satirical narratives. Felicity Nussbaum writes exclusively on the topic in her *The Brink of All We Hate*

(1984). She writes of seventeenth- and eighteenth-century British satires, "When we determine resemblances among antifeminist satires, we can elucidate the conventions and myths which allowed satirists to catch hold of deeply disturbing elements and create a poetic fiction of power and authority" (3). Furthermore, Nussbaum notes that "women in the myth of satire represent a world of disorder, and the satirists rage at the female power to seduce and overpower them. Women are accused of rebellion against all aspects of patriarchal order and authority. Society easily accepts a satire against the things it most fears" (19). Similarly, Charles Knight underscores the representation of women in satire when he writes, "One further quality of the satiric frame of mind needs to be noted, and that is its apparent gender exclusivity. . . . What makes satire more-or-less a masculine genre is not a gender exclusivity. . . . Satire of men is thus satire of human nature, but satire of women is satire of a particular variety of people" (6). At the core of these explorations into the male dominance of satire is the material reality that afforded men, in particular white men, the ability to be educated and to travel in order to gain the nuanced perspective that satire often requires of its audience. Likewise, the assumed discursive violence and combative nature of satire also deemed it a more masculine pursuit than other literary forms. As antiquated as these strict gender roles seem, they still have some relevance in contemporary African American literature, yet little has been written about both the representation of black women in male-authored satires and the obvious lack of black female-authored satires.

ZZ Packer has incorporated the satirical form into some of her prose, most successfully in several of the stories in her collection *Drinking Coffee Elsewhere* (2003). Unlike her male counterparts, however, she has written female-centered narratives without limiting her narratee-community to a particular gender, whether her own or that of her narrators and/or protagonists. Despite containing a pointed critique of racism and its effects, both within and outside the black community, her narrative remains relatively more accessible and ethically inviting to readers and therefore offers them a broader, more inclusive sense of community. Although Packer is writing short stories and not novels like Ellis, Everett, or Reed, she manages to be much more inclusive in the shaping of her social critique, creating both the kind of feminist community and visibility for which Lanser and The Combahee River Collective argue.

Packer's story, "Brownies," is about an all-black Brownie troop of fourth-grade girls from the suburbs of Atlanta who go camping for the weekend. These girls seem to loathe the notion of going camping and seem rather uninterested in the weekend's events until they instantly declare war on an all-white Brownie troop unloading from a bus in close proximity. Feeling as though these white girls from Troop 909 have invaded their territory, the black girls work themselves into a rage of racial envy and paranoia that ultimately culminates with one of the black girls fabricating a lie that a white girl called a member of the black troop a nigger. This, as planned, inflames an already volatile situation among the black girls, who equate whiteness with wealth and everything they desire but cannot have. The black girls plan to fight the white troop in the bathroom, but their plan is interrupted when they confront the girls from the white troop and realize that they are all mentally handicapped.

Although Packer's stories in *Drinking Coffee Elsewhere* deal with different periods and subject matters in women's lives, they all demonstrate both a desire for community and a desire to embrace the reader. In "Brownies" the reader immediately understands the emphasis on community in the text, but does so through a mildly satirical questioning of how and why communities are formed and maintained. The story opens as the black troop first sees the all-white troop piling out of the bus that brought them to the camp. Arnetta, one of the black girls, says after the white girls passed by, "Man, did you smell them. . . . They smell like Chihuahuas. *Wet* Chihuahuas," after which she "raise[s] her nose in the air and grimace[s]" (Packer 2; emphasis in original). Packer illustrates the implicit power play that the troop of Laurel, the narrator, experiences immediately upon seeing the white troop. The imagery of a wet chihuahua and the corresponding grimace also imply a level of disgust among the black girls, something that inherently limits any sense of seeing the white girls as part of their wider community of Brownies. As Sara Ahmed writes, "When thinking about how bodies become objects of disgust, we can see that disgust is crucial to power relations. . . . The relation between disgust and power is evident when we consider the spatiality of disgust reactions, and their role in the hierarchizing of spaces as well as bodies" (88). The ability to express disgust unifies the group internally and shows their racial prejudice. Significantly, it is a wet chihuahua and not a larger dog that Arnetta chooses for her simile, thereby both minimizing the importance that she places on whiteness as well as perhaps mitigating any fear of violent reprisal from Troop 909. The laughter among the girls in the black troop intensifies the power dynamic that is implicit in Arnetta's statement by functioning as a way for the group to agree with her exclusionary disgust. The story's conclusion, however, makes it clear that Packer's *reader* will not be allowed such an agreement, since both the words and the behaviors of Laurel's troop will ultimately be subverted satirically.

Moira Smith notes that humor often functions to maintain boundaries that mark and reify the social norms of groups: "[joking] is a key component in the regulation of social life, smoothing interactions, serving as a mechanism of social control, and promoting solidarity. . . . The flip side of solidarity is marking boundaries, which is achieved by emphasizing not only what people inside the group have in common but also the differences that distinguish them from others" (159). Thus, the laughter and attendant disgust function as dividing lines and as a sort of call-and-response utterance by which the girls can claim their allegiance to a racially defined community rather than the larger community of Brownies that makes up the entire population of the camp. In addition to their immaturity, the girls' conditioned perception of whiteness is largely to blame for the way they act. As Laurel narrates, "When you lived in the south suburbs of Atlanta, it was easy to forget about whites. Whites were like those baby pigeons: real and existing, but rarely seen or thought about. . . . The ten white girls behind us—*invaders*, Arnetta would later call them were instantly real and memorable, with their long, shampoo-commercial hair, straight as spaghetti from the box. This alone was reason for envy and hatred" (Packer 4–5; emphasis in original). It is the conception of these white girls as invaders that solidifies the boundaries of the community within the narrative. It is also their shared, if limited understanding of how racial oppression and hegemony are enacted in their broader community that forces these girls to feel as though they have to defend their specifically black community. However, it is important that Packer has Arnetta, the unreliable bully of the narrative, be the dominant voice during these moments, since the resolution of the story satirically reveals the destructive and careless blindness that comes with adopting Arnetta's point of view. Packer ensures that her reader does not share or embrace the community building that is happening through Arnetta's influence because of its source. Laurel's outermost narrative frame allows for a recognition of the historical and social forces that have negatively influenced the girls, but it does not validate the hateful, disgusted, and exclusionary response to which Arnetta gives voice.

Unlike Everett and Ellis, Packer is able to embrace her readership broadly and, in the process, advocate for a communal, feminist mindset through the satirical framing of her social commentary. In "Brownies," the community represents Packer's commentary on prejudice of all forms and the misdirected desire to avenge past wrongs against people not responsible for them. Packer does not negate the presence of racism, both real and imagined, in the story; the children vividly and compellingly recount their parents' narratives of racism. However, she does become critical when the experience of racism engenders an attitude for blacks that retards social progress, both within the black community and within a larger community (such as the Brownies, Atlanta, the U.S. generally). Laurel's troop eventually embodies a lynch mob in the way they create a lie around the supposed use of the word *nigger* and then try to enact retributive violence upon Troop 909. The imagery of a lynch mob illustrates the regressive politics of trying to get even with a perceived racist threat, even when the conventional markers of race are reversed. Trudier Harris's *Exorcising Blackness: Historical and Literary Lynching and Burning Rituals* (1984) speaks to the diseased communal aspects of lynching when she articulates the way in which this ritual was performed and maintained as a means of in-group solidarity that projected problems onto outside members (that is, blacks) and then symbolically purged them through the lynching. Therefore, the eerie turn in Packer's story satirizes the idiocy associated with modes of thinking that call for a loose form of redemption and the destructive, limited sense of community they reinforce.

Packer also features the broader black community of the Atlanta suburbs through the adult characters of Mrs. Margolin and Mrs. Hedy, the leaders of the black troop. The purpose of these women in the narrative is to provide a nonsatirical counterexample of community that maintains a genuine black identity but not at the cost of exclusionary violence like that espoused by Arnetta. For instance, Mrs. Hedy, a mother to one of the troop members, is on the verge of a divorce, and the children are very sympathetic to her. Similarly, Mrs. Margolin is devoutly religious, to the point that the majority of the Brownies' activities are religious in nature. Both of these details and the girls' sympathy toward them show the potentially positive influence of a broader community on these girls. This form of community is analogous to an extended family and is defined by care, not disgust and mockery. For instance, when the thought of her husband makes Mrs. Hedy sad, the entire troop feels the need to sing in order to cheer her up. When the plan to beat the girls of Troop 909 goes awry, it is Mrs. Margolin and Mrs. Hedy who reimpose communal discipline. ("'Oh. They *will* apologize,' Mrs. Margolin said to the 909 troop leader. . . . 'When their parents find out, every one a them will be on punishment'" [Packer 22].) But it takes an affirmation from Laurel and Daphne, Laurel's only seeming kindred spirit within the troop, in the story's final lines to make it clear that Arnetta's perspective is not to be validated by the reader in any way. On the bus ride home, Arnetta and some of the other troop's girls begin "trying to do the most exaggerated imitation of the Troop 909 girls, all without speaking, all without laughing loud enough to catch the women's attention" (25). This shows clearly that the reimposition of discipline alone will not drive home the needed lesson or undo the legacy of distrust and disgust that created the problem with Troop 909 to begin with.

In the final pages of the story, Laurel has an epiphany that serves to complete the satirical deflation of Arnetta's perspective. The process leading to this epiphany begins with Laurel explaining to the reader that upon see-ing a group of Mennonites in the mall one day, her father explained to her that they will do anything that you ask them to because it is part of their religion. He goes on to prove his point by asking them to paint his porch. When the girls in the troop ask Laurel why his father asked them to do that, Laurel responds, "He said . . . it was the only time he'd have a white man on his knees doing something for a black man for free" (Packer 27). As is the case with the girls' symbolic near-lynching of Troop 909, her father's desire to get revenge for the racial oppression that he has felt at the hands of whites eventually inverts the oppressor-oppressed binary, causing him to take advantage of others. Earlier in the story, Laurel expresses her obsession over a line from a friend's award-winning poem: "You are my father, the vet-eran / When you cry in the dark / It rains and rains and rains in my heart" (6). Laurel's infatuation with this verse at the beginning of the story begins to worry her father that something may be wrong with her. However, by the end of the story the lines represent the father and his generation's contempt toward white people and how their anger and vulnerability are magnified in the next generation. Thus, when the girls in Laurel's Troop feel that Troop 909 has invaded their space, they perhaps understandably feel the need to protect their community and their traumatized parents.

The final lines of the story, however, suggest that Packer wants her read-ers to move beyond this response to the pain of the unjust past (and possibly the present). As Arnetta predictably suggests that she would have demanded the Mennonites paint her whole house and not just the porch, Laurel pon-ders the significance of her father's response, saying "I now understood what he meant, and why he did it, though I didn't like it. When you've been made to feel bad for so long, you jump at the chance to do it to others" (Packer 27). This is precisely what Arnetta has been urging the girls of the troop to do throughout the story, so Laurel's rejection of this behavior that she both understands and abhors articulates Packer's moral position clearly. Laurel comes to an important realization: "[I] suddenly knew there was something mean in the world that I could not stop." As if to show that very mean-ness, Arnetta immediately laughs and asks if the Mennonites would "take off their long skirts and bonnets and put on some jeans" if she asked them to, a gesture that would impose Arnetta's noxious notions of "proper" com-munity for no other reason than self-validation. Daphne's answer serves as the last line of the story, but also as Packer's entreaty to the reader who may have had an epiphany similar to Laurel's in the course of the story: "And Daphne's voice, quiet, steady: 'Maybe they would. Just to be nice'" (28).

The role of community ensures that the satire is implemented in a way that promotes inclusivity. To foster this, Packer satirizes ideas instead of people. Packer uses the father's story to emphasize the problem with the girls' actions without ever saying explicitly that the father was wrong. By making the reverberations of racism everyone's responsibility, Packer allows her short story to be a potential learning tool for a much wider audience, basically anyone who hasn't closed their sympathies to the extent that Arnetta has. Laurel's desire to feel like she is a part of the troop is integral for Packer's satirical message. Just as Laurel does not want to distance herself from her community—even as they behave awfully—within the story, Packer does not want to distance herself needlessly from any potential subset of her readers that might benefit from her ethical message. By focusing on the concept of community, Packer finds a way to operate satirically in a way that remains inclusive and fosters visibility for marginalized characters, rather than relying on acts of vengeance and erasure to (re)empower them.

Pilgrims in an Unholy Land: Satire and the Challenge of African American Leadership in *The Boondocks* and *The White Boy Shuffle*

Cameron Leader-Picone

Intraracial satire focusing on major individual figures within black culture has a long history in African American literature. Wallace Thurman's *Infants of the Spring* (1932) includes thinly veiled fictionalizations of his fellow Harlem Renaissance writers as they contemplate the relationship between their race and their art. George Schuyler's *Black No More* (1931) caricatures major black political and cultural figures from W. E. B. Du Bois to Marcus Garvey within its satire of a black community that, if given the chance, would choose to become white. More recently, over the course of the second half of the twentieth century, the works of Ishmael Reed have targeted both individuals and cultural movements, including the Black Arts Movement and Black Aesthetic critics with whom Reed was often associated early in his career. In her article "The New Literary Blackface," Jennifer Jordan contrasts recent black satirists such as Paul Beatty with Reed, whom she calls their "literary forefather," saying that "Reed's apostles tend to be more anarchistic and less political" than him because they are "devoid of ideological loyalties" (28). In particular, Jordan emphasizes that the newest generation of African American satire is often "absent any heroes," as the authors "are quite willing to critique themselves as fiercely as they attack others" (28). Jordan's observations highlight the issue of what responsibility (if any) satirists have to the racial community, particularly with regards to their willingness to attack what Jordan calls the "sacred cows" of African American culture (28). Jordan's charges could similarly apply to Aaron McGruder, creator of *The Boondocks*. McGruder's work has continually and controversially satirized African American public figures across the ideological spectrum. However, while Jordan positions indeterminacy and a lack of heroes as a deficiency in contemporary African American satire, the willingness of African American satirists to target even the most sacrosanct of African American cultural and political figures does not imply an absence of political focus. In this article, I will analyze specific scenes of racial leadership in Beatty's *The White Boy Shuffle* (2001) and McGruder's *The Boondocks*, both of which are marked by the looming presence of Martin Luther King Jr., to argue that it is precisely the affirmation of a lack of "heroes" that defines the political dimension of their satire.

McGruder began writing *The Boondocks* comic strip for a University of Maryland student newspaper in 1996. The comic strip follows the members of the Freeman family—consisting of Robert Freeman and his two grandsons, Riley and Huey—as they move into a wealthy suburb from urban Chicago. Huey, named for Black Panther Huey Newton, is a politically radical black nationalist who serves as the strip's—and subsequent television show's—protagonist. Initially, the strip focused on Huey's and Riley's adjustments to their new neighborhood, but the strip began to face substantial controversy when, following the terrorist attacks of September 11, 2001, McGruder focused greater satirical attention on President Bush and the implications of the global war on terror. McGruder stopped writing the strip in 2006 following the development of the popular television version of *The Boondocks* as part of Cartoon Network's [*adult swim*] late night, adult-oriented cartoon block.[1] Paul Beatty initially gained fame as a slam poet, winning the first ever Grand Poetry Slam competition held by the Nuyorican Poets Café in 1990. He subsequently published two books of poetry prior to the appearance of *The White Boy Shuffle* in 1996. Beatty's novel is a *künstlerroman* representing the childhood and artistic development of Gunnar Kaufman, a poet who becomes a nationally recognized leader in the black community. From the very beginning of their careers, both authors demonstrated a humorous take on contemporary black popular culture in the wake of civil rights–era racial progress, a take focused particularly on the increasingly visible presence of African American political and cultural figures in a broader American context.

In their satirical depiction of black political leadership, Beatty and McGruder engage with many of the central issues within the interdisciplinary scholarship on the subject. As the political scientists Ronald Walters and Robert C. Smith state in their book *African American Leadership* (1999), while "there is a scholarly consensus" that the contemporary moment in African America is a decisive one, "there is no consensus among these scholars about the appropriate direction for the Black community and its leadership in the next century" (80). As Akwasi Assensoh and Yvette Alex-Assensoh argue, "Black political officials continue to define the Black community in ways that limit and mask the heterogeneity and different interests within its ranks" (196). It is this heterogeneity that provides the topography for the satires of Beatty and McGruder. While both authors traffic in bitterly mocking portraits of the racism in American culture more broadly, their main vitriol is reserved for intraracial satire, reflecting what Mark Anthony Neal calls "a rigorous form of self and communal critique" central to post–civil rights African American cultural production (120). The political scientist Robert C. Smith titled his book on African Americans in the post–civil rights era *We Have No Leaders* (1996) to decry the erosion of leadership structures in the black community through mainstream co-optation and marginalization. However, I argue that the satires of Beatty and McGruder suggest a different tone with which to articulate Smith's title. Instead of lamenting the lack of black leadership, as Smith does, their work suggests that perhaps it can serve as a statement of purpose, a new organizing principle through which one might embrace the heterogeneity of black culture.

In addition, an analysis of Beatty and McGruder highlights a central conflict within literary criticism over whether the label of satire is dependent on authors providing a prescriptive corrective in their work. Steven Weisenberger's book, *Fables of Subversion: Satire and the American Novel, 1930–1980* (1995), attempts to redefine the meaning of satire by distinguishing between what he calls "generative satire," detailed by critics such as Northrop Frye and David Worcester, and his own objects of study, which he describes as "degenerative satire[s]" that lack a prescriptive corrective, and whose main purpose is to "delegitimiz[e] . . . hierarchies of value" (3). In his definitive study of African American satire, Darryl Dickson-Carr specifically aligns black satirists with Weisenberger's "degenerative model" (17). While African American satire tends towards the degenerative,[2] the specific satire of black leadership in the works of Beatty and McGruder underscores the issue of whether satire is defined by the ability or desire of the author to offer something generative in the wake of its rhetorical violence. One of the questions prompted by contemporary African American satirists such as Beatty and McGruder is whether the authors are merely interested in tearing down major African American cultural and political figures or if they are obliged to temper their critique with some avenue for progress, such as by providing the "heroes" that Jennifer Jordan argues they lack.

Both *The Boondocks* and *The White Boy Shuffle* interrogate the state of contemporary black political leadership through representations of Martin Luther King Jr. While McGruder does this by directly resurrecting King in the present, Beatty's novel juxtaposes King with his protagonist, Gunnar Kaufman, to illustrate Gunnar's inability to occupy the charismatic leadership position vacated by King. Through their representations of King, Beatty and McGruder question the viability of the leadership model that

King epitomized, thereby suggesting that the dynamic and continually shifting nature of the black community assures that it can never adequately be led, even as societal change with regard to race remains necessarily immediate. Beatty and McGruder use the structures of satire to represent a black community at a crossroads defined by the continued discursive presence of the Civil Rights Movement (typified most directly in the ubiquitous scholarly description of the present era of black politics and culture as "post-civil rights") and the changing realities of a black experience that is worthy of critique. In doing so, I argue that Beatty and McGruder affirm a lack of leaders or heroes as a necessary precondition for embracing a disaggregated black community leadership that is capable of progressing beyond nostalgia for anachronistic models rooted in the civil rights era.

In discussing Beatty's and McGruder's satire of African American leadership, it is useful to focus on what Erica Edwards describes as the "charismatic scenario," which she defines as "a portable sketch, a movable set of prescriptions for body and affect" that "articulate[s] a range of performative and narrative gestures within a single pattern that determines, in broad outlines, both the single event—march, rally, convention speech—and the historical circumstances that necessitate it—scarcity, suffering, lack" (17). Both *The Boondocks* episode "Return of the King" and *The White Boy Shuffle* pivot on such events during which the authors utilize the figure of Martin Luther King Jr. to represent both charismatic black leadership and, synecdochally, the Civil Rights Movement itself. In each work, these moments operate in reverse to repudiate the structures of charisma they superficially represent by building to negation rather than affirmation. "Return of the King" culminates in the provocative image of Martin Luther King Jr. admonishing a crowd gathered to inaugurate a new African American political party while *The White Boy Shuffle* builds towards Gunnar's triumphant ascent during a speech in which he enters into a public suicide pact with the rest of the black community.

After "Return of the King" aired on King's birthday—January 15, 2006—McGruder was accused of disrespecting the legacy of King. The Reverend Al Sharpton called for an apology by McGruder and the Cartoon Network, while ABC's *Nightline* ran an interview with McGruder addressing the controversy, with most of the focus related to the King's climactic N-word laden speech.[3] The episode proposes that King was not assassinated by James Earl Ray but instead lapsed into a coma, waking up early in the twenty-first century. Following a public disgrace related to his opposition to post–9/11 Islamophobia and the steady march to war, King finds himself embroiled in the world of McGruder's fictional suburb of Woodcrest, living with the Freeman family. Flipping through channels showing a parade of racial stereotypes in black popular culture, King asks, "What happened, Huey? What happened to our people?" to which Huey responds, "I think . . . everyone was waiting for Martin Luther King to come back" ("Return of the King").[4] Juxtaposing the parade of negative images constructed by and about African Americans with Huey's statement, McGruder implies that the African American community has become paralyzed by the faith that another figure such as Martin Luther King Jr. will arise and save black America. By creating a story line in which King never died, McGruder literalizes this abstract faith. While some were offended by his representation of King, ultimately McGruder's true subversion of King's legacy is not putting the N-word in his mouth but in suggesting the damaging effects of American society's idolization of King.

King's controversial speech is the culmination of the episode's representation of the tension between civil rights–era leadership represented by King and the contemporary state of black America. The speech occurs during a social gathering intended to launch a new African American political party, which devolves into a grotesque spectacle featuring: a bouncer; a rapper arguing that it's important to honor all the kings, not just Martin Luther King Jr.; a black female host, who thanks "White Jesus for making all this positive black shit possible"; a "hustler preacher"; "the rapper truce"; and "the inevitable fight." With Huey's sardonic comment that the party was "everything you expected it would be," McGruder suggests not only that the presence of such hollow archetypes exists throughout black culture, but also that their ubiquitous normative presence illustrates the broader apathy of the black community. King's tirade responds directly to the complacency and lack of responsibility that McGruder depicts at the event, which feels more like a night at the club than a political rally: "King looked out on his people and saw they were in great need. So he did what all great leaders do, he told them the truth: 'Will you ignorant niggas please shut the hell up. Is this it? This is what I got all those ass whuppings for. I had a dream once, it was a dream that little black boys and little black girls would drink from the river of prosperity, freed from the thirst of oppression. But lo and behold, three decades later, what have I found but a bunch of trifling, shiftless, good for nothing niggas. I know some of you don't want me to say that word. It's the ugliest word in the English language. But that's what I see now: niggas'" ("Return of the King"). McGruder frames King's exhortation as confronting an element of unwillingness on the part of individual African Americans to take responsibility for creating positive change within the black community.

Avi Santo's study of the black political responses to the episode analyzes how message board posts about the show illustrate the political ideologies of viewers. Santo finds that the show's viewers took King's speech as a courageous attempt to spark outrage within the black community and to differentiate those African Americans who are carrying on the civil rights legacy from those members of the community, particularly young men, who the viewers in Santo's study suggest King accurately labels as "niggas" (259–261). As Santo's analysis suggests, such responses argue that the willingness to address uncomfortable truths about black culture is a prerequisite for contemporary black leadership. However, the message board posts that he cites tend to show an audience that, like many critics, takes the critiques voiced by King and Huey as unmediated political statements exempt from McGruder's satire. Such viewers place themselves in the privileged role of insight, assuming their alignment with the satirist in targeting social degeneration. To these viewers, the version of King represented by McGruder instantiates the idea that the failure of current black leadership rests in the inability of the black community to either capitalize on or extend civil rights–era gains. The actions associated with "niggas" in King's speech thus become representative of a community the viewers believe has drifted away from previously effective forms of black leadership, epitomized by King himself. However, this response is premised on the charismatic ideal that if those in the audience, both within the fictional setting of the party as well as of the show itself, merely listened to, and followed, insightful figures like King, there would be immediate transformative change in society.

Although McGruder targets the complacent nostalgia of the black community in this scene, he doesn't just critique its unwillingness or inability to hear or respond to charismatic leadership; he also suggests that such a leadership model is incapable of addressing the differentiated nature of the contemporary black experience. As much as McGruder may use King to voice what he sees as legitimate critiques, the structure of the speech satirizes the viewer who would re-elevate a resurrected King as a black leader as much as it does the complacency of black culture. King ends the speech by stating, "I've seen what's around the corner, I've seen what's over the horizon, and I promise you, you niggas have nothing to celebrate. And no, I won't get there with you, I'm going to Canada." With these words, McGruder starkly emphasizes the irony of the image of King as a potentially redemptive twenty-first-century leader directing his vitriol at the very community the episode implicitly revives him to lead. Instead of building to an affirmation of the potential for change and progress within the community itself and America as a whole, King's speech culminates in a negation and the rejection of his individual responsibility for the black community.

The episode's optimistic ending reinforces that while McGruder does see African Americans as somewhat complicit in their own oppression, the absenting of civil rights–era leadership models represented in the ending of King's speech is a necessary precondition for mobilizing the agency of the black community to confront and change such conditions. The episode concludes with images of African Americans storming the gates of the White House, a newspaper headline referring to Oprah Winfrey's election as president, and an obituary for King's death in Canada. Huey ends the episode with the voiceover statement, "It's fun to dream," explicitly alluding to King's "I Have a Dream" speech. Huey's ironic reference to King aligns the episode with the desire for change embodied in King's original speech while implying that it is precisely the absence of a figure like King at the end of the episode that makes such change possible. McGruder positions the episode as a type of idealistic fantasy in which black America is able to move away from its internal divisions, cease waiting for an individual black leader willing to martyr himself/herself for the entire community, and generate the revolution of which they are capable. While McGruder consistently satirizes the form of Huey's black nationalism for its anachronism, "Return of the King" argues for its own nationalism that recognizes that the reliance on civil rights–era charismatic leadership reflects the complacency of a community unable or unwilling to adjust to a changed reality in which African Americans are able to wield new forms of power in American society.

Although *The White Boy Shuffle* does not insert King as a direct character in the way that "Return of the King" does, his legacy as a political leader nevertheless hovers over the text of Beatty's novel. The novel's mostly implicit allusions to King culminate in a momentous speech by Beatty's poet-protagonist Gunnar Kaufman, a scene that strongly parallels McGruder's satire of black political leadership. Much like the speech King makes in "Return of the King," Kaufman's oration builds to negation rather than affirmation, constructing a collective suicide pact between Beatty's protagonist and the rest of the black community. Erica Edwards cites this scene as an example of "reductio ad absurdum" that "stages a protest against the civil rights model of protest, and the antileader imagines the mass suicide as an end to civil rights politics" (158, 161). McGruder and Beatty each struggle with the tension between an apathy-inducing nostalgia for a romanticized civil rights–era unity and the shifting experiences of blackness in contemporary America. In particular, both authors illustrate how the desire to merely substitute any new leader for those of the previous era mirrors the impulse to proscribe a corrective to the satirical representation of the present state of black leadership. Ultimately, both *The Boondocks* and *The White Boy Shuffle* make it clear that it is only by continually invalidating the desire for a unity premised on charismatic leadership that the black community can embrace its manifest heterogeneity.

Just as McGruder premises "Return of the King" on the presumption that there is a glaring need for charismatic leadership in the black community,

Beatty opens his novel with Gunnar's sarcastic consideration of "the perennial void in African-American leadership" he will come to fill, even though he acknowledges ruefully that "this messiah gig is a bitch." Kaufman frames the role of a black leader as a job for which "fed-up second-class citizens . . . [placed] a want ad in the Sunday classifieds" and defines it in ways that both strongly allude to and subtly undermine King's civil rights–era rhetoric: "*Negro Demagogue.* . . . Must have ability to lead a divided, downtrodden, and alienated people to the Promised Land. Good communication skills required. Pay commensurate with ability. No experience necessary" (*White Boy Shuffle* 1). When describing the process by which he came to fill this role, Kaufman avers, "I didn't interview for the job. I was drafted by 22 million hitherto unaffiliated souls into serving as full-time Svengali and foster parent to an abandoned people. I spoon-feed them grueled futility, unveil the oblivion that is black America's existence and the hopelessness of the struggle. In return I receive fanatical avian obedience" (1). Gunnar's brief description reflects the fear of a growing black nihilism described in Cornel West's bestselling book *Race Matters* (1993).[5] This sense is augmented further by Kaufman's revelation that what he has offered African Americans in exchange for this obedience is what he sarcastically calls "the Emancipation Disintegration": "In the quest for equality, black folks have tried everything. We've begged, revolted, entertained, intermarried, and are still treated like shit. Nothing works, so why suffer the slow deaths of toxic addiction and the American work ethic when the immediate gratification of suicide awaits?" (2). Finally, Beatty's opening chapter reveals that Gunnar's heritage makes him an atrocious choice, perhaps the worst one possible, as a leader for the black community: "Preordained by a set of weak-kneed DNA to shuffle in the footsteps of a long cowardly queue of coons, Uncle Toms, and faithful boogedy-boogedy retainers, I am the number-one son of a spineless color-struck son of a bitch who was the third son of an ass-kissing sell-out house Negro who was indeed a seventh son but only by default. . . . From birth my parents indoctrinated me with the idea that the surreal escapades and 'I's a-comin'' watermelon chicanery of my forefathers was the stuff of hero worship" (5). Beatty's opening thus removes any illusions the reader might harbor that the novel will represent the unity achieved by filling the gap in African American leadership as a boon for the community.

Consequently, the reader approaches Gunnar's climactic speech with ample trepidation. Beatty sets the speech at Boston University, Martin Luther King Jr.'s graduate alma mater, and Gunnar's speech assails the apathy of the black community by riffing on the inscription on a campus sculpture dedicated to King: "If a man hasn't discovered something he will die for, he isn't fit to live" (*White Boy Shuffle* 200). Stating that "I want them niggers to get theirs, but I am not willing to die for South Africa" (200), Gunnar implicates himself in the complacency he decries in the audience. What distinguishes Gunnar from the audience, and prompts his coronation as "king of the blacks" (200), is certainly not his willingness to fight or die for any cause, but rather his "candor" (199): "So I asked myself, what am I willing to die for? The day when white people treat me with respect and see my life as equally valuable to theirs? No, I ain't willing to die for that, because if they don't know that by know, then they ain't never going to know it. Matter of fact, I ain't ready to die for anything, so I guess I'm just not fit to live. In other words, I'm just ready to die" (199). The masterful twist of logic that turns an unwillingness to die meaningfully into a readiness to die meaninglessly subverts the idealistic imperative spoken by King and inscribed on the sculpture. Both Beatty and McGruder capitalize on the popular perception of King's saintliness as the basis for their satire. In each case, the seemingly endless capacity of the historical King to struggle against the oppressive forces of white racism, poverty, and state-sanctioned violence is directly contrasted against the hypocrisy of a contemporary black community that has reaped the benefits of King's actions without demonstrating a willingness to continue his struggle for social justice. By having the fictional King voice his own incapacity to endure the contemporary state of black culture, McGruder forecloses any potential continuation of civil rights–era leadership. Beatty, on the other hand, constructs a nihilistic inversion of the organic ideal of grassroots activism by constructing a collectivity around an affirmation of self-annihilating complacency. Consequently, while Gunnar derides the current state of African American leadership, saying "what we need is some new leaders. Leaders who won't apostatize like cowards. Some niggers who are ready to die" (200), Beatty makes it clear that Gunnar is no leader himself, and that he merely provides an external validation for the unwillingness to find something worth dying for.

Gunnar's position in this moment has prompted diverse interpretations of the meaning of Beatty's satire. As noted above, Edwards argues that Beatty has created a postmodern protest against both the collective memory of the civil rights era and charismatic leadership models. In her analysis of the novel, L. H. Stallings draws upon Houston Baker's concept of "critical memory" to argue that Gunnar actually does represent a new type of leader in the black community, albeit one that subverts the messianic assumptions associated with such a figure. Stallings argues that Gunnar functions as the "anti-race man . . . a revision of the race man that bridges the spiritual, intellectual, bodily and material ethos of the past" (103). Similarly, Mark Anthony Neal argues that the novel "represent[s] Beatty's effort to get at the construction and understanding of legitimate and 'authentic' leadership within black urban enclaves" (150). However, each of these analyses remains ambivalent about whether Gunnar instantiates the leadership figure they describe. Gunnar superficially fits the bill as a member of a post–civil rights version of W. E. B. Du Bois's Talented Tenth.[6] However, Gunnar's actions following the speech, instead of rejuvenating charismatic leadership in the present, serve to embrace nihilism, taunting an atomic bomb-wielding U.S. government with artistic festivals that superficially mirror the happenings and be-ins of the 1960s (and echoing his promise from the prologue that "our mass suicide will be the ultimate sit-in" [*White Boy Shuffle* 2]). The novel ends with Gunnar's father, who has served as a stereotypical Uncle Tom figure throughout the book (most specifically, by serving as a policeman in Daryl Gates's LAPD), joining many African Americans in heeding Gunnar's speech by committing suicide via his own service revolver. Gunnar's father also fulfills Gunnar's call to compose a death poem as part of one's suicide. His poem further alludes to King to illuminate the gap between the idealism of racial leadership and the lived experience of African Americans: "Like the good Reverend King / I too 'have a dream,' / but when I wake up / I forget it and / remember I'm running late for work" (226). Gunnar's father's poem serves as a bitter riposte to blind optimism, substituting the weary tone of labor in the place of political idealism. Beatty does not use his ending to redeem Gunnar's father; instead, he ironizes King's famous statement to suggest that the distance between the March on Washington and the days, and even decades, that followed do not trace an inexorable line to King's mountaintop, but are instead marked by mundane oppressiveness. Rodney King has become more salient than Martin Luther King. Beatty utilizes the gap between the idealism of activism and the reality of the more ambivalent and qualified outcomes of civil rights–era leadership to satirize the very potential the reader (and, by extension, the African American community) might see in Gunnar.

The reception of McGruder's and Beatty's work has served to elide the distinction between their fiction and their ideologies, evoking Steven Weisenberger's argument that critics of satire attempt to "ameliorate the aggressiveness" (19) of the form by seeking within it the corrective to its real-world attack. It is certainly tempting to read the critiques leveled by McGruder and Beatty against African American leaders in precisely the same terms that prompt their humor, elevating a figure like Huey or Gunnar, or McGruder and Beatty themselves, in place of a figure like King. McGruder has been consistently questioned as to the relationship between his art and his political beliefs. In a 2001 interview McGruder was asked, "How closely do Huey's opinions come to your own?," to which he responded, "It would be inaccurate to say that Huey's opinions are my own. I think there's a broad opinion being put out through the strip with a combination of all the characters' voices, and it's really up to the reader to figure out what that is" (McGruder, *All the Rage* 143). Indeed, a 2004 *New Yorker* article details how McGruder himself has gained a reputation for giving speeches that eerily mirror Gunnar Kaufman's in *The White Boy Shuffle*, reflecting his own ambivalence as to whether and how he can fulfill the expectations that various constituencies have set for him (McGrath).

Part of the elision between author and character is the product of deliberate choices on the part of the authors. Just as Beatty explicitly frames Gunnar's climactic speech through contextual evocations of Martin Luther King Jr., Howard Rambsy suggests that McGruder characterizes Huey as a "black hero" (143) by associating him with iconic images of black political struggle. Based on such a characterization, a viewer might expect an episode such as "Return of the King" to represent a metaphorical passing of the torch from a resurrected King to Huey as the repository of the tradition of African American leadership. Indeed, in the episode, it is Huey who proposes the idea of founding a new African American political party to allow King to carry on the legacy of his previous activism. However, as McGruder makes clear through his satirical representation of King, the tradition with which McGruder associates Huey is anachronistic in the present. As the founding event of this new political party culminates in King's controversial speech, McGruder exposes the distance between the idealism of Huey and King and the inadequacy of their methods.

Ultimately, McGruder is not attempting to provide any single name, especially not his own or that of his protagonist, to replace current African American leaders. Instead, it is the conglomeration of the various perspectives embodied by his characters, and the heterogeneity within African American culture that they represent, which generates the potential for progressive change. Glenda Carpio has argued that humor in African American culture is not "a moralizing discourse" (7) and that it has often functioned "as a way of affirming [African Americans'] humanity in the face of its violent denial" (5). For Beatty and McGruder, that denial has engendered a complacency that must be countered by a reaffirmation of the vital heterogeneity already present in the black community. Avi Santo's "Of Niggas and Citizens" describes how some viewers of *The Boondocks* have pointed out that the flawed "subgroups" within the black community to which each of the characters of the show belong "are represented as kin," suggesting the possibility of "family becom[ing] the space for exploring potential solidarity across classed and generational lines" (269). While Santo refers to the viewers among his sample who articulate this position as exceptions, their comments suggest a form of racial leadership that I would argue most closely aligns with the portraits of the black community contained in the works of Beatty and McGruder. Both authors stress that the disaggregation of black leadership liberates African Americans, allowing them to embrace a multivariate politics freed from the burden of nostalgia. However, it is worth noting that the works of Beatty and McGruder focus specifically on masculine leadership models, implying that their own works fail to engage with the heterogeneity in the black community they gesture toward. Jennifer Jordan specifically critiques McGruder for this lack ("Huey and Riley"), and Stallings argues that Gunnar's repudiation of a racial identity formation rooted in his father in favor of one instantiated in his mother is central to Beatty's queering of black masculinity; nevertheless, the performance of leadership in the novel is largely confined to the male Gunnar. As Erica Edwards points out, "monographs on black leadership often betray the subfield's mournful nostalgia for a kind of leadership that is always imagined as singular and male" (25). While Edwards is speaking of political science texts, *The Boondocks* and *White Boy Shuffle* illustrate that even critiques of such nostalgia may perpetuate its exclusionary masculinist tendencies.[7]

As "degenerative" satirists, both authors ultimately maintain a constant distrust of their own capability of envisioning a politically engaged, heterogeneous black community. The ambivalent endings of both "Return of the King" and *The White Boy Shuffle* manifest this distrust in order to suggest the necessity of maintaining the self-critical lens typified by satire. It is tempting to speculate that the ending of an episode such as "Return of the King" represents McGruder's prescription for change, much like the reader might perversely desire that Gunnar become a true leader for the black community. Huey's statement at the end of "Return of the King" that "it's fun to dream" mirrors Beatty's ironic signification on Martin Luther King Jr.'s "I Have a Dream" speech at the end of *The White Boy Shuffle*. The fact that both McGruder and Beatty close with explicit references to King's iconic speech emphasizes the ambivalence of their representations. The words of King's speech echo through their texts as a reminder of the incompleteness of civil rights–era progress but illustrate that no matter how great a desire there might be for the return of an individual leader like King, that very desire constructs barriers to further change.

Barack Obama is another figure who has been widely anointed as a potential heir to the legacy of civil rights–era black leadership, and in the first episode of *The Boondocks* to air after Obama's 2008 election ("It's a Black President, Huey Freeman"), Huey's affectlessness contrasts sharply with the valedictory emotions of nearly every other character. In the case of both "Return of the King" and "It's a Black President, Huey Freeman," McGruder preemptively responds to viewer expectations that a show such as *The Boondocks* would uncritically celebrate the return of Martin Luther King Jr. or the election of Barack Obama. By countering the presumption of excitement with ambivalence, McGruder emphasizes the radicalism of refusal, reaffirming his iconoclasm through the negation of unquestioning support. Similarly, the ambiguity with which Beatty ends *The White Boy Shuffle* denies the reader a prescriptive fiction, suggesting that the product of any advocacy or leadership is only a precarious instability for African Americans. By highlighting the gap between the idealistic desire for racial unity and the complexity of the contemporary African American experience, the satires of Beatty and McGruder suggest that the fantasy of a return to civil rights–era leadership unduly limits African Americans and has resulted in a cultural stagnation that verges on self-destruction.

Notes

1. See also Terrence T. Tucker's article in this collection, pp. 22–37.

2. See also Christian Schmidt's article in this collection, pp. 150–61.

3. While Sharpton was outraged at the episode, it won a Peabody Award from the University of Georgia for being "an especially daring episode" (Ball; F. Lee).

4. All dialogue from "Return of the King" is based on my own transcriptions from the DVD for *The Boondocks: Season 1*. In my transcription, I use "nigga" instead of "nigger" in keeping with McGruder's comments during a *Nightline* interview from January 2006 regarding "Return of the King."

5. West defines the "nihilistic threat" to African Americans as an absence of hope: "The self-fulfilling prophecy of the nihilistic threat is that without hope there can be no future, that without meaning there can be no struggle" (23).

6. Du Bois's concept of "the Talented Tenth" emphasizes the obligation of educated and successful African Americans to help the black community as a whole as well as the need to train such leaders at historically black colleges and universities. Beatty's novel explicitly satirizes Du Bois's essay by transforming his thesis into the basis for a reality television show called "The Talented Tenth," which he describes as "the show where a bunch of seddity motherfuckers be saving the community by rewarding exemplary African-American citizenship with a piece of fried chicken. 'By deciding to wait until marriage to have sex, Leroy and Martha are celebrating traditional African values. Here go a thigh, a wing, and a biscuit'" (*White Boy Shuffle* 145). Through his satire, Beatty implies that the "Talented Tenth" concept has been transformed into a conservative statement of individual responsibility praising those who conform to normative American values while demonizing those who do not as pathological. Beatty's representation mirrors McGruder's use of the term "niggas" in King's speech to satirize the idea that the black community merely needs to be lectured on personal responsibility to enable structural change.

7. See also Brandon Manning's article in this collection, pp. 125–36 .

Dissimulating Blackness: The Degenerative Satires of Paul Beatty and Percival Everett

Christian Schmidt

One of the distinctive criteria for defining satire and differentiating it from such related modes as parody is that satire needs to have an extra-textual or extramural target—a satiric "target that is *independent of the text itself*" (Knight 45; emphasis added). As Charles Knight acknowledges, however, the way in which satire textualizes this extra-textual target is a vexed issue. In other words, the seemingly straightforward relationship between textual representation and represented world is much more complicated than some strands of satire criticism have been willing to concede. In fact, there has been an ongoing critical discussion about whether satire is or is not a mimetic art form, that is, whether or not satires directly refer to an external reality outside the text. Dustin Griffin finds a conciliatory middle path between the two extreme positions by acknowledging that "historical particulars in satire always have a curious in-between status, neither wholly fact nor wholly fiction" (123). Along similar lines, Steven Weisenburger has convincingly singled out what he calls the "degenerative mode" of satire, a mode that complicates the notion of mimetic referentiality of satiric literary texts. Degenerative satire is aware of the inherent limitations of diegetic representation of an external world and therefore, he says, turns inward to "reflect suspiciously on all ways of making meaning, *including its own*" (3; emphasis added). Like parody, degenerative satire has as its target "another form of coded discourse," and *as* satire, it targets the extra-textual and is "social in its focus" (Hutcheon 16).

It is here that degenerative satire encounters a paradox: it acknowledges self-consciously that it cannot and will not represent anything directly, yet at the same time it is dependent on such textual representations to transmit its moral and/or ethical position on matters social and extra-textual. According to Weisenburger, this leads the degenerative satirist to "[turn] metafictionist and parodist, seeking out 'intramural' and self-referring ways of striking at the aesthetic rules hemming us in" (5). As I will show in my reading of three exemplary novels—*Erasure* (2001) and *A History of the African-American People [Proposed] by Strom Thurmond. As Told to Percival Everett and James Kincaid* (2004), by Percival Everett,[1] and *Slumberland* (2008), by Paul Beatty—the central feature of degenerative satire thus becomes the constant interplay between the spheres of the intra- and the extramural, both in terms of narrated content (such as tropes of mirrors, walls, authorial personae) and in terms of narrative presentation (for example, multilayered levels of narration, textual devices of mirroring, and a generally self-conscious and self-reflexive form of narration). Dissimulating (namely, concealing, in part or in full) blackness behind a wide array of visible and invisible walls, these three novels both parody and satirize conventional images of blackness in the African American canon.

It is only logical that degenerative satire relies heavily on parody. If we define parody as any "cultural practice which provides a relatively polemical allusive imitation of another cultural production or practice" (Dentith 9) or as an erasure of "constructions of textual authority" (Phiddian 4), we again come very close to Weisenburger's definition of degenerative satire. However, although both point to their own textuality by using, copying, and imitating other texts, degenerative satire goes beyond parody in that it points to the world "hiding" behind and within these texts. What is being dissimulated in these satires is, after all, blackness "as we know it." Yet this blackness is available only in what Weisenburger calls "the satiric diegesis" (18). That is to say, the diegeses of these satires may describe worlds, people, or actions that are very similar to our contemporary world. As fictions, however, they are not mimetic mirrors of it. Therefore, the targets of these degenerative satires, by necessity, are creations of and within the text, even if they have the same names, for example, as "real" human beings such as Percival Everett or Strom Thurmond.[2]

Since "degenerative satire [is] a form for interrogating and subverting codified knowledge and revealing it as a dissimulation of violence" (Weisenburger 11–12), these novels have chosen an apt target in blackness for their satirical arrows. By satirizing a highly complex, inherently problematic, and historically violent discourse such as blackness, these texts show the ways in which formulaic ascriptions of blackness to both texts and authors have violently curtailed the former's potential meanings and limited the latter's artistic freedoms. Rather than turning outward to a straightforward satire of the social world of blackness, however, degenerative satire turns inward in order to shed light on the machinery of fiction and the textual workings of blackness. As Weisenburger asserts, "If these fables of subversion can be said to target anything, it is fiction making, the very strategies of dissimulation by which the nuclear age seeks to mask its violent being" (19). And while I fully agree with Darryl Dickson-Carr's claim that "African American satire tends to follow [this] degenerative model in its iconoclasm" (17), I also think that one important element of Weisenburger's argument is still missing here. That is to say, what degenerative satire subverts is not so much social structures like racism, but rather the language and mindset of texts that help mediate and proliferate such violent structures. Degenerative satires, thus, do (at least) two things: first, they subvert degenerated social structures through ridicule; second, and for my argument more importantly, degenerative satires also "reflect suspiciously" (Weisenburger 3) on their own textual nature. Refusing to believe in a mimetic nature of textual representation, degenerative satire complicates the ways in which texts can be said to mirror extra-textual reality at all. Of course, this also affects the potential for social criticism and moral rebuke to be found within these texts, as their satire of social ills always has to take a detour through (other) text(s).

Weisenburger claims that degenerative satire "lacks a steady narrative voice, specific 'targets,' and fixed norms or corrective goals" (14), and even the most cursory reading of the three novels shows that they share these characteristics. All three are first-person narratives, albeit with twists that undermine those narrative voices: *Erasure* consists of Monk Ellison's first-person "journal, . . . a private affair" and a hypodiegetic novel-within-the-novel in the form of a fictional memoir by one Van Go Jenkins. *A History* consists of reams of first-person tales in the form of various letters and the character Percival Everett's first-person accounts of several interactions with Senator Strom Thurmond.[3] *Slumberland* is the most straightforward first-person narrative of the three, yet it is the tale of a collaborative effort to create the "perfect beat" as a collage or sampling of other people's sounds, and it thereby becomes more than just one narrator's individual tale. More generally speaking, these texts embed their voices into the wider cultural text of blackness, satirizing it in the process. In order to do this, they dissimulate blackness and satirically play with the visible/invisible nature of it. Yet by dissimulating blackness, they also reiterate the discourse of blackness. For Weisenburger, this is the "key paradox: by moving onto degenerate ground, the satirist reveals language as a great cover-up, but it is only with language that one keeps moving at all" (26). The degenerative satirist always is acutely aware of this paradox and his or her texts openly play with this final irony: presumably unwilling to participate in the existing discourse of blackness, they still reinscribe themselves within this very discourse. Put differently, by writing books about the end of blackness, or about the refusal to be classified as a black author, or yet again writing a history of the African American people, these novels make an ambivalent gesture: they ridicule and criticize reigning discourses of blackness and refuse to play along with them. Yet at the same time, they cannot but participate within these very discussions, albeit obliquely. In this sense, degenerative satires dissimulate their blackness by referring to it ad nauseam, by quoting the grand narratives of blackness (Ellison, Wright, and so on), and by playfully using master tropes of the text of blackness, such as the mirror scene or the trope of invisibility.[4]

Percival Everett's *Erasure* is a first-person account of the life and work of Thelonious "Monk" Ellison, a writer of experimental fiction, who happens to be black but "[doesn't] believe in race" (2). On many levels, this novel deals with the relationships between text and world and undermines the boundaries between the intra- and the extramural. *Erasure* focuses the reader's attention on the very act of artistic creation and on the tricky nature of literary representation by doubling and mirroring authors, narrations, and fictions within the text. It thus highlights the very fact of narration and explicitly thematizes authorship. The key device[5] the text employs to this effect is that of the *mise en abyme*, of putting (representation) at the abyss. The idea behind the mise en abyme is that it muddies the distinction between the subject and the object of representation; that it continuously questions the relation between artifice and reality; and most importantly, that it meta-narratively directs attention to the very process of representation by pointing out its boundaries. Mieke Bal has suggested the useful term "mirror-text" (58; compare to Dällenbach *passim*) for this device, as it indeed is a mirror-text and a mirror *in* the text. Monk's novel-within-the-novel, *Fuck*, written under the pseudonym Stagg R. Leigh,[6] is such a representation inasmuch as it mirrors several key plot elements of Monk's frame narrative in its embedded diegesis. Furthermore, *Erasure* adds mirror image upon mirror image and even includes an extended self-referential meta-comment on how to read texts in general (and therefore this text in particular), effectively dissimulating blackness within this textual hall of mirrors. Degeneratively satirizing the notion of a black text, the novel targets the ways in which a text's meaning comes to be (mis)aligned with the black face of its author. Yet by displacing the vexed issue of mirrored representation to a more abstract and metaphorical level, the text's very structure already hints at the self-referential nature of its dissimulations.

On one level, *Erasure* transposes these issues of (black) writing and the role of literary authorship to such an abstract plane of argumentation by having Monk deliver an academic paper about the boundaries of the experimental novel. The novel thus not only provides an example of a mirror-text within its own pages but also prefaces its novel-within-a-novel with its own critical apparatus, so to speak. Monk's story gets on its way when he presents his paper, titled "F/V: Placing the Experimental Novel," at the *Nouveau Roman* Society meeting (Everett, *Erasure* 14–17). With its pairing of the voiceless and the voiced fricative, it parodies Roland Barthes's essay *S/Z*. Basically, the paper does with/to Barthes's *S/Z* what Barthes's text does with/to Balzac's *Sarrasine*. Thus, Monk's paper adds another layer of mise en abyme to the analysis and takes it to a yet higher level of abstraction. More important than the details of this presentation, however, are the explicitly stated reasons for choosing this very topic. Argues Monk, "*In establishing its own subject, ostensibly Balzac's* Sarrasine, *it raises the question of whether that text is indeed its subject. And of course it is not, as S/Z tells us, its subject is the elusive model of that thing which* Sarrasine *might be argued to be a representation*" (14; emphases in original). In other words, it is a text about texts, a text about how to read other texts and how to read its own text. Through internal mirroring, Everett's novel thus reflexively presents a model for reading it, and by turning inward to the intramural, it performs the degeneration of its own textual nature that is so crucial for the degenerative mode.[7]

Throughout *Erasure*, the making visible of the invisible takes center stage, as can already be gleaned from its narrator's last name. As a novelist, "Monk" Ellison has always been too visible, or perhaps visible for all the wrong reasons. In the words of a reviewer of one of his experimental novels: "*The novel is finely crafted . . . but one is lost to understand what this reworking of Aeschylus'* The Persians *has to do with the African American experience*" (Everett, *Erasure* 2; emphases in original). As a writer, he is automatically being read as a *black* writer, irrespective of the content of his novels. In an early mirror scene, Monk is literally faced with this reductive reasoning that inextricably links the author's black face to his text. While waiting for his sister in a large chain bookstore, he decides to look for his own novels: "I went to Literature and did not see me. I went to Contemporary Fiction and did not find me, but when I fell back a couple of steps I found a section called African American Studies and there, arranged alphabetically and neatly, read *undisturbed*, were four of my books including my *Persians* of which the only thing ostensibly African American was my jacket photograph" (35; emphasis in original). Literally and literarily, his texts are being read as mirror images of his black face, a confusion of the intra- and the extramural that *Erasure* satirizes. Monk self-consciously ups the ante and writes his novel—originally entitled *My Pafology*, but later simply named *Fuck*—a parody of Richard Wright's *Native Son* (1940), the novel about a black man who is arguably all too visible as a black man in a white world. In this embedded parody, Van Go Jenkins rapes and kills Penelope Dalton, a black version of *Native Son's* white Mary Dalton, and is eventually arrested for this crime. As his apprehension by the police is being broadcast live, the novel-within-the-novel ends with Van Go staring directly into the camera eye of the nation: "I looks up and see the cameras. I get kicked again while I'm bein pulled to my feet. But I dont care. The cameras is pointin at me. I be on the TV . . . I on TV" (131). Thus, the final image of the hypodiegetic narration is a stereotypically black face, one that is guilty of murder and faulty grammar, being brought to justice in a manner reminiscent of the television show *COPS*.

Ironically, Monk Ellison continues to be invisible behind the hypervisible image of his alter ego, Stagg Leigh, which the text underlines by including repeated echoes of *Invisible Man* in its final pages. Despite Ellison's attempts to sabotage himself as a member of the jury of the "National Book Association, the NBA,"[8] *Fuck* wins "*The Book Award*," as it is "simply and pretentiously" called (Everett, *Erasure* 223; emphasis in original). The live-telecast award ceremony necessitates the simultaneous presence of both Monk *and* Stagg, which leads to the novel's climactic mirror scene. As Monk makes his way to the stage, faces of his past life flash before his inner eye, and "then there was a small boy, perhaps me as a boy, [holding] up a mirror so that I could see my face and it was the face of Stagg R. Leigh. 'Now you're free of your illusion,' Stagg said. 'How does it feel to be free of one's illusions?'" (265). These lines are, of course, from the final dream of Ellison's *Invisible Man*, a dream in which he is confronted by his enemies. Monk and the Invisible Man respond to the question using the same three words: "Painful and empty" (265; Ellison, *Invisible Man* 430). Blinded by the camera lights, Monk peers directly into one of the TV cameras and utters the novel's penultimate line: "'Egads, I'm on television'" (Everett, *Erasure* 265), thus echoing Van Go's final words almost verbatim. He is mirroring Van Go, yet with a signal difference: Monk's is a grammatically correct sentence, and he adds the interjection "egads," the use of which had marked him earlier in the text as not black enough while playing basketball as a child (2).[9] This final statement cleverly rolls into one sentence the novel's degenerative satire of blackness: it is an echo of Van Go's intradiegetic final sentence, both syntactically and in terms of content. It mirrors Van Go with a spin, namely by adding the decidedly uncool and outdated expression "egads"; moreover, it ends the novel with the reader staring at the face of Monk / Stagg, who in turn is staring into a camera that refuses to see him how he wants to be seen. It is a very subtle double play on the issues of visibility, invisibility, and hypervisibility, as it is not clear just who we see staring back at us from the TV screen. Is it the author of experimental fiction "Monk" Ellison or "black" author Stagg R. Leigh? Dissimulating blackness in this complex mirror play of faces, *Erasure* effectively satirizes the overly reductive association of text with the black face of its creator and leaves the reader stranded in an endless hall of mirrors. In the end, it is not clear whose (black?) face is looking into the camera.

The narration in Paul Beatty's novel *Slumberland* (2008) begins where *Erasure* leaves off. After having erased blackness through a musical performance, the novel's protagonist-narrator Ferguson W. Sowell, a.k.a. DJ Darky, retrospectively declares that "Blackness is passé and I for one couldn't be happier, because now I'm free to go to the tanning salon if I want to, and I want to" (*Slumberland* 4). He sojourns in (West) Berlin in 1989 and is on a journey to locate a legendary, albeit obscure black jazz musician known as "The Schwa," whom he needs to authenticate his "perfect" beat. This very condensed plot summary already underlines the degeneratively ambivalent approach to blackness the text performs: on the one hand, it satirizes racial identities, as Ferguson proudly adopts the provocatively suggestive moniker "Darky." Yet on the other hand, it also invokes "authentic" black cultural productions such as jazz and hip-hop. Instead of becoming a true racial artist, however, DJ Darky uses music to eradicate blackness as a label for art and, thereby, to dissimulate what he calls a fourteen-hundred-year "charade of blackness" (3) on the novel's opening page.

To show that received notions of blackness are, indeed, passé, *Slumberland* continually conjures images of separation, walls, and boundaries, yet always satirically undermines these very dividing lines, be they between black and white, or between the visible and the invisible. As DJ Darky, the first-person narrator of the novel, retrospectively says about his final performance with The Schwa, "Me and the greatest musician you've never heard of played two minutes and forty-seven seconds of musical perfection. . . . A beat so perfect as to render musical labels null and void. A melody so transcendental that blackness has officially been declared passé. . . . It just happened to be of indeterminate blackness and funkier than a motherfucker" (Beatty, *Slumberland* 16). The novel culminates with the construction of a new Berlin Wall made of sound, a dividing line that separates but at the same time is also permeable and invisible. Figuratively, the invisible wall also points to the more general question of the distinction between intra- and extramural realms, and by making the wall a permeable one, the distinction between inside and outside, text and world is put under erasure that is similar in many ways to the erasure of blackness in Everett's novel.

In *Slumberland*, the infamous wall that used to be set in stone and concrete is reconstructed out of sounds. The person responsible for this reconstruction is The Schwa, whose real name, ironically, is Charles *Stone*. True to the novel's degenerative subversion of clear demarcations, however, the invisible, immaterial wall is "ten meters thick and five meters high" and everyone would "have to figure out for themselves if the wall of sound was confinement, exclusion, or protection" (Beatty, *Slumberland* 198). Refusing to cling to material boundaries such as stone, walls, or skin color, the novel calls for a change of epistemologies. It moves away from a predominantly visual model that focuses on bodies, borders, and blackness and invokes an aural[10] regime that highlights the fluidity of demarcations and resists binary classifications of any kind. Exploding the boundaries of blackness, *Slumberland* offers an intertextual collage of sounds that refuses solely to be categorized in terms of blackness. And it uses jazz as an ambivalent metaphor for this, given that jazz is often viewed as a field of ultimate freedom, yet one that is routinely categorized as an inherently black idiom. It is thus the fitting metaphor for the novel's dissimulation of blackness in DJ Darky and the Schwa's "free-jazz tsunami" (221). In the live performance of their musical masterpiece, "the Schwa erected a series of African-American landmarks upon the foundation I had laid down," most explicitly by instrumentally "quoting from 'Lift Every Voice and Sing,' the Negro national anthem" (228). Darky considers this a "blatant violation of the zoning laws" of his "mental landscape where blackness is passé" and remarks that "by constructing a new black Berlin Wall in both my head and the city, [the Schwa] was asking me to improvise. . . . He was daring me to be 'black'" (228). Yet Darky holds his "compositional ground," refusing to "blacken" his perfect beat. Ironically, however, this very performance, which was meant to eradicate blackness once and for all, contributes to its very reestablishment and even trendy commodification: "Thanks to my misguided efforts, blackness is back. . . . Black is the new black," Darky states in the Ellisonian "Epilogue to the Day Before Yesterday" (234). Yet again, any effort to dissimulate blackness effects a simultaneous reiteration of blackness. Despite DJ Darky's best efforts, his music continues to be heard as specifically black music, just as much as "Monk" Ellison's texts continue to be read in terms of blackness in *Erasure*'s final pages.

Slumberland links this reiteration of blackness satirically to the African American literary tradition's preoccupation with the (in)visibility of racialized bodies via Ralph Ellison's trope of invisibility. Yet whereas Ellison's *Invisible Man* invokes a scopic regime of truth, Beatty's novel sets up a regime of aural truth that dissimulates the need for the visual order of blackness. The sonic performance of the wall riffs on Ellison's trope, but now what is invisible is not the man but the thing that separates, the wall. Given the transparency of this particular wall, the novel remains ambivalent whether this actually is a separation at all and, thus, about its success at eradicating blackness. Stone's musical tour is called "THE BLACK PASSÉ TOUR—BUILDING WALLS, TEARING DOWN BRIDGES" (Beatty, *Slumberland* 209), which obfuscates the traditional meaning of walls as separating and bridges as connecting. As the Schwa ponders after their climactic perfor-mance, "I was thinking about the phrase on the banner, 'Black Passé.' How being passé is freedom. You can do what you want. No demands. No expec-tations. The only person I have to please is myself" (230). By consciously playing on Ellison, Beatty situates his text, albeit uncomfortably, in the Afri-can American tradition and picks up on the important trope of freedom yet situates it in a wholly different context. In the end, Ellison's *Invisible Man* "shake[s] off the old skin and come[s] up for breath" because, just possibly, "even an invisible man has a socially responsible role to play" (Ellison, *Invis-ible Man* 439). If, in a certain sense, DJ Darky is the satiric reincarnation of the Invisible Man who has shed his skin and his blackness, does he try to play a "socially responsible role" in the end? Beatty's novel does a wonder-ful job of tearing down walls and rebuilding them with a twist, as invisible walls. As opposed to generative satire, however, there is no socially respon-sible role conceivable within this mode of satire. Yet by riffing on Ellison, *Slumberland* is highly successful as specifically degenerative satire in point-ing to the ways in which fictional texts render blackness. Letting go of the illusion of blackness via dissimulation may be "painful and empty"—and the final words of Beatty's novel suggest that Darky's musical innovation has not changed the fact that "these Germans, they either want to fuck you or kill you. Sometimes both. Just like everybody else" (Beatty, *Slumberland* 241)—yet that is all degenerative satire *can* do.

While *Erasure* and *Slumberland* can be read as dissimulations of black-ness, Everett's *A History* goes a step further by being an exercise in self-erasure, the ultimate act of dissimulation. Already on its cover, this novel announces that the relationship between text and world is strained within its pages. It shows a photograph of the real Senator Strom Thurmond, and the novel's very title indicates that several layers of authorial identity will be involved: it is a "history" not really authored but only "proposed" by Thur-mond, as the parenthetical insertion adds. Furthermore, it is the history "as told to Percival Everett and James Kincaid," both of whom appear as characters within the novel and function as the ghostwriters of Thurmond's history, which has been commissioned, unbeknownst by the senator, by a lunatic former aide of his. Authorial identity is thus transferred from the "real" authors to various other figures of (more or less) authority in the novel, the least of which is Strom Thurmond, whose work it purports to be. Of course, all this strains the boundaries of authorial control, textual integ-rity, and narrative voice. Already in its highly ironic copyright disclaimer does the satiric novel acknowledge these complications: "*The authors wish to make clear to the reader that this is a work of fiction (i.e., none of it is true). Though there are many references to actual people, all of our interactions with those people (and the fictitious ones as well) are, in fact, fictitious*" (Everett, *A History*; emphasis in original). Speaking from the paratext, and thus outside the fictional text proper, the authors—or possibly the intradiegetic ghostwriters—address the extra-textual readership, pointing out the intricate relationship between text and world, fiction and truth. As it turns out, the history is never written, as Thurmond's eventual death, the ghostwriters' lack of interest, and the publishing house's withdrawal from the project conspire to end "A History of the African American People." In many ways, *A History* thus is the perfect example for what Weisenburger means by degenerative satire, as it is produces its own dissolution and dismantlement. In contradiction to its own title, the text is *not* "A History of the African American People," nor was it written by Strom Thurmond or told to Everett and Kincaid. Rather, *A History* all along has been a satirical subversion of questions of authorial identity, the defining qualities of a "black" text, and whether only African Americans have the authority to write a history of their people. The satire of Everett's epistolary novel thus targets neither Strom Thurmond nor any other real extra-textual entity. By mirroring Thurmond's ostensible "A History of the African American People," Percival Everett and James Kincaid's *A History of the African-American People* revolves entirely around itself and its own textuality rather than being a true history of the African American people.[11]

As far as narrative authority in the novel is concerned, the book also proceeds along unconventional lines. It is an epistolary novel, consisting of letters by an ever-growing number of writers, leading to a more and more diversified narrative voice. Nevertheless, as the novel progresses, a central voice of authority does present itself in the form of the character of Percival Everett. The narrative authority is thus delegated from the authors of the novel—Everett and Kincaid—to the intramural character Everett, who also mirrors his extra-textual namesake. Yet even this sliver of authorial control or an integral narrative voice fades toward the end of the book. The final encounter between Everett, Kincaid, and Thurmond is no longer even narrated but presented in the form of a screenplay, containing italicized stage directions as well as primary and secondary dramatic text, but no narration. The lack of a coherent or unified narrative voice—together with the combination of white and black authors—problematizes the notion of a black text and thus leads to the ultimate irony of the novel: Thurmond's self-proclaimed amanuensis Barton Wilkes asks the tandem of ghostwriters to show that Thurmond "is, properly understood, a black writer" (Everett, *A History* 255). And while this is an outrageous thing to say about the notoriously bigoted Thurmond, it raises an important question about this degenerative satire: namely, what is a black writer, and what makes—by extension—a black text? Is a novel, jointly written by a black and a white author about the commissioning of "a history of the African American People" by a white former aide to a racist white politician, as told to a duo of ghostwriters, one white and one black, who share the names of the novel's authors, a "black" text? By complicating the levels of narration and narrative transmission, this satire dissimulates blackness and the question of black authorship in a text that consists of nothing but masquerades. Complicating things even further, the ghostwriters claim to write "authentic history," even though they "do not make any pretense of empirical justification, of giving a world outside Strom. There is, for Strom and for the reader, no world outside Strom" (285). Put differently, this history of the African American people does not refer to any extra-textual social world but only to the "intramural" world of Strom Thurmond as presented within the bounds of this very fiction. Although the novel clearly lampoons the ignorance of both Thurmond and Wilkes, the unreliability of the narration and the narrators themselves prevents the text from becoming exclusively a satire of a man who, after all, was already dead at the time of the novel's publication, but rather a satire of a range of discourses that relate to Thurmond's rather infamous place in (African) American life.

In my analysis, I hope to have shown how the various mirrors and dissimulations in these three texts contribute to a destabilization of the category of blackness as it is being used in literary discourses. Through direct and indirect allusions, these novels aim their satires at narratives of blackness in textual form. In their refusal mimetically to represent the world outside themselves, these novels dissimulate blackness behind manifold textual mirrors in their highly irreverent and outrageously humorous destabilizations of this very text of blackness. They are, in a very literal sense *de*-generative in that they rip apart reality within the refractions of their textual mirrors without reconstructing—that is, "generating"— an alternative world. In this sense, dissimulation, indeed, is the "richest source of satire," as Feinberg has claimed (23). Yet in degenerative satires of blackness, what is being dissimulated is not an underlying reality but "only" other texts.

Notes

1. Authorship of the book is ultimately credited solely to Everett in its Library of Congress entry, so I will follow that convention here, even though the copyright information, the book's title, and the content of the text suggest co-authorship between Everett and his University of Southern California colleague Kincaid.

2. Everett's hilarious *I Am Not Sidney Poitier* (2009) is another excellent case in point. The novel's protagonist, Not Sidney Poitier—the famous actor's dead ringer—relives several scenes of Sidney Poitier's various films, thus fictively reenacting a wide array of already fictional roles.

3. *A History* is not only an epistolary novel; it is one that is co-authored by Everett and James Kincaid. In addition to multiple narrative layers, the novel consists of two authorial voices that constantly tangle with the narrative voices of their namesake character-narrators, resulting in a wide-ranging satirical metaconversation about race that takes place in the interstices of text and world.

4. In this sense, dissimulating blackness is one strategy employed by what Thelma Golden has called "post-black" art. As she defines it, it "is characterized by artists who [are] adamant about not being labeled as 'black' artists, though their work [is] steeped, in fact deeply interested, in redefining complex notions of blackness" (14).

5. As many critics have pointed out, the novel also makes use of Derrida's notion of writing *sous rature*, or under erasure, in which the original term is crossed out yet remains visible/legible as a marker in discourse (cf. Russett).

6. This pseudonym is a parody of the legendary African American folk hero "Stagger" Lee Shelton, aka Stagolee (cf. Gysin 74–75).

7. See also Gillian Johns's article in this collection, pp. 85–97.

8. This, again, is a parodic mirror play: the NBA is Trey Ellis's abbreviation (itself perhaps a pun on the abbreviation of the National Basketball Association) of the New Black Aesthetic, that playful artistic bunch of experimentalist "cultural mulattoes" ("New Black Aesthetic" 235) who irreverently crossed, straddled, and dislocated the boundary between black and white arts, creating a hybrid to which no one can give a face.

9. Had he really fully adopted the Stagg persona and thus abolished Monk's identity—as several critics of the novel have argued—he would have chosen the more obvious "Fuck."

10. By operating within an aural regime, the novel also parodies the strong focus on the oral and vernacular style in much of African American fiction.

11. The fact that Everett's title hyphenates *African-American* whereas the project within the book leaves the term unhyphenated is perhaps a subtle typographic indication of this differentiation.

"It's a Black Thang Maybe": Satirical Blackness in Percival Everett's *Erasure* and Adam Mansbach's *Angry Black White Boy*

Danielle Fuentes Morgan

In her essay "What White Publishers Won't Print," Zora Neale Hurston remarks, "It is assumed that all non-Anglo-Saxons are uncomplicated stereotypes. Everybody knows all about them. They are lay figures mounted in the museum where all may take them in at a glance. They are made of bent wires without insides at all. So how could anybody write a book about the non-existent?" (118). Although Hurston wrote this statement in 1950, the sentiment still reverberates today in the mainstream commodification of African American experience.[1] The experiences of people of color are systematically simplified and consciously homogenized, as though the experiences of one cannot be distinguished from another, particularly if that experience is negative. Differences of class, education, and background are all dismissed in favor of a limiting, monolithic organization of nonwhiteness wedged into categorical subculture.

Percival Everett's *Erasure* (2002) and Adam Mansbach's *Angry Black White Boy, or The Miscegenation of Macon Detournay* (2005) address the troubling nature of this particular desire to confine blackness—specifically, black masculinity—to the static, easily identifiable, and quantifiable. In *Erasure*, the presence of stereotypical black masculinity is figured through the projection of performative characteristics onto physical black masculinity. In *Angry Black White Boy*, the fear of the black masculine becomes so insidious that its presumed characteristics entirely efface white masculine physicality. Even in the presence of white maleness, black masculinity is so fearsome that it has the potential to subsume all other categorizations. Through this understanding of racialization, Everett and Mansbach demonstrate that the cultural stereotype of the violent, criminal black male is so pervasive that it persists even in the absence of signifiers.

Broadly, this mythology surrounding blackness gestures toward what makes a text specifically black and addresses the malleability of post-soul blackness. In *Playing in the Dark: Whiteness and the Literary Imagination* (1993), Toni Morrison argues that when it comes to race, "silence and evasion have historically ruled literary discourse" (9). *Erasure* and *Angry Black White Boy* operate with a clear awareness of the calculated reticence around race, and so their satirical representations of race thrust blackness to the forefront in nontraditional and important ways. If whiteness seems to exist in and to permeate American literature through its absence of signifiers, then it is blackness that requires demarcation and introduction. This is particularly important in consideration of the post-soul questioning of racialization and the subsequent rejection of racial quantifiability. Racial essentialism is eschewed, but this does not mean that race becomes invisible. There is instead acknowledgement of the failure of language to define race in satisfactory ways. Race here relies on virtuality, not what is physically present but what is presumed to be present. Ultimately, it is this idea of racial intangibility that begins to contextualize the post-soul literary movement. Black texts are traditionally identified simply by the author's race, but the idea of the post-soul complicates that narrative. Instead, within the frame of the post-soul aesthetic, black texts are better defined as those that shirk the primacy of white privilege within their own narration and instead bear witness through a kaleidoscopic lens of blackness. They are reliant upon an authorial perspective that privileges nonwhiteness without intentionally fetishizing it for mainstream consumption.

In fact, both *Erasure* and *Angry Black White Boy* gain additional significance in the context of post-soul. Macon Detournay, the protagonist of *Angry Black White Boy*, is initially identified by the public as black despite his phenotypically non-black characteristics, thus problematizing the reliance on simple stereotypes in racial essentialism. Likewise, in *Erasure*, Monk's created persona, Stagg R. Leigh, is presumed to be black for the same reason as Macon: their convincing use of violence and heated language is tantamount to purportedly black rhetoric.[2] Throughout his literary oeuvre, Everett has consistently been concerned with the seeming ineffability of blackness in both the public and private realms, but the very fact of Mansbach's presence within post-black literature demonstrates a new racial fluidity implied by the post-soul aesthetic. Certainly *Angry Black White Boy* is not African American literature in the easiest, most literal sense because it is not written by an African American author, but if hip-hop is used as a signifier of black cultural thought, then *lit-hop*—one way to potentially classify the novel—functions as its literary equivalent. Lit-hop, like hip-hop, is defined not by its blackness but by its outsider status in relation to both the literary canon and whiteness. *Angry Black White Boy* can only truly reside in the category of African American literature in a post-soul context. It is through this playful engagement with quantifiable blackness that both

Everett and Mansbach demonstrate the arbitrary yet significant nature of racialization in the twenty-first century.

Erasure's protagonist, Thelonious "Monk" Ellison, is a writer, but his writing is not selling. His books, written with a decidedly academic flair, are suffering from the preconceptions of the readers and publishers alike: he's a black author, but where are his books about the black experience? It is out of this anger that he adopts the pseudonym Stagg R. Leigh and writes *My Pafology*, a satirical novella focused on an over-the-top ghetto and its downtrodden residents. In doing so he imprecisely attempts to indict a well-meaning public for their oversimplified and ultimately harmful construction of black masculinity. It is important to note that while Monk's creation of *My Pafology* erupts from raw emotionality and frustration, Everett uses the novella in a more calculated and intentional satirical manner. The novella, in this larger dimension, critiques the market for literature and images that limit blackness to a small range of particular, negative portrayals. Monk explains that the need to write the book suddenly consumes him, saying, "I remembered passages of *Native Son* and *The Color Purple* and *Amos and Andy* and my hands began to shake, the world opening around me, tree roots trembling on the ground outside, people in the street shouting *dint, ax, fo, screet* and *fahvre!* And I was screaming inside, complaining that I didn't sound like that" (Everett, *Erasure* 61; emphases in original). The juxtaposition of *Native Son* (1940) and *The Color Purple* (1982) with *Amos and Andy* is particularly significant in considering his disgust with the widespread acceptance of negative blackness. His work is ultimately not a condemnation just of white America; otherwise Monk could claim inspiration from *Amos and Andy* and other white-authored parodic portrayals of blackness in isolation. But his inclusion of *Native Son* and *The Color Purple*—both critically acclaimed, black-authored, and beloved by racially diverse audiences—indicates the presence of and his recollection of these belittling characteristics in perhaps unexpected spaces.

Although Monk's anger at the willingness of the public to accept these trite stereotypes of blackness is the catalyst for writing *My Pafology*, he is able to write it only because he has likewise internalized these characteristics; his ability to instantly recall these stereotypes of blackness significantly precipitates the creation of the novella. *My Pafology* bridges the gap between the real and the absurd as Everett personifies common stereotypes of blackness and plays them out to an outlandish conclusion—so outlandish, it would seem that no one could possibly accept either *My Pafology* or Stagg R. Leigh as being in earnest. Yet the novella is taken at face value as audiences either ignore or fail to recognize its satirical elements and project the stereotypical black masculine on the pseudonymic author, an author ironically received simultaneously as mysterious and (to paraphrase Hurston) as someone audiences already know all about. As a result, the text is well received as a window onto supposedly typical black life. In Monk's attempt to point out the ridiculousness of racialization, he ultimately highlights race and reinforces its status as inextricable from public consciousness.

My Pafology is intended to be received as a satire-within-a-satire by the audience of *Erasure*. Yet with Stagg as the author, Monk inadvertently only reestablishes racial salience within the novel. The audience of *My Pafology* is unaware of the work's existence as a satire and consequently accepts Stagg's account as true. Everett is satirizing both mainstream American culture and the African American literary communities that allow these negative performances to stand in for blackness. Thus, while Everett effectively censures mainstream perception, Monk's very personal anger overwhelms his text, and consequently he lacks the critical stance necessary for a full evaluation of race in American society. Monk explains to his agent, "Look at the shit that's published. I'm sick of it. This is an expression of my being sick of it" (Everett, *Erasure* 132). While Monk's frustrations are valid, to be sure, Everett structures them in such a way that audiences must see Monk's effort toward articulating his anger as problematic, to say the least. Ultimately, Monk achieves nothing more than momentary catharsis in his writing. His novella becomes impotent as he furthers the Stagg R. Leigh charade. When an editor hopes to meet with Stagg, Monk asks his agent to "tell her I'll call her. . . . Tell her Stagg R. Leigh lives alone in the nation's capital, Tell her he's just two years out of prison, say he said 'joint,' and that he still hasn't adjusted to the outside. Tell her he's afraid he might *go off*. Tell her that he will only talk about the book, that if she asks any personal questions, he'll hang up" (153; emphasis in original). Monk is far too cavalier about any ramifications of his portrayal. If his racialized frustrations stem from mainstream willingness to accept the basest stereotypes of blackness, Monk is only embracing them rather than agitating against them.

Portrayals of the kind of subversive blackness that Monk aspires to write are plentiful in literature. In *Constructing the Black Masculine* (2002), Maurice O. Wallace argues that in Ralph Ellison's *Invisible Man* (1952), "the black masculine virtuality obtains in the affective power of shadows" (35). This power of shadows is endemic to Monk's understanding of blackness and his ability to create and to sustain Stagg R. Leigh. Blackness is paradoxically situated within American culture as that which is quantifiable and commodifiable by all, yet simultaneously alien and hidden—something so outside of the norm that its motivations and behaviors become animalistic and can never be fully understood by the mainstream. In *Erasure*, the mythic Stagg R. Leigh is empowered by forced clandestinity; yet even this anticipated cover is fraudulent as Monk characterizes Stagg according to his most readily accessible notions of blackness. Stagg is most convincing because Monk subconsciously believes and accepts the stereotypes as well. Finally, it is significant that it is not only the general public that legitimizes Stagg's existence, but also the educated elite, including Monk himself.

Ultimately, it is for this reason that audiences of *Erasure* can determine that, despite his arguments otherwise, Monk is not truly attempting to write a satire. This fact is made evident not only by his facile narration, but also in the creation of a pseudonymic authorial persona. *My Pafology* has all the signifiers of a work to be taken seriously, at least when presented to an audience already largely inured to a complex signification regarding black masculinity. Monk's narrative is bolstered only by grotesque, caricatured blackness, and he smugly places the burdensome onus of discerning it as satire on the audience. In fact, without Stagg's performative blackness as the author, the novella would be far less compelling because it would lack autobiographical intrigue as propellant. Thus, the reliance on audience discernment is problematic for two discrete reasons. First, his text is unable to function as a fully articulated satire because Monk is unable to establish any distance between himself and his narration; satire presumes authorial understanding of the situation being satirized, while providing space for simultaneous audience awareness of authorial distance from the actual plot as it occurs. Second, and even more troublingly, *My Pafology* never works as a satire quite simply because Monk did not truly write it as a satire. This dimension is easily overlooked, but it cannot be overemphasized in understanding why Monk's satire fails and, likewise, why Everett is able to so skillfully satirize Monk's behavior in the text. Monk wrote the narrative as cathartic invective, possessed by hideous, stereotypical blackness and nothing more. In addition, it is not until he decides the work is publishable that he retroactively determines the work to be satirical and insists the title be changed from *My Pafology* to *Fuck*. This distinction is important. It is as if to absolve himself from wrongdoing for his addition to the canon of black-belittling literary exercises, he must claim to have written the work as a satire. It is doubtful that Monk even believes his own rationalization, as he is more diligent in creating Stagg than his text itself. The impetus for his writing was that these simplistic stereotypes are so readily consumed, and yet he provides no indication to his readers that his work is not merely following in this tradition of cashing in on a wildly limited vision of blackness. He is, at best, incredibly careless with his handling of his emotions. For the audience of *Erasure*, it is evident that Monk has merged the frustrations of past aggressions with performative blackness and satirical inclinations, but even we remain unconvinced as Monk indicts everyone except himself. How could the readers of

My Pafology—without having information about Monk's purported intentions—be cued to receive the work as satire, especially in the presence of so many other contemporary literary works that touch on similar themes and are presented and received in earnest? In this case, context is everything. Satire must contain signifiers of satirical intention, and Monk's novella is grossly unsuccessful as it teaches nothing, seems to emerge from nothing, and reinforces the stereotypes he sought to dismantle.

It is this lack of coding that ultimately harms not only the text but also Monk himself. As a result, as Houston Baker explains, "The ordinary reader might have a very difficult time empathizing with Monk as he proceeds, with creepy, solipsistic self-certainty, through the world—believing he alone is capable of placing the contemporary culture industry *sous rature* [under erasure]" (*I Don't Hate the South* 136; emphasis in original). Because Monk narcissistically assumes on one level that mainstream audiences should share his perspective upon reading his text—despite his previous articulation that he is well aware they cannot, and despite his unwillingness to give them any signposts to guide them as they read—he distances himself from both the readerly and writerly audiences, ultimately disconnecting himself from reality and being absorbed into blackness as commodity.[3] Finally, it is his emotionality that causes him to so fully miss the mark. Monk is so angry about what he perceives as reader apathy surrounding the portrayal of blackness that he is unable to channel his feeling into something productive, rather than explosive, simplistic racialization. In fact, Monk seems to imagine that somehow his writing should jar audiences out of their complacency while disregarding his own inability to do so. Although readers are guilty for so eagerly devouring Stagg's tale, Monk is even more culpable for writing a supposed satire containing no satirical markers.

Everett centers the satirical action squarely on Monk and examines the significant damage these preconceptions of black masculinity do to him as an individual. This is an important satirical choice as Monk begins to represent unexpectedly a microcosm of black masculinity. While Monk's own experiences may initially seem personalized, it is worth considering the fact that the negative effects on his life are socially constructed and that the damage done to individuals ultimately compounds to widespread social impact. It is the implied communality of fractured identity that gives the text its satirical significance in a post-soul context. Monk worked actively in both his early writing and his personal life to reject the stereotypes of blackness by shirking what he viewed as expected African American scholarly interests and instead involving himself in those traditionally associated with the white avant-garde and the white leisure class. However, his efforts are ultimately futile, as he becomes so immersed in quantifiable blackness that he

cannot be distinguished from it. The monolithic nature of the black masculine stereotype confines the individual black man and ultimately attempts to
stifle black manhood.

In *Angry Black White Boy*, Adam Mansbach further complicates stereotypical notions of the black masculine. The novel opens with a young white
Columbia University student, Macon Detournay, working as a cab driver
and lamenting the fact that his knowledge of and appreciation for black
culture has not gotten him "scratched from the [white] devil list for good"
(17). His youthful frustration at being unable to alter his privileged racial
identity led to an anger directed initially at the very people with whom he
most strongly identified: "How dare black people not see him as an ally,
not recognize that he was down? He retaliated by studying their history,
their culture: he was a thirteen-year-old whiteboy in a Malcolm X T-shirt,
alone at the first annual Boston Hip Hop conference, heart fluttering with
intimidation and delight as scowling bald-headed old schoolers pointed at
his chest, demanding 'Whatchu know about that man?'" (17). After an adolescence spent at "work constructing a rhetorical identity that would allow
him to embrace the Five Percenters' truths without capitulating his soul:
White people aren't evil, but evil is white people" (18; emphasis in original),
Macon goes away to college in New York, starts working as a cabbie, and one
day begins robbing his white fares out of aggravation at what he perceives
to be their willingness to accept white privilege without question. He holds
them at gunpoint and engages in racialized rhetoric, threatening to "bust
a cap in your flabby white ass" and snarling that "you people are a fucking
plague on this planet" (98). Later, his victims report having been robbed by
a black man based purely on inferred racial performativity: "He'd done it:
found some kind of worm hole in the white psyche, some uncharted reflex,
and here he stood, divorced from his own color by the violence and conviction of his own actions. Those fools hadn't seen white knuckles gripping that
gun. They couldn't. Their brains weren't wired to link whiteness to the words
Macon had hurled at them, the fear he'd made them feel. It had to be a nigger. Macon was invisible. Shock fluttered his stomach" (109). This misper-
ception might merely be humorous if the implications weren't so horrifying
in reality, which seems to be the source of the "shock" that Macon feels and
that Mansbach wishes to convey to his audience.

Mansbach himself is certainly familiar with the problematizing of racial
identity as he and his protagonist share a number of characteristics: both are
white, Columbia-educated Boston natives, both came from upper-middle-
class backgrounds, and both embraced hip-hop culture at an early age. In
Angry Black White Boy, Mansbach skillfully and satirically addresses the
problem of the preconceptions of black masculinity by imagining it out to

its absurd conclusion—what happens when a man seems to exhibit some of the basest stereotypes of black masculinity, but lacks black skin? Maurice Wallace believes that "it is the insufferability of the inescapable afterimage of the absent black antecedent that would seem to worry the effort, at least in the white imagination, to 'cover [one's] tracks and traces.' For the traces of black male visibility are retained in the white unconscious 'permanently'; they defy cover" (33–34). Black masculinity is defined then not by literal physicality but by an expectation of exotic degeneracy and so it need not physically be present for its threat to emerge. It is then, as Mansbach argues in his essay "The Audacity of Post-Racism," that "white kids all over the country believe, based on the signifiers flashing on their TV screens, that blackness equals flashy wealth, supreme masculinity, and ultra-sexualized femininity—interrupted occasionally by bursts of glamorous violence, and situated in a thrilling ghetto that is both dangerous and host to a constant party" (73). Like Everett, Mansbach uses satire not simply to examine the stereotypes surrounding race, but even more importantly to dissect the damage these preconceptions do to both black and white individuals and to society more broadly.

Mansbach dismantles race by significantly demonstrating its arbitrary nature without ever implying that race doesn't matter or that it is inherently negative. The fact that Macon is white and, after being mistaken for black, becomes some sort of pseudo-black, pseudo-Nationalist figurehead requires a suspension of disbelief merged with understanding the reality inherent in the absurd that is almost always a characteristic of satire. Satire is absurd, to be sure, but not wholly unbelievable, and this distinction is especially important for literature dealing with and problematizing race. Rather than merely indicting their readers for being ignorant, these satirical representations force readers out of their comfort and complacency by demonstrating unchecked racialization in a familiar literary universe. Furthering this satirical inventiveness, Mansbach mirrors Everett / Monk by confounding racial expectations in aligning his text with Wright's *Native Son* and Ellison's *Invisible Man*. Like *Native Son*, *Angry Black White Boy* is broken into three books, and like *Invisible Man*, it features an outbreak of racialized violence in Harlem, but the similarities extend well beyond the superficial. Macon explains in the prologue that "I was hoping someone would call me the white Bigger Thomas, but nobody had the nutsack even though it's an obvious comparison, what with Bigger being a chauffeur and me a cabbie. I talked a lot more shit than Bigger ever did, though. And I did what I did on purpose. And I got away" (Mansbach, *Angry* 2–3). Bigger's threat of black violence against whites is reimagined here as the threat of white-initiated black violence against white, demonstrating the strange evolution of American racial politics through a lens of post-blackness; blackness has presumably become so post-black that even a sympathetic white kid from Boston may at least temporarily be wedged into it, with or without his consent. Indeed, here even the figure of Depression-era black tragedy, Bigger Thomas, can be aligned with a privileged, white college student in the twenty-first century. It is the forced parallelization of black and white masculinity that holds a microscope up to social understandings of racialized gender roles and allows *Angry Black White Boy* to agitate against public apathy and indifference.

In a phone interview, Mansbach touched on the development of his satire technique during the writing of *Angry Black White Boy*: "There were earlier platforms and iterations of this book that were much more earnest and it was revelatory for me to realize, 'OK, what I need to do is take this over the top and go crazy with it and really use humor and be funny and be absurdist with it.' It was really liberating and I really enjoyed that. But you know, satire is tricky because the world is increasingly self-satirizing" (Telephone Interview). Mansbach, like Everett, demonstrates a clear understanding of the high degree of absurdity necessary for effective post-soul satire. Mansbach's comment about the "increasingly self-satirizing" nature of the world, implies that failing to go "over the top" runs the risk of an audience mistaking a satirical gesture for an earnest one, as has happened on numerous occasions in which seemingly unmistakably satirical news items from *The Onion* have been re-reported as genuine stories by actual news outlets. Perhaps though it is only through audience knowledge of authorial intention and the subsequent acceptance of their protagonists that these works can be regarded as satire; one of the surest ways for a satire to fail as social criticism is through audience inability or unwillingness to accept the material as satirized, which often comes from a lack of coding by the author.[4]

The impetus to read a text as satire is often based on our knowledge of the author or the extra-textual framing of the book, even though there are also usually signposts in the text itself. Due to the lack of such markers, Monk's and Macon's efforts at effecting change are at best misunderstood and at worst ineffectual or even counterproductive. As Monk speaks to his publisher, this ineffectuality is crystallized. His publisher asks, "'So what do you want me to do?' 'Send it out.' 'Straight or with some kind of qualification? Do you want me to tell them it's a parody?' 'Send it straight,' I said. 'If they can't see it's a parody, fuck them.'" (Everett, *Erasure* 132). Again, the absurdity apparent to the audience of *Erasure* is not enough, because it does not resonate with the relatively unsophisticated readers of *My Pafology*. Although *My Pafology* written by Thelonious "Monk" Ellison could be coded as satire, the same text written by Stagg R. Leigh is at best unclear.

Similarly, after he is arrested for his taxicab robberies, Macon recognizes the potential he has to explain his act of frustrated violence upon discovering the "worm hole in the white psyche" as an act of satirical didacticism: "Macon nodded, astounded at his own serenity. The stress headache, the grime of jail, were gone. He gazed calmly into the throng, thought, Yes, this makes perfect sense, and felt his heart thump an amen. Yes, I will talk and they will listen. Ready or not, motherfuckers, here I come" (Mansbach, *Angry* 140). From this initial impulse arises what Macon will eventually call the "Race Traitor Project," intended to give "white people, especially white people with money" a chance to "consider how they go to where they are" (190). As Macon describes his philosophy for leveling the racial playing field in the United States by encouraging more white-on-white crime, radio host Joe Francis states that "I don't know if I'm supposed to take that seriously or not, Macon" (191), an indeterminacy that is echoed at various other stages of the book by both white and black characters who come into contact with Macon's movement.

Despite efforts at shirking his privilege, it is ultimately Macon's whiteness that allows him a platform to speak on racial issues. He is initially permitted youthful naiveté and miscalculations because his race is seemingly incongruous with his actions; ironically, because he appears to have less at stake in a conversation about race, his audience is more receptive to his perspective: "Radio, TV, newspapers, Web sites, magazines—everybody wanted the well-spoken white criminal race traitor" (Mansbach, *Angry* 147). Macon does not fully comprehend the nature of the authority suddenly granted to him until his roommate, Andre, explains, "I've decided to believe in you until you give me reason not to. . . . Somebody's gotta light a fire under white people's asses. Every time a brother does it, somebody up and kills him, so it might as well be you" (149). As he takes the stage at a poetry reading a few days later, Macon begins to recognize his role as a critical mirror for other whites (that is, an agent of satire): "People were listening. There were other kids like him out there—right here—skating along the edges of whiteness as disgusted as he was, looking for a leader, a mouthpiece, someone to tell them what to do and validate their angst before it turned sour or misfired or faded. . . . For the first time, Macon thought about the legions of white people out there who, if they weren't as committed as he was, were at least highly suggestible. Perhaps even open-minded enough to learn to be self-critical—and it would be cake to make people feel good about being self-critical, venturing far enough outside themselves to analyze and bat around the forces that made them think the way they did" (165). Gradually, though, this impulse to set the record straight gets subsumed within Macon's desire for acceptance (in other words, his desire to be seen as "down" by black people), and his motivations become increasingly muddled and self-serving, eventually unleashing a destructive riot in the midst of a "Day of Apology" meant initially to allow white America to begin to atone for the sins of its racialized past. It isn't until Macon fully and articulately engages in the rhetoric of disabling white privilege that he endangers himself, a process that comes full circle in the startling act of possibly redemptive martyrdom that closes the book.

Satire is especially effective in the present because the cynicism of the twenty-first century does not necessitate strict didacticism. Neither of the protagonists of the novels discussed here come to a good end, ending up as casualties of the very racializing processes they wish to resist. Everett and Mansbach anticipate the trajectory of society unaltered and imagined out to its absurd conclusion, spurring critical self-reflection from readers rather than readers' censure. These are satires about race, but in nontraditional ways they also engage in subtle critiques of the African American literary canon and the uses to which that canon has been put. These post-soul novels tackle issues of post–civil rights significance—questions of definitional blackness, gendered race, and individual place in a society that confounds the personal and the communal. Importantly, these are not satires that simply ridicule white, mainstream society, a relatively easy target. Rather, they are examinations of the margins based on the idea that within the black experience, the tragic is never wholly invented. Roger Rosenblatt explains that "when the central character is black, the abuses are authentic. No black American author has ever felt the need to invent a nightmare to make his point" (171). Even within the satirical, these "abuses" are only logically extended, rather than purely fabricated, and they are extended by necessity to shun complacency. This is why satire is so significant in African American literature; the tragic elements of race are so expected and normalized that it is helpful to dismantle them to disallow complacency among readers. Satire jars readers out of their traditional readings by virtue of the new absurdity within a familiar plot, forcing analysis and introspection. It is for this reason that there is a notable history of satire in African American literature, or certainly at least some elements of it, even in texts that are not classified as strictly satires.[5]

So the fact that *Angry Black White Boy*—a narrative featuring a white male protagonist and written by a Jewish American author—seems to fall neatly into the contemporary African American literary tradition is perhaps the most significant aspect of its satirical bent. Mansbach offers a unique perspective on race relations not only because of his decades-long engagement with hip-hop culture as a fan, a spoken-word artist, and a hip-hop scholar but also because he is Jewish American, thus a member of a group that has been systematically oppressed and only recently absorbed into monolithic whiteness.[6] Likewise, the title itself takes the idea of the "angry black man" and makes it racially ambiguous—black acting but white looking. Additionally, by shifting the focus from a "black man" to a "white boy," Mansbach satirically highlights the supposed incongruence between black and white masculinity. This is perhaps even the most overt way in which he makes whiteness visible and forces audiences to be conscious of the detrimental preconceptions of not only black masculinity but white masculinity as well. Mansbach aligns Macon with black cultural thought without appropriation. He goes to lengths to validate Macon's role in hip-hop culture while forcefully explaining that he can never fully claim the position within it that he desires. It is Macon's acknowledgement of his final inability to be absorbed by blackness—that his white privilege is perhaps basically as pervasive as the myth of the black masculine—that ultimately allows him to move through the narrative arc without becoming a wholly laughable or pathetic character, even if certain aspects of his personal philosophy are held up for satirical ridicule. If African American satires already move through modes of discourses with great fluidity, then Macon's additional voice is simply a new facet, particularly appropriate in an age preoccupied by the idea of post-blackness.

Toni Morrison explains that "Africanism is the vehicle by which the American self knows itself as not enslaved, but free; not repulsive, but desirable; not helpless, but licensed and powerful; not history-less, but historical; not damned, but innocent; not a blind accident of evolution, but a progressive fulfillment of destiny" (52). As a result, blackness often necessitates specific signifiers so it can serve as contextualization for whiteness; whiteness simply exists, and what whiteness is not, blackness is. As Macon explains to Joe Francis, "My job is to make whiteness visible. I want people to look at me, Joe, this crazy kid who won't shut up about race, and realize, maybe for the first time, that hey, whiteness is an identity" (191). It is this effort at making whiteness visible that disallows the comfortable privilege subconsciously anticipated by some of his readers. For these reasons, satire is especially useful in dissecting and addressing issues of blackness and racialization more broadly. Because Everett and Mansbach provide context both within and without the texts, they are able to articulate their concerns around racialization and thus confound its simplistic binary logic. Everett's and Mansbach's utilization of satire highlights the fear of the black masculine, a fear so profound and far-reaching that it exists even when blackness itself is absent. Indeed, blackness is phantasmatic and operates not only as a cultural presence, but also through spectrality. By addressing this difficult subject matter from a satirical angle, the authors create a fictitious American public that is abhorrent enough to shock readers out of their own complacency and self-absolution, but familiar enough to simultaneously highlight audience culpability. These satires create a space for a conversation about the more complicated, transient, and often transgressive nature of blackness in America.

Notes

1. Perhaps this commodification is most evident today in the prevalence of "the gangsta," "pimp," or "thug" tropes as they appear in mainstream culture. Notable examples include fictional characters such as Nino Brown of *New Jack City* (1991) and Huggy Bear, a character in the 1970s series *Starsky and Hutch* who has found resurgence in popularity after a 2004 movie remake and the subsequent use of his image on clothing marketed to teenage boys. In real life, these tropes figure in the popularity of gangster rappers and the glamorization of a "thug life" sensibility as embodied by The Notorious B.I.G. and Snoop Dogg, who himself played Huggy Bear in the remake of *Starsky and Hutch*, seeming to blur the line between fact and fiction. Most recently and egregiously, it is worth considering the appearance of a hologram of deceased rapper Tupac Shakur at the 2012 Coachella Music Fest, seeming to gesture toward a desire to capitalize on the threatening performance of black masculinity even after the death of the fetishized black man.

2. It is important to note here Everett's allusion to "Stagger" Lee Shelton. Stagger Lee was a known pimp convicted of murder in 1895. Both Stagger Lee and the murder have since been immortalized in song and popular culture as a symbol of fearsome black masculinity. These songs and images still circulate to this day.

3. See also Gillian Johns's article in this collection, pp. 85–97.

4. Even this assertion is somewhat questionable in the face of Dave Chappelle's well-documented discomfort as to the nature of his audience's laughter by the end of his popular television series, which could hardly be accused of masking its satirical intentions. The distinction between being laughed at and being laughed with is, after all, absolutely essential to conveying satirical intent.

5. This trajectory includes George Schuyler's *Black No More* (1931), Ishmael Reed's *Mumbo Jumbo* (1972), and Paul Beatty's *White Boy Shuffle* (1996). More recently, there is Issa Rae's web series, *The Mis-Adventures of Awkward Black Girl*.

6. African Americans and Jewish Americans have a long, complicated history marked by cooperation as marginalized minorities within the United States; parallels have been drawn through American chattel slavery and the enslavement of Jews in Egypt, ghettos in America and Europe, and aligned goals in civil rights movements. However, this relationship has been marked by tension as separatist tendencies emerged in Black Nationalist movements and as Jewishness began to signal whiteness in America.

Coal, Charcoal, and Chocolate Comedy: The Satire of John Killens and Mat Johnson

Keenan Norris

The critical divergence between the two satires that are this essay's subjects, John Killens's *The Cotillion, or One Good Bull Is Half the Herd* (1971) and Mat Johnson's *Hunting in Harlem* (2003), arises from the different ethical-political viewpoints from which they approach black Harlem. The former is infused with the righteous convictions of the Black Arts Movement (BAM), and its moral calculus accordingly glorifies the modish Afrocentricity of the 1960s. By contrast, the latter satire is written at a later point in history and finds the affirmation of African American pride an insufficient philosophy in view of the chaos that characterizes life in the city. Johnson's ridicule is broadcast in all directions, at all philosophies and agendas; there are no affirmations and the conclusion verges on nihilism. The drastic difference between these two books indicates the deep disillusionment that came to characterize black intellectual space in the decades between 1968 (when Dr. Martin Luther King Jr. was killed, taking with him much of the vitality of the mainstream Civil Rights Movement) and 2008 (when President Obama's election symbolized for many an evolved American mentality). Johnson's *Hunting in Harlem*, published in 2003, marks this nearly four-decade interval between significant periods of black hope.

In his foreword to a 2002 reprint edition of *The Cotillion*, Alexs D. Pate writes that the novel "was written for the black reader of the Black Power era" (xi). As such, the material therein might seem dated, relegated to the year in which it was written. Pate goes on to write that Killens "was at the forefront of delineating the details of what it meant to be a black writer in the Black Arts Movement" (xiii). Killens's status as an acclaimed novelist, a founder of the Harlem Writer's Guild, and a representative spokesperson for BAM lends his work cachet as an intellectual manifesto for both Black Arts and Black Power, two deeply intertwined artistic and sociopolitical discourses. When Killens published his grand satire, these movements most certainly had not yet moved on, as Mat Johnson writes some thirty-five years later (6); they were a significant part of the then-existing reality. Pate claims *The Cotillion* remains significant as "one of the few glimpses of the transformational power of resurgent black consciousness rendered in fiction" (x).

"My name is Ben Ali Lumumba, and I'm free, Black and twenty-three" the novel's narrator-protagonist declares in its fictionalized, unpaginated foreword, which is subtitularly addressed "To Whom It May Concern (and to all of you who ought to be)" (Killens xxiii). This is the first of many rhetorical challenges that Lumumba will lob at America's elite, which he and the book characterize as essentially white, wealthy, and ideologically white supremacist. Lumumba, a would-be memoirist, is determined to tell the tale of his experiences at sea, where he claims to have gone at the age of seventeen in order to escape the Vietnam War. "I wandered," he writes, "carousing, reading, brawling, learning, looking, drinking, fornicating from Tashkent to Johannesburg" (xxiii).

Despite this bevy of experience, his initial forays into the literary world have been frustrated by the limitations, cultural in nature, of literary life itself: "I went to one of them downtown white workshops for a couple of months and got all screwed up. . . . I was uptight with the craft shit. Can you dig it? I decided to write my book in Afro-Americanese. Black rhythm, baby. Yeah, we got rhythm, brothers, sisters. Black idiom, Black nuances, Black style" (Killens xxiv). Lumumba's tangent suggests the assumptions on which his ideas are based. First, that white and black are more than mere racial designations; that they are also class and cultural affiliations essentially determining the way one writes, one's idiom, rhythm, style, and location within the city.

Hence the "white" creative writing workshops are situated "downtown," presumably in the middle of Manhattan, whereas Lumumba signs his fictional foreword, "BEN ALI LUMUMBA, *son of* Harlem, U.S.A." In place of the conventional academic jargon of the creative writing classroom, Lumumba pledges to write in a distinctly black manner: "Nevertheless and basically, this is a Black comedy. I mean a Black black comedy" (Killens xxiv). Thus, the ideological basis for the book is set down in the prelude that leads to it: that which is white is oppressive and out-of-date, while that which is black is enlivening and artistic. Lumumba's clarity of vision will allow for *The Cotillion*'s blistering satire against white and white-identified institutions.

Lumumba concludes his fictional foreword by informing the reader that the story will not be about him, but rather about a beautiful young woman named Yoruba. Yoruba is introduced on *his* book's first page (as opposed to Killens's book, which begins with Lumumba's framing foreword) and is quickly marked as the story's heroine: "Pure, beautiful, untampered-by-the-white-man, Yoruba. Black and princessly Yoruba, as if she'd just got off the boat from Yoruba-land" (Killens 1). Again, that which is good—"princessly," in this case—is explicitly identified as black and any trace of whiteness is denounced as impurity. To be "pure," by Lumumba's rhetorical logic, is to remain "untampered-by-the-white-man," unlike Yoruba-land.

The first chapter essentially functions as Yoruba's introduction to the reader; it even opens with a free-form introductory ode in quintessential BAM style: "Hey! / CALL HER YORUBA, RIGHT? / High Priestess of the Nation! You ready for that? / . . . Black and comely was this Harlem princess. / Yoruba, her father named her" (Killens 1). Actually, her full name, Yoruba Evelyn Lovejoy, is a compound of her father's and mother's wishes. Her father, Matthew Lovejoy, named her Yoruba, an indication of his "wondrously angry and terribly frustrated nationalism"; her mother added Evelyn, "like the woman made from Adam's ribs," Lumumba glosses, "and like Christmas Eve and the night before the New Year" (1). Her name foreshadows the principal question of the book, which is whether the girl will choose her father's (and Lumumba's) clenched militancy, to which she is partly heir, or her mother's colonial mentality.

Yoruba's mother, Lady Daphne Braithwaite Lovejoy, a black woman from Barbados, is the curiously zealous defender of all things British. She idealizes the United Kingdom and sees herself as a rightful inheritor of its glory, such as it is. "Daphne's father was a Scotchman," Lumumba informs, "with eleven Black concubines, one of whom was Daphne's lucky mother" (Killens 37–38). Instead of seeing him as a colonial rapist, as her militant husband (among others) would, Daphne thinks of Angus Braithwaite as "a gentleman for true" (39). Lumumba laments that Lady Daphne "lack[s] a sense of humor, which should have been her heritage as a colored woman" (113). While this disqualifies her as a character in a serious drama about black folk, it makes her a perfect vehicle for Lumumba's censure and, thus, Killens's satire. "Daphne was a slender woman, almost thin, who ate like seven lean years of drought and famine were just around the corner. And food was going swiftly out of style, decidedly. The dear one ate only one meal a day, continuously all day long" (39–40). Daphne's identification with white mores is cast here in physical terms: if whiteness is sterile, ineffectual, and lifeless, then its acolytes must be skinny, underfed, breathing corpses.

Her curious esteem for whiteness is reflected in her religious practice as well. "The nation," Daphne enthuses, "is working for an integrated society, and our church is a shiny example. The dear Vicar is giving up his entire career as a white man, just to give us an integrated experience" (36). Daphne advocates for the white vicar at her family's church. The vicar, she argues, is doing Harlem a service by integrating his whiteness into their hopelessly black milieu. That Daphne idealizes whiteness and despises blackness is obvious enough; more interesting are the desperate devices by which she tries to deal with the fact of her blackness and the fact of her daughter's blackness. She knows she lives in the Negro section of apartheid America, so she attempts to alter her given space with as many white conventions as possible. Lady Daphne's delusional elitism is so deep and her Anglophile tendencies so pronounced that she quickly establishes herself as the most one-dimensional character in the novel and thus the most susceptible to satire. She is, in fact, a perfect satirical vehicle. Her complete identification with the United Kingdom, with her scoundrel Scottish father, and with all things white make her an apt character for ridicule in a book advocating for Black Power, whether Killens's actual one or Lumumba's metafictional one.

In his definitional 1968 essay "The Black Arts Movement," Larry Neal writes that "Black Art is the aesthetic and spiritual sister of the Black Power concept" (29). Neal's essay, published in the same year as Killens's novel, provides the clearest articulation of the foundational philosophy of *The Cotillion's* satirical attack on the black bourgeoisie (as represented by Lady Daphne and the other members of Harlem's high black society). "The Black Arts Movement proposes a radical reordering of the Western cultural aesthetic. It proposes a separate symbolism, mythology, critique, and iconology," Neal states (29). Directly confronting Eurocentric bias, Neal asks, "Whose vision of the world is finally more meaningful, ours or the white oppressors'?" (30). Through the vehicle of satire, Killens quite clearly answers this question, lampooning those blacks who orient themselves toward a value system steeped in white supremacist ideology. In *The Cotillion*, all of Daphne's Eurocentric desires coalesce under the banner of the Grand Cotillion that she wants desperately for Yoruba to join. The Cotillion is the closest thing black America can offer Daphne to match her nostalgic memories of Barbados.

Another Harlem social climber, a Mr. Patterson, is equally status conscious but less disciplined than Daphne. As the socialites of Harlem coo over their church's sweetly ringing chimes on one pre-Cotillion morn, Mr. Patterson dissents: "Especially did he not appreciate those heavenly chimes at six o'clock of a Saturday morning when he had just gotten to bed at five a.m. and was in that land beyond the river known as Hangoverville" (Killens 68). Mr. Patterson's station and his carousing behavior do not seem to correspond. To borrow a line from later in the book that refers to a similar character, "He was of the high and Black society. He could not possibly be as uncouth as he obviously was" (221). Mr. Patterson cannot stand the church, the chimes, or religion in general. He dreams of recruiting the street gangs and "pay[ing] them to blow up the goddamn church, chimes and all." He finally "puts the ladder up against the church and starts up the ladder with his cocktails à la Molotov and a pocketful of matches. And a lighted cigar in his mouth. Sweating, cursing, stoned for days. . . . Halfway up the ladder, he is accosted by two policemen, friends of his, who bring him laughingly home . . . calling God and the Devil's choicest damnations down upon the church, the chimes, the police, people in general, Black folks in particular" (70). This sally into terrorism by one of the black community's leading men highlights many points of hypocrisy: first, the obvious charade that is his self-ordained status as a gentleman; second, the maintenance of that charade by his circles of "friends," in this case the policemen who will not reprimand his psychotic behavior; and third, the people in general and black folks particularly who let church chimes ring at all hours to paper over the obscene world with superficial gestures of piety.

The lampooning of Mr. Patterson is in line with the spiritual ideology of Black Arts. Neal notes that Black Arts scorns the "old" spirituality that ostensibly elevates a white supremacist version of Christianity. Whatever artistic form the scorn takes, though, the final attitude is preordained by the Black Arts ideology: "Where the Old Spirituality would live with oppression while ascribing to the oppressors an innate goodness, the New Spirituality demands a radical shift in point of view. The colonialized native, the oppressed, must, of necessity, subscribe to a separate morality. One that will liberate him and his people" (L. Neal 39). In this vein, black high society's real crime in *The Cotillion* is its denial of its rightful heritage as a segment within black America. "Implicit in the Black Arts Movement is the idea that Black people, however dispersed, constitute a *nation* within the belly of white America," Neal argues (39; emphasis in original). Unable to acknowledge their actual position, the black upper class becomes haughty, debased, and ultimately superfluous.

The Cotillion is in many ways simply a comedy of manners, bad manners. As Yoruba is initiated into the rites of propriety by the Cotillion supervisors, she notes that they prefer to refer euphemistically to their predecessors' "previous condition of servitude" (Killens 73). Her cosmetologist teaches her and the other girls "how to curtsey, how to sip their tea, and all the other white cultured graces. Likewise how to walk, again" (105). She is compelled to pick her date for the Cotillion ball from a prearranged list of deserving black lads from "superior family background, first family and all that, second-generation Brooklyn at the very least; doctor's, lawyer's, preacher's son . . . [who] must be suave, urbane, presentable, must have a good reputation, regardless of his character" (124). The efforts made at teaching the girls the "white cultured graces" are so many denials of the black culture with which the girls grew up and can consequently only unlearn. The insistence that Yoruba bring as her date to the Cotillion an heir of the black haute monde suggests that none but the most financially fortunate (and presumably the most assimilated) black boys have anything to offer her. Worse than simple elitism, these class prejudices display self-hatred on the part of the black upper class.

When Yoruba falls in love with Lumumba and determines to take him to the ball, Lady Daphne musters all her elitism and race hatred: "He's a wort'less black woolly-head nigger, and I should have got me a pistol and blowed his brains out when he was seven or eight years old the first time I saw him grinning in your face" (Killens 132). It is a statement that hardly needs parsing: Daphne is saying that she would love to exterminate all signs of blackness that threaten to contaminate her family. What she imagines herself and her daughter to be if they are not black is harder to define. Lumumba tells Yoruba that "the white establishment is one thing, your mother is a different establishment altogether" (183). The only "establishment" Lady Daphne represents is the self-hating black bourgeoisie. *The Cotillion* relentlessly satirizes the nonsensicality of this self-hate.

But if Lady Daphne is a paragon of the Negro's hateful, recalcitrant past, Lumumba represents a hopeful future for the race. In his essay "Towards a Black Aesthetic," Hoyt Fuller argues that blacks who would emphasize the similarities between themselves and whites are wasting their time sympathizing with a fundamentally hostile culture. Lumumba, by contrast, embodies all the clarity of vision and pride of purpose that a black man at the forefront of the culture should possess. Lumumba has come to understand his place in America and is acting upon that revelation. Fuller writes, "The world of the black outsider . . . by its very nature is inheritor and generator of values and viewpoints which threaten the insiders. The outsiders' world, feeding on its own sources, fecundates and vibrates, stamping its progeny with its very special ethos, its insuperably logical bias" (202). The presentation of Lumumba functions in precisely this manner.

At first, Lumumba seems to choose the mask of worldliness. He boasts—in the third person—not only of traveling the world, but also of having sex with women of all ethnic descriptions, spreading his seed far and wide: "In love passionately, entirely, all the way, to the Philippines and back, by way of Timbuktu. In love, oh my yes, and with no holds barred . . . from Hong Kong to Honolulu. All colors and denominations. He did not discriminate" (Killens 77). Lumumba is so infatuated with his persona as world traveler that he has even embarked upon writing a book called *From Harlem All the Way to Timbuktu*, a specimen of escapist literature. Escapism, in this context, refers to the avoidance of or inability to confront the pressing issues at hand. If Ben Ali follows this literary path, then he has simply traded on a false brand to further his own ends, and the judgment he levels at the various fake black militants that pass throughout the book would apply equally to him: "Thugs and hoodlums who had skimmed through a few books and memorized a few catch phrases, bought a few dashikis, put their do-rags in hiding for a season. . . . But they were not the Movement. Not even were they of the Movement. They had been pimps before and were still pimps" (61). This highlights the complete impasse that the moral logic of the book sets between those inside and those outside the Black Power Movement. Those who cannot or choose not to claim allegiance might as well have generated from an alien species, for they are not even "of the Movement." Eventually, Lumumba adopts pure black militancy, replacing false airs ("The cause was not hair or beard or dashiki" [156]) with a more substantive ideal: "'I'm just a cat who's trying to get his thing together. So when I do say something, it will have some small significance for Black People'" (159). What Lumumba ends up "saying" is, of course, not the escapist travelogue *From Harlem All the Way to Timbuktu*, but *The Cotillion*.

As Lumumba and Yoruba commit themselves to the Movement, the satire gains momentum because now the specific "targets" to be satirically undermined are unambiguous. They go to the downtown white Cotillion ball. Here, the "beaucoup ambivalent" nature of the "cream of the crap" is on full display (Killens 195, 190). Rich white kids get stoned and wild and unsuccessfully proposition both Yoruba and Lumumba. Sex of all descriptions is perpetrated on the dance floor, in the dining halls, in doorways, and in bathrooms. Lumumba happens in upon "a four-eyed rosy-cheeked dude who had been giving Yoruba and him such a bad time. . . . Apparently, he had forgotten his gender and had sat down to make water [and] had somehow managed to get his cutest little fellow caught between the toilet seat and the commode." He begs Lumumba for help, professes to be a member of "the CORE, Snickers [that is, members of SNCC, the Student Nonviolent Coordinating Committee], Panthers." But instead of heeding his pleas, Lumumba smashes the toilet seat on his penis, causing him to faint clean away. "Shouting 'Nigger! Nigger! Nigger!' Even after he lost consciousness, from deep in his unconscious, he kept mumbling 'Nigger! Nigger! Nigger!'" (197). His cravenly superficial attempts at political solidarity are belied by the fact that the white boy still continues screaming "Nigger!" after he is unconscious, further suggesting that even in their most innocent and unguarded moments, whites harbor hatred toward blacks. There is no common ground between the sides and conflict, even in the realm of the unconscious, is inevitable.

Although the novel ends with the hero and heroine dressed in African garb at the Harlem Cotillion, it is this scene in the bathroom that most ruthlessly brings home the message of the book. Ultimately, the novel is satirical, not simply polemical; its promotion of a pro-black ethos founded in politically radical and racially essentialist sensibilities does not exist in a vacuum but rather acquires its force from its absurdist dismantling of the black and white bourgeoisie alike. Indeed, *The Cotillion* has very conscious moral and ethical designs upon its readers. In both its negative satirical mode and its promotion of Black Power, it is as propagandistic as any pamphlet. It is, therefore, unlikely that such a book, grounded in a Black Power ideology as it is, would have been written in any previous or succeeding American generation. It is, instead, solely a novel *of* 1968 and the radical black ideology of that moment, a compelling testimony to the erstwhile currency of that ideology.

Johnson's *Hunting in Harlem* summons forth this late 1960s Black Power zeal only to dismiss it within the novel's opening pages. The father of one of the book's protagonists, Cedric Snowden, is described as "a man who wasted his life raising banners no one wanted to read, following his conscience wherever it led him—even though that was usually jail. . . . By his last release from a federal penitentiary twelve years later, the reception had been reduced to a bucket of drive-through chicken and Snowden's uncle in the front seat, saying, 'It's 1983 and nobody gives a damn about that shit no more, so just shut up and stop hogging all the white meat'" (6). The deterioration of Snowden's father and his small Philadelphia branch of the Black Power Movement is given as an example in microcosm of the criminality, apathy, and useless rhetoric that beset the Movement as a whole during the seventies and led to its complete demise. Snowden's father is reminiscent of such Black Panther militants as Huey Newton and David Hilliard who increasingly found themselves the object of criminal prosecution rather than the spokespersons for social progress. The dismissive comment by Snowden's uncle is only one way of saying that the Black Power Movement was a passing moment in history. This anecdote strikes an opening chord of pervasive disillusionment with the loud dogmas of the past. As a powerful example of this sense, Snowden kills his own father in a fit of disillusioned rage, though by that point "there really wasn't much left of the man that hadn't already died anyway" (6). Thus, *Hunting in Harlem*'s opening scene swiftly lowers the curtain on its archetypal Lumumba-like figure, triumphant not only in *The Cotillion* but in the ideology of the Black Power Movement.

It is instructive to note the difference between Killens's heroic race man, Ben Ali Lumumba, and Johnson's troubling update of that character type, Cyrus Marks. In *The Cotillion*, Harlem is more than a simple venue for the novel's action; it is a space implicitly deserving of what is actually quite an earnest contest of visions. On the one hand, there are the Lady Daphnes of Harlem, who are attempting to shape the iconic, predominantly black neighborhood as an imitation (specifically, a parody worthy of satirical scorn, from Killens's perspective) of white-dominated spaces. On the other, there are young radicals like Lumumba who seek to unleash the iconic neighborhood's transformative capacities, seeing it as a seminal space where black Americans can do their own thing and ultimately create a nation within a city that is all but detached from white-dominated downtown. The common thread uniting these otherwise contradictory visions is the recognition of Harlem as a space of symbolic significance, which is somewhat obscured by its blight and decay. This notion of Harlem as somehow special is undermined in the opening pages of *Hunting in Harlem*. "Harlem," the novel dryly reads, "was a ghetto . . . perhaps the most romanticized ghetto in the world" (M. Johnson 9). The popular idealization of Harlem as an African American Mecca is the reason why Cyrus Marks, the self-aggrandizing congressman and founder of Horizon Realty, chooses its squalid tenements for his urban renewal efforts. It is crucial to Marks's ultimate design that Harlem does not lose this romantic veneer.

To that end, he has hired a team of Philadelphia and Chicago ex-cons to do the manual labor required to rebuild the tenements, despite "the contradiction that there was no reason to import cheap labor to Harlem" (M. Johnson 57). This includes patricidal Snowden, as well as Bobby Finley and Horus Manley, who compete against each other throughout the book for a promotion within Horizon's ranks. Marks is a rabid proponent of his quasi-messianic vision of civic rebirth. "Harlem is more than a place," he proclaims, "it's a symbol. It's our Mecca, it's our Jerusalem, the historic cradle of our culture" (15). In Johnson, idealistic rhetoric is figured not as heroic, but rather as rabid: "'Harlem is ours!' Marks yelled, spittle shooting forward, tears dripping straight down" (15). Disdaining the poetical propaganda of those bygone days, Marks, Lester Baines, and the rest of Horizon Realty favor a plan of radical economic action; by converting Harlem's worst tenements into brownstones for the young and upwardly mobile, they feel that they are creating a practical economic foundation for the uplift of black Harlem. By replacing the old tenants dependent upon welfare with young black professionals, they feel they are maintaining the racial solidarity of the ghetto while at the same time bringing back that class of blacks who left for the suburbs and took with them their middle- and working-class values.

Unlike Killens's Black Power trio of Lumumba, Yoruba, and Matthew Lovejoy, Congressman Marks believes that white racism is essentially irrelevant to black success. Recent replicas of this simplistic and bombastic political type are not hard to find among the relatively few but voluble and often-televised black superconservatives. For example, the Reverend Jesse Lee Peterson, a minister based in South Central Los Angeles, argues that "most black Americans are suffering not because of racism but the lack of moral character" (Klavan). Casting his critical net beyond black America, 2012 Republican presidential candidate and former Godfather's Pizza CEO Herman Cain reacted to the Occupy Movement by stating that the unemployed and homeless should blame themselves for their inability to find reliable work and shelter (Cain). Even President Obama, whose views do not generally qualify as conservative when compared with America's center-right norm, has gotten in on the act from time to time. For instance, he concluded his 2011 address to the Congressional Black Caucus (CBC) with a bizarre exhortation that seems the pale sister to Peterson's and Cain's typically dismissive rhetoric: "Take off your bedroom slippers, put on your marching shoes. Shake it off. . . . Stop complaining, stop grumbling, stop crying. We are going to press on. We've got work to do, CBC" (Obama, "Remarks"). Such talking points by both conservative and ostensibly liberal public figures assert that black people are the sole cause of their own problems. Any grumbling, crying, or complaining about racism or structural inequities should be converted into self-flagellation and personal improvement.

In this vein, Johnson's character of Congressman Marks chides that "we were raised [in the 1960s] to fight white oppression, and guess what? We won! Not every battle, but that war is basically over, as we knew it. Nowadays, black folks' biggest problem isn't white racism, it's *ourselves*. White people aren't breaking into our homes, attacking us on the streets, or selling drugs to our children. . . . We need new blood, new ideas to fight new enemies. That's why you're here. This is your destiny. This is our last stand" (121; emphasis in original). That the "war" against white oppression has effectively been decided is the assumption upon which Marks bases his philosophy. Asserting this opinion as fact allows him the rhetorical leverage to claim that black people are their own worst enemies. Marks's rhetoric runs the risk of making a monolith out of a complex society. Even in Harlem, black people are not a community with a single destiny or problem to solve. Viewing Harlem as something more than the neighborhood it is allows Marks the rhetorical leverage to employ a romantic vocabulary of war and noble resistance.

According to Marks, blacks now have "new enemies." Thus it is that Marks and Lester Baines have devised a speedier solution to Harlem's woes than gentrification could ever bring: they are killing off the criminals and welfare cases to clear space for the incoming young professionals. In the final phase of their plan, they propose to unsubtly disappear the neighborhood drug czar in the following manner: "Shove a pound of C4 explosives against the adjoining living room wall, walk through the burning hole, and shoot everything living" (M. Johnson 231). From the first, Snowden suspects this brute method of neighborhood takeover when his work for Horizon Realty entails cleaning out the rooms of all the people who die in Harlem every week. A startling number of people seem to die from week to week. Confronted by Snowden with the evidence, Lester rationalizes the process with all the murderous nonchalance Jonathan Swift satirically attributes to the English gentry by immodestly proposing that the starving Irish solve their famine problems by devouring their young: "Social gardening," Lester terms Horizon's heinous program (118).

Indeed, it is this idea that killing the undesirables is a form of neighborhood beautification that allows the men the ideological leverage to carry out their program of socioeconomic cleansing. Marks tells Snowden that "almost all drastic social improvement is the result of moments of inhumanity. It was the staunch disregard for the humanity of blacks and Indians that made America the great nation it is today" (M. Johnson 121). Marks willingly takes on the mindset and the rhetoric of his historical oppressors and argues that it is now his duty to be similarly inhumane. The novel satirizes how radical ideology replaces ethical judgment with moral rhetoric. Marks claims to do good and therefore would have Snowden disregard the evidence of his eyes and believe what he is told. The evil that ideologies condone is the dominant theme of *Hunting in Harlem*. Whereas Killens portrays ideological commitment released from the slightest ambivalence as virtuous, ideology is analogous to insanity for Johnson. After he uncovers the entirety of the Horizon plot, Snowden thinks to himself, "They were all mad, the men of Horizon, even the best of them" (139). Johnson's critical satire of these black ideologues signals the intellectual progress out of the militancy of the late 1960s and into post-ideological space.

Trey Ellis's essay "The New Black Aesthetic" (1989) defined a cultural phenomenon integral to black intellectual and artistic space. Ellis and his peers constituted "a minority's minority mushrooming with the current black bourgeoisie boom—[that] have inherited an open-ended, New Black Aesthetic from a few Seventies pioneers that shamelessly borrows and reassembles across both race and class lines" (234). Defining this new mindset in dynamic, almost evolutionary relation to not only the "Seventies pioneers" of aesthetically hybridized black creative space but also to the socially segregated (and consequently artistically confined) artists of the 1960s and earlier, Ellis attempted to stake out unique intellectual territory for his young, black, and gifted generation. Coining the term "cultural mulatto" to describe his demographic, Ellis enthused over "young blacks getting back into jazz and the blues; the only ones you see at punk concerts; the ones in the bookstore . . . who admit liking both Jim and Toni Morrison" (234).

Hunting in Harlem is without the enthusiasms that propel "The New Black Aesthetic." Instead, what it shares with this cultural signpost is that it conveys the recognition that a sea change in sensibility has occurred. At the end of *Hunting in Harlem*, Olthiduis Cole dies and his son takes over Harlem's paper of record, the *New Holland Herald*. Lucretia Yates, a student from NYU, sends the younger Cole an employment application whose accompanying writing sample argues that "this [is] a less sentimental group, secure enough for the harshest of self-criticism. They [are] the first generation of black leaders not formed by the struggle against a hostile white world . . . more likely to be focused on their own world's internal dilemmas" (M. Johnson 282). Yates's thesis parallels Johnson's authorial position. The central conflicts in *Hunting in Harlem* have nothing to do with white people or white-controlled and white-identified institutions. It is an evolved Harlem satire taking as its target of ridicule not the hostile white and white-identified world, but black people in their own environs.

Johnson's satire is separated not only by thirty-five years but also by considerable ideological space from Killens's work. Whereas Killens is firm in his ideology, Johnson has none. *Hunting in Harlem* occupies negative ideological space. It disowns and savages not only the specific ideology of the Black Power Movement but also ideology itself as a means toward desirable ends. In its place is disillusionment; Snowden's disillusionment is parallel not to Killens's creations in *The Cotillion* but to the existential breaking-point in Ralph Ellison's *Invisible Man* when the narrator is left in a state beyond shock, at the mercy of total pain, his genitals skewered by Communism, white pseudo-philanthropy, and black demagoguery. The stark differences between the respective heroes in *Hunting in Harlem* and *The Cotillion* best illustrate the rejection of hope at the core of Johnson's novel. Ben Ali Lumumba is a hero through and through, and the narrative sentiment of *The Cotillion* rewards him with all the trappings that a traditional male hero enjoys: a beautiful girl, fine robes, and the attention of a vast readership (not to mention the amazed audience at the Cotillion ball). Yoruba, too, is granted the charms of the classic heroine. Both are exalted figures whose actions lead to the successful Africanization of Harlem's black Cotillion. They are beautiful in their Afros and dashikis.

By contrast, Snowden is the central man in *Hunting in Harlem* and he is a lost man, much like his namesake, a character in one of the foremost American satires of the twentieth century. In Joseph Heller's *Catch-22* (1961), the young soldier Snowden appears over and over in the memory of another character, but always in the same characteristic pose, lying prone and bleeding to death in the gunnery turret of a World War II fighter plane. Long incarcerated and incapacitated, Johnson's Snowden re-emerges into the world a beaten man looking for a handout. As the bodies pile up and the murderous plot of Cyrus and Lester becomes clearer to him, Snowden is repelled but does nothing. He has frequent recourse to alcohol and his closet. When Lester seeks him out for one of many covert assignments, Snowden prepares by trying to drink himself into a stupor: "In disbelief and defiance, Snowden swallowed another double of the same, determined to make himself useless if no alternative presented itself" (M. Johnson 179). Actually refusing to participate in the work would place him in willful opposition to Marks and Lester, and Snowden does not want that. While he is disgusted by the killings, he is even more disgusted by the possibility of his own death and will not do anything to hasten it. Caught between endorsing Horizon and rejecting it, he wanders, often drunkenly, through the space of the book. Snowden goes into seclusion in his apartment after witnessing the death of Piper Goines, a reporter investigating Horizon and his occasional lover: "At first Snowden's inaction was out of shock and hysteria, but after a couple of naps his motivation for immobility had evolved into resistance and passive aggression" (222). That he could come to view his inaction as a form of resistance is a radical reinterpretation of the methods of black resistance to injustice when contrasted with black militancy. Because he simply refuses to act, Snowden becomes the opposite of Ben Ali and Yoruba, an antihero. When he finally does determine to act, Snowden sides against heroic confrontation. He carries out Marks's grand plan by shooting the Harlem crack kingpin, Parson Boone. For this act, Snowden wins the informal competition between the three ex-cons and becomes Horizon's newest lead spokesman, in the process attaining a false sense of self-worth.

That an institution as indifferent to humanity as Horizon could become the focal point of a city and the source of a man's personal renaissance is the disturbing note on which *Hunting in Harlem* ends. Snowden, in the final analysis, becomes the antihero twice over, first for his refusal to act, then for his determination to act in the service of a cause he knows to be morally bankrupt. Before his metamorphosis into true believer, Snowden had observed that "A dream was a drug. In a world without meaning, belief was an aphrodisiac" (M. Johnson 86), which essentially is the book's ethical thesis. Mat Johnson's severe criticism of inner-city renewal efforts warns that zealous belief is always ill-fated. In a world without final truths, the only real virtue is honesty, which comes with harsh consequences; conversely, lies founded in moribund ideology sustain those who live by them.

Between John Killens's outraged and ideologically committed satire and the disillusionment and despair of Mat Johnson's novel is a thirty-five-year movement from Black Power to intellectual severity and detachment. In many ways, I strongly favor a work like Johnson's, which forgoes the (too-) easy truths of ideological certainty. On the other hand, I sympathize with the Black Arts critic Ernest Kaiser, who once wrote that politically uncommitted writing is a cop-out in an exploiting, murdering, dying capitalist nation (88). *The Cotillion* is a book that mobilizes ideologically inspired satire in the fight against two of America's deepest cancers, elitism and white supremacy. The disconnect between Killens and Johnson is finally indicative of the tragic predicament by which a marginalized people is forced to choose between truth and power.

How a Mama on the Couch Evolves into a Black Man with Watermelon: George C. Wolfe, Suzan-Lori Parks, and the Theatre of "Colored Contradictions"

Jennifer Larson

Oren Jacoby's 2002 film *The Topdog Diaries: An Intimate Portrait of Suzan-Lori Parks* chronicles the journey of Parks's Pulitzer Prize–winning play, *Topdog/Underdog* (2001), from idea to Broadway. George C. Wolfe appears in this documentary as a kind of mentor to Parks, first as she attempts to find a stage home for the play and then later as she prepares for its off-Broadway debut at the Joseph Papp Public Theater under Wolfe's direction. As actors Don Cheadle and Jeffery Wright read through Parks's initial script, Wolfe tells Parks what works and suggests where to further develop her ideas.

This collaboration between Parks and Wolfe, though, did not begin with *Topdog/Underdog*. On a practical level, Wolfe served as the artistic director at the Public Theatre when Parks's *The America Play* appeared there in 1994. In a more abstract sense, though, Wolfe's influence on Parks shows throughout her oeuvre. Specifically, echoes of the artistic and social goals of Wolfe's groundbreaking satirical production *The Colored Museum* (1986) appear in many of Parks's major works, most obviously *The Death of the Last Black Man in the Whole Entire World* (1990), but also in *Imperceptible Mutabilities in the Third Kingdom* (1989), *The America Play* (1994), *Venus* (1996), and *Getting Mother's Body* (2003).

In a 1993 interview with *Callaloo* editor Charles Rowell, Wolfe details the criticism he received, especially from "the guardians of black culture" (read: black intellectuals and artists) for what they perceived as *The Colored Museum*'s ruthless attacks on black culture and expression (Rowell 616–617). He explains, "If you come along and you don't speak with a reverential tone, then you are a renegade or you've surrendered to white culture or you've sold out. Or if the white people get you then that really means you've sinned" (617). Wolfe maintains in this interview and others that he meant the play to be a call to all audiences and writers, black and white, to not define black people solely by their reactions to white oppression.

Parks's plays, and especially the satirical elements therein, reflect *The Colored Museum*'s values because they remind audiences to pay special attention to the "bones" of the ancestors (in other words, their literary, cultural, and historical legacies), providing an aesthetic perspective that both honors and challenges black history and black culture.[1] Parks, however, does not simply respond to Wolfe's call; she also issues a call of her own to audiences and to dramatists, a call to not only reexamine but also to reform potentially imprisoning paradigms of race, language, and patriarchy.

Both Wolfe's ideas and Parks's response to them align the playwrights with the values of the post-soul movement and the New Black Aesthetic. In his definitive 1989 essay, Trey Ellis explains that the writers of the New Black Aesthetic "are creating [their] own definitions of blackness no matter how loudly either white or black people might complain" ("New Black Aesthetic" 241). Ellis names Wolfe as part of a group of artists who "aren't flinching before they lift the hood on our collective psyches now that they have liberated themselves from both white envy and self-hate" (238). Similarly, in his introduction to *African American Review*'s 2007 special issue on the post-soul movement, Bertram D. Ashe asserts, "Central to the post-soul aesthetic is the idea that no one—no white establishment, no black identity police, and, certainly, no peer pressure—can limit the imagination of the black artist" ("Theorizing" 612). As a writer of the post-soul movement, Wolfe uses his work to reclaim and reopen the literary and cultural past as well as to show that even the most revolutionary artistic models have flaws to satirize. Parks furthers this work with her ever-challenging and ever-evolving narratives as well as with her focus on developing a dramatic aesthetic committed to artistic freedom.

The Colored Museum presents a series of acts, or "exhibits," featuring characters that channel specifics tropes, themes, and even stereotypes from African American literature and culture. These characters include a slave ship airline stewardess, an insane soldier, a transvestite, talking hairpieces, a man and his angry former self, a diva, and a girl who laid an egg. All offer biting satiric commentary on the cultures they represent or in which they participate, but all remain metatheatrically aware of their own participation in the drama as they question the audience, criticize each other, and even comment on theatre's paradoxes. According to Brandi Wilkins Catanese, "the juxtaposition of exhibits, whose placement puts them in dialogue with one another, responds simultaneously to the divisions within the black community (over issues such as class, sexuality, politics, and standards of beauty)" (18). Wolfe's play uses the confrontation Catanese describes to explore history, theatre, and the ways in which theatre has defined and shaped African American identity's relationship to history. Wolfe believes that *The Colored Museum* unsettled its African American critics because it "dared to self-examine"; he adds, "And to use humor to do it? Horror, horror" (Rowell 617).

Based on both *The Colored Museum*'s content and on Wolfe's comments in interviews, though, Marc Silverstein asserts that "Wolfe has no interest in creating a new paradigm for black plays or colored museums, but in exploring and critiquing how the representational practices and ideological operations of the theatre and the museum have systematically alienated African-Americans from a viable engagement with their history—a history, as Wolfe's character Topsy asserts, consisting of 'colored contradictions' that demand acknowledgement as a prerequisite for empowerment" (96). Wolfe resists artistic definitions and mandates, especially those that prescribe a singular approach to understanding identity or reading history. Wolfe himself explains, "I wrote [*The Colored Museum*] so that I could write any other play that I wanted. The power of American culture, of black American culture exists not in its purity but in its contradictions.... We try to come up with all these absolute definitions and we are a mutt culture and we are mutt people just like everyone else in America, and our power is in our mutt behavior" (Rowell 619–620). In other words, Wolfe calls his audiences to awareness of the power and persistence of theatre's racialized past as well as awareness of the power that comes from both claiming and rejecting that past.[2]

Many of the elements that sharpen Wolfe's satire are also nearly ubiquitous in Parks's plays. Among these are metaperformative nods (discussions about theatre or plays within the plays), disruptions of the page / stage dichotomy (including footnotes and significant action / narration within stage directions), and audience indictment (through the breakdown of the "fourth wall" or through criticism of the actual or figurative theatregoer / spectator). Like Wolfe, Parks also rejects the notion of a drama defined by its relationship to whiteness or to oppression in general. In her essay "An Equation for Black People on Stage" (1994), she writes that "there are many ways of defining blackness, and there are many ways of presenting Blackness onstage. The Klan does not always have to be outside the door for Black people to have lives worthy of dramatic literature" (19). Both Wolfe and Parks use satire to show just how much audiences—white and black—have relied on the proximity of "the Klan" (that is, the threat of white oppression) to create "drama."

While Wolfe, as Silverstein asserts, may not be trying to establish "a new paradigm," Parks's plays and essays suggest that she does, in fact, want to create a new paradigm for black theatre, a paradigm that embodies the very contradictions it seeks to represent. In "New black math" (2005), Parks returns to "the same crossroads asking the same questions" she engaged in her earlier essay "An Equation for Black People Onstage" ("New black math," 576). Motivated by August Wilson's illness and the disaster of Hurricane Katrina, Parks revisits the question: "what is a black play?" She writes, "what Im talking about today is the same and different. I was tidy back then. And now Im tidier. Tidier like a tidal wave" (576).[3] Parks then goes on to present a series of definitions for "a black play," many of which are as humorous and paradoxical as her introduction. Among the most intriguing are: "A black play is on broadway, the great white way. / A black play is not on broadway, and furthermore, aint studying no broadway" (577); "A black play wants to uplift the race. / A black play just might set the race back 10 years. / A black play is not political—that term don't even begin to approach its complexity, especially these days, dog" (578); and finally, "A black play is simple / A black play is COMPLICATED" (583). The last lines of "New black math" read simply: "A black play is free. / PEACE / and / POWER / To the PEOPLE" (583). Thus, Parks's new paradigm seems to advocate for the absence of paradigms. A black play can be whatever it wants to be, or whatever it doesn't want to be. The one line that repeats in Parks's manifesto—"A black play fights the power"—suggests, though, that a black play must have an agenda, and it must be an underdog (578, 582). The play need not be political or subscribe to a specific artistic / cultural mandate, but it has "got a mission," even if that mission is to reject the idea of missions (578). Such a paradigm may seem contradictory, but Parks's series of paradoxes in "New black math" suggests that even the total or partial rejection of an agenda is an agenda in itself. As in Wolfe's play, these contradictions underscore Parks's satirical goals by demonstrating how a playwright can be simultaneously reverent and irreverent and still contribute to black culture and black art while questioning— or even rejecting—its values.

Such a paradigm of inclusivity recalls Parks's closing lines in "An Equation for Black People Onstage." Here, Parks explains of her own work, "I write plays because I love Black people. As there is no single 'Black Experience,' there is no single 'Black Aesthetic' and there is no one way to write or think or feel or dream or interpret or be interpreted. As African-Americans we should recognize this insidious essentialism for what it is: a fucked up trap to reduce us to only one way of being. We should endeavor to show the world and ourselves our beautiful and powerful infinite variety" (21–22). The liberating mission of black drama in Parks's paradigm, then, is to reject "insidious essentialism" and not only to embrace but also to demonstrate the beauty and power of "infinite variety" in black theatre, be that in the form of "colored contradictions" or something altogether new.

Parks's mission also links her explicitly to the post-soul movement. Ashe explains that, in this movement, "artists and texts trouble blackness, they worry blackness; they stir it up, touch it, feel it, and hold it up for examination in ways that depart significantly from previous—and necessary—preoccupations with struggling for political freedom, or with an attempt to establish and sustain a coherent black identity," but "this 'troubling' of blackness by post-soul writers is ultimately done in service of black people" ("Theorizing" 614). Parks "troubles"—often through satire—her literary and cultural ancestors, but she does so "in service" of her mission to create a new, more liberating paradigm for black art in general and black theatre specifically.

Connections between the satirical moves in one of *The Colored Museum*'s most oft-referenced and enigmatic exhibits, "The Last Mama-on-the-Couch Play," and in Parks's *The Death of the Last Black Man in the Whole Entire World* show the extent of Parks's and Wolfe's artistic relationship. Specifically, these connections demonstrate how Parks pays homage to Wolfe and his aesthetic while also suggesting a need for a still stronger, more paradigmatic focus on theatrical inclusivity.

In "The Last Mama-on-the-Couch Play," Wolfe directly satirizes Lorraine Hansberry's *Raisin in the Sun* (1969) and Ntozake Shange's *For Colored Girls who Have Considered Suicide When the Rainbow is Enuf* (1975), criticizing both plays' visions of gender, poverty, family, and the influence of race on each of these elements. Wolfe's oversized MAMA's exaggerated physical and emotional dominance make her a sharp parody of Hansberry's powerful Mama Lena Younger. Her son, WALTER-LEE-BEAU-WILLIE-JONES, a conglomeration of *Raisin in the Sun*'s emasculated Walter Lee Younger and *For Colored Girls*'s infanticidal Beau Willy Brown, is married to the anti-Shange LADY IN PLAID. These characterizations suggest that the black women writers who came before Wolfe portrayed black mothers and sons as helpless and/or witless, destined to be victims of their circumstances.

In *The Death of the Last Black Man in the Whole Entire World*, Parks takes aim at a number of minstrel caricatures with her "figures" (as she calls the folks on her *Dramatis Personae*), who include BLACK MAN WITH WATERMELON and BLACK WOMAN WITH FRIED DRUMSTICK. BLACK MAN WITH WATERMELON is repeatedly killed and resurrected over the course of the play while the chorus tries to explain the significance of this cycle. This chorus features biblical parody HAM and literary parody AND BIGGER AND BIGGER AND BIGGER.

Even the implied finality of these dramas—this is the *Last* mama-on-the-couch play and *Last* black man in the whole entire world—links their satirical agendas through the common use of sarcastic exaggeration. *The Colored Museum* suggests that mama-on-the-couch plays are not only too comfortable and too popular with both white and black audiences and critics to go away, but that they are also just another incarnation of a problematic performative lineage that extends back to blackface minstrelsy.

The police shoot WALTER-LEE-BEAU-WILLIE for "overacting" (Wolfe 29), but he later rises from the dead "and joins in the dancing. A foot-stomping, hand clapping production number takes off, which encompasses a myriad of black-Broadwayesque dancing styles—shifting speeds and styles with exuberant abandonment" (32). Then, "they continue to dance with zombie-like frozen smiles and faces" and "around them images of coon performers flash as the lights slowly fade" (32). In this de-evolution from the Broadway chorus line to the minstrel shuffle, *The Colored Museum* links contemporary black characters to blackface parodies of African American identity and thus denounces the performers and playwrights who mindlessly subscribe to the cultural and artistic conventions that created both models. Just as the play resurrects WALTER-LEE-BEAU-WILLIE, mama-on-the-couch plays will continually be resurrected to perform and perpetuate racialized stereotypes.

The Death of the Last Black Man in the Whole Entire World follows a similar death-resurrection pattern. Near the beginning of the play, BLACK WOMAN WITH FRIED DRUMSTICK explains, "Yesterday today next summer tomorrow just uh moment uhgoh in 1317 dieded thuh last black man in thuh whole entire world" (Parks 102). Another character, VOICE ON THUH TEE V, later announces, "Good evening. I'm Broad Caster. Headlining tonight: the news: is Gamble Major, the absolutely last living Negro man in the whole entire known world—is dead. Major, Gamble, born a slave, taught himself the rudiments of education to become a spearhead in the Civil Rights Movement. He was 38 years old. News of Majors [*sic*] death sparked displays of controlled jubilation in all corners of the world" (110). These anachronistic declarations, combined with the constant killing and reanimation of the play's protagonist, BLACK MAN WITH WATERMELON, suggest that even if there were a last black man, his ritualistic deaths—and the associated white desire to kill him violently—would live eternally.

With their ironic assertions of finality, both plays' titles also point to the complex intersections of history and theatre. For Wolfe, these intersections are revealed through humorous metadrama. The characters in "The Last Mama-on-the-Couch play" consistently reflect on their participation in the exploitive theatre. MAMA, THE LADY IN PLAID, and the sister MEDEA accept "awards"—faux Tonys or Oscars—after particularly melodramatic monologues. Frustrated WALTER-LEE-BEAU-WILLIE shouts, "This is my play. It's about me and the Man" (Wolfe 28), and THE VOICE OF THE MAN emerges to say, "Walter-Lee-Beau-Willie, this is the Man. You have been convicted of overacting. Come out with your hands up" (29). Once WALTER-LEE-BEAU-WILLIE is shot, MAMA reflects, "If only he had been born into a world better than this. A world where there are no well-worn couches and no well-worn Mamas and nobody over emotes. / If only he had been born into an all-black musical / Nobody ever dies in an all-black musical," and the women pull out church fans and begin "singing a soul-stirring gospel" (29).

This relapse into stereotypical theatrical and liturgical performance suggests that audiences and critics—likely predominantly white, but certainly black as well—have rewarded only those black plays that fit within their narrow expectations for representations of black life and black history. The scene shows WALTER-LEE-BEAU-WILLIE's total emasculation by dominant, successful black women as well as by "the man," a militarized, faceless (and, therefore, colorless) über-masculine power. The dress that MAMA wears matches her drapes and couch, suggesting the extent to which her environment and her role in past and enduring constructions of domesticity define her. Harry J. Elam explains, "The couch and Mama's dress are constructed of the same 'well-worn' fabric. Together they symbolize the outmoded but recurrent themes of African-American drama. Just as this large unwieldy couch, situated center stage, inhibits the possibility for inventive staging, the recurrent Mama on the couch realism impedes the creative experimentation of African American theatre" (300). The couch and WALTER-LEE-BEAU-WILLIE's tragicomic death both represent a stasis in black drama and black life. Wolfe exaggerates these themes and makes them absurd to show that rather than the "searing domestic drama" it claims to be, a mama-on-the-couch play is nothing more than an updated minstrel show.

In *The Death of the Last Black Man in the Whole Entire World*, Parks expands Wolfe's focus on the relationship between drama and history. Whereas Wolfe relies primarily on narrative as the vehicle for his satire, Parks looks to the structures and abstract significations of language. In "from Elements of Style" (1994) she explains, "My interest in the history of words—where they came from, where they're going—has a direct impact on my playwriting because, for me, Language is a physical act. It's something which involves your entire body—not just your head" (11). This emphasis on the physical recurs in the same essay's definition of humor: "Playwrights can come from the most difficult circumstances, but having a sense of humor is what happens when you 'get out of the way.' It's sorta Zen. Laughter is very powerful—it's not a way of escaping anything but a way of arriving on the scene. Think about laughter and what happens to your body—it's almost the same thing that happens to you when you throw up (15). Even Parks's attempts to classify black drama in "New black math" rely on humorous wordplay to express their intricacies. Not only does Parks's intention in this essay stem from being "tidier . . . like a tidal wave" (576), but she later posits, "A black play knows that racerelations sell. / A black play knows that racerelations are a holding cell" (580). The tidy / tide and cell / sell "puns," as Philip Kolin has labeled them,[4] call attention to the words' root meanings and histories while also pushing the reader to consider the connections between the ideas that the sound of the language has linked. To borrow a metaphor from the slave ship airline stewardess MISS PAT in *The Colored Museum's* first exhibit, "Git on board," the English language by nature comes laden with historical "baggage" needing to be "claimed" (Wolfe 5).

In her *Laughing Fit to Kill: Black Humor in the Fictions of Slavery* (2008), Glenda Carpio argues that Parks "has developed a number of formal strategies to remember aspects of a painful past, including a combined use of the aesthetics of conjure and postmodernism as well as nuanced and abstract use of the features of minstrelsy. Most important, Parks also experiments with language to produce a kind of humor that is sometimes derived from simple wordplay, as in punning, but that more often becomes a part of the larger process of signifyin(g)" (192). Responding to Kim Euell's suggestion that signifyin(g) playwrights such as Wolfe are evoking minstrel traditions in order to "ask the audience to participate in the ritual of adjudication, either actively or as witness" (Euell 668), Carpio suggests that Parks moves beyond this model because she "neither replicates the features of minstrelsy, nor does she create rituals of adjudication" (Carpio 206). Rather, "Parks creates comedy by inverting, juxtaposing, and otherwise de-familiarizing the features of minstrelsy," particularly through language (206).

One of the most stunning examples of Parks's satirical use of minstrel language to reflect on the historical and the dramatic in *The Death of the Last Black Man in the Whole Entire World* occurs in the section titled "Ham's Begotten Tree" (121). This biblical parody begins, "NOW: She goned begotten One who in turn begotten Ours. Ours laughed one day uhloud in from tuh sound hittin thuh air smakity sprung up I, you, n He, She, It" (121). It then proceeds to give an intricate lineage involving incest, miscegenation, and "odoriferous bodily emissions" to arrive at the final assertion: "Mines joined with Wasshisname and from that union come AllYall" (122). The characters in this section are a complete abstraction; they do not directly name or symbolize any specific players. Ham's "Begotten Tree" thus not only signifies on the biblical form; it also reduces its subjects to labels not unlike those in the rest of the play and in Wolfe's "Last Mama-on-the-Couch Play."

According to Carpio, "the laughter that Ham's speech incites affirms life through irony: it satirizes the corruption of an ideal, the integrity of personhood, and it recognizes the repeated loss of kinship" (214). In sum, it's a blues utterance; laughing to keep from crying, HAM remembers the past and reclaims it through the unexpected power and complexity of satire and irony. The play links the parody to the literary and dramatic traditions through call and response—characters interject variations of "Thuh list goes on in on" or "Shame on his family"—as well as through the character YES AND GREENS BLACK-EYED PEAS CORNBREAD's call to "write *that* down" (Parks, "Death" 122; emphasis in original).

Parks's satire is also distinct from Wolfe's because while both take aim at well-worn narratives and even revered texts—Shange's and Hansberry's plays in *The Colored Museum* and the Bible and *Native Son* (1940) in *The Death of the Last Black Man in the Whole Entire World* —in Parks's plays, audiences do not need to know all of the backstory behind a name or character to understand the satire. The message is humorous because of the language that presents it, not necessarily because of (and certainly not only because of) the narrative on which it signifies; therefore, this message, and the play that delivers it, accomplish Parks's mission of dramatic inclusivity: her plays are "come as you are," with no previous knowledge of black theatre required. In contrast, Elam notes that because of *The Colored Museum*'s "references to specific texts, the success of this parody depends not only on Wolfe's familiarity with the musical and classic African-American drama, but on the spectator's knowledge of them as well" such that "the effectiveness of this exhibit depends on the spectators' awareness of African-American theatre" (301). Audiences need to have read *A Raisin in the Sun* and *For Colored Girls* to fully understand Wolfe's message about those plays.

In fact, the seemingly ungrateful use of Hansberry's and Shange's works—works that are among the most beloved in American literature—in "The Last Mama-on-the Couch Play" draws the most criticism for Wolfe. Even Elam, who otherwise applauds Wolfe's goals in *The Colored Museum*, notes that when it comes to women, Wolfe "contradicts his own ideals" (302), for his "sexist attacks on black female writers . . . dissipate his message of cultural diversity and inclusion" (301). Other critics, meanwhile, try to exonerate Wolfe. Silverstein, for example, argues that Wolfe's parody does not actually target Hansberry's or Shange's works, but "the social use to which they are put" (112).

"The Last Mama-on-the Couch Play," however, is not the only exhibit in *The Colored Museum* with a questionable relationship to gender. Wolfe's MISS ROJ, the transvestite protagonist of "The Gospel According to Miss Roj," generally "assails the limitations of heterosexual orthodoxy"

(Elam 302); yet the play does not allow her the feminine identity that she chooses for herself. Throughout the exhibit, Miss Roj refers to herself in the third-person feminine. In one such moment, she says, "So come on and dance with Miss Roj and her demons. We don't ask for acceptance" (Wolfe 17). Yet when the stage directions speak of Miss Roj, they always use the masculine pronoun, suggesting a privileging of masculine identity even for a character that actively seeks to reject that identity. Such a privileging underscores Elam's assertion that *The Colored Museum*'s "negative refiguring parody of black female playwrights does not foreground their place within the matrix of African-American cultural diversity, but instead affirms the dominant and conventional patriarchal hegemony" (302). The play may allow Miss Roj to perform femininity, but it does not accept her rejection of the masculine in order to "foreground" the feminine in her self-definition. She does not "ask for acceptance," and the play doesn't offer it.

Satire as a mode in general, though, often raises gender questions. In her introduction to *African American Humor, Irony, and Satire* (2007), Dana A. Williams notes the dominance of male-authored texts examined in the collection and suggests that this dominance "simply reminds of the work that is yet to be done on women who work in the traditions of humor, irony, and satire" (3). Also, in his introduction to *African American Satire: The Sacredly Profane Novel* (2001), Daryl Dickson-Carr points out that "certain types of sexism have dogged satirists and besmirched their reputations almost as frequently as their general iconoclasm" (3).

Parks's works, however, respond to these questions by evoking past and present literary icons of both genders. Such conjuring is nearly omnipresent in Parks's texts (plays and prose), and the influence of black female writers such as Shange and Adrienne Kennedy on Parks's aesthetic has been well documented.[5] Yet while Parks's works may use humor to signify on these icons, they do not mock them. With an eye toward a paradigm of expanded inclusivity, her "revisions do not seem to advocate that we wholly dismiss these earlier representations. Rather, her new version of the story suggests that we see these works again with more modern, more critical eyes—eyes that see beyond the surface of the work to the contexts that inform its creation" (Larson 3).

Instead of "negative refiguring," the roots of Parks's satire trace back to her unique Rep & Rev, or repetition and revision, a signifyin(g) move in which she is "working to create a dramatic text that departs from the traditional linear narrative style to look and sound more like a musical score"; through this process, she explains in "from Elements of Style," Parks is "asking how the structure of Rep & Rev and the stories inherent in it—a structure which creates a drama of accumulation—can be accommodated under the rubric of Dramatic Literature" (Parks, "from Elements" 9).

In Parks's *The Death of the Last Black Man in the Whole Entire World*, the character of AND BIGGER AND BIGGER AND BIGGER stands out as signature Rep & Rev. AND BIGGER AND BIGGER AND BIGGER, a humorous nod to the embattled Bigger Thomas of Richard Wright's *Native Son*, not only clearly identifies with BLACK MAN WITH WATERMELON, as many of his lines speak of being bound and asking for freedom; he also reflects on his plight as a misused literary figure. He laments, "Rise up of uh made-up story in grown Bigger and Bigger. Too big for my own name. Nostrils: flarin. Width: thickly. Breath: fire-laden and smellin' badly" (115), and declares, "I would like tuh be fit in back in the storybook from which I camed" (116).

This satirical representation of Bigger Thomas does not criticize Wright's character but, rather, examines this character's legacy. Carpio explains that although AND BIGGER AND BIGGER AND BIGGER "is the strongest voice of anger in the play, he is not violent. LIKE BLACK MAN WITH WATERMELON, he is stuck, unable to move his hands. His name thus also implies that the frustrations of being bound grow bigger and bigger with the generations, often exploding into violence, as in Wright's novel" (209). AND BIGGER AND BIGGER AND BIGGER, like WALTER-LEE-BEAU-WILLY, wants freedom. However, AND BIGGER AND BIGGER AND BIGGER does not to want to escape from Wright's text; he wants to escape from the narrow, racist vision of vengeful black masculine identity that created him and perpetuated the stereotype that his character came to embody.

The Death of the Last Black Man in the Whole Entire World also privileges the feminine by making BLACK WOMAN WITH DRUMSTICK a hero of the play. She is the survivor, and she voices many of the play's most critical messages, including the first explanation of the play's title (Parks 102) and its final call to action: "Re-member me. Call on me sometime. Call on me sometime. Hear? Hear?" (131). She comforts BLACK MAN WITH WATERMELON and helps him makes sense of his trauma; she's also genuinely witty, showing the audience a humor based not in minstrel-like imitation, but rather in the creative shaping of language. At the beginning of the play, for example, she caps even the darkest commentaries on BLACK MAN WITH WATERMELON's repeated death with offers of food, specifically "hen" or "hen leg" (109), and later, when she banters with her husband about how to deal with the tree branch stuck in his collar from being lynched, she says with a twist of irony and creative wordplay, "Your days work aint like any others day work: you bring your tree branch home. Let me loosen the tie let me loosen thuh neck-lace let me loosen up thuh noose that stringed him up let me leave thuh tree branch be" (118).

Thus, in *The Death of the Last Black Man in the Whole Entire World*, Parks is able to build on Wolfe's satirical work in *The Colored Museum* while also advocating for a new dramatic paradigm, a paradigm with a mission of inclusivity that privileges language and that honors women's roles in the tradition. As such, Parks extends an aesthetic trajectory that Elam asserts begins with Adrienne Kennedy's *Funnyhouse of a Negro* (1964): "Kennedy asks the audience to appreciate the complex and contradictory nature of black identity, while Wolfe asks African Americans not only to recognize the contradictions but embrace them" (298). In turn, Parks asks audiences to not only embrace the contradictions, but to live them and re-sing them in order to create a more vibrant theatre, a theater in which there is space for all of black life—past, present, and future—and all of the contradictions therein.

Notes

1. In her essay "Possession," Parks writes, "Since history is a recorded or remembered event, theatre, for me, is the perfect place to 'make' history—that is, because so much of African American history has been unrecorded, disremembered, washed out, one of my tasks as a playwright is to—through literature and the special strange relationship between theatre and real-life—locate the ancestral burial ground, dig for bones, find bones, hear the bones sing, write it down" (4).

2. Wolfe's "mutt culture" and its "colored contradictions" resonate with Ellis's description of the "mulatto culture" that shaped the development of the New Black Aesthetic. Ellis writes, "Just as a generic mulatto is a black person of mixed parents who can often get along fine with his white parents, a cultural mulatto, educated by a multi-racial mix of cultures, can also navigate easily in the white world" ("New Black Aesthetic" 235). The idea that "post-soul artists often grapple with the 'cultural mulatto' archetype" is also the first point in Ashe's definitive "triangular post-soul matrix" (613).

3. The formatting in these quotations is indicative of Parks's unorthodox typographical choices and linguistic experimentation. She often omits punctuation and/or capitalization, runs words together, and uses phonetic spellings to emphasize how her aesthetic interrogates the relationship between the signifier and the signified.

4. Kolin writes at length about Parks's use of such puns in her earlier play, *Imperceptible Mutabilities in the Third Kingdom*. He explains, "Parks's puns are subversive, explosive. . . . But her puns—her language—do more than upset syntax and semantics. They shake up language, memories/identities, as well as the human anatomy" (48).

5. Deborah R. Geis, for example, explains that "while Kennedy's work inspired Parks's fragmentation of characters and diminishment of plot in favor of repeated unfolding stories, Shange influenced her freedom with language, specifically the freedom to rebel against white, Western standardizations of English. In both playwrights, language is deeply connected to the speaking characters bodied forth on stage; the unconventional look of the text reflects a need to find an Africanist-feminist way of speaking" (9).

"Slaves? With Lines?": Trickster Aesthetic and Satirical Strategies in Two Plays by Lynn Nottage

Aimee Zygmonski

Trickster figures operate in stories and folklore from many cultural groups across the world: Chinese folktales tell of the Monkey King, southwestern Native American tribes have Coyote, the Inuit retain the Raven, and Yoruba myths invoke Eshu and Anansi. In each of these cultures, the trickster operates in various ways, translating messages from the gods to mortals, though sometimes the significance may be skewed, veiled, or coded. Tricksters wander, roaming either across lands or between worlds, and their unresolved hunger propels their journeys. Due to this constant instability, tricksters straddle the boundaries between one world and another in a liminal existence, always at the threshold of something new, keeping one eye focused on the past while looking straight into the future. Tricksters outwit, outsmart, and outtalk any foe, always one step ahead. Jeanne Rosier Smith notes in *Writing Tricksters: Mythic Gambols in American Ethnic Literature* (1997) that a "trickster's medium is words. A parodist, joker, liar, con-artist, and storyteller, the trickster fabricates believable illusions with words—and thus becomes author and embodiment of a fluid, flexible, and politically radical narrative form" (11).

Satire also employs the trickster's tool of a coded message. Relying upon the traits of destabilization, illusion, and manipulation of words to create a desired effect, satirical writing delivers an inherent social or political critique, often couched within absurd humor or fantastical tales. African American satire in particular uses the trickster figure to critique cultural and social norms, with folktales or folk culture serving as a basis for the satire. Depending on the situation (or the time period in which a particular trickster figure was created), the trickster's persona can vary from selfish to selfless, and "she or he consistently reifies the potential for the witty and idealistic to effect an alteration of material conditions" (Dickson-Carr 35).

In this essay, I argue that Lynn Nottage—a contemporary African American female playwright, Pulitzer Prize winner, and MacArthur "genius grant" recipient—utilizes the trickster figure and the satirical technique of polyvocality to destabilize well-known African American stereotypes in her plays *Fabulation* (2004) and *By the Way, Meet Vera Stark* (2011). Both plays feature a main character imbued with trickster characteristics, but also Nottage's satirical voice. Both scripts question how black stereotypes such as the happy slave, the dutiful maid, the welfare queen, and the bourgeois negro impart their insidious traits in the construction of identity. Playing the trickster herself, Nottage strategically provides a metacommentary on her own plays, using elements of satire not only to provoke the audience, but also to urge the audience toward deeper inquiry. Through these multi-layered, multivoiced texts, Nottage as trickster questions identity construction; the effects of derogatory stereotypes on a culture; and, ultimately, how harnessing and redirecting the power of a stereotype may actually hinder its continuation.

Fabulation develops within a complex satirical mode in order to complicate African American stereotypes via a traditional folk-story framework. Nottage's modern-day trickster tale challenges the boundaries of traditional theatrical discourse by offering a twenty-first-century take on the trickster figure. *Fabulation* actually begins at the end of the story, and as the play progresses, it hurtles toward the beginning. Within the first scene of the play, main character and narrator Undine Barnes Calles discovers that her husband has drained their joint bank account and disappeared. To further complicate the story, Undine also finds out that she is pregnant. Virtually insolvent, she must leave her upper-middle-class life and return to her parents' home in Brooklyn public housing. Through interactions with people in jail, a drug therapy group, and the local welfare office, the play charts not only Undine's fall but also her subsequent rise from social, emotional, and financial destitution in a slow reclamation of her true self. In *Fabulation*, Nottage uses the satirical format of a fantastical narrative, where stories and people may not always be what they seem.[1]

Fabulation's satire depends upon the audience's recognition of a variety of contemporary African American stereotypes, such as the welfare queen, the drug pusher, and the bourgeois black lady. As the audience learns throughout the play, fabricating outrageous fictions has been the cornerstone of Undine's life. The stereotypes trafficked throughout the play feature in many of Undine's stories. For example, to succeed in the high-powered business world of New York City, Undine concocts a story about her family tragically dying in a fire so no one knows she was associated with "low-class" folk. In Act Two, while trying to buy heroin for her ailing grandmother, Undine is sentenced to drug rehab classes. She ends up liking the group's camaraderie and crafts an involved tale of a nonexistent drug addiction to stay in it. It is essential that Undine's fabulations be ridiculous because the idle humor of her fantastical tales offers Nottage dramatic moments in which to rearrange and expose the stereotypes pervasive in each exchange. The play's comic elements, thinly veiled as simple mocking humor, initially attract the audience's attention. However, their structural position within the text provides a more subversive, satirical context that undercuts the very stereotypes that initially evoked laughter.

Fabulation's polyvocal satire finds its expression in the performance of Nottage's trickster. By understanding how the character of Undine operates, Nottage's trickster aesthetic may be better understood. Instead of turning to Henry Louis Gates's signifying monkey as an example of an African American trickster, I liken Undine to Brer Rabbit, the crafty antihero in southern slave stories who outwits his fellow animals by always being one step ahead. As Moira Smith points out, "Brer Rabbit's position as trickster in African American folklore and culture is a highly controversial one because he is often maligned as a sneaking, selfish, greedy dissembler" (113). Brer Rabbit's daily survival depends on his ability to lie and his mastery of wit and cunning. In the play's opening scene, Undine is no different. Her insatiable desire for wealth and status transformed her into her current self from what she was fourteen years before the play's beginning, when Undine was Sharona Watkins, a soon-to-be graduate of Dartmouth College with a family living in the Walt Whitman projects in Brooklyn.[2] It is fitting that Undine is a publicist, a job well-suited to the manipulation of language and image. In her estimation, to become a successful businesswoman, Undine had to mask her past. This sort of masking is an element of trickster existence that is particularly apparent in African American folktales, as masking constitutes survival, figuratively and literally, for tellers of tales. The way Undine tells it, her desire to rid herself of her family's poverty and her stereotypically precarious social position seems equally as urgent as a slave's desire to "steal away" off the plantation. For her, "survival" constitutes upward mobility and monetary stability, all afforded by a better social position and career.

Clearly, Undine's tenacity has led her to her current social status. She tells her doctor that she "decided years ago never to view [her]self as a victim" (Nottage, *Fabulation* 88) and instead uses her trickster skill set to her advantage. Her use of the word *victim* is particularly telling in relation to the cultural history of trickster tales. Slaves who created and retold these stories actually were victims. "Because the American slave system involved living with whites in daily power-based relationships," writes Smith, "African American trickster tales strongly reflect the necessity for the trickster's subversive, masking, signifying skills" (113). Thus, the traits of the trickster could never be too ridiculous or outlandish if, in the end, the goal was met. A variety of literary examples of African American satire also follow this logic: the more outrageous, the more provocative the satirical turn.[3] As the narrator of the play, Undine tries to coerce the audience into siding with her, absolving her of her guilt by accepting the reasons why she denied her past to climb the social ladder. Yet by immediately inserting her precipitous downfall at the opening of the play, Nottage undermines her own protagonist and creates an inherently unreliable narrator. I argue that this move is strategic. For the satirical counternarrative to be effective and stereotypes to be challenged, it is essential that Nottage play the trickster. The destabilization of norms and the attention to floating boundaries aid Nottage in the play's slippery strategy of subverting particular stereotypes. The only "victim" in this play may well be the audience, which becomes implicated in Undine's storytelling. *Fabulation*'s satirical intent operates through the mode of provocation, and I argue that the audience is provoked (and ultimately educated) through the play's stereotypical content.

Nottage's fabulations and the humor derived from the various fables rely on the knowledge of particular African American stereotypes at work within the play. Undine embodies two opposing contemporary stereotypes: the black bourgeois lady and the welfare queen. Wahneema Lubiano considers the welfare queen and black lady narratives complementary "social taxonomies" and "recognized by the national public as stories that describe the world in particular and politically loaded ways" (330). The stereotype of "black lady" as a recurring social signification works in tandem with dominant ideology, reinscribing the presumed impossible: a bourgeois black woman with goals of upward mobility.[4] On the other hand, the welfare queen "is the agent of destruction, the creator of the pathological, black, urban, poor family from which all ills flow" (339). A modern-day female version of the lazy coon, the welfare queen is "content to sit around and collect welfare, shunning work, and passing her bad values to her offspring" (Collins 77). Trapped in the urban ghetto, the welfare queen has little hope of changing her status and moving out of her position. In Undine, Nottage plays with each of these stereotypes. Initially, Undine follows the role of the black lady, but since, as Lubiano argues, such a role in society is inconceivable for the dominant white culture, Undine is stripped of her social position at the start of the play, effectively becoming a welfare queen. By structuring the development of character in this particular way, Nottage does not follow convention by using the stereotype; rather, because Undine achieved her status position fraudulently, Nottage exposes the ridiculousness of the stereotype.

For example, in bemoaning the loss of her solvency, Undine admits to her friend Allison that she has "returned to [her] original Negro state" and is "on the verge of becoming a statistic" (Nottage, *Fabulation* 93). I find the particular usage of "Negro" and "statistic" to be intriguing word choices; through them, Nottage parodies the language conservative pundits might use to describe a welfare queen. Undine then changes tactics, instead suggesting she create a "deprivation narrative" and emulate her "ancestors . . . shackled in wooden ships" rather than admit failure (85). Instead of a welfare case, she brands herself a slave. Playing into notions of historical victimhood offers more benefits for Undine at a time when referencing slave ancestors and travelling to West African slave ports has more societal cachet than admitting that one grew up in public housing, yet another trickster move by Nottage. In both instances, Nottage's ironic twist links slavery and welfare control, which both contain and regulate black bodies. Undine moreover jokes that she will "attend church or give alms . . . tend to some limbless African children in the middle of a malaria zone" (93). From "Negro statistic" to slave to philanthropist, Undine tries out all the available options, each one more ridiculous than the next. After this exchange, Nottage places the stage direction "they share a laugh at the notion" directly after Undine's suggestion. While subtle, this prescribed laugh is Nottage's double-voiced satire at work. The dialogue operates on two levels, the literal level of the story within the play and the larger societal subtext. Thus, the satire critiques the type of characters the women represent within the context of the play and the audience that may compartmentalize or stereotype "these" people. The shared laugh of the stage direction is localized between two characters, but the uncomfortable, knowing laugh of the audience, and ultimately, Nottage's satirical derision is directed more broadly at the behavior displayed by those characters.

Undine's refusal to inhabit the welfare queen stereotype continues throughout the rest of the play, as she tells the audience at the end of Act One, "my entire life has been engineered to avoid this very moment" (Nottage, *Fabulation* 104). The connotation of "engineered" references Undine's detailed life plan, meticulously executed to circumvent the stereotype. Yet here she is, six months pregnant with a fatherless child, living in the projects, ready to buy heroin for her grandmother. Nottage engineers her as a perfect stereotype: "I don't belong here," Undine tells another woman after she has been placed in jail for buying the drugs. The woman responds, "Guess what? I don't belong here, she don't belong here, but we here." (108). Undine's path to the jail cell may be based on confusion, but the woman's thinly veiled comment clearly references the high rate of African American arrests and imprisonments. In fact, each of the social services Undine interacts with as the play continues (welfare office, doctor's clinic, drug therapy group) explores another facet of the poor black stereotype and, in each exchange, characters comment on the stereotype they inhabit. This duality of portraying the stereotypes while at the same time commenting on the performance is a clear example of the polyvocality in Nottage's play.

It is in the voiced and unvoiced, the dialogue and the subtext, that the mechanics of Nottage's satire can be exposed. In a waiting room at a clinic, a "very young pregnant woman" tries to engage Undine in conversation. "You're my mother's age," she tells Undine, and Undine tells the audience, "I say nothing, though I want to let her know that I don't belong here, that my life experience is rich and textured and not presented well in the low, coarse clinic lighting. As such, I show her a touch of condescension, perhaps even pity" (Nottage, *Fabulation* 123). Undine immediately sees the woman as a stereotype, when in actuality they are really both the same thing: unwed mothers on welfare. Undine does, in fact, belong in the clinic. "I'm scared," the woman admits, and in a moment uncharacteristic for Undine, she admits that she is scared as well (124). Through Undine's position as narrator, a conduit to the audience, Nottage seduces audiences into thinking they are "down," feeling that they are on the "inside" of the joke, and this moment is where Nottage complicates the stereotype. As Glenda Carpio argues in her study on the satire of slavery in African American art, literature, and performance, "Black Americans have not only created their own stereotypes of white Americans—of 'peckerwoods' and 'honkies'—but have also directed their laughter at the stereotypes with which they have been represented, appropriating those images in order to diffuse their power of humiliation. They have also used jokes about stereotypes of blackness to laugh at, and thus chastise, those who were complicit in perpetuating such images" (Carpio 86). Nottage's use of humor through stereotypes highlights this complicity. Tricking the audience into thinking they should align with the narrator—and then providing a deceptive narrator—creates instability within the play. As tricksters thrive in an unstable world, Nottage may feel quite at home. This textual destabilization and concurrent unsettling of the audience is an ideal position in which to deploy suggestions for correction, a common if not absolutely necessary feature of the satirical mode. Undine's sarcastic rhetorical flourishes, like the "rich and textured" line above, engage the audience, and then Nottage's quick trickster turn—for example, Undine's subsequent admission that "I look at her and I realize, she's looking back at me with a touch of condescension"—admonish the audience for accepting Undine's stereotypical judgment (Nottage, *Fabulation* 123).

Fabulation encapsulates the trickster paradox that Lewis Hyde articulates, saying "that the origins, liveliness, and durability of cultures require that there be space for figures whose function is to uncover and disrupt the very things that cultures are based on" (9). Through Undine's shape-shifting between class and racial inequities, Nottage as trickster emphasizes the fabulous nature of the various narratives in which Undine participates, thereby exposing the stereotypes associated with each particular situation. The black bourgeoisie is undone, the welfare queen is dethroned, and the unwed mother finds support and comfort in a community of recovering drug addicts. As Undine's brother Flow admits in his epic poem, "It that ghetto paradox, / When we rabbit and we fox" (Nottage, *Fabulation* 131). Nottage may offer us a protagonist in the guise of Brer Rabbit, but she also plays the antagonist Brer Fox as well.

By the Way, Meet Vera Stark pushes the envelope even further by directly engaging one of the institutions most responsible for creating and sustaining African American stereotypes: American cinema. The play's unique structure of parodies within parodies affords Nottage multiple levels on which to address the anonymity of black actors in the early days of the film industry. Leaping across decades through the life of Vera Stark, Nottage's composite creation is inspired by the real-life Hollywood actress Theresa Harris. The play satirizes everything from institutionalized racism and passing to the film industry and academia. Early scenes take place in 1933, when the audience meets Vera Stark working not only as an actual maid to America's sweetheart actress, but also vying for the role of a theatrical maid in the actress's upcoming film. In the second act, the play jumps to a present-day conference at which academics discuss Stark's days in early Hollywood and reflect on her last public appearance on a popular 1970s talk show. Both the conference and the talk show are portrayed onstage, complicating the various stereotypes the play presents. By employing well-known stereotypes while at the same time deriding them, Nottage calls into question the development of America's racist past through the media and our equally unstable present. *Fabulation* may provoke audiences with its satirical turn, but *Vera Stark* urges audiences toward substantive inquiry into their own cultural history.

From the start, Vera clearly embodies many of the trickster characteristics described above. As was the case for many black actors in Hollywood at that time, she is stuck in a state of limbo, able to participate in a desirable profession but only being offered roles that left much to be desired. Working as a maid to Gloria Mitchell, formerly "America's little sweetie pie" but now an aging starlet, Vera helps Gloria prepare for a new film that she hopes will make her a comeback star. Vera's early exchanges with Gloria clearly place Vera in charge as she preys upon Gloria's insecurities. True to her trickster nature, she is quick-witted, matching Gloria's anxiety-ridden outbursts with sly asides and insults masked in deferential phrases. For example, as Gloria pops yet another chocolate in her mouth in nervous desperation, Vera mentions that the studio backlot gossip has been focused on "when, if ever, you'll lose the baby fat . . . for it appears you're wearing it more comfortably than they like" (Nottage, *Vera Stark* script 8). She then makes a show of going to get Gloria's audition dress, saying "I'll 'fetch' the red dress," although Gloria does not seem to understand the double entendre of "fetching" to which Vera alludes (9).

Vera also displays the trickster's tenacity for survival. Determined to be considered for the film as well, she works all angles to snag an audition. She asks Gloria to set one up, but not counting on her, she goes to the studio backlot and flirts with the director's chauffeur. However, her greatest trickster turn comes in a performative tour de force during Gloria's dinner party for the film's producer and director. So strong is her trickster hunger for survival that she goes to any length to score the role. As the director discusses his need for "real Negroes" in the film, Vera transforms before his very eyes, from sassy maid to field slave, crafting on the spot the most ridiculous and stereotypical representation of a "real Negro" for the director. In the presence of such trickster mastery, he buys into every moment. Her trickster wiles end up paying off, and Vera does get the part of the maid in what ends up being a career-defining film for Gloria. Yet for all her trickster cunning, Vera is still subject to the institutionalized racism of early Hollywood, and the audience learns that the film also becomes ironically defining for Vera, as her role as the faithful maid is the only surviving trace of her acting career.

The scenes juxtapose moments of Vera with her friends and Vera interacting with Gloria and other white characters. These scenes reveal Nottage's complication of the concept of what is real, which is further explored in the second act of the play during the on-stage colloquium where the characters decipher who the "real" Vera Stark may be. Although fraught with complexities, it is this very narrative of the "real" that Nottage complicates in the play, where the tension between the "real" Vera and how Hollywood sees the "real" clash in unexpected ways.[5] Vera admits after her ridiculous performance of a "Real Negro" at the party that she "did something I vowed I'd never do" but "got to thinking about what I'd be willing to do to have a taste of what Gloria's got. Be a star! And tonight I crossed a bridge, and I'm telling you, I ain't going back!" (Nottage, *By the Way* script 54). To interrogate the nature of the "real," Nottage reproaches audience complicity through parodic satire, sending up stereotypes while sending out critique. As Paul Gilroy notes, "signifyin(g) and shape-shifting can still be tactical as well as playful; contestatory as well as compensatory" (16). As in *Fabulation*, the subversion of stereotypes proves a strategic tool.

Through Vera's trickster nature, the play calls attention to the pervasive limitations of the stereotypes that the film industry imposed upon African American actors. A scene with Vera and her fellow actor roommates vividly shows the lengths to which the women will go to carve a space for themselves as artists of color in the golden age of film. Both Vera and her friend Lottie work menial jobs and audition for even more menial roles, namely those of slaves. But even then, Lottie explains, "You gotta be high yella mellow or look like you crawled outta Mississippi cotton patch to get work in this rotten town" (Nottage, *By the Way* script 22). Vera's roommate Anna Mae even passes as Brazilian, hoping that identifying with the eroticization and exoticization of South American beauties will help her win the affections of powerful white male producers and, in turn, valuable film roles.[6] Although each woman fantasizes about the ways in which she will rise to the top, each sacrifices her own "real" self to conform to the deformative and racist demands of casting. Lottie continually hums spirituals, at once commenting critically on the stereotype of the happy, singing slave and yet also showing how complacency perpetuates that stereotype. Anna Mae willingly submits to inventing her past to play into Hollywood's colorism out of short-term self-interest.

As mentioned above, Vera also ends up participating in her own objectification when, at Gloria's party, she transforms herself from feisty maid into downtrodden house slave. This scene best illuminates Nottage's satirical craft through the dialogue and accompanying stage directions. The misguided Russian émigré director speaks of his intent with the film, telling the guests, "I vant the Negroes to be real, to be Negroes of the earth, I vant to feel their struggle, the rhythm of their language, I vant actors that . . . no, I don't vant actors, I vant people" (Nottage, *By the Way* script 45). Here Vera slowly changes before his very eyes, "giving the performance of a lifetime" as the stage directions note (45).[7] As Maxmillian notices her for the first time, she launches into the most stereotypical "poor black folk" story that she can muster: "My Mama died in child birth cuz there wasn't no doctor there to birth me proper, and you see my Pappy wuz a blues man, and he guitar was the onliest thing he luv. My pappy dun own heself a jukejoint. And as a chil' I work-did dere cuz he couldn' afford no other help. Nah, suh. I work-did like a grown woman, though I was nuthin' but a chil'. I dun seen plenty of ugly things, things no chil' need see. But my Pappy was a good man, but mister sometime in de South a good man hafta do ugly things just to survive" (45). Vera pulls out all the stereotypical stops in her over the top dialect: poverty, the blues, juke joints, prostitution. The director is riveted, using Vera's "life story" as the reason for the making of the film as the producer fires back that "slavery ain't exactly a pick me up. All I'm asking is that if you're gonna give 'em slaves, give 'em happy ones" (47). Vera's stereotypical tale, and the ensuing exchange between the two white men, is farcical, but it also provokes an uncomfortable laugh from both white and black audiences. As Bambi Haggins puts it in *Laughing Mad: The Black Comic Persona in Post Soul America* (2007), "I know what I'm laughing at, but what are you laughing at?" (236). Mel Watkins notes that this discomfort is a specific trait of African American humor in that it "ridicules both those outside and those inside the ethnic group and frequently embraces the profane" but that there is a fine line between satire and "self-derogatory 'coonery'" (xxiii). But who makes that distinction? Can Nottage expect audiences to possess a level of sophistication that they understand race as a social construct, that targeting particular African American stereotypes from multiple perspectives is not a form of perpetuating the stereotype but rather exposing the system of stereotypes that undergirds American racism and identity politics?[8]

Capitalizing on a trickster aesthetic, Nottage makes a strategic move with the addition of contemporary characters in Act II. The second act begins with film footage of a melodramatic scene from the movie featuring Gloria as the dying southern belle and Vera as the maid.[9] The scene then abruptly cuts to a present-day table of panelists participating in an academic colloquium, "'Rediscovering Vera Stark, the legacy of *The Belle of New Orleans*'" (Nottage, *By the Way* script 59). Through these panelists, Nottage guides theatre audiences to critically examine the stereotypes Nottage has been toying with through Act I. For example, Herb, the organizing panelist, speaks to the "audience" at the conference and calls attention to "Vera Stark's subversive and nuanced performance. . . . She is at once in the role and commenting on it. It is a revolutionary performance, dare I say political performance" (60). Nottage, the ultimate trickster, provides a meta-meta-commentary, at once commenting directly on Vera's various performances but also alluding to the multiple levels in which the character of Vera has been operating throughout the play itself.

To add yet another meta-level to this already nuanced and complex text, Herb and his fellow panelists themselves embody stereotypes. Discussing Vera's last televised appearance on a 1970s talk show, the two women panelists—Carmen, a mousy academic and Afua, an angry black lesbian—are at odds with each other. The former references academic theories of identity, the latter responds by reciting slam poetry and updated black power slogans. The feminist shouts that Vera is "a volcano on the verge of erupting, ready to release the pressure of years of battling patriarchal hegemony," while the professor calmly explains that Vera shows an "internal tug of war, between what she was and could have been, and what she has come to represent" (Nottage, *By the Way* script 70, 71). Through these comical panelists, Nottage offers multiple viewpoints on the idea of the "real" as they try to uncover the trajectory of Stark's career. Through each panelist, Nottage gives the audience the various voices in the debate over authenticity, on representations of blackness on film, and the divide between the roles one may play on film, in public, or in private.[10] Put succinctly by Afua about Vera's volatility as her career progresses, "She got tired. She got angry. She got, how should I say it, she got real. She got real" (65). Declaring the idea of the "real" Afua alludes to the very nature of performance, of playing a role, and the various roles, in and out of film that Vera played.

However, like Undine in *Fabulation*, even the panelists are unreliable narrators. Toward the end of the play, the panelists speak over each other, and although overlapping in dialogue, the arguments clearly state the precarious position of African American actors in early Hollywood, and ultimately, the delicate balance between Nottage's pointed satire and reckless stereotypical humor. Carmen asks, "Can we fully hold [Vera] responsible for perpetuating images that have come to define how people still view African American women on the screen today?" and Herb, the moderator, counterattacks with "ultimately she still was just another shucking, jiving, fumbling, mumbling, laughing, shuffling, pancake making mammy in the kitchen" (Nottage, *By the Way* script 89). In many ways, both of these points are valid and could be opinions of the theatre audience members on the actual play they are watching. As Charles McNulty writes of the New York production in the *Los Angeles Times*, "[Nottage's] irony detector can't help beeping as it surveys all the social progress that has been made. But she's also aware of how anyone in the public eye is forced to sell a part of his or her soul. In this regard, she's an equal opportunity satirist, sending up the performing seal in all of us."

Indeed, the play operates within the liminal boundary between buffoonery and satire just like the trickster figures of old. As Vera sardonically explains, "It's a burden to be a Negro woman in this town. What has all of my enviable talent given me? Mammy Jane, Josie, Bitsy, Petunia and Addie, forty years of characters who they didn't even bother to give last names. That's something to celebrate, honey!" (Nottage, *By the Way* script 84). Nottage's strategic use of stereotypes, the commentary from her protagonist and secondary characters, and Nottage's own metacommentary provide an important intervention.

Work that engages in the delicate deconstruction of stereotypes provides a locus in which to understand why these images and qualities are still so potent in American society today. Nottage's strategic use of stereotypes imbues the plays with the necessary tools with which to circumvent the uncomfortable laugh. Through the trickster figure embodied by both Undine and Vera, each play embraces the delicate balance between picayune and parody, between sophomoric and satirical. Nottage's polyvocal writing style asks audiences to re-envision an alternative future, a future that rejects singular stereotypical portrayals of African Americans for a future that favors expanded notions of blackness. For at their core, satire and the lessons of the trickster tales must not only attack but also correct; provoke, but also move one toward inquiry.

Notes

1. Jonathan Swift this is not, but I would argue that the various fabulations that weave in and out of the play do correspond with the traditions of the fantastical satire.

2. While it is common for many public housing units to be named after famous Americans (and there are actual Walt Whitman Houses in Brooklyn managed by the New York City Housing Authority), I do not think this choice to ascribe Undine's childhood home to the Walt Whitman housing was idle. Over his life, Whitman constantly worked and reworked his seminal book *Leaves of Grass* (1855). Within its pages, scholars have questioned the various clues to who Whitman was himself (his sexuality, relationships, politics), which is seemingly detailed in his epic "Song of Myself" (1855) and may indeed call attention to his various selves, as well as the myriad facets of humanity. This relates (subtly) to how Undine has also edited and reworked the stories in her life.

3. Examples of such outlandish wit range from early African American satire, such as George Schuyler's *Black No More* (1931), to Baratunde Thurston's more recent *How to Be Black* (2012).

4. In Lubiano's argument, the Anita Hill-Clarence Thomas hearings exposed hegemonic animus against such a possibility, shunning Hill's accusations against the conservative, Bible-toting Thomas, while simultaneously chastising her for suggesting Thomas's guilt and showcasing the fact that her social position seemed incomprehensible to a white, male–dominated establishment on Capitol Hill.

5. I recognize that the idea of "real" is an anxious term. For the purposes of my argument, I consider the idea of the real as read through the theories of Paul Gilroy ("'…to be Real'") and the argument concerning authentic blackness by E. Patrick Johnson (*Appropriating Blackness*).

6. Ironically, in the New York production at Second Stage in 2010, this role was actually played by a Latina, Karen Olivo. She originated the role of Vanessa (the female lead) in the play *In The Heights* (2007) and won a Tony for playing Anita in the 2009 revival of *West Side Story*.

7. In the Second Stage production, all of the servants onstage made this transformation simultaneously, attempting to "out-slave" one another by singing spirituals, speaking in dialect, and making grotesque physical gestures. This moment got one of the biggest laughs of the evening as the audience recognized the characters' deployment of stereotypical traits.

8. In the West Coast premiere at the Geffen Playhouse, audience reaction to this scene was mixed. The mostly white and elderly matinee audience members either laughed

uncomfortably or, at times, not at all. I wondered if they felt that they were not "supposed" to laugh. The minority of African American audience members enjoyed the moment intensely, their laughter making up for the sometimes awkward quiet.

9. Nottage's filmmaker husband Tony Gerber directed the footage, very reminiscent (purposefully, I believe) of a black and white *Gone with the Wind*.

10. In both the Second Stage and Geffen productions, the moderator and two panelists were double cast. The moderator was the chauffeur from the first act, and the two panelists were Vera's friends / fellow maids. This proved an interesting directorial choice as audiences watched them embody the stereotypes that they then critically "unpack" in the second act, while at the same time referencing entirely new, contemporary stereotypes.

Satirizing Satire: Symbolic Violence and Subversion in Spike Lee's *Bamboozled*

Luvena Kopp

Black American satire is truly black when it is genuinely American. That is to say, the blackness of black American satire lies in the satirist's experience with America's "problem of the color-line" (Du Bois v) that, in the new millennium, continues to be among the fundamental organizing principles in American society. However, the formerly overt racist borders drawn by the color line have gradually transformed into more subliminal patterns of discrimination. In *Laughing Fit to Kill* (2008), Glenda Carpio argues that the notion of a supposedly color-blind society that emerged during the last decades of the twentieth century created an avenue for a steady and successful retreat from the accomplishments made by the Civil Rights Movement and, in the process, also amplified the legitimate use of racial stereotypes for the implicit corroboration of white supremacist ideas:

> A great reversal occurred almost as soon as the major civil rights acts passed: the focus was no longer on white racism—because segregation in public accommodations and proscribed discrimination in employment and disenfranchisement had been outlawed—but on the moral deficiencies of minorities.
>
> For African Americans, such backlash included the reemergence of long-standing stereotypes regarding their character. Stereotypes of blacks as lazy, irresponsible and "in violation of core American values" have been used to explain the undeniable inequalities that persist in the brave new world in which racial discrimination apparently no longer exists. (3–4)

In accordance with the proverb, "The more things change, the more they remain the same," which Michelle Alexander cites in her introduction to *The New Jim Crow* (2010), our seemingly post-racial or color-blind society relies as much on black stereotypes as did the era of slavery and the subsequent period of Jim Crow (1); black stereotypes are pivotal for the clandestine maintenance of the orthodox social order, a social order that was founded on racial separation and white privilege. Charles W. Mills stresses the idea of a racial contract that "underwrites the modern social contract" (62) and ensures the "differential privileging of the whites as a group with respect to the nonwhites as a group, the exploitation of their bodies, land, and resources, and the denial of equal social economic opportunities to them." (11). The myths of post-race and color blindness actually blind us "not so much to race," as Alexander writes, "but to the existence of racial caste in America" (241).

Under the capitalist dictates of mass consumption and multimedia technology, in which "life is presented as an immense accumulation of *spectacles*" and "everything that was directly lived has receded into a representation" (Debord 1; emphasis in original), black stereotypes circulate more widely than ever and ultimately *create* people's social reality. The entertainment industry forms the cultural space in which black stereotypes materialize and transform into marketable commodities. "I knew from the days of the minstrel shows to the musicals and movies then current, that many non-Negro outsiders had reaped fame and fortune by assuming the stereotyped mask of blackness," writes Ralph Ellison in "An Extravagance of Laughter." "I also knew that our forms of popular culture, from movies to comic strips, were a source of national mythology in which Negroes were the chief scapegoats, and that the function of this mythology was to allow whites a more secure place (if only symbolically) in American society" (628).[1] Consequently, black stereotypes function as symbolic forms that configure a white supremacist national mythology.

With the assistance of such symbolic forms that impose themselves on the perceptions and actions of social agents, this white supremacist national mythology becomes naturalized. As we—literally and figuratively—buy into stereotypes that explicitly picture blacks as silly, violent, or irresponsible while implicitly equating blackness with those traits, we practically promote a social discrimination that is fundamentally racial. In a cultural environment in which portrayals of blacks as hypersexual gangsta rappers and clownish mammy types can ensure fame and economic success, consumers and producers of all races join in a "collective denial" (Bourdieu, *Outline* 196), in which the "reality effect" (Bourdieu, *On Television* 21) of stereotypes—that is, their power to create and separate—is tacitly misrecognized. Twenty-first-century America's problem of the color line, therefore, rests upon a "symbolic violence" that, according to the French sociologist Pierre Bourdieu, is "imperceptible and invisible to its victims, exerted for the most part through the purely symbolic channels of communication and cognition (more precisely, misrecognition), recognition, or even feeling"

(*Masculine Domination* 1–2). It is furthermore "known and recognized both by the dominant and by the dominated" (2).

It comes as no surprise, then, that Spike Lee's first feature film of the new millennium, *Bamboozled* (2000), features a biting satire on contemporary America's enthusiastic embrace of minstrel show conventions. Commenting on the subtle contours of modern racism, the director explains, "What we hope that this film shows is that in the twenty-first century, in the new millennium, you don't have to wear blackface to be a minstrel performer" (Iverem 238). *Bamboozled* is told from the perspective of its main character, Pierre Delacroix, who is the only African American writer at the fictional Continental Network System (CNS). Thomas Dunwitty, his white boss, believes he is "blacker" than Delacroix; he confidently underscores this claim not only by referencing his black wife and children but also by the constant use of racial slurs in his manifestly artificial black vernacular.[2] When Dunwitty urges Delacroix to deliver a cutting-edge African American show, the latter decides to pitch a televised minstrel show in the hopes that its blatant racism will get him fired and thereby allow him to leave CNS without violating his contract. Ironically, *Mantan: The New Millennium Minstrel Show* becomes a national craze. In the course of his unexpected success, Delacroix begins to justify the show's grotesquely racist nature by claiming that it is intended as satire. In the end, the alleged satirist and nearly all of the black characters who have engaged in the fabrication of black stereotypes lose their lives, thereby revealing that they had been "bamboozled" into misrecognizing the true social impacts of stereotypes.

In the extensive amount of commentary that *Bamboozled* has generated, many critics have commented on the modes in which Lee pillories the reinforcement of black stereotypes by African Americans themselves. Susan Gubar notes that "Lee . . . mocks the victims of racism as complicit keepers of America's prison house who prove that what African Americans continually confront is not survival after or despite racism, but the survival of racism" (26). According to Daryl Dickson-Carr, African American satire generally argues

> that some, if not most, blacks are more than willing to fulfill the stereotypes racism constructs as a means of getting ahead in an untenable economic situation. . . . Racism and racists are not stable, monolithic quantities any more than the black Other is. Racism may range from the individual and personal to the systemic, extending into all levels of American social and economic spheres. For this reason, it is altogether possible, even probable, that African Americans participate in their own oppression, with or without their conscious consent. A more chilling possibility that African American satire suggests is that even

if some individuals are able to decipher racism's ubiquitous coding, they may not have the will to counter and destroy racism in whatever form it takes. To do so might require sacrifice of material comfort, and in the vision of the black satirist, blacks stand shoulder-to-shoulder with the rest of humanity in being venal, greedy, selfish, and self-sabotaging. (32–33)

Both Gubar and Dickson-Carr indicate that the African American contribution to racism is largely motivated by deliberate calculation. However, an analysis of the symbolic dimension of Delacroix's actions dislodges the notion of conscious deliberation because "symbolic violence accomplishes itself through an act of cognition and of misrecognition that lies beyond— or beneath—the controls of consciousness and will" (Bourdieu and Wacquant 171–172). Symbolic submission is furthermore "durably embedded in the bodies of the dominated and in form of schemes of perception and dispositions . . . which *sensitize* [the victims] to certain symbolic manifestations of power" (Bourdieu, *Masculine* 40; emphasis in original). For Delacroix and other African Americans—particularly those in the entertainment industry—acting according to the demands of the industry (or against those demands) therefore means acting according to schemes of perception and disposition that ultimately reinforce their symbolic domination.

In his October 2000 review of *Bamboozled*, Roger Ebert claimed that "Delacroix isn't very black." Although Delacroix unquestionably identifies as African American, Ebert is not entirely wrong. Delacroix's stereotypical whiteness is engendered by a *habitus*, a practical sense that reflects the white corporate norms and demands that organize the objective space of CNS. Habitus, according to Bourdieu, is a system that produces social practices by generating and organizing the "schemata of perception, apperception, and action" (Bourdieu and Wacquant 126–127). As the product of incorporated objective structures, habitus permeates the physical dimension of social agents, thus becoming "a durable way of standing, speaking, walking, and thereby of feeling and thinking" (Bourdieu, *Logic* 70). *Bamboozled*'s opening scene foregrounds Delacroix's embodiment of CNS's objective structures and, thus, his practical sense for the network's immanent laws. The camera leads the viewer through the huge open spaces of his clock tower apartment and reveals a spotless interior that lacks any trace of homely living, in the process conveying a sterile and detached atmosphere that is characteristic of the corporate world. The predominance of blue in Delacroix's apartment and clothing adds a sense of coolness to this sterility and detachment (Zeinbau 17). Delacroix has not only embodied the network's corporate notions, as the mise-en-scène suggests; he also reinforces them in his objective environment. In so doing, he practically acknowledges CNS's

corporate norms and misrecognizes its endemic racial hierarchization. Ste-
vie Wonder, *Bamboozled*'s voice of conscience, defies Delacroix's misrecognition in the fashion of an ancient Greek chorus.[3] His song "Misrepresented
People" underpins the scene acoustically, reemphasizing the continuous
subordination of blacks in America and highlighting the film's main theme
by admonishing that African Americans "must never be a misrepresented
people" (*Bamboozled* 0:01:29).

The apartment's excessive illumination signifies Delacroix's efforts to
overcome the stigma of his dark skin.[4] In her brilliant exploration of the film,
Rachel Delue remarks that Lee's use of light works to "eliminate all traces of
darkness and shadow" (75) and moreover communicates a "desire to be seen"
(75–76). Damon Wayans, who plays Delacroix, explains that his character's
"goal is . . . to be like his mentor, Mr. Dunwitty, and . . . [to] have some power,
some say so, and creative control" ("Making of Bamboozled" 0:03:06–0:03:21).
Wayans consequently asserts Delacroix's desire for visibility and, by referring to Dunwitty as Delacroix's "mentor," also highlights Dunwitty's symbolic power within the asymmetrical power relation between the two men.
Dunwitty's symbolic power, which includes the "power to make things with
words" (Bourdieu and Wacquant 23), reveals itself ironically, yet blatantly,
when he prefigures to "squeeze" a coon show out of Delacroix "even if it kills"
the latter (*Bamboozled* 0:09:57). Delacroix's desire for visibility is triggered
by the subordinated status he occupies within the hierarchical structure of
CNS, where he is neither recognized—as his abandoned birth name, Peerless,
indicates—nor in any kind of control. The film illustrates Delacroix's lack of
recognition when he enters the network building and receives no response
to his morning greetings. It seems as though his colleagues refuse to see him
for the black man that he is.[5] This, instantly, recalls the opening remarks of
Ellison's invisible man: "I am invisible, understand, simply because people
refuse to see me" (*Invisible* 3). The parallels between Delacroix's invisibility
and the protagonist of Ellison's *Invisible Man* (1952) are unmistakable; to wit,
Delacroix's apartment displays countless lamps, much as the invisible man's
cellar contains 1,369 lights. Whereas the invisibility of Ellison's protagonist
eventually leads him to an enlightened "understanding of his human condition," which is symbolized by the heat, light, and power his cellar provides
(Ellison, "Change" 111), Delacroix's invisibility merely increases his desire
for recognition within CNS and, at that, strengthens his implicit belief in
the network's "fundamental axioms" (Bourdieu, "Some Properties" 74). The
initial sense of enlightenment that *Bamboozled*'s opening evokes, therefore,
chiastically marks Delacroix's delusion.

The metamorphosis from Peerless Dothan to Pierre Delacroix[6] suggests
the latter's symbolic migration from a rural / southern African American

background (since Dothan is a small city in southeastern Alabama) to the white corporate world of the urban / northern metropolis of New York City.[7] However, Delacroix's African American heritage, on which these Eurocentric ideals are superimposed, continues to bear their relative weight. Bourdieu explains that "early experiences have particular weight because the *habitus* tends to ensure its own constancy" (*Logic* 60; emphasis in original). The African American cultural tradition is most vibrantly expressed by Delacroix's father Junebug, a comedian and a "strong man with conviction, integrity, [and] principles" (*Bamboozled* 0:59: 40) who introduced his son to the entertainment business. Junebug's comedy represents the black working-class comedy of the Chitlin' Circuit that spawned such notable sociocritical comedians as Richard Pryor.[8] Lee's film highlights the antagonism between America's institutionalized white hegemonic popular culture and a defiant, independent black comedy tradition. In this black comedy tradition, the comedians implement their subversive strategy by exploiting the ambivalence that, as Homi Bhabha maintains, "is central to the stereotype" and "gives the colonial [or, in this case, modern white supremacist] discourse its currency" (18). As Ellison notes, "the blackness of *Afro-American* 'black humor' is not black; it is tragically human and finds its source and object in the notion of 'whiteness'" ("An Extravagance" 642; emphasis in original). Whereas *Mantan*'s orthodox implementation of black stereotypes reinforces the idea of black inferiority, Junebug's heretic implementation of black stereotypes ultimately exposes the hypocrisy and, therefore, the arbitrariness of white supremacy. In one of Junebug's jokes, Mother Theresa craves the enormous genitals of a black male; in this way "that 'otherness'" that Bhabha stresses in his exploration of the stereotype becomes "at once an object of desire and derision" (19).

At the intersection of his African American heritage and his white corporate network experience, Delacroix's habitus thus constitutes a "divided or even torn habitus" (Bourdieu and Wacquant 127). The victims of symbolic violence, as Bourdieu remarks, suffer from an "internal conflict and division of self" (Bourdieu, *Masculine Domination* 39). In similar terms, Delue notes that "Delacroix is Du Bois's split self, always looking at himself through two sets of eyes and thus unable to see himself as anything but the image he is made out to be" (74). Delacroix's split self is cinematically underscored when the camera depicts the protagonist facing his reflection while brushing his teeth in front of a mirror. This establishing close-up of Delacroix conjoins with a voice-over in which he defines satire, thereby introducing the film's protagonist to the viewer in terms that allude to his internally divided self. The shot renders the mirror invisible, thus making it seem as if two manifestations of Delacroix were facing each other. By applying white shaving cream to his scalp, Delacroix antithetically references the film's core ritual, in which the minstrel performers blacken their faces with a paste of burnt cork (compare to Delue 75). When skimming the cream off he also removes the nappy hair that, according to Orlando Patterson's *Slavery and Social Death* (1982), registers as a primary marker of blackness (61). Following Patterson's argument in which the shorn head presents a symbol of powerlessness (60–62), Delacroix's shaving may also compare to a "symbolic act" (60) that manifests his powerlessness toward the network's representations of power.

At the end of the scene, Delacroix introduces himself as a "television writer, a creative person" (*Bamboozled* 0:00:59), thereby using the network's dominant categories for his self-description. The classifications that the victims of symbolic violence employ to "perceive and appreciate" themselves are, as Bourdieu remarks, "the product of the embodiment of the—thereby naturalized—classifications of which [their] social being is the product" (*Masculine Domination* 35). Delue maintains that "we cannot see Delacroix as he is . . . nor can Delacroix fashion himself except by way of imposing other masks . . . on his own person" (68). The seemingly heretic, ironical tone of Delacroix's speech eventually identifies as a resigned cynicism. This becomes particularly clear during his cynical remarks at the end of the film. His irony can therefore not "take the form of true resistance" (Bourdieu, *On Television* 38).

A reading of Lee's *Bamboozled* that accounts for the symbolic modes of action and reaction poses Delacroix's subjective contribution to black stereotypes in relation to the objective social structures in which his practice is embedded.[9] His reinforcement of racist images is not the result of a deliberate calculation. If "the various fields provide themselves with agents equipped with the *habitus* needed to make them work," as Bourdieu indicates (*Logic* 67; emphasis in original), then Lee's protagonist is equipped with the practical sense, or, as Bourdieu also termed it, the "feel for the game" that CNS demands from its agents in order to function and persist. Since Delacroix is inclined to acknowledge the network's representations of power, he unconsciously contributes to Dunwitty's schemes even as he believes himself to be resisting them. In his defiant stance against CNS, Delacroix consciously "intend[s] to give" Dunwitty a coon show (*Bamboozled* 0:13:13) in order to expose the network's racism, as he makes clear in a conversation with his assistant; his engagement in racist stereotyping ensues unconsciously, however, because Delacroix fails to recognize the symbolic truth that underlies his intention. Symbolic violence "is instituted through the adherence that the dominated cannot fail to grant to the dominant (and therefore to the domination)" (Bourdieu, *Masculine Domination* 35). *Mantan* thus articulates the self-alienation and false consciousness of Delacroix who, while deliberately attempting to counter his domination, is unable to apply any other categories than those that reinforce this very domination.

Apart from CNS, *Mantan* appears as another means by which the black characters reinforce their symbolic domination. By playing the roles of ignorant coons, the black actors collaborate in confining themselves in what Stanley Crouch defines as "the prison of stereotypes" ("Making of Bamboozled" 0:02:01). The minstrels' imprisonment is most significantly marked by their symbolic prison uniforms, consisting of blackface and grotesquely stereotyped costumes. During their performance of the show, Lee further emphasizes this symbolism by having the members of *Mantan*'s house band wear actual prison uniforms. In a racial dimension, this echoes a point Bourdieu makes about the symbolic role of clothing in gendered subjugation: "[The] symbolic *confinement* is secured practically by their [i.e., women's] clothing which (as was even more visible in former times) has the effect not only of masking the body but of continuously calling it into order (the skirt fulfills a function entirely analogous to that of the priest's cassock) without ever needing to prescribe or proscribe anything explicitly . . . because it contains movement in various ways" (*Masculine Domination* 28–29; emphasis in original). By casting The Roots, a politically activist hip-hop combo, for the show's blackfaced house band, Lee inserts a reality (Baldwin, "Devil" 493) into *Mantan*'s figures that, in its complexity, transcends the confinements of the show's stereotypes. He also demonstrates, however, how the symbolic effects of America's white supremacist national mythology constrains the complicity of all subjects, their political commitment notwithstanding.

It is in the light of satire that Lee's film exposes and subverts the mechanisms of symbolic violence that operate within *Mantan*, CNS, and America's national mythology at large.[10] He reveals the absurdity and discriminatory power of stereotypical images through a satirical exaggeration that magnifies "the distortions that crystallize in stereotypes" (Carpio 15). By bringing this truth back into the collective memory, the director defies the historical process that fosters its symbolic concealment and, ultimately, its collective denial. Lee's satire, furthermore, accomplishes a denaturalization of the racial concept and its hierarchical order. Like Junebug, Lee also signifies on the arbitrariness of white supremacy. He does so by satirically exaggerating Delacroix's stereotypical whiteness, in particular his diction and gestures. Delue argues that the film works "to make whiteness strange and . . . obscene (at least to those for whom whiteness was not already these things), thereby dismantling its false normativity and dislodging its authority" (74). Lee also spotlights the interchangeability of racial categories by having his main black character, Delacroix, act stereotypically white and his main white character, Dunwitty, act stereotypically black (Delue 75). It is again Delue who observes that "the ease with which one identity is substituted for another . . . assists in laying bare and *de*naturalizing, through analogy, the rhetorical and historical process whereby racial and/or ethnic differences are established and naturalized" (62; emphasis in original). In light of Ellison's claim that "America is a land of masking jokers" ("Change the Joke" 109), this easy and ubiquitous substitution of race signifies on America's reliance on arbitrary racial categories. Race is, then, more functional than natural. All of *Bamboozled*'s characters (including *Mantan*'s audience) wear blackface or whiteface or both faces at once and are, therefore, minstrels in Lee's own great modern-day minstrel show.

The dichotomy between Delacroix's minstrel show and Lee's minstrel show correlates with the dichotomy between the false satire *Mantan* and the true satire *Bamboozled*. Lee's cinematography underscores this dichotomy. In reference to what Ed Guerrero defines as "Hollywood's plantation mythology" (10), *Mantan* is set in a watermelon patch and was shot on actual 16 mm film, thereby emulating the visual style of "classic" Hollywood movies. Paula Massood remarks that "[*Mantan*'s] antebellum idyll is characterized by a specific spatiotemporal dimension, a seemingly static plantation-like space. In it, characters and narratives exist outside of history and have no relationship to a contemporary context" (217). The show's supposedly carefree and fun[11] idyll is among the main catalyzers of *Mantan*'s symbolic subjection of blacks. Saidiya Hartman elaborately deciphers this "complicated nexus of terror and enjoyment" (21), as she calls it. In *Scenes of Subjection*, she notes that "the indiscriminative use of the black body made possible the pleasure of terror and the terror of pleasure. Within this framework, suffering and shuffling were complementary" (29). In contrast to *Mantan*'s pastoral setting, *Bamboozled* is set in New York City. "Everywhere the satirist turns," writes Alvin P. Kernan, "he finds idiocy, foolishness, depravity, and dirt. . . . It is no accident that most satire is set in the city, particularly in the metropolis with a polyglot people" (254). Unlike *Mantan*'s embellished design, *Bamboozled* was shot with hand-held digital cameras that give the film an uneven, fuzzy look. Gilbert Highet remarks that "where they [i.e., other patterns of literature] use carefully posed models and work in a skillfully lighted studio, the satirist cries, 'I am a camera! I am a tape-recorder!' If the results which he offers us are not always smooth with the contours of perfect art, and if their tints are not harmoniously blended, they at least have the urgency and immediacy of actual life. In the work of the finest satirists there is the minimum of convention, the maximum of reality" (3). Even though Highet's remarks refer to satirical literature, they nevertheless resonate with the film's dichotomy between a false and a true satire. Whereas the world of Delacroix's false satire is characterized by orthodoxy, stagnation, conservation, and conformity, Lee's true satire is characterized by heresy, chaos, Brechtian alienation, change, and ambiguity.

The director juxtaposes *Mantan*'s historically remote static temporal space with the postmodern time and space of *Bamboozled*, where history is practically produced by the characters' struggle over the legitimate representation of blackness. The film's concept of time is shaped by Lee's implementation of the African American oral tradition. The past and present converge in Delacroix's recapitulation of the events leading to his death. In "Time and the African-American Experience," Ulfried Reichardt notes that "the oral transmission of the past is performative: the past merges into the present recitation. When these cultural elements are integrated into the [work], non-linear time is juxtaposed with linear processes, to the effect that they intersect with and perspectivize each other" (479). The incorporation of the historical form of blackface minstrelsy into *Bamboozled*'s contemporary setting signifies a dialectic intersection of present and past in Delacroix's storytelling; the film's opening scene, furthermore, juxtaposes the voice-over of the murdered and thus past Delacroix with the action of the living and therefore present Delacroix. By disrupting the idea of a monolithic, linear temporality and demonstrating that history is always inherent, and operative, in the present, Lee argues against the belief that blackface minstrelsy and its stereotypes are relics of the past. In the film's first image, the camera depicts a giant clock that is filmed from behind. This shot not only symbolizes the moral regression of today's mass-mediated black imagery to the times of blackface minstrelsy; it also indicates that due to this moral regression of black images, time for African Americans like Delacroix (who, in this take, is lying directly beneath the clock) is moving in a reverse (that is, wrong) direction.

Lee also performs a satirical subversion of a satire in which the satirist Delacroix eventually becomes the satirized (compare to Black 20). Glenda Carpio explains that "for centuries black humorists have used . . . aspects of voodoo and conjure to signify on chattel slavery's transformation of people into objects" (16). She stresses, however, that voodoo and conjure are not utilized "in any nostalgic or essentializing manner," but "through formally innovating means" (15). Lee's complex use of satire signifies on the stereotypes' transformation of people into objects. The director conducts his signifying practice by weaving the false satire *Mantan* into the frame narrative of the true satire *Bamboozled*, or more precisely, by satirizing an alleged satire, thereby objectifying the objectification of the black agents. The methodological distance thus created discloses a more informed view on the symbolic power mechanisms that operate in Lee's film and America's national mythology at large. Lee's satire eventually reveals that African Americans are (as alluded to by Delacroix's adopted last name) the "chief scapegoats," as Ellison called it or, more precisely, the "symbolic instruments" (Bourdieu, *Masculine Domination* 43) of white supremacist cultural politics.

In the end, almost all of *Bamboozled*'s black characters who have reinforced racist stereotypes die violently. Their deaths do not mark the transition from symbolic to physical violence, but rather emphasize the physicality of symbolic violence. When the members of the Mau Maus kill *Mantan*'s star actor out of a supposedly black nationalist conviction, they "resort to the weapons of the weak" (Bourdieu, *Masculine Domination* 59) that reinforce the very stereotypes they sought to attack. The police, the executive force of America's white supremacist national mythology, in turn shoot the Mau Maus, sparing only one member, One-Sixteenth Black, who in their view identifies as white.[12] One-Sixteenth Black begs to be killed in recognition of his blackness but the policemen arrest him instead. White privilege—in this case the privilege to live—is a systematic automatism that overrules individual will and benefits even those who oppose it. The film suggests that "legitimate" blackness is not a question of individual choice or self-fashioning (as Touré claims in his book, *Who's Afraid of Post-Blackness?*); it is, rather, predetermined by the state, which holds the monopoly over, and "imposes common principles of vision and division" upon, its agents (Bourdieu, *Practical* 46). In *Bamboozled*, "authentic" blackness, then, does not mean begging to be shot by law enforcement, as One-Sixteenth Black believes in his stereotypical idea of blackness; it means actually, in fact, being shot by law enforcement because the state does not invest the black body with the same amount of symbolic value as the white body.[13] Delacroix's female assistant Sloan Hopkins eventually shoots Delacroix, in whom she sees the ultimate source of all this violent mischief. The fact that Sloan, as Donald Bogle criticizes, "doesn't attempt to wipe out the white TV executive who after all is in the power seat that has led to Delacroix's compromise and corruption" (361), indicates that she also acknowledges Dunwitty's symbolic power. These instances in which the black characters kill among themselves or are killed by the police demonstrate that symbolic violence and physical violence are not two separate entities. They coincide and, borrowing from Reichardt's formulation, perspectivize each other.

The deaths of *Bamboozled*'s black characters do not ultimately induce renewal and improvement as a Bakhtinian reading of Lee's satire would suggest. However, in his dying moments, Delacroix gains a more refined understanding in two contrasting ways. On the one hand, he finally acknowledges the discriminating force that underlies the symbolic forms of stereotypes;

he demonstrates this by quoting from James Baldwin's "No Name in the Street": "People pay for what they do, and, still more, for what they have allowed themselves to become. And they pay for it very simply: by the lives they lead" (386). On the other hand, when reciting his father's advice to "always keep 'em laughin'"[14] (*Bamboozled* 2:02:01), Delacroix also reveals that he has gained an enhanced cognition of *his* condition, namely, as a token, a symbolic object, a scapegoat. Baldwin remarks: "The scapegoat, eventually, is released to death: his murderer continues to live" ("No Name" 386). In this light, *Mantan* continues to air after the actors have been quickly replaced. *Bamboozled*'s last image, a daunting close-up of the show's main actor, whose grinning, jet-blacked face is running with perspiration, symbolizes this troublesome predicament in which the black stereotypes and the white supremacist national mythology they foster persist despite Delacroix's intellectual growth.[15]

Although renewal and improvement are not the ultimate effects within the world depicted in *Bamboozled*, the film nevertheless carries the possibility of change in the world the audience inhabits. Lee prompts his audience to scrutinize the world's representations and images that impose themselves as natural. In so doing, he aims "to break the *doxa*" (Bourdieu, *Masculine Domination* 89; emphasis in original), to reestablish the illogic of "this experience [that] apprehends the social world and its arbitrary divisions . . . as natural, self-evident, and as such contains a full recognition of legitimacy" (9). The potential for change is grounded in the fact that "there is always room for a *cognitive struggle* over the meaning of the things of the world . . . [that offers] the dominated a possibility of resistance to the effect of symbolic imposition" (13–14; emphasis in original). This possibility allows the viewer to reassess the montage of stereotypical black images that *Bamboozled* displays at its end. Lee explains that he wants the "people to think about the power of images, not just in terms of race, but how imagery is used and what sort of social impact it has" (Crowdus and Georgakas, 9). His satire is therefore not a source for cathartic relief. It provides a critical understanding of the subtle mechanisms that govern America's problem of the twenty-first century: a color-blind color line. In this way, Lee's *Bamboozled* qualifies as a true black American satire.

Notes

1. Although Ellison's essay was written in 1985, the entertainment culture he describes in this essay is that of the mid-1930s. It was the era of Jim Crow in the South and a time in which the Negro Servant in Hollywood "provided a down-hearted Depression age with

buoyancy and jocularly," as Donald Bogle notes in *Toms, Coons, Mammies, Mulattoes, and Bucks* (36). "As [these black servants] delivered their wisecracks or acted the fool," Bogle further writes, "the servants were a marvelous relief from the harsh financial realities of the day. Not only their joy and zest but their loyalty, too, demonstrated that nothing in life was ever completely hopeless" (36). Therefore, in spite of the fact that Ellison's experience dates back almost a century, his words nevertheless echo strongly with today's entertainment industry. The African American actress Octavia Spencer, who received the 2012 Academy Award in the category of Best Supporting Actress for playing the outspoken maid Minny in Tate Taylor's *The Help*, serves as a vibrant example for this presence of the past.

2. Dunwitty's artificial black language reflects the equally distorted black vernacular used (especially by white performers) in the minstrel shows of the nineteenth and early twentieth centuries.

3. See also Thomas R. Britt's article in this collection, pp. 56–57.

4. Symbolic power, as Bourdieu explains in *Masculine Domination*, is generally exerted through "a distinctive property, whether emblem or *stigma*, the symbolically most power- ful of which is that perfectly arbitrary and non-predictive bodily property, *skin colour*" (2; emphases added).

5. It is only after he has created the new millennium minstrel show and, thus, ultimately proven his practical sense for the immanent white supremacist laws of the network, this "proleptic adjustment to the demands of the field . . . [that] is called, in the language of sport, 'a feel for the game'" (Bourdieu, *Logic* 66), that Delacroix is finally recognized by Dunwitty and the other staff members of CNS.

6. Except for Delacroix's father and his assistant, Sloan Hopkins, all of the film's main black characters change their names. Whether in an act of submission, as in the case of the two street performers, Manray and Womack, who transform into the minstrels Mantan and Sleep 'n Eat, or through a false heresy, as exemplified by the Mau Maus. Especially the latter's name change signifies the symbolic power of America's white supremacist national mythology that is utterly affirmed by its subjects, even if they believe they are engaging in subversive strategies.

7. This antinomy between southern ruralism and northern urbanism that resurfaces in the dichotomy between Mantan's pastoral setting and *Bamboozled*'s urban setting is a recur- rent theme in Lee's African American discourse. It is also indicative of the Great Migration of African Americans in the twentieth century. His thesis film, *Joe's Bed-Stuy Barbershop: We Cut Heads* (1983), already thematizes this dualism in the conflict between Zacharias Homer, who runs a barber shop in the Brooklyn neighborhood of Bed-Stuy, and his wife Ruth, who wants to move to Atlanta, Georgia. In this regard, it is worth mentioning that Lee's personal biography is marked by a migration from Atlanta to Brooklyn.

8. Junebug's connection to the comedy of Richard Pryor is underscored by the fact that the character is played by Paul Mooney, a social critic / comedian who wrote many of Pry- or's routines and was a close friend of his. Junebug's orange outfit might, then, serve as an allusion to the orange suit Pryor wears during his famous show *Richard Pryor: Live on the Sunset Strip* (cf. Black 22).

9. Bourdieu's remark that "people . . . are manipulated as much as they manipulate [and that they] manipulate even more effectively the more they are themselves manipulated and

the more unconscious they are of this" (*On Television* 17) shows that victims of symbolic violence are by no means incapable of exerting it. Delacroix's symbolic power over the homeless street performers works by way of class distinction, while his symbolic power over his female assistant is mainly exerted through a symbolic violence that is colored by masculine domination. This symbolic power relation between Delacroix and these characters manipulates the latter into contributing to Dunwitty's derogatory plans for the minstrel show.

10. *Mantan* is a symbolic analogue for real-time modern-day minstrel shows such as Lee sees them in commercialized gangsta rap (cf. Sragow 195), whereas CNS represents America's scope-driven television industry that, in its greed for ratings, ruthlessly perpetuates derogatory black images (cf. Crowdus and Georgakas 4).

11. Dunwitty's media consultant, Myrna Goldfarb, enhances the symbolic concealment of *Mantan*'s racism by explicitly pointing to the aspect of fun. Her "Mantan Manifesto" demands, "Lighten up, man . . . this is about fun, nice wholesome fun" (*Bamboozled* 1:08:04–1:09:09). It is in this instant that the viewer realizes how naively, and therefore most effectively, the symbolic separation of blackness is reinforced in the name of "nice wholesome" entertainment.

12. Within the film's ironic discourse about who is "truly" black, the character of One-Sixteenth Black (played by the Jewish American hip-hop artist MS Serch) is Lee's parodic comment on such absurd historical race categorizations as the "one-drop rule" or "octoroons." It is also a comment on the way in which the commodification of gangsta rap (and blackness in general) allows for a white American appropriation of a black (gangsta) culture with "everything but the burden" (as Greg Tate eloquently titled his book on the subject) of actually being black in America. "Everybody wanna be black but nobody wanna be black," says Junebug in his comedy routine (*Bamboozled* 0:56:26–0:56:28). See also Danielle Fuentes Morgan's article in this collection, pp. 162–74.

13. The actual killings of young black males at the hands of New York Police Department officers—victims such as Amadou Diallo and Sean Bell—to which *Bamboozled* alludes in this sequence, are gloomy evidence in support of this argument.

14. This quote is a reference to a key scene in Ellison's *Invisible Man* in which the protagonist's grandfather utters his cynical advice to "overcome 'em with yesses, undermine 'em with grins, agree 'em to death and destruction" (16).

15. The perspiration also allegorizes the recurring dream of Ellison's invisible man, which repeatedly ends with the grandfather's instruction to "Keep This Nigger-Boy Running" (*Invisible* 26) and is, ultimately, echoed in Dr. Bledsoe's alleged letter of recommendation. Lee's allusion to this episode of Ellison's novel at the end of his film indicates the kind of future the director envisions for black people if their cultural misrepresentation is continuously fabricated in this ongoing, unreflective manner.

Charlie Murphy: American Storyteller

James J. Donahue

In his landmark study of African American satire, Darryl Dickson-Carr asserts that "the picaro, especially the black picaro, is the quintessential African American satiric figure" (36). And while he notes that not all picaresque narratives are satirical in nature, "most do create a commentary upon the social mores of the society in which the picaro lives" (35). The picaro—a rogue or rascal—thus functions as one possible focal point for audiences through which African American artists can provide satirical commentary. More specifically, Dickson-Carr suggests that the black picaro "seeks the bridges between two worlds, the heroic and the ironic" (36); as such, the picaro is a figure that can be productively employed by African American artists to provide satiric commentary along both the internal and external vectors identified by Derek C. Maus.[1] In this chapter, I will examine one of the more popular of such picaros in contemporary African American satire: Charlie Murphy. Despite the small number of appearances as a storyteller in "Charlie Murphy's True Hollywood Stories"—a twice-run skit in the successful but abruptly ended Comedy Central series, *Chappelle's Show* (2003– 2006)—Charlie Murphy had an arguably profound impact on a generation of American viewers; his humorous retellings of encounters with Rick James and Prince gave occasion to some of the most oft-repeated lines from the series.[2] More importantly, as I will demonstrate below, these "True Hollywood Stories" operate as a multilayered satire, demonstrating the dual vectors that Maus claims define post-soul satire. They simultaneously provide both Horatian satirical commentary (mild satire directed at an in-group, in this case the African American community) and Juvenalian satirical commentary (scornful satire directed at political and social institutions that we might call American society at large). In these stories, Murphy smartly satirizes particular aspects of the African American community, including definitions of masculinity and latent homophobia, as well as the "authenticity police" and gradations of skin color. Just as significant, however, is the satiric treatment of the entertainment industry and the role of the black male performer in American popular culture. And it is important that these skits are presented as "True Hollywood Stories," as mock-documentary presentations, since this allows *Chappelle's Show* to satirically engage in one of America's longest-lived and most iconic forms of entertainment: the tall tale. Charlie Murphy as roguish picaro thus functions as a contemporary teller of tall tales, those stories often deemed too fantastic to be true, yet also operating to define American cultural values.

Dickson-Carr takes his definition of the picaro from Charles H. Nichols's essay "The Slave Narrators and the Picaresque Mode: Archetypes for Modern Black Personae," part of which I would like to repeat here: "In each account the writer presents a welter of realistic detail designed to drive home the brutality and inhumanity of his experience as a victim" (Dickson-Carr 107). While Murphy is not a slave, nor do the skits depict the historical institution of slavery, he certainly presents himself as the victim. In the first episode,³ he is the victim of Rick James's capricious and at times vicious attacks. In the second episode,⁴ Murphy and his friends suffer an embarrassing defeat by Prince and the Revolution in a game of basketball. Additionally, Murphy is also the "naïve persona" that Linda A. Morris identifies as the figure in American satire "who inadvertently, and in an understated manner, reveals social truths" (377). These stories reveal Murphy to be an inadvertent participant in events that demonstrate painful social truths. In other words, Murphy does not engage in these events in order to critique either the African American community or American society; in fact, his character as presented in the sketches seems largely unaware of the satiric implications of the stories he tells. Charlie Murphy as narrator is able to effectively comment on the actions of Charlie Murphy the character, assisting the viewing audience in coming to terms with the complex social critiques of the satire.

However, given *Chappelle Show*'s repeated use of slavery as a motif for presenting the black male artist—most pointedly and provocatively in the Pilot Boys Production "vanity card" of a shirtless Dave Chappelle in shackles holding fistfuls of $100 bills⁵—it is not a stretch to read all *Chappelle's Show* skits as veiled critiques of the institution of slavery and the modern, economic forms of slavery to which black male artists are subjected. If, as Dickson-Carr claims, "African American satire's earliest purpose . . . was to lampoon the (il) logic of chattel slavery and racism itself" (3), then *Chappelle's Show* demonstrates that one of the aims of post-soul African American satire is to lampoon the contemporary forms of bondage for African American performers, who are reduced to stock racialized caricatures and stereotypes.

In his 1989 essay "The New Black Aesthetic," Trey Ellis claimed that "NBA [New Black Aesthetic] artists aren't afraid to flout publicly the official, positivist black party line" (236). This is the Horatian satire Maus notes as the first of the dual vectors of post-soul satire. Part of the satiric thrust of "True Hollywood Stories" results from the ways that these skits illuminate and critique certain negative stereotypes about the African American community.[6] One such satiric play involves Murphy's relationship to Rick James. Throughout, Murphy and James are shown to have a friendly relationship that also involves intensely violent episodes. Their first encounter in the skit shows James sucker-punching Murphy in the nose to the laughter of the crowd at Studio 54. James notes that he wore a ring with the word UNITY in raised letters, thus leaving a mark that was "imprinted in that black head of his for at least a week." James then taunts Murphy with the word "unity," leaving Murphy to decide between shrugging off the action because of James's stardom or listening to his "ghetto side," which was telling him to "stomp this muthafucker out." Murphy eventually retaliates against James in his hotel room, kicking James to exaggerated effect. The use of physical violence as a means to dominance aptly demonstrates Robyn Wiegman's claim that "physical strength ... emerges as the black male's claim to both power and natural masculinity" (107). Additionally, when James calls in his security guards, he employs a nickname that Murphy bears for the rest of the skit: Darkness. James still calls the Murphy Brothers by such racially significant epithets as "Black Evil Midnight," "Black Magic," and "Darkness" even as they beat his legs. As such, these episodes can be read as an example of what is commonly called "black-on-black crime." One reading, then, of these violent episodes is as satiric commentary on "black-on-black crime" that enforces the stereotype of the black man as violent provocateur. (In James's mind, he is not the provocateur, and he attributes his violent actions to cocaine.[7]) That is, Charlie Murphy is violent because of his dark complexion.

Certainly, such a series of episodes does not work to enforce what Ellis calls "the official, positivist black party line"; similarly, Kathy Russell and colleagues open their study on the politics of skin color by asserting that "intraracial color discrimination is an embarrassing and controversial subject for African Americans" (1). When this skit employs the word "UNITY" as the very marker of violence, the skit is suggesting that there is no such unity in the black community, or at the very least that such unity is more of a surface concern: ideology as costume jewelry. As such, this installment of "True Hollywood Stories" plays out a possibility for African American satirists as articulated by Dickson-Carr in the exposure of "African Americans participat[ing] in their own oppression, with or without their conscious consent" (32–33). The above examples of what Dickson-Carr would call "colorism, or intraracial racism" demonstrate the "chilling possibility" that African American satire suggests some individuals are incapable of "decipher[ing] racism's ubiquitous coding," denying themselves "the will to counter and destroy racism in whatever form it takes" (33). While such actions and language as portrayed in this skit may appear playful—and both Murphy and James note their continued friendship through the years—the skit mildly satirizes this relationship by suggesting the damage it does to the black community, on two levels. First, such fighting—especially when it involves the use of racist characterizations—betrays the very unity that is at the core of "the party line." Second, and perhaps more damaging, is the possibility that such examples of violence will be read by non-African Americans as characteristic behavior; in other words, if James can attribute Murphy's violence to his "darkness," what's to stop others from doing so, too? At this point it becomes important to note that both James and Murphy are high-profile stars (though by his own admission, and as part of the humor of the skits, Murphy presents himself as a second-tier celebrity) and that multiple examples of their violent behavior take place at high-profile clubs (Studio 54 and the China Club). Because of the celebrity status of the participants and the venues, these episodes become very public examples of high-profile "black-on-black" violence. Throughout his series, Chappelle demonstrated a keen understanding of how black male entertainers are looked upon as community leaders (a role he actively rejected); it is not uncommon for such performers to be taken to task for not providing leadership via "advancing the race" in their cultural productions.

As Murphy suggests, these episodes are an escalation of "ghetto" thinking, and when James complains of the Murphys that "they should have never gave you niggers money," he is suggesting that economic opportunities do nothing to change the "ghetto" mentality, and that African American celebrities are nothing more than well-dressed and finely accessorized "ghetto" thugs. And the comedic affectation of many of the violent episodes—from the unrealistic imprint of "UNITY" in Murphy's forehead to the various slow-motion fight scenes that evoke blaxploitation films—encourages the audience, particularly the in-group audience, to laugh with these scenes as gross exaggerations of a stereotype too widely held. A similar gross exaggeration is demonstrated in the second installment of "True Hollywood Stories" in the characterization of Prince (another high-profile celebrity who, even more than Rick James, has enjoyed success outside the black community). This time, however, the "house business" that Murphy airs is the homophobia that lies beneath heteronormative constructions of the black male athlete.

The exaggerated fights between Murphy and James in the first installment of "True Hollywood Stories" can be read as a critique of the hypermasculine desire to assert physical dominance. As such, Murphy's later encounter with

Prince and the Revolution takes this assertion one step further, exposing and then satirizing the undercurrent of homophobia in the African American community, particularly with regard to the black male celebrity. At the beginning of the second installment, Murphy immediately highlights the gender tensions of the episode, claiming that in the 1980s, "The guy that looked most like a bitch was gettin' all the women." Note here that he not only sets up a gendered dichotomy, but that he marks the feminine as "bitch." This derogatory word is often employed as a means of constructing a negative association with femininity; in this context, a "bitch" is a non-masculine male. Note that in the previous episode, James uses "bitch" to refer to women as well as the Murphys. So when Murphy opens this episode by distinguishing a man from a "bitch," he does so to prime for the reader the negativity that should be associated with Prince and the Revolution for their apparent lack of masculine attributes.[8] Of course, immediately following this setup, Murphy notes that even he played into this cultural moment, thus frustrating the clear dichotomy he just delineated. Focusing his attention on clothing, Murphy states that Prince's outfit "looked like somethin' that a figure skater would wear," employing thinly veiled code for homosexuality, a code based both on the flamboyant outfits figure skaters wear as well as the denigration of figure skating as an effeminate sport. This association takes on greater importance when Murphy and his crew are challenged by Prince and the Revolution to a game of basketball, a sport that, unlike figure skating, is often defined as masculine and is dominated by African American players.

When Prince first suggests a game of basketball, Murphy and his crew— all of whom are dressed similarly, in flashy but clearly masculine suits— immediately laugh. Accepting the challenge, they then change into properly "masculine" athletic attire. Prince and the Revolution, however, opt to play in their club clothes, prompting Murphy to call this "the shirts against the blouses." Signifying on the traditional playground separation between "shirts and skins" for teams, Murphy again highlights the gender dichotomy by noting his opponents' feminine attire, taunting Prince with "you know where you got that shirt from, and it damn sure wasn't the men's department." Having firmly established the gendered dichotomy and humorously suggesting to his audience Prince and the Revolution's distinct lack of masculine attributes,[9] Murphy's tone abruptly changes, lecturing the audience to never judge a book by its cover. This is because "this cat could ball"; Prince and the Revolution proceed to humiliate Murphy and his crew ("it was a landslide victory"). However, even within this display of masculinity, Murphy still refers to "fruity picks," complaining about how the Revolution would play defense, suggesting once again a fear of homosexuality in his desire not to be "bent over in front of a cat like that." The sexual tension reaches its peak when Prince is shown simulating sexual acts on the basketball, here a symbol of masculine athleticism, suggesting that Prince is "genderfucking" traditional concepts of black masculinity. As a result, Murphy angrily calls out those who don't believe him to challenge Prince to basketball and to "make sure your people is there to see the game"; this challenge to traditional black masculinity is too unbelievable, too much an affront to cultural norms, to be accepted on its face.

As Julia Round notes, "Prince has confirmed the story in an interview with MTV, saying 'the whupping is true' (although he denies the high heels)" (99). Very likely, Murphy-as-storyteller embellished the story in order to emphasize the satire, just as Chappelle-as-actor embellished the presentation of exaggerated fight sequences in the earlier episode; by highlighting this gender-based tension, Murphy more clearly frustrates traditional notions of black masculinity. In this regard, Murphy engages in what Bertram D. Ashe called "*blaxploration*—or the propensity to trouble blackness*" (614; emphasis in original). Prince's characterization as feminine in dress and manner, as well as dominant on the basketball court, simultaneously challenges and affirms his black masculinity. Prince frustrates overly simplistic definitions and blurs the boundaries between the traditionally masculine and feminine. He continues to blur these lines after the game; still dressed in his "figure skater" outfit, Prince serves pancakes to Murphy and his "flunkies," not unlike how a traditional *Leave It to Beaver*–style mother would serve her family.[10] And here Prince has finally turned the tables on Murphy and his crew, who "got served" in the metaphorical sense that they got beaten on the court, after which Prince literally served them pancakes, at which point he calls them "bitches." While actively performing femininity, Prince here ironically employs the very word that was used to deny "feminine" men their masculinity. So by the end of this episode, the previously clear gender dichotomy is frustrated, along with traditional notions of blackness. As such, just as Murphy earlier satirized the notion of racial unity, here he satirizes the notion of black masculinity, engaging in the kind of explorations of "post-Blackness" that Touré explores in his *Who's Afraid of Post-Blackness?* (2011). For Touré, "Blackness" should not be subjected to what is commonly called "the authenticity police," but rather defined by how African American individuals choose to portray Blackness.[11] Prince's "Blackness"—both his skills on the court as well as his flamboyant stage persona—is thus given cultural credibility by Murphy's story.

In addition to their Horatian, in-group satire aimed at the African American community, the "True Hollywood Stories" also operate as Juvenalian satire in their scornful denunciation of the entertainment industry at-large.

From the very beginning of the series, though with increasing scorn and vitriol (and culminating with Chappelle's surprising resignation from the show), Chappelle aimed his satiric guns at an entertainment industry that (among its other crimes) operates as modern-day slaveholders with respect to African American performers. For instance, the Pilot Boys Productions graphic mentioned above already appears at the end of the first episode. Over the course of its two-plus seasons, *Chappelle's Show* featured numerous skits—such as "Inside *Chappelle's Show* Studio," "R. Kelly's 'Piss on You' Videos," "Wu Tang Financial," and "A Moment in the Life of Lil' Jon"—that attacked the entertainment industry and highlighted to comedic effect the various racist stereotypes that exist in how African American celebrities (especially male celebrities) have been portrayed by mainstream American media. For instance, the humor behind "Wu Tang Financial" arises from the idea that African American rap artists could provide sound financial advice, despite the fact that individuals such as Sean Combs (a.k.a. "Puff Daddy" and/or "P. Diddy") and Jay-Z are arguably more famous today as successful entrepreneurs / impresarios than as rappers. It thus important that both installments of "True Hollywood Stories" feature successful mainstream artists, both of whom enjoyed popular success as well as enduring very public legal battles (albeit for different reasons). Rick James and Prince were both wildly successful African American artists who appealed to diverse audiences during their careers, not unlike Dave Chappelle and Charlie Murphy. In addition to their connection to Murphy, both James and Prince provide examples of some of the pitfalls associated with celebrity, particularly celebrity that comes with crossover success.[12]

Noted for his drug use—his line "cocaine is a hell of a drug" is among the most famous of the entire run of *Chappelle's Show*—Rick James also saw his personal life spiral out of control throughout the 1980s and 1990s. In addition to his career-long drug problems, James was eventually found guilty of multiple charges of kidnapping and assault. James certainly brought this upon himself, and *Chappelle's Show* in no way suggests that his legal problems are related to his race.[13] However, it is nearly impossible to discuss James's career without discussing race. James's drug problems worsened in the late 1980s after he left the Motown record label with which enjoyed his highest record sales. (His most popular single, "Super Freak," was released by Motown in 1981.) As such, Rick James's career can be viewed as a cautionary tale; the mordantly comic repetition of "cocaine is a hell of a drug" during "True Hollywood Stories" (a line James uttered only once during the actual interview that is spliced into the skit) can be read as a not-so-subtle warning to the audience: with great fame comes the potential for a great fall. James's body was found on August 6, 2004; the autopsy found a variety of drugs in his system, including cocaine, the drug he will be most remembered for (thanks, in part, to *Chappelle's Show*). Chappelle's over-the-top performance of James—as a celebrity who demanded to be the center of attention, licked the faces of women while slapping the faces of men, and engaged in ludicrously (self-)destructive antics—is thus presented as a caricature of the successful African American artist, as modern-day minstrelsy.

Chappelle continues such minstrelsy with his portrayal of Prince (who, unlike James, does not appear as part of the skit), as noted above in terms of costume and mannerisms. Like James, Prince is known for his flamboyant performance style. And like James, Prince was involved in several legal battles. However, these legal battles involved financial control over his music as well as several copyright issues over the use of his name and likeness. Most famously, in 1993 Prince changed his name to a symbol (known as "Love Symbol #2") and performed under a variety of pseudonyms because his first name "Prince" (which he was using as his stage name) had been trademarked by his record company, Warner Bros. In public appearances at this time, Prince would write "slave" on his cheek, drawing attention to the same corporate quasi-slavery that Chappelle would later attack. Prince was also involved in several copyright suits regarding unlicensed use of his music and likeness, including cases involving the increasingly popular website Youtube.com. Although unpopular with many fans and fan groups, these actions can be read, alongside Prince's legal battle with Warner Bros., as part of his desire to control his output and image. As a corporate "slave," Prince was fighting for the right to control the fruits of his own labors, a freedom denied to many artists certainly, but a freedom that *Chappelle's Show* suggests is particularly denied to African American artists. Although none of this is explicitly addressed in "True Hollywood Stories," the audience familiar with Prince could not but help recall his public legal battles.[14] Chappelle's embodiment of another African American artist who has worked to escape the bonds of corporate slavery reminds the audience of his own mounting battles with corporate servitude, alluded to in various ways throughout the series and coming to a very public conclusion when he walked out on his contract in 2005, abruptly ending his series during filming of the third season. As such, while Dickson-Carr notes that the generation after slavery "reinterpreted the struggle against oppression in new terms that depended less upon the specter of chattel slavery" (9–10), Chappelle is actively working to reclaim and to recast that specter as a means to understand the challenges faced by contemporary African Americans, particularly celebrities, whose artistic freedom is ironically often challenged by the very system that provides them with financial freedom (compare to the Pilot Boy Productions "vanity card" image). And while the two installments of "True Hollywood

Stories" do not explicitly address these underlying themes of the precipitous downfall of public figures and the shackles of corporate slavery, their use of controversial subjects from the entertainment industry—and the intertextual play with other aspects of *Chappelle's Show*—certainly remind the larger audience of these issues. As such, the "True Hollywood Stories" operate as part of *Chappelle's Show*'s larger attack on the entertainment industry and the particular challenges faced by African American artists.

This facet of the satiric work of "True Hollywood Stories," of course, focuses more on Dave Chappelle than on Charlie Murphy, reading these skits alongside Chappelle's larger body of work. However, it is important to note that these skits are in fact Charlie Murphy's stories, presented to the audience through the figure of the picaro. While Chappelle often makes such critiques himself—or, as seen in the series's second episode, in a thinly veiled manner[15]—"True Hollywood Stories" employs a narrator, a witty raconteur whose delivery often serves to advance not only the humor but also the satiric critique. Given such successful parodies as "Frontline: Clayton Bigsby," "The Niggar Family," "The Mad Real World," "Trading Spouses," and "The World Series of Dice," *Chappelle's Show* has demonstrated a keen understanding of narrative form; how the material is presented, in other words, is just as important as the material itself. Thus, the question must be asked: why is this material best presented through Charlie Murphy? Certainly, as Chappelle himself notes, they are Murphy's stories and he tells them well. However, I would like to submit that their presentation as oral narratives—specifically as over-the-top oral narratives that employ carefully choreographed visual representations which include repeated appeals to their veracity[16]—serves to subtly satirize one of America's most popular artistic forms: the tall tale.

Tall tales, in the American literary-historical context, have often been employed to recount the unbelievable exploits of characters who have taken on mythic stature in American folk history, such as Johnny Appleseed, Daniel Boone, Paul Bunyan, and Davy Crockett. Popular during the nineteenth century and often used to help develop the mythology of the American frontier, the tall tale has survived in popular American culture and has been adopted by such post-soul African American artists as Percival Everett (in his novels *God's Country* [1994] and *Glyph* [1999]) and Colson Whitehead, whose *John Henry Days* (2001) alludes to perhaps the most notable African American subject of the traditional tall tale. John Henry, the steel driver who worked himself to death demonstrating his ability to out-work a machine, serves as an interesting—though admittedly vague—parallel to Dave Chappelle's own career. I make this observation to emphasize the importance of the narrative form of "True Hollywood Stories." It is a fitting coincidence that the most notable African American subject of a tall tale worked himself to death fighting against a symbol of corporate industrialization, not unlike Chappelle's own battles against the entertainment industry. What is important, in terms of the narrative form, is Murphy's participation in the larger tradition of American tall tales, reclaiming them from their traditional association with the American West and employing them in the service of his multilayered satire of contemporary African American life.

Though based in fact, Murphy's "True Hollywood Stories" certainly bear several of the hallmarks of the traditional tall tale: larger-than-life characterization of the subject, exaggeration of the subject's exploits, and appeals to the audience regarding their veracity. Both skits employ backlighting to give their subjects a special glow when they are first described, and in both skits Chappelle's performance is exaggerated to give the impression that the characters have borderline superhuman abilities: Prince, at the conclusion of the basketball game, appears to hang in midair even after letting go of the rim following a dunk, while Rick James appears to have a superhuman ability to abuse his body (through both his drug use as well as his ability to recover from Murphy's comically exaggerated beatings). And just as importantly, Murphy repeatedly affirms the veracity of his stories, beginning with the title "True Hollywood Stories" (itself a reference to the long-running *E! True Hollywood Story* documentary television series) through his various appeals to the audience to believe his otherwise outlandish claims about celebrities who already have firmly established public personae. Murphy's "True Hollywood Stories" are thus mocking the popular series devoted to salacious coverage of troubled celebrities while at the same time co-opting a traditional narrative form employed to mythologize public heroes. The satire, in this regard, plays in two directions: on the one hand, Murphy is calling out the entertainment industry for its portrayal of celebrities' personal problems (Rick James) or privately held personae (Prince); on the other hand, Murphy, through his picaresque stories, elevates these figures to the status of folk heroism. This, of course, is the double standard that *Chappelle's Show* repeatedly notes for African American celebrities: even when celebrated by the popular media, such celebration is accompanied by some form of vilification. Or, as was also the case with John Henry, public success comes with heavy personal cost.

Many *Chappelle's Show* skits are dark, even downright grim; at various points throughout the show's run, Chappelle and others targeted many of America's most profound and public—if not productively addressed—social tensions. The skits do not shy away from portrayals of violence, drug use, or other criminal behavior, for these are the realities faced by many African Americans. Socioeconomic conditions in many black neighborhoods, public injustices perpetrated by the forces of law and order, and the repeated indignities of day-to-day living in a country that has yet to fully address the problem of race, have inspired *Chappelle's Show* to create multilayered satire that comments upon multiple communities simultaneously. As part of that larger satiric project, Charlie Murphy's "True Hollywood Stories" exists as a reminder that a "post-soul aesthetic" does not in any way reflect a "post-racial society." As Murphy's stories demonstrate, there are far too many problems both within and beyond the African American community for black artists to drop their guard.

Notes

1. See also Derek Maus's introduction to this collection, pp. xi–xxiii.

2. As Mark Anthony Neal has noted, "I mean, Chappelle, the Chappelle thing is really fascinating because he's working on a water cooler level. Right? When you consider the way 'I'm Rick James, bitch' circulated, he's working on that kind of level" (Ashe et al., 798).

3. Season 2, episode 16; original air date February 11, 2004.

4. Season 2, episode 17; original air date February 18, 2004.

5. When this graphic airs at the end of the episode, it is accompanied by an audio clip from season 1, episode 4 (original air date February 12, 2003), "I'm rich, bee-yatch!" It is significant that this audio clip comes from a skit on reparations for slavery.

6. All of the issues that I will discuss with respect to *Chappelle's Show* have also been satirized—and in some cases more blatantly—by the animated series *The Boondocks*. Which is to say that both the cultural norms being satirized, and the satires themselves, are not limited to *Chappelle's Show*. See also Terrence T. Tucker's article in this collection, pp. 22–37.

7. Where Dave Chappelle-as-Rick James is often seen as the provocateur, Rick James himself at times contradicts Murphy's version of the events. The two versions of Rick James highlight the constructed nature of the narratives; these are Charlie Murphy's stories and not documentary accounts.

8. As Kathy Russell and her co-authors assert, "historically, [it] has long been the case" that in visual media, African American women have been lighter-skinned than their male counterparts, noting specifically that "Black actors who are light are often turned down for roles that call for virility . . . or sexiness" (135). Keeping in mind that Prince is lighter-skinned than Murphy, we see that the politics of color cannot be separated from the politics of gender.

9. Throughout his career, Prince has played with the conventions of masculinity. In addition to his flamboyant dress and stage presence, many of his songs challenge stereotypes regarding gender and sexuality, such as "Controversy" (1981) and "If I Was Your Girlfriend" (1987), as well as the album *Lovesexy* (1988), with cover art that arguably presents Prince as feminine (nude, surrounded by flowers, wistfully gazing off-camera).

10. I make this reference specifically because *Chappelle's Show* parodies *Leave It to Beaver* earlier in season 2 (episode 2, original air date January 28, 2004) with "The Niggar Family."

11. Touré also provides a useful analysis of *Chappelle's Show* in chapter 3, discussing post-black art with respect to such clips as "Clayton Bigsby," "The Niggar Family," and "The Racial Draft."

12. For an interesting analysis of Chappelle's own battle with crossover celebrity, see Bambi Haggins's "In the Wake of 'The Nigger Pixie': Dave Chappelle and the Politics of Crossover Comedy," where she explores "the price of de facto crossover . . . when those of us in the audience may—or may not—be discerning the politics of racial representation embedded in the satire" (234).

13. However, in several skits and intros, Chappelle does announce his immediate distrust whenever African American celebrities are arrested, a distrust shared by many in the African American community.

14. As noted above, Prince has confirmed the veracity of (most of) the story being told. Although Prince's absence from the skit itself may suggest his continued desire to control his public image, he also released a single titled "Breakfast Can Wait" in 2013 that featured a still shot of Chappelle's portrayal of him on the cover.

15. "Pretty White Girl Sings Dave's Thoughts" opened the second episode of the first season, original air date January 29, 2003.

16. The "True Hollywood Stories" operate as multileveled satire, with Charlie Murphy's oral narratives providing the first layer, followed by Dave Chappelle's reenactments of these stories within the larger framework of their inclusion as sketches in *Chappelle's Show* (for which Dave Chappelle, as host, provides meta-narrative commentary). Both Chappelle and Murphy at times attest to the veracity of the stories, raising doubt in their audiences as to their truth. Ultimately, their truth value is not important for the satire. In fact, by subtly suggesting their value as stories (as opposed to historical events), Chappelle and Murphy highlight their satirical nature; these sketches are not merely events, but instead carefully constructed moments of social critique.

Embodied and Disembodied Black Satire: From Chappelle and Crockett to *Key & Peele*

Marvin McAllister

Blackface minstrelsy was one of this nation's first popular entertainment sensations. It transformed black bodies, particularly black male bodies, into visual spectacles saddled with outrageous—yet strangely limited and eventually burdensome—expectations. In the early 1920s, pre-eminent theatre critic Theophilus Lewis assessed the cultural and artistic damage wrought by blackface. For a three-part series on Negro theatre published in A. Philip Randolph and Chandler Owen's *The Messenger*, Lewis lamented that a "luscious low comedy" defined and dominated Negro performance in his era ("Survey of Negro Theatre" 301). He noted how black and white audiences overwhelmingly preferred black performers in lowbrow "horseplay and bawdy comedy" as opposed to highbrow forms of entertainment that intellectually engaged wit and social commentary. Lewis feared this nation's narrow public tastes and black performers' calculated surrender to physical comedy not only strangled the probative potential of black humor, but also hindered the maturation of African American culture.

More recent critics of black comedy challenge Lewis's dire assessment. Writing about Richard Pryor's one-man show *Black Ben, the Blacksmith* (1968), Glenda R. Carpio illuminates how Pryor's response to blackface minstrelsy—peppered with satiric takes on white bodies—transcended the regulatory norms of the minstrel monster. She contends that Pryor's single black body alternating among white, black, male, and female roles was "not subject to the tension it performs. Instead, it is a conduit for a laughter that releases that tension in a play that celebrated the body's freedom to *perform* rather than be defined by stereotypes" (Carpio 87; emphasis in original). Theophilus Lewis would agree with Carpio that Negro performers did become innovative, first-class spectacles despite the fixed imagery propagated by a blackface tradition. From Billy Kersands to Bert Williams to George Walker, early-twentieth-century black vaudevillians perfected a brand of fully embodied comedy about which Lewis wrote, "What it lacks in subtlety and cleverness, it more than makes up for in sensuousness and daring" ("Survey of Negro Theatre" 301). Yet Lewis also identifies a serious peril for African American art and culture when black comedians show-case physical brilliance and sensual daring to satisfy a ravenous public. He explained, "Our way of living is naturally fecund and exuberant and we have a frank way of facing life. When colored actors dwell on the mere play of a passion in a single mood instead of showing its significance in various veins, they are simply giving a literal duplication of life with a certain amount of exaggeration which is the lowest form of art and the work of petty artists" ("Survey of Negro Theatre" 301).

Twenty-first-century comedians and writers like Dave Chappelle, Affion Crockett, Jordan Peele, and Keegan-Michael Key are by no means "petty artists," but they all have confronted or fallen victim to this black comedic conundrum of an excessively physical comedy fixated on "a single mood." In our cultural and performative moment, these artists represent what Bambi Haggins terms "post-soul . . . media babies," meaning they are post-civil rights, post-Black Arts products of fixed and fluid cultural imagery circulating through various old and new media outlets: film, television, video, the Internet (*Laughing* 5). As conscious or unconscious consumers of earlier racial representations and as creators of the latest transmedia versions of commodified blackness, whiteness, and brownness, these black performers actively contest, reshape, and reinscribe the historical expectations of black comedy.

Their unique identities as "post-soul media babies" have been shaped by specific journeys to old and new media stardom. Chappelle found his niche through the conventional professional comic route. He developed his stand-up "chops" as a teenager, moved on to small and large roles in feature films, signed on for various failed situation comedies, and finally unleashed his brilliant but brief cable series *Chappelle's Show* (2003–2006). Affion Crockett entered the entertainment world as a pre-teen breakdancer, and after graduating from college with a business degree, he also pursued the traditional stand-up path. Crockett appeared on *HBO's Def Comedy Jam* and graduated to minor roles in comedic films, but after several grinding years, he discovered his market niche in new media. Like other internet comedic sensations, notably Dane Cook and Bo Burnham, Crockett built a comedic presence online, which led to bigger opportunities like a web series with Russell Simmons ("Hustle with the Russells") and eventually a short-lived sketch comedy series, *In the Flow* (2011), for Fox television. As they relate in early episodes of *Key & Peele*, Jordan Peele and Keegan-Michael Key earned theatre degrees, developed their skills in sketch and improv comedy, and achieved relative stardom as featured players on Fox's *MADtv* (1995–2009). From there, Key moved to supporting roles in situation comedies, while Peele booked the occasional film role as a nonthreatening black friend, but in 2011 they returned to sketch comedy to develop *Key & Peele* for Comedy Central, the same network on which *Chappelle's Show* appeared.

This comparative analysis of embodied and disembodied black satire will assess Chappelle's, Crockett's, Key's, and Peele's work in old media, specifically commercial television. The plan is to measure their small-screen work against Theophilus Lewis's excoriation of "luscious low comedy" and his call for a black social comedy rooted in ideas and consequence. How do these black comedians execute physical comedy and what are the hazards of their embodied satire? This is not to suggest that performing black bodies are inherently problematic or that every black comedian must devolve into "single-mood" buffoonery. To the contrary, I agree with performance ethnographer Joni L. Jones (Omi Osun Olomo), who locates culture, knowledge, and authenticity within the performing body ("Performance Ethnography"). I am simply acknowledging that black comedic bodies, if not staged with great care, can abdicate the core responsibilities of satire. Finally, as Lewis once hoped, can these talented black artists produce disembodied wit with "significance in various veins"? And to what extent can their comedic commentary sustain ongoing conversations on race, representation, and American culture?

In referring to embodied satire in particular, I am referencing Juvenalian forms of comedy in which artists like Chappelle, Crockett, Key, and Peele rely on physical, gestural, and aural signs of difference to capture and skewer their satiric targets. As for the difference between embodied and disembodied performance, I have previously examined this distinction in my work on "whiting up," an African American tradition of performed whiteness. The dual components of "whiting up" include body-centered, materially focused stage Europeans and the more perception-based, socially and politically attuned whiteface minstrels (McAllister 1–2). To realize stage Europeans, black artists have recreated, in naturalistic, parodic, and satiric modes, the visual trappings of whiteness, such as blonde wigs and blanching face paint. Beyond physiognomy, these imitative acts typically involve reproducing a white tone of voice, a white walk, and even a white attitude or presence.

For their respective television series, Chappelle, Crockett, Key, and Peele have all crafted notable crossracial, transgendered, and intraracial impersonations, but I want to begin with Chappelle's characterization of a timid white husband in his parodic satire of ABC's *Wife Swap* and Fox's *Trading Spouses: Meet Your New Mommy*, a reality series that premiered in 2004. Late in the twelfth episode of the first season of *Chappelle's Show*, head writers Dave

Chappelle and Neal Brennan unfurled "*Chappelle's Show* Trading Spouses," a groundbreaking version of the domestic reality show that "for the first time . . . [is] going interracial." The sketch imagines a black dad named Leonard who moves in with a white family and Todd, a white dad who experiences life with a black family. Chappelle executes Leonard with an Afro wig, bushy beard, abrasive language, and a constantly dangling cigarette. To produce his contrasting stage European, Chappelle dons a platinum-blonde wig and applies mauve makeup to his face and hands. Vocally, Chappelle slips into a deep, hypercorrect, "white" tone of voice. In terms of behavior, Todd is a fully domesticated male partner who cooks and even does dishes.

The satiric target here is not simply "corny" white males, but perceived racial, class, and sexual differences, the kinds of easy contrasts featured in a brand of observational stand-up known as "white people be like" comedy (Haggins, *Laughing* 192; McAllister 201). This unrelenting comedic juxtaposition of white versus black appearances, attitudes, and activities dates back to comic pioneer Jackie "Moms" Mabley and was perfected by the legendary Richard Pryor. For their sensuous comparison of black temerity and white timidity, Chappelle and Brennan actually reference and build on elements of Pryor's work. In a bedroom scene, the cigarette-wielding, supremely confident Leonard is forward and demanding with his "traded" white spouse, while Todd is obsequious, nervous, and sexually awkward around his temporary black partner. However, by the end of the sketch, Chappelle and Brennan reveal that Todd secretly enjoys sniffing (and apparently pilfering) female undergarments.

Sexual perversity aside, the sketch does tease its audience with some insightful commentary. During an interaction between Leonard and his rap-obsessed, "traded" white son, we learn how cloistered white kids can mythologize urban culture, and so to expose his borrowed progeny to reality, the no-nonsense Leonard drops the boy off in the "hood." Regrettably, Chappelle's ridiculously wigged, mauve-faced, hypercorrect white caricature dominates the piece and overwhelms any satiric insights on how cultural difference is romanticized. And this was not the first time an excessive stage European caused a satiric misfire on *Chappelle's Show*. In episode four of season one, Chappelle gets trapped in a similar "single mood" of white maleness when he enlists white anchorman Chuck Taylor to report on slave reparations finally arriving in the "hood." Like the laughable white husband Todd, this stiff, white anchorman becomes the low-comedy focal point, and a potentially consequential sketch never fully imagines what reparations might mean for lower-class black urbanites.

Chappelle and his writing team were diverted by the physical; they got lost in what Theophilus Lewis once called the "mere accessories of comedy"

("Magic Hours" 1). In a *Pittsburgh Courier* reminiscence on black comedy, Lewis painted all "colored" performers as body-dominant, low-comedy artists and damned their work as "the humorous expression of vulgar ideas and behavior of coarse and unenlightened people." He protested that the most gifted actors on Negro stages were "devoting their talents to depicting the conduct of bumpkins, hoidens, rogues, and other picaresque characters" (1). Lewis saw wasted genius and suggested that "one would expect to see this form of amusement develop to a very high degree of excellence." Yet here is how Lewis explained the lack of development: "too often our comedians ignore ideas and behavior, the true sources of comedy, and spend all their ability on the mere accessories of comedy, such things as a black makeup, enlarged lips, clodhopper clothes, and elephantine feet. This is one of the fundamental weaknesses of our stage" (1). Such weaknesses—an overreliance on the physical and a concurrent neglect of compelling ideas—arose from a popular thirst for easy, affirming laughter; and sadly, this corporeal fixation persists as a core problem in Chappelle's and Crockett's embodied satire.

For the August 2011 debut of his series *In the Flow*, Affion Crockett immediately and firmly aligned himself with this same fundamental weakness. Crockett just happens to be a talented dancer, so during the opening sequence of every show, he showcases his dance skills in a rewound film of him breaking, popping, and locking in archetypal B-boy style. In addition, on the very first episode, Crockett establishes a firm linkage between his new show and Fox's legendary sketch comedy hit *In Living Color* (1990–1994); he invites the younger generation of the Wayans brood—Damon Wayans Jr. and Damian Dante Wayans—to lounge on his couch between sketches. With two "baby" Wayans serving as cosigners, Crockett announces that their comedic forefathers—Keenen Ivory and Damon, Shawn, and Marlon Wayans—have all endorsed his series and passed the mantle on to him. Coincidentally, Jamie Foxx, a dynamic contributor to *In Living Color*, served as co-creator and executive producer for Crockett's new venture.

As for embodied satire, Crockett performs a problematic cross-racial impersonation of Filipino boxer, elected official, and aspiring singer Manny Pacquiao in the first episode of the series. The premise: various celebrities are auditioning for a highly prized judge's spot on Fox's megahit singing contest, *American Idol*. To embody Pacquiao, Crockett lightens his already fair skin and wears a straight black wig, with a whisker-like goatee. For costume, Crockett's Pacquiao wears red boxing gloves and a red "ring" robe to ensure immediate audience recognition. Later, in a behind-the-scenes outtake, Crockett shares his transformation process, especially the straight hairs that were glued to his face, and he explains that his grandfather was

Chinese, which somehow helps justify his stereotypical rendition of a Filipino cultural icon.

The most distinctive and demeaning feature of Crockett's embodied satire is the language. Pacquiao's English is severely broken, and as the Filipino boxer struggles to communicate with the *Idol* contestants, his speech wanders into incredibly long, song-like pauses. Interestingly, Crockett's Pacquiao shares this linguistic difficulty with the comedic actor impersonating his boxing trainer, Freddie Roach, who in real life suffers from Parkinson's disease. For an easy, juvenile laugh, Crockett and his writing team developed an unfortunate merger of Roach's neurological disorder and Pacquiao's language deficiency. And if that peculiar combination is not regrettable enough, Crockett taps into a persistent rumor—kept alive by boxing rival Floyd Mayweather Jr.—that Pacquiao is a dirty fighter who relies on performance-enhancing drugs. The sketch lands on this satiric target, illegal drug use, when Freddie Roach provides Pacquiao with his "vitamins," a syringe filled with steroids, and from there, the scene rapidly devolves into a cartoonish lampoon. A "juiced" Pacquiao goes on a rampage of shadowboxing, singing into a microphone while doing push-ups, and finally punching out a show contestant and a crew member. Sadly, Crockett's Pacquiao gets trapped in this "single mood" of broad physical comedy, and any potential social commentary about an allegedly drug-abusing fighter gets muddled amidst whiskers, mangled English, and cheap steroids humor.

In the market of online short videos, where Crockett has arguably had his greatest success, the most outlandish yet familiar representations tend to earn the page-views and achieve "viral" status; therefore, one can understand why he would push for "luscious low comedy." Much like new media content, Chappelle's and Crockett's old media cross-racial impersonations are designed to elicit recognition from the lowest common denominator, as broad a television public as possible; and in this world of embodied satire, fixed signifiers of color, masculinity, ethnicity, ability, and class get the job done. Glenda R. Carpio offers Richard Pryor as that exceptional black comic whose career skyrocketed when he discovered urban folk humor and successfully navigated the minefield of blackface cultural remnants. Media scholar Bambi Haggins once identified the same transcendent potential in "post-soul media baby" Chappelle, but he may have failed to equal Pryor.

Novelist and journalist Touré, in his work on post-blackness, characterizes Chappelle as a comedic talent who was seduced by the allure of a post-black representational aesthetic but was then ruined by the high cost of being a performing black body. Touré first lauds Chappelle as the quintessential post-collective artist, liberated from white and black gazes and unafraid to offend and potentially "set the race back" with his comedic sketches. However, over a week of taping for the third season of *Chappelle's Show*, doubt crept into Chappelle's mind about racial responsibility and how his flirtations with the minstrel monster played to a largely white viewing audience. He suddenly questioned the freedom of his post-black cultural moment, in which black artists supposedly no longer had to confront anxiously centuries of racial imagery. In a stand-up routine years after his departure, Chappelle would claim he walked away from his show because he felt "pimped" by Comedy Central, but Touré argues Chappelle actually exploited himself and that, in essence, his "comic mouth has written checks that his body is afraid to cash" (Touré 74). But as an astute cultural observer, Chappelle has always recognized the vulnerability of black comedic bodies. In his stand-up, Chappelle often appears sheepish, physically awkward, never quite at ease with how his body reads or plays. So it is no surprise Chappelle experienced an existential crisis when he became a national star, simultaneously realizing that his Juvenalian impersonations of whiteface dads or blackface coons might still be too volatile even for post-black fluidity.

Pushing this racial "noise" aside, Affion Crockett positions himself in the vanguard of a new generation of black comedic talent that is truly free of racial gazes and unconcerned with the pitfalls of embodied satire. Following his photo opportunity with the young Wayanses, Crockett cements this generational distinction through a "Passing the Torch" sketch, in which he browns up to impersonate "old-head" Chappelle as a bitter, paranoid, cannabis addict who fixates on white folks. As a fallen television icon, "Dave" gives Crockett advice: he warns him to watch out for the "coalition of the white folks" because they are supernatural beings that can float and control your behavior by putting white skin flakes in your food. To cap this racially obsessed version of Chappelle, Crockett's "Dave" says "have fun making shows with the white devils." With this parodic satire of Chappelle, Crockett sends an important message to mainstream audiences, Fox executives, and national advertisers: I am not Dave and I will not flip out over racial imagery and leave a megahit show. Crockett signals that he is braver than Chappelle, truly unconcerned with doing damage to the race. In doing so, he embraces a painfully familiar physical brand of comedy with limiting implications for black bodies and African American culture.

In the second episode of the first season of *Key & Peele*, Keegan-Michael Key and Jordan Peele offer an excellent, self-reflexive satire on how black performers "pimp" the physical. For this sketch, Key and Peele represent two actors performing in a community theatre production about a fictional meeting between Malcolm X and Martin Luther King, perhaps a reference to Jeff Stetson's one-act play, *The Meeting* (1984). In the sketch, the two iconic black leaders are drawn into a battle to see who can elicit the most applause and vocal approbation from this community theatre audience. The two powerful speakers initially move the crowd with the best-known lines from their expansive rhetorical repertoires, but the game of linguistic gymnastics quickly degenerates. The showdown moves from ideas and insights to broad physical gestures, even dance moves, to elicit the largest reaction from this predominantly black public. Key and Peele suggest that as the stakes are raised in this political competition for hearts and minds, what wins the crowd is not wisdom, but the body, specifically physical comedy. Ultimately, the fixation on the physical, this "single mood," robs Martin and Malcolm of their accustomed, hard-earned gravitas, and by the end of this brutal yet revealing sketch, two black political heroes are reduced to vaudevillian clowns.

Despite Lewis's early-twentieth-century desire, enlightened, comedic treatment of ideas was still losing to "luscious low comedy" in the early twenty-first century. With their cross-racial impersonations, Chappelle and Crockett gesture toward perceptive social commentary, but that hint of substantive discourse gets drowned in a swirl of too-obvious physical humor and their satires ultimately miss their marks. Two episodes into their series, Key and Peele exposed how easy it is for black performers to succumb to the physical and abandon the intellectual. However, what can happen when Chappelle and Crockett abandon the wigs and whiskers and fully pursue ideas, behaviors, and consequences through disembodied, non-Juvenalian satire? What happens when comics like Key and Peele push beyond the body and develop varied conversations on social and political dynamics in this country?

Effective satiric performance is about using the body to reference disembodied social practices, or put another way, artists manipulating constructed, theatrical identities to comment on and maybe correct specific social mores. So by disembodied satire, I mean comedic explorations driven by intense observation and committed to creating a deep discourse far surpassing the "mere accessories of comedy." When comedians pull back from reductive whiskers, laughable wigs, and physical pandering, their comedy can potentially achieve the level of reflection and consequence that Lewis envisioned: a comedy fully rooted in the social.

The best practitioners of satire realize that the stakes are high, and their work accepts the awesome responsibility of altering cultural and personal conceptions. The seventeenth-century French dramatist Molière understood that the higher purpose of all satire was to reprove, not reassure or reaffirm the public. He once wrote that "the finest strokes of high moral philosophy are less powerful, most often, than those of satire, and nothing reproaches most men more effectively than a painting of their faults"

(Norman 4). Larry F. Norman has analyzed the codes governing Molière's satiric "painting," with an emphasis on how his comedy is "both theatrical and social in origin" (5). According to Norman, Molière's theatrical production is about the combination and occasional collision of embodied, theatrical spectacle with disembodied, culturally defined social practices. To expose man's faults, foibles, and predilections, Molière deployed various dramatic weapons and took many representational liberties with his real-life targets. As a result, he crafted a series of vibrant, inventive, yet recognizable comedies of manners that played well beyond "static moral commentary" (7). The endgame for Molière's blend of the theatrical and the social, the embodied and the disembodied, was to reform Parisian society.

This corrective function of satire has been equally prevalent in African and Afro-diasporic performance. Historian William Piersen writes about the efficacy of West African satirical songs in speaking truth to power and resolving private and public grievances. According to Piersen, such songs "were especially useful in fostering social harmony because they permitted socially approved criticism without fostering unpleasant and dangerous personal face-to-face confrontations." In practice, potentially divisive criticism—leveled at neighbors, relatives, or even powerful officials—was softened by culturally sanctioned lyrical wit. West Africans trusted that most serious issues could and should be resolved through this disembodied satire predicated on "social pressure and communal wisdom" (Piersen 54).

Molière, William Piersen, and Theophilus Lewis would all agree that communal pressure and critical artistic insights were the true strengths of French and Afro-diasporic satire. Confronted with the lingering impacts of blackface in the 1920s, Lewis would add that, "contrary to the belief that prevails in some quarters, comedy is not just sheer nonsense or exaggerated imbecility. True comedy springs from the inner nature of man, his attitude toward life and the consequence of his conduct" ("Magic Hours" 1). Based on an understanding of disembodied satire as a social practice rooted in conduct, pressure, and consequences, comedians like Chappelle, Crockett, Key, and Peele become immensely responsible for how race, gender, and other cultural positions signify for their publics. More importantly, the true social significance of their work resides in its ability to expose certain attitudes and potentially police conduct.

For this televisual discussion of disembodied humor, ideas, and conduct, I want to start with the game show parody, a long-standing staple of television sketch comedy. Chappelle and Crockett have returned some vitality to this format by using the game show to explore racial constructions and assumptions. This variety of comedic inquiry is right up Dave Chappelle's alley, because as he explained in a *Fresh Air* interview with Terry Gross, he grew up listening to the dean of conversational black comics, Dick Gregory. Also, during the segments of stand-up sandwiched between his sketches— highlights of the television series—Chappelle is allowed to showcase his slightly detached, cerebral comedic style.

In episode eight of season two, Chappelle proved he could master disembodied satire in a highly original game show sketch titled "I Know Black People." Chappelle uses in-between commentary to establish the segment, as he matter-of-factly explains how the idea sprung from a disconcerting encounter with a white person who claimed *Chappelle's Show* was offensive to black people. In the wake of this confrontation, Chappelle decided he was not going to discount this particular viewer simply because he was white. Instead, he reasoned (his tongue likely planted firmly in his cheek) that some white people might have a gut instinct for how black people feel about various serious issues. In the resulting sketch, Chappelle plays a straightforward, well-spoken game show host in a sensible suit, who grills a panel of real contestants as they compete to prove they know black people. Leading off the panel is a white male professor of African American studies; a white female police officer from Washington Heights in New York City; a white writer on *Chappelle's Show*; a Korean male grocery store worker; a Filipino-looking DJ who claims to have many black friends; a white female social worker from Delaware; a fair-skinned Latino high school student who goes to a majority-black school; and, finally, a black male barber from Brooklyn with a 100 percent black clientele.

The verbal banter builds and cultural attitudes are revealed as Chappelle playfully interacts with the contestants, putting the same questions to each in order to elicit their genuine, idiosyncratic responses. Several questions— like "why do black people like menthol cigarettes?" or "how can black people rise up and overcome?"—have multiple, even contradictory correct answers. The sketch relies on this variability to demonstrate the complexity of African American experience and to allow Chappelle to showcase his improvisational skills. Case in point, with the question, "Is pimping easy?," most contestants answer with some version of "no"; the white professor even references the original Big Daddy Kane song. But when the final contestant, the black barber from Brooklyn, answers with an emphatic and braggadocio-laden "hell yeah," Chappelle-as-host improvises and declares, very much in the moment, that his answer is "also correct."

Chappelle cleverly uses the game show to confront cultural assumptions not individual identities, and his most poignant exchange arises from a highly specific question: "What was Mr. Bookman's job on *Good Times*?" The Korean grocer, who admits to having never seen this iconic black sitcom, guesses that Bookman was a janitor, which prompts host Chappelle to comment on how amazing it is that the contestant has never seen the show yet can still intuit "that Bookman was cleaning up." In this moment, Chappelle's target is not Korean grocers or black custodians; rather, he is laser-focused on occupational and racial hierarchies that persist in the United States. By slyly accenting this assumed economic disparity, and ending the sketch with a question that has a seemingly inexhaustible list of answers ("How can black people rise up and overcome?"), Chappelle's skit explores a larger conversation with significant economic, political, and social consequences.

Chappelle and Crockett differ greatly in how they use disembodied satire to launch interventions into the social. Chappelle's game show is premised on the idea that nonblack people have some familiarity with black people, while Crockett's game show, "Put That on Something," from the fourth episode of *In the Flow*, is inspired by an in-group phrase that he assumes nonblack viewers do not know. After prancing and dancing on screen as the nattily attired, ebullient host Mark Johnson, Crockett clarifies for his white public, in a silky smooth "white" broadcaster voice, that "Put That on Something" is not a game show about condiments. To further clarify his "hood" terminology, he explains the phrase is a challenge you make when you do not believe a person's claim and you want to force them to "put up something" they love to support the veracity of their assertion. Unlike Chappelle's wide array of contestants, Crockett reduces his game show to two interchangeable black male contestants, A.J. and Reggie, "play cousins" who have known each other since junior high. By building his show around an in-group phrase and two contestants "from the block," Crockett tightly controls the interpretation of this particular world, unfortunately limiting the potential social resonance of his commentary at the same time.

The rules involve betting back and forth based on a claim made by one contestant, specifically, "I slept with sexy Janet from the block." One contestant puts up the entire "hood" that his adversary is lying about this sexual encounter, while the claimant trots out his mother as collateral for his assertion. To resolve the bet, host Mark Johnson brings on "sexy Janet," who promptly denies the hookup, causing the claimant to lose both his mother and Janet to his "play cousin." This understandably short contest, involving only one claim, does not take us anywhere or provide any new perspectives on "hood" dynamics. The main agendas in the sketch are to spring an exotic phrase on mainstream audiences, ridicule whites for their ignorance of inner-city vernacular, and launch demeaning asides at the contestants to generate easy laughter.

One potential satiric target could be the prevaricating "play cousin" who risks and loses his mother, with the potential corrective message being "watch out, because the lies you tell have serious and unforeseen conse-quences." Another target could be Mark Johnson and his irrepressible clowning, but Crockett's peripatetic host actually steals the show and under-mines the sketch. Once he hits the stage, Johnson is in constant motion, indulging in hip-hop dance moves, even sliding across the floor after an especially cutting "snap" from one contestant. Sadly, Crockett lapses into what Lewis would call a "single mood" of representation, that mood being purely physical, "luscious low comedy." He rapidly morphs into the uncon-trollable physical caricature Key and Peele expose and ridicule in their Mar-tin and Malcolm sketch.

With respect to on-air longevity, both Chappelle and Crockett enjoyed relatively brief runs on the small screen, which could suggest the tenuous-ness of black satire on broadcast and cable television, but also the failure of both artists to strike a productive balance between embodied and disem-bodied satire. Over three seasons of *Chappelle's Show*, Chappelle was clearly more comfortable with observational humor, especially when riffing on social conceptions of race. Chappelle's "I Know Black People" sketch suc-ceeds because it takes a cerebral, physically disengaged approach to generate multiple conversations on the past, present, and future of African American culture. It was when Chappelle got caught in the rapids of racial signifiers, when he was overwhelmed by the historical expectations projected onto black comedic bodies, that he froze and cancelled himself.

Crockett, by contrast, willingly delivers culturally legible, full-bod-ied black comedy familiar to most audiences, but his series failed to earn another season because his brand of embodied satire could not hold our collective attention. In his rare moments of disembodied satire, like the exotic "Put Something on That," Crockett never struck his targets squarely or effectively critiqued specific social selves. True, one "play cousin" loses his mother because of an inane boast, but a sense of real consequence for his conduct remains absent from the sketch. As he establishes in his very first episode, Crockett is not overly concerned with race like Chappelle, but because of this disengagement, his potential satire of urban youth never matches Chappelle's self-reflexivity. Instead, Crockett's attempt at socially responsible humor retreats to derisive "snaps" and regresses into a distract-ingly broad and often superficial comedy that once again compromises the black body. His exposé "Put Something on That" misses its marks not just because host Mark Johnson fails to discipline his roaming body, but because Crockett and his writing team are just not interested in building an instruc-tive conversation about this particular "hood."

During the first three seasons of their new Comedy Central series, Key and Peele have managed to meld embodied and disembodied satire in

contributing to an important conversation on the political, racial, and personal implications of having a black man in the Oval Office. For their debut
episode, the duo crafted a dualistic or bifurcated Obama impersonation
rooted in the widespread perception that he is detached, almost Vulcan in
his emotions. Peele coolly embodies a dry, witty Obama—an impersonation that simultaneously skewers and justifies the president's lack of emotional affect—while his collaborator, Key, high kicks and karate chops his
way into an "anger translator" named Luther, who has been hired by the
White House to communicate the beleaguered president's rage. In the initial weekly address from the Oval Office, President Obama runs through
a litany of concerns, including Middle Eastern dictators, uranium enrich-
ment in Iran and North Korea, the Tea Party, and the "birther" controversy.
On each topic, Luther provides fully enraged, foul-mouthed counterpoints
to Obama's aesthetic of cool; Luther calls the dictators "bitches," refers to the
Tea Party as "them motherfuckers," and dismisses the "birthers" as "dumb-
ass crackers." Beyond the colorful language, Luther is a human maelstrom,
pacing on- and off-camera, throwing his hands up in frustration, and pushing right into the camera to punctuate Obama's fury. Meanwhile, the president remains calm and composed in his plush, antique chair.

At the heart of this embodied-disembodied conversation on race, representation, and politics is a significant cultural truth: the first black / biracial
president must remain circumspect because he is working against the cultural imaginary of Luther. The stereotypical, verging on archetypal, "angry
black man" is a powerful political trope; in fact, the notion of a raging Barack
Obama has become quite marketable. Conservative critic Dinesh D'Souza's
2011 book *The Roots of Obama's Rage* and his highly successful 2012 documentary *2016: Obama's America* both depict Obama as governing with a postcolonial agenda rooted in the dreams of his dead Kenyan father (Guzman).
D'Souza, Key, and Peele would all agree that Obama harbors some anger, but
the core difference is conservatives believe his rage is unfounded, unpatriotic,
and ultimately destructive, while black satirists like Key and Peele believe that
his anger is justified, even productive, when channeled properly.

During their second season, Key and Peele's "dualistic Obama" sketches
take direct aim at Governor Mitt Romney, the dynamics of the 2012 election
campaign, and Obama's poor performance in the first televised debate. Peele's
restrained Obama opens the address by explaining how the two campaigns
will be respectful of each other's personal lives, families, and religions. But
Key's impatient Luther immediately breaks that truce with a religious rant.
He cries double standard, raging that Obama has to continually explain he
is not a Muslim, while it is off limits to talk about Mormon Mitch Romney's "magic underwear." Obama immediately checks Luther—essentially

checking himself—and for the first time in the series, Luther is allowed a self-reflexive moment. He admits he went too far on this hot-button issue and asks himself whether "[he has] no sense of decorum? Goddamn!"

Of course, the point of Luther is precisely his excess, especially the physical extremes, with his mugging into the camera and his high kicks aimed at Obama's opponents. However, after reprimanding himself in this address, for the next installment Luther is again allowed much more room to vent. In the wake of Obama's lackluster first debate performance, Luther laments that he, the embodiment of Obama's rage, was not allowed onstage for that intellectual tussle. Luther criticizes the president for not bringing his passion to the first debate and properly channeling his aggression against an extremely vulnerable Mitt Romney. Deploying wit and not his martial arts skills, Luther unloads a string of zingers he would have used at the debate, including one about Mormons and multiple wives. Notably, this time an unrepentant Luther does not chide himself for dipping into the troubled waters of religion.

Apparently, Key and Peele's social commentary has reached its intended target. In a 2012 interview on *Late Night with Jimmy Fallon*, President Obama explained how his aides showed him a YouTube clip of one of *Key & Peele*'s sketches, because his staff felt the piece accurately captured the current political climate. Obama was so impressed by the duo's work that he invited them to a sit-down. For the debut of their second season, Key and Peele proudly recounted their meeting with President Obama in their inter-sketch commentary. The duo gushed over how Obama sympathized with them about how hard it was "for a brother on television," a comment that echoes Lewis's original articulation of the black comedian's conundrum. Obama was alluding to the problems faced by a self-cancelled Chappelle or a network-cancelled Crockett, and he frames these troubles in explicitly male terms. Key and Peele are the latest in a line of male bodies that testifies indirectly to the profound lack of black female comedians heading their own sketch comedy programs, with Wanda Sykes being the rare exception.

In closing, the duo shares President Obama's parting words to them: "by the way, don't let me do anything too crazy." Not surprisingly, the sketch immediately following the commentary features a collegiate "Barry O" who is totally obsessed with a "diversity of babes" and "righteous bud." Clearly, Key and Peele's encounter with the president did not compromise their satirical acuity. Hopefully this latest crop of "brother[s] on television" (which also includes W. Kamau Bell and his FX series *Totally Biased*, which premiered in October 2012) will last long enough to resolve the problem of black comedic bodies on television, to develop more productive critical relationships between those bodies and cultural discourse, and to define what comes next for African American comedy.

Television Satire in the Black Americas: Transnational Border Crossings in *Chappelle's Show* and *The Ity and Fancy Cat Show*

Sam Vásquez

Dave Chappelle made headlines when he left his critically and commercially successful comedy sketch, *Chappelle's Show* (*CS*) in May 2005. Initially hiding away in South Africa while his third season was scheduled to start filming, Chappelle eventually reemerged, making numerous television appearances in which he explained the disturbing realizations that prompted his departure. On *The Oprah Winfrey Show* he noted that while shooting one of his typically racially provocative sketches, "somebody on the set [who] was white laughed in such a way—I know the difference of people laughing with me and people laughing at me—and it was the first time I had ever gotten a laugh that I was uncomfortable with. Not just uncomfortable, but like, should I fire this person?" This moment instantiated what Chappelle described as "a complete moral dilemma," and he wondered whether he was being "socially irresponsible" ("Chappelle's Story").

In these insights, the African American comedian implicitly raises a question: how should black satirical works, particularly those that rely on racial and ethnic stereotypes, be interpreted? Despite his compelling notion that his racially informed sketches were failing in their larger social mission—so much so that he forfeited a $50 million contract with the Comedy Central network—scholars have often challenged this very premise as limiting. In his groundbreaking study *African American Satire: The Sacredly Profane Novel* (2001), Darryl Dickson-Carr rightly states, "The Western literary canon tends to deem African and African American literature and culture as primarily social protest literature, a restrictive designation not normally given to traditional, European literatures and cultures" (2). Certainly, such a position raises an important concern about the need for closer attention to the aesthetic contributions of black literary and cultural production. Yet if one acknowledges Chappelle's investment in the productive social signification of his work, one must also interrogate commonly held assumptions about the particular kinds of "social protest" that black artistic forms are expected to undertake. Dickson-Carr astutely clarifies some of the stakes of this satire in ways that seem to mirror Chappelle's aims, noting that "African American satire spends less time upon *protesting* the existence and persistence of racism as a sociological phenomenon *per se* and more upon examining its effects . . . upon the African American" (32; emphases in original).

Still, there are startling and significant limitations to the general perception Dickson-Carr conveys and other key terms it invokes. First, in light of increasingly accepted notions of a "transnational Americas," I suggest the need for additional interrogation of who is included/excluded in the category of "African American literature and culture." Focusing on Dickson-Carr's attention to cultural production, I would add that despite lip service paid to increasingly transnational explorations in the Americas, studies of humor and black satirical culture are often limited to the continental Americas, with contributing, noncontinental cultural and ethnic groups glibly subsumed or overlooked in this scholarship. Notably, even Dickson-Carr's early caveat in his study about using the terms *black* and *African American* interchangeably and "people of color as a general descriptor of the major ethnic minority groups in the United States of America" fails to elicit a specific reference to one of the most obvious groups that might be included in such conversations: Afro-Caribbeans (xv).[1]

This tendency in humor studies to treat communities in the black Americas as discrete and/or unrelated is evident in other important contributions, including Glenda Carpio's *Laughing Fit to Kill* (2008), Daryl Cumber Dance's *Honey, Hush!* (1998) anthology; the "Black Laughter" section of Lawrence W. Levine's *Black Culture and Black Consciousness* (1978), and Mel Watkins's *On the Real Side* (1994), which all focus almost exclusively on an African American context. Although Dance's broader body of scholarship extensively engages with both African American and Caribbean folklore, humor scholars' overall tendency to separate these traditions is evident in her publication of different works such as *Shuckin' and Jivin': Folklore from Contemporary Black Americans* and *Folklore from Contemporary Jamaicans* (1981). Roger Abrahams's pioneering text *The Man-of-Words in the West Indies* (1983), which focuses on humor in the Anglophone Caribbean, offers one of the most sustained comparisons of blacks' deployment of humor in various New World contexts. Yet it is an invitation to a critical conversation that few scholars have accepted. Such oversights are particularly surprising given many artists' transnational explorations.

The notion of black satire being an expressive mode heavily invested in social examinations suggests other areas in need of closer scrutiny. Which society is being interrogated and which specific aspects of that society are being singled out for examination? The underlying assumptions that these forms of black "social" explorations in the Americas focus on black/white relationships (or at best colorism within an African American context) are also too narrow. Many of the hierarchies that humor subverts and reveals are within the diverse marginalized communities themselves, not between blacks and whites, as is the focus of most scholarly discussions of blacks' satirical works.[2]

There is yet another reason to utilize a transnational and comparative approach in black humor studies. Focusing specifically on television, Matt Sienkiewics and Nick Marx question literary scholars' close textual analyses of racially loaded satirical programs, noting that "work focusing specifically on offensive representations of ethnic minorities . . . remains largely relegated to the textual level" (6).[3] They suggest that narrow interrogations remain intellectual and centered around individual experiences. However, I examine shows that open themselves up to a larger discursive community, as is the case in Chappelle's negotiation of transnational exchanges and his parodic satire of well-known shows. Rather than dwell on the personal experiences of racism, these programs "show such prejudice as a systematic, social problem, not one that can be blamed on certain 'bad' individuals" (Sienkiewics and Marx 5). In this way, even descriptions of social protest / examination—and the attendant nationalistic connotations—are expanded. Personal accounts have numerous advantages, including offering nuanced and intimate depictions of social atrocities. Nevertheless, in an allegedly post-racial era, broader examinations remind contemporary audiences of the systematic, engrained nature of racism, highlighting some of the ways in which it continues to thrive. Furthermore, a transnational approach demonstrates that for "black" Americans, "society" is limited neither to the United States nor to a primarily black/white, African American context.

In light of burgeoning African diasporic studies, my discussion of *Chappelle's Show* considers the noncontinental African diasporic community Chappelle most often examines outside the United States: Afro-Caribbeans. In these explorations, one does not simply encounter malicious, all-inclusive racial and ethnic stereotyping, but complex representations of black identity. I specifically focus on moments in which Chappelle depicts Caribbean individuals, and particularly Jamaicans, as being "inside" and "outside" African American communities in the course of his examinations of black life in the United States.

Although complex racial dynamics emerge, Chappelle's own ambivalence regarding a Caribbean community is periodically evident in his sketches. If satire "makes fun of human folly and vice by making people accountable for their public actions," might this unstable genre not also reveal the shortcomings of the speaker's own "folly and vice?" (Marc ix) In other words, if satire is meant to question and interrogate widely held social views, then might it not also question the producers of satire, holding the satirist's feet to the same comedic fire he wields? As much of Chappelle's humor relies on linguistic play, then not surprisingly, when he mocks differences between African American and Caribbean individuals, linguistic variations are often central. Therefore, I also explore these moments of intragroup typecasting within African diasporic communities, particularly when linguistic play and a flip-flopping, unstable satire raise questions about racial and ethnic belonging.

Despite *Chappelle's Show*'s relatively short run, it had a broad international impact on approaches to comic representations of race. Specifically, its profound influence on Jamaicans is concretized in the critically and commercially acclaimed Jamaican comedy sketch program *The Ity and Fancy Cat Show* (*IFCS*), which Television Jamaica contracted in 2006 right on the heels of Chappelle's departure from *CS*. In fact, one of the creators and stars, Ity, describes his show as "a cross between Dave Chappelle, *In Living Colour* [sic] and a kinda Chris Rock ting" (T. Evans). I explore *CS*'s problematic stereotyping, and *IFCS*'s departure from these paradigms. Therefore, I complete a close analysis of *CS* before moving to a discussion of *IFCS*. I argue that although both programs usefully explore racism as being indebted to long-established, institutional paradigms, *CS* tends to represent the Caribbean (and specifically Jamaicans) as being related to, yet always outside of, the black community in the United States. Conversely, its Caribbean counterpart more inclusively represents nonblack immigrant groups as having originated apart from an Afro-Jamaican community but nevertheless being able to become a part of a wider Jamaican community.

Well before *CS*, the program most often cited for its trailblazing satirical interrogation of race in the post–civil rights era was Norman Lear's *All in the Family*, which aired on the CBS network from 1971 to 1979. Although *All in the Family*'s second spinoff, *The Jeffersons* (CBS, 1975–1985), was less pointedly political, this later show was also a pioneer in using humor to question race relations in the late-twentieth-century United States. Chappelle also benefited from the emergence of satirical television as its own subgenre with the growing prominence of the cable network Comedy Central and shows on this and other television stations that exhibited an impressive political savvy. These programs included *Saturday Night Live, The Simpsons, The Daily Show, The Boondocks*, and *South Park*. The prominence of other controversial black comedians like Redd Foxx, Dick Gregory, Richard Pryor, Eddie Murphy, and Chris Rock had also paved the way for and created a climate in which *CS*'s brand of humor could thrive.

Offering a more sustained critique of transnational racial stereotyping, one of *Chappelle's Show*'s most nuanced explorations emerges in episode twelve of the show's first season, in the sketch "*Chappelle's Show* Trading Spouses," which parodies a show of the same name (*Trading Spouses: Meet Your New Mommy*) that aired on the FOX network from 2004 to 2007. The sketch highlights two suburban families, one black and one white, who trade husbands. Playing both roles, Chappelle dons a large Afro wig to depict the black husband (Leonard) and a bad light brown wig and whiteface to play the white husband (Todd). Typical of *CS*'s satirical approach, the sketch is rife with racial stereotypes.[4] In the scenes that juxtapose Leonard and Todd reading different magazines whose covers are visible to the audience, *CS* offers wickedly astute commentaries on intragroup typecasting. The advertisement on each back cover beckons visitors to Jamaica and reveals a wealth of information about black and white Americans' stereotyping of the Caribbean. The magazine Leonard reads in what is usually Todd's bathroom features two well-groomed men—one black, one white—both wearing golf attire and standing on a manicured lawn. The surrounding caption is Jamaica's national motto, "Out of Many, One People." In contrast, Todd reads a magazine in Leonard's bathroom called *Mahogany*. The front of the periodical lambastes whites with captions like "How fast food makes you fat and makes the white man rich." The back cover shows a seminaked black man on a raft, on a stream in a wooded area. Above and below him are the words "Come Back to Jamaica for the Big Bamboo." The man looks upward to a long bamboo pole that pours water toward his face. It is unclear whether he is drinking or bathing from the stream. In both scenes, much of the humor results from the mental flip-flopping implicitly demanded of the audience: both black and white characters haltingly read messages that are ostensibly intended for someone else, yet Chappelle's playing of both roles destabilizes and fractures this dyad. Instead of remaining stable, the epistemological grounds of the "juxtaposition" continue to shift, heightening the humor.

Unlike the seemingly more "civilized" and "culturally inclusive" world of the magazine we see Leonard perusing, in the scene with Todd, the ostensibly black publication sells an image of an atavistic return to nature and "natural" pleasures, including play with the metaphorical "big bamboo" (read: phallus).[5] The muscular black gentleman in the picture is shirtless, wearing only shorts. The largely unclothed figure, conflated semiotically with the "big bamboo" and the lush landscape, also suggests this return to an idealized Eden, even as the glossy magazine reminds viewers of the scene's constructedness. Of course, such representations of blacks as closer to nature have a long and well-rehearsed history in essentializing discourses. In *Paradise and Plantation* (2002), Ian Strachan describes "centuries old erotics of conquest" that depict the Caribbean and its inhabitants as prime targets of Western visual cannibalization (30).⁶ In regard to the depiction of *Mahogany*, these discourses take on particularly inimical implications, operating as they do within this African diasporic cultural world. That is to say, in this African diasporic community, this "in-group"—another primarily black community—is marked using the generalizations that colonizers, an "out-group," created. *Chappelle's Show* positions the targeted audience of *Mahogany*—urban African American tourists—as distinct from Jamaican individuals ripe for pleasure and exploitation. Despite tendencies to collapse cultural variations in the United States (that is, Afro-Caribbean identity sometimes becomes conveniently subsumed within African American identity), the sketch distinctly outlines the differences in this African diasporic community in locating Jamaican inhabitants firmly outside a larger Western milieu that includes African Americans. Therefore, the publication in Leonard's bathroom suggests African Americans' visual consumption of the Caribbean.

However, lest one rest too comfortably on the notion that African Americans can just as easily assume a neocolonial position, *CS*'s stereotyping also turns this notion on its head, implicitly suggesting that blacks who seek this sexual escape are themselves hypersexual. This complexity is perhaps best described by Avi Santo's sense that, "a populist impulse in our society to tell jokes that subvert existing power hierarchies and . . . the joker's disruptive ability to render elite sense nonsensical by adopting the 'tonalities of common sense' expose underlying—if alternative—truths about the social fabric of reality that are shared by the audience being addressed" (260). The elite sense rendered nonsensical is the paradigm of white Western racism. It soon becomes apparent that the typecasting projected onto Afro-Caribbeans shares similar origins as the typecasting of African Americans. The sketch relies on signifiers like the term *mahogany*, which is familiar to viewers from numerous black cultural contexts, notably Hallmark's line of "Mahogany" gift cards, which is explicitly marketed to black audiences. In light of well-rehearsed arguments that Western norms dictate visual representations of blacks in advertising, the publication's title raises interesting questions about the impetus for *Mahogany*'s marketing of Jamaica. Chappelle's sly wordplay is a reminder of the ubiquitous, though often hidden, hand of white commercialism that perpetuates stereotypes from "outside" while pretending that such discourses are manufactured within the black community. Todd's presence as a white/black character/performer reading *Mahogany* is also a reminder of the complex racial politics underlying the advertisement and its dissemination. True, this scene suggests the ways in which blacks in different but related cultural contexts might imbibe racist neocolonial paradigms. However, the sketch also reveals the systemic nature of the underlying, contradictory, self-serving discourses used in tourism.

Chappelle's satire of the *Making the Band* reality show that aired on ABC and MTV between 2000 and 2009 offers another provocative, if more problematic, example of his interrogation of stereotyping in a broad African diasporic context. In the reality show, Sean "P. Diddy" Combs auditions prospective musicians, and Chappelle's sketch satirically explores a moment from the actual show when a Grenadian American cast member named Dylan sang for the Haitian musician Wyclef Jean. Chappelle, as Dylan, stubbornly performs an unintelligible song, despite Jean's attempts to steer him in another direction. The "Making the Band" skit pokes fun of the difficulties Combs and Jean had in integrating Dylan, the self-professed and patently unhappy "black sheep," into their artistic fold. As was the case for the singer in the actual show (in which Dylan's African American castmates mocked his Grenadian accent), *CS* highlights the ways in which Caribbean speech and performance become indelible markers of difference. Citing Shawn-Marie Garrett, Glenda Carpio argues that "many professional critics and scholars have condemned the new art of stereotype for 'not establishing distance between [artists] and their material, for underestimating the destructive power of these images'" (23). Unlike the more nuanced and complex attention to stereotyping within the Caribbean community that Chappelle explores in pieces like "Trading Spouses," this sketch does not go far beyond mocking Dylan's speech as unintelligible and representing him as a violent nonconformist.[7] To paraphrase Garrett / Carpio, Chappelle does not "establish distance between himself and his material." One can readily point to the violence and/or uniqueness of other cast members, but as the sketch makes clear, for Chappelle the most marked distinction worthy of humor and ridicule is Dylan's accent.

Even if one dismisses such shenanigans as typical of the ever-vacillating absurdity that characterizes Chappelle's work, perhaps the most obvious clues to his own complicity in perpetuating stereotypical representations emerges in the captions to the gibberish he spouts. Although Dylan is Grenadian American, the subtitles included on the DVD release[8] of *Chappelle's Show* reveal a homogenizing gesture in calling specifically for a "Jamaican accent" for his words, a detail absent from the original televised sketch. This addition does not enhance the scene's humor, and indeed appears to be the primary "odd note" in the subtitles provided. Seemingly intended to clarify one's viewing of the piece, it adds a disturbing discordant note. Dylan ostensibly represents an ideal African diasporic subject, mentored by both American Sean Combs and Haitian-born Wyclef Jean; yet the sketch's treatment of language risks eliding both cultural specificity and inclusivity, seemingly beyond its intended satirical gestures. One might argue that this instance evinces a joker's ability to recognize a maligned individual and "turns deceptively aside and revokes the suffering in the form of jest" (Kierkegaard 459). However, the humor here depends too heavily on an unrelenting taunting that seems to expand beyond the comedian's intended purview, unwittingly revealing the extent to which stereotyping is systematically ingrained. This shortcoming supports my earlier contention that satire, as a slippery, unpredictable, and complex tool sometimes highlights its practitioners' shortcomings, in this case elucidating distance within the African diasporic community.

Following in Chappelle's important, if at times wayward, footprints, *The Ity and Fancy Cat Show* debuted on Television Jamaica in April 2008 to tremendous critical acclaim and popular success. Previously, the stand-up comedian duo of Ian "Ity" Ellis and Alton "Fancy Cat" Hardware had toured comedy circuits throughout Jamaica and the Caribbean generally. Such comedic performances have a rich and varied past in modern Jamaica, dating from mid-twentieth-century pantomimes to the more boisterous and sometimes outright raunchy traveling comedy sketches and plays of today. Although Ity and Fancy Cat emerged out of and benefited from this tradition, thanks to television and to the Internet, they and individuals like Jamaican duo Delcita and Shebada have achieved unprecedented wealth and recognition.[9] Until recently, the particularly lucrative world of television had been the almost exclusive playground of well-known mainstream comedians like Oliver Samuels. Not since Samuels's *Oliver at Large* (*OL*) has a comedy show been as popular with a Jamaican audience as *IFCS*. However, *OL* tended to focus on the more innocuous storylines typical of many Caribbean sitcoms rather than venturing into politically sensitive territory or engaging the controversial issues that *IFCS* tackles. David Marc's observation that "sitcoms . . . tend to flatter their viewers by ridiculing personal behavior rather than the people who run things" is applicable to Samuels's sitcom, and this is precisely where *IFCS* departs from its famous predecessor (x). Ity captures this sense, declaring, "It's not TV, it more unorthodox" (T. Evans). When racial and ethnic humor is in question, one runs the risk of audiences dismissing attendant discourses as unique to those individuals. Rather than limiting itself to the personal, *IFCS* verbally lambastes a wide range of political and other public figures in unprecedented ways, illustrating the systemic nature of stereotyping even as it highlights a tendency toward embracing racial and ethnic differences.

Not surprisingly, given the long shadow of the United States on the Global South and a long history of cross-pollination among African diasporic artists in the Americas, Ity credits African American comedians with this turn to a more outspoken form.[10] Structurally, *IFCS* mirrors *CS* in obvious ways. The former's brand of racial and ethnic humor uses a similar satirical paradigm, parodying popular television programs and commenting on racial and ethnic relationships in society. As in *CS*, many of the most pointed critiques are offered through the characters dressed in poorly constructed and obvious blackface or whiteface. Still, *IFCS* moves beyond this influence by more pointedly engaging provocative topical issues and by frequently venturing into the community to involve local individuals in sketches. Most interesting for my purposes are the show's explicit critiques of transnational exchanges.

One of the most provocative of these sketches, "The Bigga Shopping Show," parodies "The Mega Shopping Show," a regular Jamaican infomercial in which Columbian television personalities Diego and Pablo market "As seen on TV!"–type of wares to Jamaican viewers. In the sketch, Ity and Fancy Cat adopt new names (respectively, António and Papi Liad [Liar]) and replace the seemingly extraordinary gadgets of the infomercials with satirically grotesque items aimed at their Caribbean audience. The sketch offers two primary critiques: first, that the Colombian personalities are outright liars, marketing false, outlandish goods; and second, that the items, which include nonscratch wigs, bleaching creams, "chicken" pills that can enhance women's derrières, a mask to hide facial imperfections, and a Mandingo drink that enlarges men's sexual organs, are problematic imported goods aimed at literally and figuratively whitening Jamaican women while conversely satisfying these women's overly libidinous natures.[11]

Reminiscent of Chappelle's contrasting magazine covers that assail white and black Americans' stereotyping of the Caribbean, the products suggest contradictory expectations regarding Afro-Caribbean women. On the one hand, these individuals are expected to adhere to European norms of beauty, wearing wigs and bleaching their skin to achieve lighter complexions. On the other hand, they seemingly desire large bottoms and men with large phalluses. The privileging of lighter skin and straighter hair (read: white features) has a long and complex history in New World race relations, while the invocation of the large black phallus hauntingly evokes other disturbing images from the silver screen, such as D. W. Griffith's *Birth of a Nation* (1915) and its hunts for violent, threatening, and oversexualized black men. Analogously, the promise of expanding black women's derrières has a long and problematic history, evoking Sarah Baartman (the Hottentot Venus), whose spectral presence haunts many representations of black womanhood and reminds us of "the dangers of the dominant visual field for black female subjects" (Coly 657). Still, the absurdity of the items and their implicit significance, coupled with the foreign vendors who glibly endorse psychologically and physically damaging goods, implicitly offer a strident critique of foreign capitalistic endeavors while usefully highlighting the systemic and schizophrenic nature of the expectations placed on black women.

Revealing yet another problematic expectation of Afro-Caribbean male sexuality, the lie regarding the Mandingo drinks is obvious, as António declares, "If he [one's spouse] was a beenie man, he beenie man no more. He big man." Obviously this drink is not capable of changing penis size. Yet Papi Liad confirms the ludicrous statement, responding, "I drink and I get man." Then he hastily amends, "I man. I man." António notes, "Oh . . . I was worried Papi" (*Ity and Fancy Cat Show*). Either stating the truth or recognizing that such a claim is unwelcome in the Caribbean, Papi Liad corrects the implication that he might "get man"—that he might be gay— with the assertion "I man." Linguistic play allows for a complex range of possibilities. As the sketch tackles homosexuality in Caribbean / Jamaican society, the foreigner asserts a sense of belonging by denying what is taboo. Equally important, he does so using a rastafari proclamation—"I man"— unwittingly or wittily marking himself as Jamaican in this performance of cultural literacy.

Numerous other *IFCS* sketches address homophobia. Fancy Cat, who is much more comfortable with physical comedy, generally plays the role of the character whose sexual orientation is ambiguous. One such sketch depicts Fancy Cat on a psychiatrist's couch dressed in pink pajamas and gesturing flamboyantly as he describes his obsession with women and his confusion about the numerous altercations that ensue between him and other men. The psychiatrist pointedly asks, "Have you considered the possibility that your obsessive desire for women may actually be a psychosomatic delusionary perception that has evolved subconsciously as a mechanism to camouflage what is probably repressed confusion about your true sexual orientation?" (*Ity and Fancy Cat Show*). This question is met with Fancy Cat's hilarious confusion. Most importantly, the sketch dramatizes the lengths to which gay men must go to conceal their sexuality in an often homophobic society and the psychological ramifications. Yet another pointed interrogation of sexuality contrasts African Americans and Caribbeans, specifically, Michael Jackson and Bob Marley. The sketch, "The After Life," shows Jackson and Marley conversing in the "after life." Jackson sings the first line of his song "Bad" ("Your butt is mine") and, misinterpreting this gesture as flirtatious, Marley shuns the African American performer and walks away. The sketch suggests that the rastafari Jamaican singer is homophobic and intolerant of Jackson's perceived advances, highlighting homophobia's long-standing and far-reaching presence in the Caribbean ("ITY AND FANCY CAT").

Such exchanges also illustrate that "contemporary satire TV often says what the press is too timid to say, proving itself a more critical interrogator

. . . than the press itself" (Gray, Jones, and Thompson 4). These treatments of sexuality elucidate *IFCS*'s departure from Chappelle, as the former examines topics particularly poignant for its Jamaican audience. In keeping with issues at the forefront of the Jamaican popular imagination—thanks in part to dancehall music's controversial themes and performances, which also enjoy an international platform—the show offers a more nuanced critique of representations of gender and sexuality. Since homophobia has long been rampant in Jamaica and still receives uneven and problematic media coverage, sketches like these undoubtedly offer more candid, unflinching attention to such topics than the local press. Ultimately, as the sketches capitalize on flip-flopping, they highlight Jamaican society's inclusion of other historically marginalized communities (Colombians) even as it problematizes the exclusion of other individuals (homosexuals).

Similarly, the sketch "2 Fortune Cookie to Go" also elucidates the ways in which minority groups from a variety of linguistics contexts are simultaneously marked as different from, yet are a part of, Jamaican society. "Fortune" targets a community that has long been present in this society: Chinese Jamaicans. In the sketch, a Chinese man pulls up to a Kentucky Fried Chicken window ordering, among other things, "two fortune cookie to go." The female teller struggles to explain to him—first in Standard English, then angrily in Jamaican patois—that the restaurant does not carry fortune cookies. As he pulls away, order unfilled, he sees the teller, notices she is Chinese, and says animatedly, "Oh! You looka lika me!" ("Ity and Fancy Cat"). She agrees in an Asian accent. He angrily repeats the order and they argue in Chinese. Humor is also problematically compounded by the fact that both individuals wear very poor Asian costumes with painted faces. Still, as the woman switches between four accents / idioms, the complexity of this undeniably Jamaican figure is revealed.

Mikhail Bakhtin's description of the carnival and marketplace as spaces in which misbehaving folk figures cross numerous boundaries and deploy humor to critique authority is blatantly displayed in this sketch.[12] Gordon Rohlehr similarly argues for public displays, particularly at Caribbean carnivals, as primary spaces for the disruption of order and hierarchy through humor and verbal aggression.[13] Here, the satirized infomercial represents the modern marketplace. Although one might argue that hierarchy is momentarily reestablished (given that Caribbean television is accessible and caters primarily to those of certain classes), status is ultimately dismantled semiotically through the performers' behavior and the effects of their exaggerated costumes, what Bakhtin would label the "grotesque."

A certain inclusivity is also communicated linguistically as António / Ity / Pablo sings lyrics from Queen Ifrica's "Mek Mi Grow." The chorus changes marginally throughout the song, but the first iteration declares, "No bwoy caan drive mi round no corner / Fi [to] go show mi no iguana / So low mi mek mi grow [So allow me to grow up] / A dat you fi know [You should know] / A bwoy caan drive mi round no corner / Fi [to] go show mi no banana." Since Pablo sings this song in his infomercial, there is a rich irony in the male Jamaican comedian, dressed as the male Columbian vendor who sings the Jamaican female performer's song that encourages young girls to abstain from sex with older men (or metaphorical play with the iguana / banana, or *Chappelle's Show*'s "bamboo"). In contrast to "a mono-logic approach . . . [in which] another person remains wholly and merely an object [as] monologues pretend to be the ultimate word," the polyvocality or a dialogic approach, which sees the other as a subject with individuality, is utilized here (Bakhtin, 1984 292–293; Bakhtin, "Discourse" 1981 183–184). *The Ity and Fancy Cat Show* capitalizes on such linguistic complexity and flip-flopping throughout this sketch and in others, upending any notion of a stable or privileged identity. Entering the diegesis of the humor, one might accept that the characters are Colombian. Yet the show's investment in a sort of documentary satire, interweaving real-life individuals into the sketch in equal parts with fictitious characters (the real-life vendors appear later in the sketch), muddies the "reality" of the world that humor creates and increases the potential for laughter as one moves back and forth between characters and their multiple worlds. The focus on linguistic code switch-ing also suggests that linguistic, and by extension national, difference is at the heart of the tensions involving the Columbian personalities. Yet *IFCS's* flip-flopping humor simultaneously marks this difference and provides the grounds for enjoyable and equal exchange. António and Papi Liad are simul-taneously revealed to be Ity and Fancy Cat, even as they remain these pro-vocative Latino characters who evoke yet another individual, Queen Ifrica. Tackling escalating numbers of incest and sexual assault cases, polyvocal-ity allows Colombian and Jamaican male performers to maintain a comic tone while they simultaneously echo a grave warning to young girls to be vigilant against sexual entrapment.[14] Evincing yet another departure from *CS* and coming after *IFCS* viciously lambastes the marketing of goods that belittle and stereotype black women as hypersexual, this moment emerges as another rich and powerful critique of gender, consumerism, and racism, voiced from the unified, national chorus of Jamaicans and Columbians.

As Bakhtin highlights the ability of humor and language to disrupt hier-archy, linguistic hegemony is further undone through the complex display of numerous and contrasting social voices, or heteroglossia—Bakhtin's "other-languagedness"—"the internal differentiation, the stratification characteris-tic of any national language" (*Dialogic Imagination* 66, 67). By questioning the use of Spanish, *IFCS* implicitly establishes a normative language as the counterpoint that highlights Spanish's marginalized position in this Anglophone society. However, unlike in *CS*'s "Band," it is not another more popular standard idiom—English—that serves as the barometer of difference, but patois and, specifically, often-maligned reggae lyrics. If the seemingly marginalized question authority, there is a wonderful irony in the historically marginalized language being positioned as the master (or mistress) idiom. As Roger Abrahams eloquently notes (in an echo of Bakhtin), "There is no joking . . . unless there is an order that can be overturned or at least challenged by the establishment of new continuities and relationships" (75). The multilayered voices juxtapose and question various categories and relationships, including high/low classes, formal/informal, standard/non-standard idioms, men/women, insiders/outsiders. A democratizing gesture is also evident in the embrasure of marginalized ethnic and racial groups. This is not to celebrate a simplistic inversion of hierarchy, but it is certainly important to recognize humor's reevaluation of the often-disparaged mode of vernacular speech. Even as the flip-flopping and linguistic play promote inclusivity, they do so on their own terms.

Abrahams's notion of "two types of man-of-words" in many Caribbean contexts offers another way of understanding the humor in this sketch. Abrahams describes the "broad talker who, using license, brings creole into stylized . . . use in the form of wit, repartee, and directed slander . . . ; and the sweet talker, who emphasizes eloquence and manners through the use of formal Standard English" (57). Of course, much of the humor lies in the sketches' co-opting of even this recognizable paradigm. Usually, these "men-of words" are two distinct individuals. However, in "Bigga," Papi Liad is merely a foil for António, who embodies both types. Although the latter's mastery of both linguistic strategies might be questionable (given his accent), António nevertheless confidently wields Creole and standard idioms, thereby parodying familiar Caribbean archetypes and the very form of the joke on multiple levels. These moments of dramatic rupture, where the blueprint of humor is revealed, cause uproarious laughter for an audience that simultaneously recognizes and is alienated from this reimagined "man-of-words." More importantly, this linguistic fluidity communicates the fluidity of Jamaican identity and a penchant for cultural inclusivity.

Transnational studies of satire such as this one aim not only to provide a broader sense of who constitutes black communities in the Americas, but also to illustrate the systemic nature of racism that often crosses national and cultural borders. Such an approach also opens up new discursive terrains for understanding different African diasporic communities that overlap continuously. Notably, comparing works such as *Chappelle's Show* and *The Ity and Fancy Cat Show* demonstrates that race, ethnicity, and linguistic differences do not operate in precisely the same ways as these programs' primary cultural contexts. For example, simultaneously introducing the grounds for cross cultural alliances through strategic uses of satire and language, *IFCS* closely interrogates even more culturally, ethnically, and nationally diverse group of individuals as part of a shared community. On the other hand, *CS* usefully illustrates the dangers of satire, elucidating the ways in which comedians are also susceptible to the very paradigms they problematize. Nevertheless, such complexities highlight the significant insights that a fearless polemical mode like satire allows and the importance of examining it in a transnational context.

Notes

1. After all, African American and Caribbean cultures overlap, but they are not always the same. Conversely, of course, although they differ, their cultural discourses are not antithetical to each other.

2. As I discuss below in regard to *The Ity and Fancy Cat Show*, the operative notions of a marginalized black community manifest themselves very differently in primarily Afro-Caribbean spaces as opposed to in the United States.

3. Specifically, Sienkiewics and Marx discuss *South Park*.

4. See also Marvin McAllister's discussion of this sketch in his article in this collection, pp. 240–53.

5. In an African American context, the film *How Stella Got Her Groove Back* (1998) popularized notions of middle-class blacks visiting the Caribbean to reawaken their sexual potency. *Heading South* (2005) depicted similar possibilities for white middle-class women.

6. This approach differs from the image on the magazine Leonard reads, which depicts a tamed landscape. This periodical's caption self-servingly declares that all are welcomed and implies that white visitors "will be safe from harm" (Strachan 102). For a more detailed discussion of the contradictory and self-serving stereotypes perpetuated through tourism see Strachan's *Paradise and Plantation* (2002).

7. The notion of the violent, nonconforming, and visually or aurally different Caribbean individual is one Chappelle returns to continuously in other sketches. In yet another moment, Chappelle questions whether the famous late night psychic Miss Cleo is really Jamaican. Controversy arose when the Federal Trade Commission charged Miss Cleo with fraudulent billing practices and the *Smoking Gun* website revealed that she was not Jamaican, already evident in her unconvincing "Jamaican" accent. In this questioning of Miss Cleo's nationality, Chappelle highlights his ability to read differing cultural codes, but he collapses these differences in "Making the Band."

8. Much the same way that artists in numerous other fields are held responsible for the final production of their materials, I similarly hold Chappelle responsible for representations of his speech in the DVDs that bear his name.

9. Of course, one traveling performer from an earlier era, Louise Bennett, one of the co-founders of Jamaican Pantomime, stands as an exception. Wealthy, internationally known, and critically acclaimed, this folk icon produced a less raunchy humor, but nevertheless pioneered extensive uses of Jamaican patois and provocative representations of the working poor.

10. One has only to look at the complex history of Jamaica's popular music being influenced by American popular forms in the mid-twentieth century, and in turn Jamaica's influence on the emergence of early rap music in the South Bronx in the late twentieth century, for some of the most fruitful and obvious examples of such artistic mirroring.

11. I say "conversely" because of the historical tendency to typecast white women as pure and chaste while depicting black women as oversexualized. For a more detailed discussion of this phenomenon in the Caribbean see, for example, Patricia Mohammed's "'But most of all mi love me browning': The Emergence in Eighteenth and Nineteenth-Century Jamaica of the Mulatto Woman as the Desired" (2000).

12. These elements are also present in CS—for example, in the "Playa Haters" sketches—but IFCS explodes them here. Ironically, in CS the typecasting in sketches like "Making the Band" reestablishes hierarchy. CS's precise negation of the very principles that define carnivalesque environments highlight Bakhtin's postulations.

13. For a more detailed discussion of this phenomenon, see Rohlehr's Calypso and Society in Pre-independence Trinidad (1989).

14. The song was also a direct response to controversial dancehall artist Vybz Kartel, whose song "Virginity" graphically boasts about the violent process of taking a girl's virginity. In this instance, both men side with Ifrica in taking a stand against the misogynistic lyrics.

Afterword: From Pilloried to Post-Soul: The Future of African American Satire

Darryl Dickson-Carr

When author Trey Ellis published his controversial essay "The New Black Aesthetic" in 1989, he was attempting to define the state of African American literature, culture, and art as it stood between the nationalism of the Black Arts Movement of the late 1960s and 1970s and an unprecedented future. Not coincidentally, Ellis allies his generation with that of the "New Negro" or Harlem Renaissance in the 1920s and 1930s. A young Alain Locke discovered and presented evidence of a "New Negro in the latest phases of social change and progress, but still more in the internal world of the Negro mind and spirit" ("Foreword" ix). Ellis argues that a younger generation of artists "misunderstood by both the black worlds and the white" and "alienated (junior) intellectuals" who came of age after the Civil Rights and Black Power Movements of the 1960s have come into their own as "cultural mulattoes" who combine "zeal, *Glasnost* [openness], and talent . . . across both race and class lines" ("New Black" 234). Locke's New Negro arose from several causes, including the national post–World War I zeitgeist that returning black war veterans spurred, along with a new respect for the riches and indelibly *American* quality of African American history and folk culture.

Ellis's "cultural mulatto," by contrast, has benefited directly from past social justice movements—including the New Negro Renaissance and the Black Arts Movement—but may not feel completely obliged to embody their often conflicting ideals and principles, especially when such efforts circumscribe the concept of blackness. In Ellis's terms, cultural mulattoes "just have to *be* natural" but "don't necessarily have to *wear* one," meaning the "natural" or "Afro" hairstyle ("New Black" 236; emphases in original). This generation's reluctance to manifest the ideals of the Black Power era allows it both to respect its predecessors and to lampoon them for their oversights. It also makes it possible for African American artists to work on projects that transcend instrumentalism. That is to say, like certain New

Negro or Harlem Renaissance artists before them, New Black aestheticians create for their own purposes rather than solely for a white intelligentsia or a particular form of Black Nationalism. Ellis's project ultimately concludes that cultural mulattoes "no longer need to deny or suppress any part of our complicated and sometimes contradictory cultural baggage to please either white people or black" (235). It is Ellis's most overt homage to Langston Hughes's 1926 essay "The Negro Artist and the Racial Mountain," in which Hughes declares, "If white people are pleased, we are glad. If they are not, it doesn't matter. We know we are beautiful. And ugly too. The tom-tom cries and the tom-tom laughs. If colored people are pleased we are glad. If they are not, their displeasure doesn't matter either. We build our temples for tomorrow, strong as we know how, and we stand on top of the mountain, free within ourselves" (694). Hughes and Ellis alike envision a future for black art without strict ideological boundaries, agendas, or sociological projects controlling the artist's impulses. Both writers broadly define the black artist to be inclusive and democratic; ironically, this presents several problems, as we shall see.

A survey of satire by African Americans from the 1980s until the present would seem to indicate that some aspects of the New Black Aesthetic's moment—"the most exciting period [Ellis] has ever known"—ring true. African American writers have embraced the New Black Aesthetic's call for an openness of subject matter, especially when the subject is defining "race"[1] and African American culture in the wake of the Black Nationalism of the 1960s and 1970s, along with evolving conceptions of gender and sexuality within African American communities. This, however, may be said of countless works of fiction and poetry in the greater African American literary corpus since 1980; what, beyond standard generic differences, makes African American satire of this period distinct? How might it continue to distinguish itself in an era that has now been identified as not only "post-soul" and postmodern, but also "post-racial," when an African American has finally been elected president? The last term has taken on innumerable ironies, as the rise of the various Tea Party factions—almost entirely coincident with Barack Obama's election as president—seems to indicate. Despite arguments from Tea Party leaders that their movement is not racist, numerous rank-and-file members display a seemingly heightened awareness of the president's "race." If the term *post-racial* means in this case that an African American president provides the final evidence that racism has no place in American society, then the "post-racial" era ended before it began. Yet "post-racial" remains a common sobriquet in the 2010s, one that commentators and critics apply often to African Americans who have apparently transcended "race." In effect, this means either writing about subjects that have little or no explicit reference to "race" or that do not follow a commonly perceived agenda. As Alex Abramovich writes in the *London Review of Books* about novelist and satirist Percival Everett, "America's pre-eminent post-racial novelist, Percival Everett . . . started off writing about characters who weren't necessarily black, or weren't described as such, or were only described as such in passing and incidentally. His 22 books include modern-day reworkings of Greek myths, genre spoofs, straight-faced westerns, broad satires, domestic novels, novel-length fables, surgically precise satires, an apocalyptic science fiction novel" (33). We may surmise that Everett has published in each of the genres Abramovich lists because of his interest in those genres, in mixing them for intellectual purposes, rather than for any particular constraint or agenda. Everett once noted about his character Thelonious "Monk" Ellison (the protagonist of *Erasure*)—who writes the same genres as his creator—"What is most interesting to me about Monk is not his colour, but his selfless examination of himself. He does not want to be constrained or reduced by society's demands or expectations. He's alert to that all the time" (O'Hagan).

Everett's conception of Monk's antipathy toward social expectations offers perhaps the best positive definition of "post-racial." It also jibes somewhat with Ellis's "cultural mulatto," who may eschew past generations' or contemporaries' expectations for black arts in favor of an independent, even improvisational ethos. The term remains problematic, though, for at least one reason: any idea or movement "post-" another never is quite *past* it. All too often, "post-racial" or even "post-soul" reveal the speaker's desire to get past a disturbing notion—"race" easily qualifies—without ever confronting the problem in the first place. If Percival Everett's work, then, is "post-racial," does that mean it relinquishes us from thinking about "race" qua racism? Does Everett therefore allow his readers not to think about either their own racism or the continuing relevance of "race" in contemporary society? Does this apply to "post-racial" satire or people in general?

Even a cursory reading of Everett's novels and stories indicates that he does none of the above. His best-known work, *Erasure* (2000), satirizes the publishing industry, academia, the general public, and African American writers for circumscribing African American literature into such limited categories as "urban" realist or "ghetto" fiction, southern pastoral narratives, and others, all for the sake of a crippling and false authenticity. Everett and James Kincaid's *A History of the African-American People [Proposed] by Strom Thurmond, as Told to Percival Everett and James Kincaid* (2006) hardly eschews "race" as it lampoons the late U.S. senator. *I Am Not Sidney Poitier* (2009) also places "race" in the foreground. If Everett is "post-racial" in any respect, it may be that his works highlight how often Americans beg the question with regard to "race"; its reality is assumed rather than demonstrated, which is inherently absurd. Everett's novels reveal that "race" and/or "blackness" stand as a markers for an elusive authenticity that writers and publishers are quite willing to exploit at every opportunity, primarily for profit, but also with the secondary effect of reifying "race" as eternally exploitable. "Race" and "blackness" thus become parts of tautologies; "ghetto" fiction is "black" because "blackness" is a "ghetto" fiction, always ready for consumption.

Everett, of course, is hardly alone in facing this dilemma. Such works as Ishmael Reed's *Reckless Eyeballing* (1988), Darius James's *Negrophobia* (1992), Paul Beatty's *The White Boy Shuffle* (1996) and *Slumberland* (2008), Alexs D. Pate's *The Multicultiboho Sideshow* (1999), Connie Brisco's *P.G. County* (2003); Mat Johnson's *Hunting in Harlem* (2003) and *Pym* (2011), George C. Wolfe's play *The Colored Museum* (1985), Spike Lee's film *Bamboozled* (2000), and damali ayo's *How to Rent a Negro* (2005) highlight commercial, ideological, and intellectual forces carrying African American culture to foreign and domestic markets full of consumers craving an authentic, primitive black subject. This market demand reinforces narratives positing slavery, the Jim Crow South, poverty, gritty urban realism, or puerile romances between black characters as the essence of blackness, despite African Americans' own knowledge and experience otherwise. In Mat Johnson's *Hunting in Harlem*, author Bobby Finley concludes that "there were only two roads to success for a male writer of African descent, such as he was. The first was to write a romance novel with an illustration of three or fewer attractive black people on the cover, preferably done in a comic book style so as not to scare off the illiterate. One written in flat descriptions of every action so that the prose was completely subservient to the plot. . . . [The other] was to create a work in the vein of Richard Wright or the great Ralph Ellison, not in the sense that the works be original and energetic, but that they focus on inner-city strife and racism. Whites, who made up the majority of sales in the literary category, felt their own writers could handle the other issues in the universe just fine, they just wanted the black guys to clarify the Negro stuff" (49–50).

Finley's assessment of the current literary scene highlights how publishers and non–African American readers have reduced African American experiences to a commodity, often one experience for white readers and another, equally reductive, cartoonish, and overdetermined experience for a black reading audience supposedly incapable of appreciating complexity. In both cases, that commodity reinforces common beliefs and stereotypes, even among purportedly sympathetic readers and critics. Finley, Johnson notes, "insisted on calling his toilet Irving Howe . . . just so he could take pleasure in shitting on it daily" (50). Irving Howe was the critic whose essay "Black Boys and Native Sons" (1963) criticized such younger authors as James Baldwin and Ralph Ellison for not fully absorbing and appreciating Richard Wright's innovations. Howe's essay spurred a heated written debate with Ellison, who upbraided Howe for assuming or arguing that African American writers' primary influences should be other black writers, when those influences are often far more diverse and complex.[2]

Bobby Finley's (and Mat Johnson's) apprehension regarding the state of African American literature reveals the irony at the heart of being "post-soul" in the latter part of the twentieth century and the new millennium. The thinly veiled models Finley describes include, on the one hand, novels focusing upon romance in the style of Terry McMillan's *Waiting to Exhale* (1992) or Omar Tyree's heavily promoted and marketed tales of contemporary black (romantic) life. On the other hand are the works that Kenneth W. Warren's *What Was African American Literature?* (2011) focuses upon: exemplars of protest literature designed to bring the (white) reader's attention to the horrors of racism and the richness of African American history. Warren's book generated considerable controversy for its argument that African American literature's true raison d'être has been to counter the invidiousness of de jure segregation. In the absence of legal barriers to enfranchisement, Warren suggests, African American literature lost its distinct identity. What black authors have produced in the last four decades is a distinguished body of work, but not African American literature, or more precisely, *Negro* literature, written in part to establish a tradition that implicitly and explicitly insisted on African Americans' humanity. "African American literature," Warren writes, "took shape in the context of [the] challenge to the enforcement and justification of racial subordination and exploitation represented by Jim Crow. Accordingly . . . the coherence of African American literature has been correspondingly, if sometimes imperceptibly, eroded as well" (1–2).

Warren argues that such imperceptibility leads critics and readers of African American literature to conflate the work authors currently produce with a literary tradition that had a markedly different purpose. Thus, Ellis's New Black Aesthetic and its "cultural mulattoes" take black humanity for granted, even if their editors, readers, and critics do not. They may write about black lives and satirize racism; the work they produce might not stridently decry the invidiousness of racism, even if the author posits a critique of American conceptions of "race." Yet African American authors—satirists in particular—may still have their works pigeonholed as "Black Studies," a fate that Everett's "Monk" Ellison endures, much to his chagrin. How might the African American satirists of the future prevent having their work circumscribed as the sort of "racial" fiction that Warren argues neither serves the same purposes nor has the same cachet as the works written by their predecessors? Put another way, we can attempt to address comedian Nick Adams's rhetorical question in *Making Friends with Black People* (2006) regarding the use of the word *nigger* (or *nigga*) among African Americans: "Can't we have anything to ourselves? Damn! Black people don't get to be president, and white people don't get to use the word nigger. Can we just call it even now?" (9). After the ultimate symbol of racial progress—Obama's election—and the purportedly post-racial society it heralded, what is the new vocabulary for African American satire?

We may discover possible answers not only in Trey Ellis's essay, but also in his telling blind spots. As provocative as Ellis's essay may be, it emerges from a decidedly middle-class perspective, one which privileges the achievements of artists reared and educated in middle-class or elite environments. As Tera Hunter notes in her critique—published in the same issue of *Callaloo* in which Ellis's essay originally appeared—he never clearly defines the criteria that place disparate artists within a New Black Aesthetic. "I am hard-pressed to discern," Hunter writes, "what aesthetic values and commitments [comedian and actor] Eddie Murphy and [jazz trumpeter] Wynton Marsalis have in common." Hunter goes on to point out that Eddie Murphy, while a gifted artist, does not push the boundaries of his art form; he "demands the minimal from Hollywood in pursuit of a vibrant artistic autonomy." She also argues that "the most striking feature of this new profusion of black talent, according to Ellis, is its class background: second generation college-educated youth are preeminent," as are males, with very few women artists mentioned at all (247). In the same issue, Eric Lott also cautions against overvaluing the work of Murphy or other artists such as Spike Lee vis-à-vis Marsalis, George Wolfe, and Lisa Jones (245). Hunter and Lott both remind their readers that not all black art can be presumed to have the same ambitions simply as a result of emerging during the same epoch; given his insistent critique of Alice Walker as a collaborator with white feminists out to demonize black men, Ishmael Reed qualifies as her ideological or artistic ally about as much as Bobby Finley adores Omar Tyree, or as "Monk" Ellison aspires in *Erasure* to break bread with Juanita Mae Jenkins, author of the exploitative novel *We's Lives in da Ghetto*.[3]

African American satire since 1980 has actively rejected the notion that all black artists serve any particular aesthetic at all. For all too many writers, in fact, the primary aesthetic worth serving is one that embraces and privileges the green paper and black ink of U.S. Treasury notes. Contemporary African American satire neither agrees with Warren's or Ellis's claims regarding the state of African American literature and art, nor does it fully reject them. Black satirists still struggle to define African American culture as something rich and diverse, but independent of any single definition of *blackness, literature,* or even American identity. The moment satire becomes any single entity or adheres to a particular agenda, it can be controlled and modulated and thereby deprived of its power. Satire, by definition, resists such attempts; it wishes to skewer sacred cows and roast them in full sight of those who either venerated or vilified them previously. For this reason, satire and satirists tend to be pilloried and condemned for their irreverence; nothing is sacred, except the right to make the sacred profane.

At the height of Black Nationalism's influence in the 1960s and 1970s, a satirist exerting that right could nearly guarantee that he (or, rarely, she) would be misunderstood or ostracized, hence Ishmael Reed's charge that "there was a nonaggression pact signed between the traditional liberal critics and the black aesthetic critics" that prevented the latter from engaging in intellectually honest critiques of African American culture and literature and excluded some authors (such as Reed) from better exposure in the publishing world (Martin 177). The shift that Ellis identifies, however, indicates that the world Reed described had changed by the late 1980s, allowing the satirist greater acceptance; such popular television shows as Keenan Ivory Wayans's *In Living Color* (1990–1994) and Dave Chappelle's innovative *Chappelle's Show* (2003–2006) incorporated withering satire.

These examples of satire's popular success, ironically, do not escape the same problem facing its literary form: commodification. In the most famous case, comedian Dave Chappelle ended his show at the height of its popularity because the phenomenon that was *Chappelle's Show* overshadowed his individuality and complexity. As Chappelle told *Esquire* magazine:

But the bottom line was, white people own everything, and where can a black person go and be himself or say something that's familiar to him and not have to explain or apologize? Why don't I just take the show to BET—oh, wait a minute, you own that, too, don't you? Same thing happened with the Rick James episode. They gave us the notes and there were like forty-six or some insane number of bleeps that we would've had to put over it. "Well, Dave, then why don't you go in and explain to them yourself." So now I'm sitting in a room, again, with some white people, explaining why they say the *n*-word, and it's a sketch about Rick James, and I don't want to air a sketch with that many bleeps over it; it will render it completely ineffective. . . . And so then there was a compromise. It was the only episode that aired with a disclaimer. But again, it was a position where I was explaining to white people why the *n*-word. It's an awful, awful position to put yourself in. I'm just saying it's a dilemma. It's something that is unique to us. White people, white artists, are allowed to be individuals.

But we always have this greater struggle that we at least have to keep in mind somewhere. (Powell; emphases in original)

Chappelle links his individual struggle for self-expression with the greater dilemma facing the African American artist, particularly one relying upon satire and other forms of humor: African American culture continues to sell, with the black body, the exotic physical presence itself a prized possession to be traded, sold, and manipulated.[4]

Little coincidence, then, that performance artist damali ayo's *How to Rent a Negro* (2005) focuses specifically on African Americans as cultural commodities, the perennial sites of the hip and cool. Both the book and the original website (the now-defunct rent-a-negro.com) from which it grew present a fictional service that allows non–African Americans to employ black "friends" to provide evidence of the renter's hipness and cultural sensitivity; after all, the presence of a single black body acts as an instant synecdoche signifying that the renter is inclusive to all African Americans, at least the acceptable kind. "Since the purchase of African Americans was outlawed," the book's faux rental agent informs us, "renting has become a tradition taught and refined through generations. Now that you know that you want a black presence in your life, exactly what kind of presence do you want? Do you want your guests challenged or just entertained? Are you looking to create waves or appear in-the-know? What are your expectations? Renters are as unique as snowflakes" (ayo 9). The "renter," in nearly all cases, seeks to dispel the notion that he or she holds any racist views or may be otherwise ignorant of African American culture in an era when— *pace* both Ann duCille and Langston Hughes—the black American is in vogue. In "The Occult of True Black Womanhood" (1993), duCille marvels at the fact that "racial and gender alterity has become a hot commodity that has claimed black women as its principal signifier" (81); in 1940, Langston Hughes joined his voice with others musing upon the "Negro vogue" of the 1920s (*Big Sea* 223). The black body, of course, may still be used for physical labor, but in the post–civil rights era, the enlightened American would never admit to seeing his fellow citizens in such retrograde terms. Instead, the black presence has to be tokenized and treated as an exception, thereby affirming the renter's exceptionality.

How to Rent a Negro reveals through relentless irony that the beneficiaries of Jim Crow racism never desired to relinquish the roles that allowed them to accrue wealth upon the free or cheap labor of their fellow citizens. Ayo pretends that the labor—answering inane questions about cultural differences, being tokenized, being rendered eternally hip, being *othered*—has remained free, at least until her service's founding. The spoof implicitly argues that nonblacks continuously and ineptly exploit black individuals' supposedly innate racial cachet while offering a radical solution: make the renters / exploiters pay until it hurts financially and psychologically, since providing inanities to the inane already taxes the rented. Hence the "Rent-a-Negro Invoice," which charges renters $1,500 to "provide a 'Tell them I'm not a racist' vouch," or $250 per hour to "give dance lessons to the rhythmically challenged," each multiplied by the number of incidents (ayo 142). Ayo satirizes the exploiter and the exploited, each locked into a pathetic commodity exchange requiring one party to quit. As in most satire, the one least conscious of the relationship is least likely to recognize the exit. Like the narrator of Ralph Ellison's *Invisible Man* (1952), African Americans remain invisible to the renters but also fail to recognize how they enable that invisibility (3). Little wonder, then, that Ellison's magnum opus remains an *ur*-text of contemporary African American satire. Ellison's invisibility metaphor—the narrator is invisible only because people "*refuse* to see [him]"— resonates with a generation that has witnessed the obvious brutality of Jim Crow transform itself into a nearly maddening invisibility in which African Americans are popular until they become either serious, angry, or the president of the United States.

The future of African American satire depends upon black artists' desire and ability to straddle the gap between whatever desire they may have to tell the truth about the complexities of African American lives and history and the commodification process that remains an anathema on work by black creative artists. That desire—virtually identical to what Alice Walker identifies as the "moral and/or physical struggle . . . expected [to result in] some kind of larger freedom"—may vary widely, and does ("Saving" 5). By simply writing satire, African American satirists published since 1980 have implicitly declared the satiric muse's centrality to the literature to show how African American literature and culture have always embraced irony, understatement, and invective and turned them into mirrors that reflect all Americans' distorted and distorting idiocies back at themselves, perhaps clearer than they might otherwise be. In the current era, the black satirist will have to work immensely hard; when Tea Party members gleefully sell and wear t-shirts that declare, "Yup, I'm a Racist," without irony (K. Johnson), Juvenal's argument maxim, "difficile est saturam non scribere"—it is hard *not* to write satire—carries less purchase (*Satires* 1.30). How does a satirist lampoon those who have already rendered themselves absurd, accepted their own absurdity, and subsequently reveled in it?

I realize that in attempting to predict the future of African American satire, I risk committing the same fallacies that appear in Trey Ellis's "New

Black Aesthetic." Forecasting cultural or artistic trends inevitably veers toward glibness, with the works of a handful of artists standing for a protean whole. Although contemporary authors have found a role for satire in a world in which the genre has gained greater acceptance, they have not necessarily found a greater audience. If satire seemed anomalous, even retrograde to the intense nationalists of the 1960s, it has become part of the acceptable range of literary expression. Yet African American literary satirists far too seldom enjoy acclaim remotely close to the vast wealth, fame, and cultural cachet of Everett's fictional Juanita Mae Jenkins. On occasion, works by writers such as Everett, Colson Whitehead, or Mat Johnson may deservedly attract popular interest and awards; in the main, though, literary satire remains relatively marginal, even as its televised brethren (such as *The Daily Show*, *South Park*, *Chappelle's Show*, *The Boondocks*, and *Key & Peele*) have made substantial inroads into the American collective consciousness.

In a post-Obama age, American racial and cultural politics will continue to grow more complicated as a milestone that millions of Americans and countless foreign observers once considered either unthinkable or impossible—the (re)election and stable administration of a moderate-to-liberal African American president—becomes just one more part of the nation's historical threads. How will the nation reconsider "race"? How will African American artists reconceive the once inconceivable at all levels of African American culture? This remains to be seen.

Without question, though, the commodification of black lives and bodies in the United States will continue to attract satirists' attention; as damali ayo and Mat Johnson demonstrate, black lives, bodies, and cultural markers have obsessed the nation since the arrival in 1619 of enslaved and indentured Africans in Jamestown, Virginia, the soil of the future United States. Ellis's own novel *Platitudes* (1988) concerns author Dewayne Ellington's attempts to define his novel against the epic pastoral narratives of Alice Walker-esque novelist Isshee Ayam. *Platitudes*'s satire depends upon frustration with a black literary scene that has grown stale and stereotyped, where prize juries and readers shower fame and financial rewards upon authors who pretend that the only sites where African Americans reside are hopelessly pathological and depressed urban jungles or rural southern landscapes in which redemption comes solely through acceptance of either a romantic Afrocentrism or quasi-primitivist idyll.[5] Contemporary satire challenges this dualism, presenting other worlds where black people live. In Paul Beatty's *Slumberland* (2008), this impulse drives protagonist Ferguson "DJ Darky" Sowell to seek challenging black music and culture in the most improbable site: Germany around the time of the Berlin Wall's collapse.[6] Among many other discoveries in his search for the sublime, Sowell reveals one of the great dilemmas of contemporary black life: "Whenever two black quarterbacks face each other in a football game, black America gets a collective migraine because we don't know which team to cheer for" (Beatty, *Slumberland* 93). The presence of a black quarterback may be a sign of racial progress—albeit one not quite akin to an African American president—but black America also finds a war within itself: regardless of which achievement it cheers, it both loses and wins. Yet it often feels more like a loss, especially to the satirist, who asks why anyone would measure progress by achievement in sports in the first place.[7]

If the satirist habitually stands outside any era's prescribed norm and is at heart an iconoclast, then we may speculate that the iconoclastic genius will remain the dominant trope. Barack Obama's election demonstrated not only that an African American could be elected to the highest office in the land, but also that another of Trey Ellis's observations rings true: "We realize that despite this current buppie artist boom, most black Americans have seldom had it worse. But what most all the New Black Artists have in common is a commitment to what Columbia University philosopher Arthur Danto calls 'Disturbatory Art'—art that shakes you up" ("New Black Aesthetic" 239). Satire is that art, and it will shake the icons to their foundations.

Notes

1. In this article I place "race" in quotation marks to indicate that the term is problematic. Although "race" has social significance and little biological basis, it remains in common use, whether in American society or by the authors discussed herein. I also define the term *post-racial* vis-à-vis "race" later in the essay.

2. See Howe, "Black Boys and Native Sons"; Ellison, "The World and the Jug"; Howe, "A Reply to Ralph Ellison"; and Ellison, "A Rejoinder."

3. Reed summed up his criticisms of Walker as follows:

My disagreement with some feminists and womanists is that they have, out of ignorance or by design, promoted such myths in the media, a situation which adds to the problems that Black men face in everyday life.

In the film *The Color Purple* (1985), directed and produced by white males, all of the myths that have been directed at black men since the Europeans entered Africa are joined. In this film, black men commit heinous crimes against women and children, and though defenders of Walker's book, upon which the movie was based, argue that these creations were merely one woman's story, critics in the media have used both the book and the movie as excuses to indict all black men. This is not Ms. Walker's fault; however some of her public statements, such as her description of black men as "evil," gleefully printed in the magazine section of the neo-conservative *New York Times*, haven't helped. (Gates, ed., "Black Person" 8)

It is worth noting that in the *New York Times* article Reed mentions, Alice Walker never characterizes black men as "evil"; author David Bradley quotes selectively from an interview with Walker in which she says, "It is possible that white male writers are more conscious of their own evil . . . than black male writers, who, along with black and white women, have seen themselves as the recipients of that evil and therefore on the side of Christ, of the oppressed, of the innocent." If anything, Walker says here that black male writers, along with black and white women, are sometimes blind to their own "evil," their own faults, due to racist and sexist oppression (Walker, "From an Interview" 251; Bradley SM25).

4. See also Michael B. Gillespie's article in this collection, pp. 68–84.

5. See also Brandon Manning's article in this collection, pp. 125–36.

6. See also Christian Schmidt's article in this collection, pp. 150–61.

7. Such satirical questioning is by no means limited to the literary realm, either, as is shown by both Dave Chappelle's "Racial Draft" skit (season 2, episode 1) and Hank Willis Thomas's provocative visual art conflating images of athletics and slavery (such as "Cotton Bowl"; "NBA Trade"; "Basketball and Chain").

Composite Bibliography

"Aaron McGruder Nightline Interview." *YouTube*. 19 Feb. 2010. Web. 21 Dec. 2012. http://www.youtube.com/watch?v=9wpWI43SZuc.

Abel, Elizabeth. *Sign of the Times: The Visual Politics of Jim Crow*. Berkeley: U of California P, 2010. Print.

Abrahams, Roger D. *The Man-of-Words in the West Indies: Performance and the Emergence of Creole Culture*. Baltimore: Johns Hopkins UP, 1983. Print.

Abramovich, Alex. "Phenomenologically Fucked." *London Review of Books* 31.22 (19 Nov. 2009): 33–34. Print.

Adams, Nick. *Making Friends with Black People*. New York: Kensington, 2006. Print.

Ahmed, Sara. *The Cultural Politics of Emotion*. New York: Routledge, 2004. Print.

Alexander, Michelle. *The New Jim Crow: Mass Incarceration in the Age of Colorblindness*. New York: The New Press, 2010. Print.

Anderson, Benedict. *Imagined Communities: Reflections on the Origin and Spread of Nationalism*. London: Verso, 1983. Print.

Anderson, Dawolu Jabari. *Gullah Sci-Fi Mysteries*. 2008–2010. Web. 21 Dec. 2012. http://gullah-sci-fi-mysteries.blogspot.com.

———. "Re: Question." Message to Michael Gillespie. 19 Aug. 2012. E-mail.

Appiah, Kwame Anthony. "Is the Post- in Postmodernism the Post- in Postcolonial?" *Critical Inquiry* 17.2 (Winter 1991): 336–357. Print.

Ashe, Bertram D. "Theorizing the Post-Soul Aesthetic: An Introduction." *African American Review* 41.4 (2007): 609–623. Print.

Ashe, Bertram D., et al. "'These – Are – The – 'Breaks': A Roundtable Discussion on Teaching the Post-Soul Aesthetic." *African American Review* 41.4 (Winter 2007): 787–803. Print.

Assensoh, Akwasi, and Yvette Alex-Assensoh. "Black Political Leadership in the Post–Civil Rights Era." In *Black Political Organizations in the Post–Civil Rights Era*. Ed. Ollie A. Johnson III and Karin L. Stanford. New Brunswick, NJ: Rutgers UP, 2002. 193–201. Print.

ayo, damali. *How to Rent a Negro*. Chicago: Lawrence Hill, 2005. Print.

Baker, Houston A., Jr. *Blues, Ideology, and Afro-American Literature: A Vernacular Theory*. Chicago: U of Chicago P, 1984. Print.

———. *I Don't Hate the South: Reflections on Faulkner, Family, and the South*. New York: Oxford UP, 2007. Print.

Bakhtin, Mikhail M. *The Dialogic Imagination: Four Essays*. Ed. Michael Holquist. Trans. Caryl Emerson and Michael Holquist. Austin: U of Texas P, 1981. Print.

———. "Discourse in the Novel." *The Dialogic Imagination: Four Essays*. Ed. Michael Holquist. Trans. Caryl Emerson and M. Holquist. Austin: U of Texas P, 1981: 259–422. Print.

———. *Problems of Dostoevsky's Poetics*. Ed. and trans. Caryl Emerson. Minneapolis: U of Minnesota P, 1984. Print.

———. *Rabelais and His World*. 1965. Trans. Hélène Iswolsky. Bloomington: Indiana UP, 1984. Print.

Bal, Mieke. *Narratology: Introduction to the Theory of Narrative*. 2nd ed. Trans. Christine van Boheemen. Toronto: U of Toronto P, 1999. Print.

———. "The Point of Narratology." *Poetics Today* 11.4 (1990): 727–753. Print.

Baldwin, James. "The Devil Finds Work." In *James Baldwin: Collected Essays*. Ed. Toni Morrison. New York: The Library of America, 1998. 477–572. Print.

———. "No Name in the Street." In *James Baldwin: Collected Essays*. Ed. Toni Morrison. New York: The Library of America, 1998. 349–475. Print.

Ball, Ryan. "Boondocks Wins Peabody Award." *Animation Magazine*. 5 Apr. 2007. Web. 9 July 2012. http://www.animationmagazine.net/events/boondocks-wins-peabody-award.

Bamboozled. Dir. Spike Lee. Perf. Damon Wayans, Jada Pinkett-Smith, Savion Glover, Tommy Davidson, Michael Rapaport. New Line Cinema, 2000. DVD.

Barthes, Roland. *The Pleasure of the Text*. Trans. Richard Miller. New York: Hill and Wang, 1975. Print.

———. *S/Z: An Essay*. Trans. Richard Miller. New York: Hill and Wang, 1974. Print.

Baucom, Ian. *Specters of the Atlantic: Finance Capital, Slavery, and the Philosophy of History*. Durham, NC: Duke UP, 2005. Print.

Beatty, Paul. *Slumberland*. New York: Bloomsbury, 2008. Print.

———. *The White Boy Shuffle*. 1996. New York: Picador, 2001. Print.

Beatty, Paul, ed. *Hokum: An Anthology of African-American Humor*. New York: Bloomsbury, 2006. Print.

Bennu, Pierre. "Black Moses Barbie commercial #2 of 3." 1 Mar. 2011. Web. 21 Dec. 2012. http://vimeo.com/20514202.

———. "Black Moses Barbie commercial #3 of 3." 30 Dec. 2011. Web. 21 Dec. 2012. http://vimeo.com/34392154.

———. "Black Moses Barbie (Harriet Tubman Commerical) (1 of 3)." 9 Feb. 2011. Web. 21 Dec. 2012. http://vimeo.com/19748484.

———. "Re: Question." Message to Michael Gillespie. 4 Aug. 2012. E-mail.

Berger, Maurice. *For All the World to See: Visual Culture and the Struggle for Civil Rights*. New Haven, CT: Yale University Press, 2010. Print.

Bernstein, Robin. *Racial Innocence: Performing American Childhood from Slavery to Civil Rights*. New York and London: New York UP, 2011. Print

Best, Stephen M. *The Fugitive's Properties: Law and the Poetics of Possession*. Chicago: U of Chicago P, 2004. Print.

Bhabha, Homi K. "The Other Question—Homi K. Bhabha Reconsiders the Stereotype and Colonial Discourse." *Screen* 24.6 (1983): 18–36. Print.

Black, Ray. "Satire's Cruelest Cut: Exorcising Blackness in Spike Lee's *Bamboozled*." *The Black Scholar* 33.1 (2003): 9–25. Print.

Bogle, Donald. *Toms, Coons, Mulattoes, Mammies, and Bucks: An Interpretive History of Blacks in American Films*. 4th ed. New York: Continuum, 2001. Print.

The Boondocks: The Complete First Season. Dir. Anthony Bell et al. Writ. Aaron McGruder, Rodney Barnes et al. Sony, 2006. DVD.

The Boondocks: The Complete Second Season. Dir. Seung Eun Kim et al. Writ. Aaron McGruder, Rodney Barnes et al. Sony, 2008. DVD.

Bourdieu, Pierre. *The Logic of Practice*. Trans. Richard Nice. Stanford, CA: Stanford UP, 1990. Print.

———. *Masculine Domination*. Trans. Richard Nice. Stanford, CA: Stanford UP, 2001. Print.

———. *On Television and Journalism*. Trans. Priscilla Parkhurst Ferguson. London: Pluto, 1998. Print.

———. *Outline of a Theory of Practice*. Trans. Richard Nice. New York: Cambridge UP, 1977. Print.

———. *Practical Reason: On the Theory of Action*. Trans. Randal Johnson and Richard Nice. Stanford, CA: Stanford UP, 1998. Print.

———. "Some Properties of Fields." In *Sociology in Question*. Trans. Richard Nice. 1984. London: Sage, 1993. 72–77. Print.

Bourdieu, Pierre, and Loïc Wacquant. *An Invitation to Reflexive Sociology*. Chicago: U of Chicago P, 1992. Print.

Bradley, David. "Telling the Black Woman's Story: The Powerful Yet Sensitive Works of the Novelist, Poet, and Writer of Short Stories Have Earned Her Much Critical Acclaim, Including a Pulitzer Prize." *New York Times*, 8 Jan. 1984: SM25. Print.

Brown, Bill. "Reification, Reanimation, and the American Uncanny." *Critical Inquiry* 32.2 (Winter 2006): 175–207. Print.

Brown, Kimberly Nichele. *Writing the Black Revolutionary Diva: Women's Subjectivity and the Decolonizing Text*. Bloomington: Indiana UP, 2010. Print.

Brown, Sterling. "Our Literary Audience." *Opportunity* 8 (Feb. 1930): 42–46, 61. Print.

Bucholtz, Mary, et al. "Hella Nor Cal or Totally So Cal?: The Perceptual Dialectology of California." *Journal of English Linguistics* 35.4 (2007): 325–352. Print.

Cain, Herman. "Big Interview Excerpt: Cain Comments on Wall Street Protests." Video of interview by Alan Murray. *Wall Street Journal Live*. 6 Oct. 2011. Web. 21 Dec. 2012. http://live.wsj.com/video/cain-to-protesters-dont-blame-wall-street/36E27C75-B8B4-4D94-84E1-2772407EF3EB.html#!36E27C75-B8B4-4D94-84E1-2772407EF3EB.

Carbado, Devon. "When and Where Black Men Enter." In *Black Men on Race, Gender, and Sexuality: A Critical Reader*. Ed. Devon Carbado. New York: New York UP, 1999. 1–20. Print.

Carpio, Glenda. *Laughing Fit to Kill: Black Humor in the Fictions of Slavery*. New York: Oxford UP, 2008. Print.

Cassel, Valerie. *Splat, Boom, Pow: The Influence of Cartoons in Contemporary Art*. Houston: Contemporary Art Museum, 2003. Print.

Cassuto, Leonard. *The Inhuman Race: The Racial Grotesque in American Literature and Culture*. New York: Columbia UP, 1997. Print.

Catanese, Brandi Wilkins. "'And the Rest Is La History': Autobiographical Strategies in *The Colored Museum*." *Journal of American Drama and Theatre* 14 (2002): 15–28. Print.

Chappelle, Dave. Interview by Terry Gross. *Fresh Air*. National Public Radio. 10 Jun. 2005. Web. 21 Dec. 2012. http://www.npr.org/templates/story/story.php?storyId=4698236.

Chappelle's Show: Season One, Uncensored! Writ. Dave Chappelle, Neal Brennan et al. Comedy Central Home Video, 2004. DVD.

Chappelle's Show: Season Two, Uncensored. Writ. Dave Chappelle, Neal Brennan et al. Comedy Central Home Video, 2005. DVD.

"Chappelle's Story." *Oprah.com*. Harpo Production Inc., n.d., n. pag. Web. 21 Dec. 2012. http://www.oprah.com/oprahshow/Chappelles-Story.

Cheney, Charise L. *Brothers Gonna Work It Out: Sexual Politics in the Golden Age of Rap Nationalism*. New York: New York UP, 2005. Print.

Chery, Carl. "Little Brother's 'Too Intelligent' Says BET, Network Responds to Allegation." *SOHH.com*. 8 Sep. 2005. Web. 15 Jul. 2012. http://www.sohh.com/articles/article.php/7519.

Childish Gambino. *Culdesac*. Independently produced, 2010. CD.

Christian, Barbara. "The Race for Theory." *Cultural Critique* 6 (Spring 1987): 51–63. Print.

Collins, Patricia Hill. *Black Feminist Thought: Knowledge, Consciousness, and the Politics of Empowerment*. Boston: Unwin Hyman, 1990. Print.

Coly, Ayo. "A Pedagogy of the Black Female Body: Viewing Angèle Essamba's Black Female Nudes." *Third Text* 24.6 (Oct. 2010): 653–664. Print.

The Combahee River Collective. "The Combahee River Collective Statement." In *Home Girls: A Black Feminist Anthology*. Ed. Barbara Smith. New York: Kitchen Table, 1983. 264–274. Print.

Cotter, Holland. "A Nightmare View of Antebellum Life That Sets Off Sparks." *New York Times*, 9 May 2003: E36. Print.

Crenshaw, Kimberle. "Mapping the Margins: Intersectionality, Identity Politics, and Violence against Women of Color." *Stanford Law Review* 43.6 (1991): 1241–1299. Print.

Crowdus, Gary, and Dan Georgakas. "Thinking About the Power of Images: An Interview with Spike Lee." *Cineaste* 26.2 (2001): 4–9. Print.

Cuddon, J. A., ed. *The Penguin Dictionary of Literary Terms and Literary Theory*. 4th. ed. New York: Penguin, 1998. Print.

Dällenbach, Lucien. *The Mirror in the Text*. 1977. Trans. Jeremy Whiteley and Emma Hughes. Chicago: U of Chicago P, 1989. Print.

"A Date with the Health Inspector." *The Boondocks: The Complete First Season*. Dir. Joe Horne and Lesean Thomas. Writ. Aaron McGruder, Rodney Barnes et al. Sony, 2006. DVD.

Debord, Guy. *The Society of the Spectacle*. 1967. Trans. Ken Knabb. Bureau of Public Secrets. Feb. 2002. Web. 21 Dec. 2012. http://www.bopsecrets.org/images/sos.pdf.

De La Soul. *De La Soul Is Dead*. Tommy Boy/Warner Bros. Records, 1991. CD.

———. *De La Soul's Plug 1 & Plug 2 Present . . . First Serve*. Duck Down Music, 2012. CD.

———. *3 Feet High and Rising*. Tommy Boy/Warner Bros. Records, 1989. CD.

Delue, Rachael Z. "Envisioning Race in Spike Lee's *Bamboozled*." In *Fight the Power! The Spike Lee Reader*. Ed. Janice D. Hamlet and Robin R. Means Coleman. New York: Peter Lang, 1998. 61–88. Print.

Dentith, Simon. *Parody*. London: Routledge, 2000. Print.

Dickson-Carr, Darryl. *African American Satire: The Sacredly Profane Novel*. Columbia: U of Missouri P, 2001. Print.

Do the Right Thing. Dir. Spike Lee. Perf. Danny Aiello, Ruby Dee, Spike Lee, Ossie Davis, John Turturro. Criterion, 2001. DVD.

Du Bois, W. E. B. (William Edward Burghardt). *The Souls of Black Folk*. 1903. Ed. Candace Ward. New York: Dover, 1994. Print.

duCille, Ann. *Skin Trade*. Cambridge, MA: Harvard UP, 1996. Print.

Dyson, Michael Eric. "Tour(é)ing Blackness." Foreword. *Who's Afraid of Post-Blackness?: What It Means to Be Black Now*. New York: Free Press, 2011. xi–xviii. Print.

Ebert, Roger. Review of *Bamboozled*. *RogerEbert.com*. 6 Oct. 2000. Web. 21 Dec. 2012. http://rogerebert.suntimes.com/apps/pbcs.dll/article?AID=/20001006/REVIEWS/10060301/1023.

Edwards, Erica R. *Charisma and the Fictions of Black Leadership*. Minneapolis: U of Minnesota P, 2012. Print.

Elam, Harry J. "Signifyin(g) on African-American Theatre: *The Colored Museum* by George Wolfe." *Theatre Journal* 44 (1992): 291–303. Print.

Elliot, Robert C. "The Satirist and Society." In *Satire: Modern Essays in Criticism*. Ed. Ronald Paulson. Englewood Cliffs, NJ: Prentice-Hall, 1971. 205–216. Print.

Ellis, Trey. "The New Black Aesthetic." *Callaloo* 38 (Winter 1989): 233–243. Print.

———. *Platitudes*. Boston: Northeastern UP, 2003. Print.

Ellison, Ralph. "Change the Joke and Slip the Yoke." In *The Collected Essays of Ralph Ellison*. Ed. John F. Callahan. New York: Modern Library, 1995. 100–112. Print.

———. "An Extravagance of Laughter." In *The Collected Essays of Ralph Ellison*. Ed. John F. Callahan. New York: Modern Library, 1995. 613–658. Print.

———. *Invisible Man*. New York: Random House, 1952. Print.

———. "A Rejoinder." *New Leader* 47 (3 Feb. 1964): 15–22. Print.

———. "Twentieth-Century Fiction." In *Shadow and Act*. New York: Vintage Books, 1953. 24–44. Print.

———. "The World and the Jug." In *The Collected Essays of Ralph Ellison*. Ed. John F. Callahan. New York: Modern Library, 1995. 155–188. Print.

English, Darby. *How to See a Work of Art in Total Darkness*. Cambridge, MA: The MIT Press, 2007. Print.

"Episode #1.2." *Key & Peele*. Writ. Keegan-Michael Key, Jordan Peele et al. Comedy Central. 7 Feb. 2012. Television.

"Episode #2.1." *Key & Peele*. Writ. Keegan-Michael Key, Jordan Peele et al. Comedy Central. 26 Sept. 2012. Television.

"Episode #2.2." *Key & Peele*. Writ. Keegan-Michael Key, Jordan Peele et al. Comedy Central. 3 Oct. 2012. Television.

"Episode #2.3." *Key & Peele*. Writ. Keegan-Michael Key, Jordan Peele et al. Comedy Central. 10 Oct. 2012. Television.

Eshun, Kodwo. "Further Considerations of Afrofuturism." *CR: The New Centennial Review* 3.2 (2003): 287–302. Print.

Euell, Kim. "Signifyin(g) Ritual: Subverting Stereotypes, Salvaging Icons." *African American Review* 31 (1997): 667–675. Print.

Evans, Patrice. "If You Can't Take A Joke . . ." *EbonyJet Online*. 16 May 2008. Web. 21 Dec. 2012. http://stage.ebonyjet.com/culture/literature/boondocks.aspx.

Evans, Teino. "The Ity And Fancy Cat Show." *The Jamaica Star Online*, 12 Aug. 2006: n. pag. Web. 21 Dec. 2012. http://jamaica-star.com/thestar/20061208/ent/ent6.html.

Everett, Percival. *Erasure*. Hyperion: New York, 2002. Print.

———. *A History of the African-American People [Proposed] by Strom Thurmond. As Told to Percival Everett and James Kincaid*. New York: Akashic Books, 2004. Print.

———. "Signing to the Blind." *Callaloo* 14.1 (Winter 1991): 9–11. Print.

Favor, J. Martin. *Authentic Blackness: The Folk in the New Negro Renaissance*. Durham, NC: Duke UP, 1999. Print.

Feinberg, Leonard. *Introduction to Satire*. Ames: Iowa State UP, 1967. Print.

Fitts, Mako. "'Drop It Like It's Hot': Culture Industry Laborers and Their Perspectives on Rap Music Video Production." *Meridians* 8.1 (2008): 211–235. Print.

"The Freedom You Will Take." *I'll Make Me a World: A Century of African-American Arts*. PBS. 3 Feb. 1999. Television.

Frye, Northrop. *The Anatomy of Criticism: Four Essays*. Princeton, NJ: Princeton UP, 1957. Print.

Fuller, Hoyt W. "Towards a Black Aesthetic." In *Within the Circle: An Anthology of African American Literary Critics from the Harlem Renaissance to the Present*. Ed. Angelyn Mitchell. Durham, NC: Duke UP, 1994. 199–206. Print.

Funkadelic. "Mommy, What's a Funkadelic?" *Funkadelic*. Westbound Records, 1970. CD.

Gates, Henry Louis, Jr. *"Race," Writing, and Difference*. Chicago: U of Chicago P, 1986. Print.

———. *The Signifying Monkey: A Theory of Afro-American Literary Criticism*. New York: Oxford UP, 1988. Print.

Gates, Henry Louis, Jr., ed. "The Black Person in Art: How Should S/He Be Portrayed." *Black American Literature Forum* 21.1–2 (Spring–Summer 1987): 3–24. Print.

Geis, Deborah R. *Suzan-Lori Parks*. Ann Arbor: U of Michigan P, 2008. Print.

George, Nelson. *Buppies, B-Boys, Baps and Bohos: Notes on Post-Soul Black Culture*. New York: HarperCollins, 1992. Print.

Gillespie, Michael B. "Reckless Eyeballing: *Coonskin*, Film Blackness, and the Racial Grotesque." *Contemporary Black American Cinema: Race, Gender, and Sexuality at the Movies*. Ed. Mia Mask. New York: Routledge, 2012. 56–86.

Gilroy, Paul. "'After the Love Has Gone': Bio-politics and Etho-poetics in the Black Public Sphere." *Public Culture* 7.1 (1994): 49–76. Print.

———. *Against Race: Imagining Political Culture beyond the Color Line*. Cambridge, MA: Harvard UP, 2000. Print.

———. ". . . to be Real': The Dissident Forms of Black Expressive Culture." In *Let's Get t On: The Politics of Black Performance*. Ed. Catherine Ugwu. Seattle: Bay Press, 1995. 12–33. Print.

Glaude, Eddie S., Jr. "Introduction: Black Power Revisited." In *Is It Nation Time?: Contemporary Essays on Black Power and Black Nationalism*. Ed. Eddie S. Glaude Jr. Chicago: U of Chicago P, 2001. 1–21. Print.

Golden, Thelma. "Introduction." In *Freestyle*. New York: The Studio Museum in Harlem, 2001. 14–15. Print.

Gray, Jonathan, Jeffrey P. Jones, and Ethan Thompson. "The State of Satire, the Satire of State." *Satire TV: Politics and Comedy in the Post-Network Era*. Eds. Jonathan Gray, Jeffrey P. Jones, and Ethan Thompson. New York: New York UP, 2009. 3–36. Print.

Griffin, Dustin. *Satire: A Critical Reintroduction*. Lexington: UP of Kentucky, 1994. Print.

Gubar, Susan. "Racial Camp in *The Producers* and *Bamboozled*." *Film Quarterly* 60.2 (Winter 2006): 26–37. Print.

Guerrero, Ed. *Framing Blackness: The African American Image in Film*. Philadelphia: Temple UP, 1993. Print.

Guzman, Rafer. "*2016: Obama's America*' Review: Diatribe." *Newsday*, 24 Aug. 2012: n. pag. Web. 21 Dec. 2012. http://www.newsday.com/entertainment/movies/2016-obama-s-america-review-diatribe-1.3925652.

Gysin, Fritz. "The Pitfalls of Parody: Melancholic Satire in Percival Everett's *Erasure*." In *Reading Percival Everett: European Perspectives*. Ed. Claude Julien and Anne-Laure Tissut. Tours, France: Presses Universitaires Francois Rabelais, 2007. 63–80. Print.

Haggins, Bambi. "In the Wake of 'The Nigger Pixie': Dave Chappelle and the Politics of Crossover Comedy." In *Satire TV: Politics and Comedy in the Post-Network Era*. Eds. Jonathan Gray, Jeffrey P. Jones, and Ethan Thompson. New York: New York UP: 2009. 233–251. Print.

———. *Laughing Mad: The Black Comic Persona in Post-Soul America*. New Brunswick, NJ: Rutgers UP, 2007. Print.

Hannaham, James. "Napkin Ring." *Significant Objects . . . and how they got that way*, created and curated by Joshua Glenn and Rob Walker. 15 Jun. 2010. Web. 21 Dec. 2012. http://significantobjects.com/2010/06/15/napkin-ring-james-hannaham-story.

———. "Re: Question." Message to Michael Gillespie. 5 August 2012. E-mail.

Harris, Michael D. *Colored Pictures: Race and Visual Representation*. Chapel Hill: U of North Carolina P, 2003. Print.

Harris, Trudier. *Exorcising Blackness: Historical and Literary Lynching and Burning Rituals*. Bloomington: Indiana UP, 1984. Print.

Harrison, Anthony Kwame. *Hip Hop Underground: The Integrity and Ethics of Racial Identification*. Philadelphia: Temple UP, 2009. Print.

Hartman, Saidiya V. *Scenes of Subjection: Terror, Slavery, and Self-Making in Nineteenth Century America*. New York: Oxford UP, 1997. Print.

Highet, Gilbert. *The Anatomy of Satire*. Princeton, NJ: Princeton UP, 1962. Print.

hooks, bell. "George C. Wolfe." *BOMB* 50 (1994–1995): 46–51. Print.

Hopkinson, Natalie. "Aaron McGruder: Post-Racial Obama Hater?" *The Root*. 5 May 2010. Web. 21 Dec. 2012. http://www.theroot.com/views/aaron-mcgruder-post-racial-obama-hater.

Howe, Irving. "Black Boys and Native Sons." *Dissent* 10 (Autumn 1963): 353–368. Print.

———. "A Reply to Ralph Ellison." *New Leader* 47 (3 Feb. 1964): 12–14. Print.

Hudson, Julius. "The Hustling Ethic." In *Rappin' and Stylin' Out: Communication in Urban Black America*. Ed. Thomas Kochman. Chicago: U of Illinois P, 1977: 410–424. Print.

"A Huey Freeman Christmas." *The Boondocks: The Complete First Season*. Dir. Anthony Bell and Lesean Thomas. Writ. Aaron McGruder, Rodney Barnes et al. Sony, 2006. DVD.

Huey, Steve. "Little Brother." *AllMusic*. n.d. Web. 21 Dec. 2012. http://www.allmusic.com/artist/little-brother-mn0000255964.

Hughes, Langston. *The Big Sea.* New York: Alfred A. Knopf, 1940. Print.

———. "The Negro Artist and the Racial Mountain." *The Nation* 122 (23 Jun. 1926): 692–694. Print.

Hughes, Robert. "The Whitney Biennial: A Fiesta of Whining." *Time* 22 Mar. 1993: 68–69. Print.

Hume, Kathryn. "Ishmael Reed and the Problematics of Control." *PMLA* 108.3 (May 1993): 506–518. Print.

Hunter, Tera. "'It's a Man's Man's Man's World': Specters of the Old Re-newed in Afro-American Culture and Criticism." *Callaloo* 38 (Winter 1989): 247–249. Print.

Hurston, Zora Neale. *Moses, Man of the Mountain.* 1939. New York: HarperPerennial, 1991. Print.

———. "What White Publishers Won't Print." 1950. In *Within the Circle: An Anthology of African American Literary Criticism from the Harlem Renaissance to the Present.* Ed. Angelyn Mitchell. Durham, NC: Duke UP, 1994. 117–121. Print.

Hutcheon, Linda. *A Theory of Parody: The Teachings of Twentieth-Century Art Forms.* 1985. Rev. ed. Urbana, IL: U of Illinois P, 2000. Print.

Hyde, Lewis. *Trickster Makes This World: Mischief, Myth, and Art.* New York: Farrar, Straus and Giroux, 1998. Print.

Iser, Wolfgang. *The Act of Reading: A Theory of Aesthetic Response.* Baltimore: Johns Hopkins UP, 1978. Print.

"The Itis." *The Boondocks: The Complete First Season.* Dir. Joe Horne and Lesean Thomas. Writ. Aaron McGruder, Rodney Barnes et al. Sony, 2006. DVD.

"It's a Black President, Huey Freeman." *The Boondocks: Season 3.* Sony, 2010. DVD.

"Ity and Fancy Cat." *YouTube.* 1 Oct. 2011. Web. 21 Dec. 2012 http://www.youtube.com/watch?v=iEnRiW7NhI4.

The Ity and Fancy Cat Show: 100 Minutes of Jamaican Laughter. Ellis International Presentation, 2009. DVD.

"ITY & FANCY CAT SHOW [THE AFTER LIFE—MICHAEL JACKSON & BOB MARLEY (HD)]." *YouTube.* 13 Oct. 2010. Web. 21 Dec. 2012. http://www.youtube.com/watch?v=4--Mso1QShk.

Iverem, Esther. "Interview—Spike Lee—October 20, 2000." In *We Gotta Have It: Twenty Years of Seeing Black at the Movies, 1986–2006.* New York: Thunder's Mouth, 2007. 238–241. Print.

James, Darius. *Negrophobia: An Urban Parable.* New York: St. Martin's Press, 1993.

Johnson, E. Patrick. *Appropriating Blackness: Performance and the Politics of Authenticity.* Durham, NC: Duke University Press, 2003. Print.

Johnson, Kirsten Boyd. "Kentucky Tea Party Sells 'Yup, I'm A Racist' Fourth of July T-Shirts." *Wonkette.* 5 July 2011. Web. 21 Dec. 2012. http://wonkette.com/448772/kentucky-tea-party-sells-patriotic-yup-im-a-racist-fourth-of-july-t-shirts.

Johnson, Mat. *Hunting in Harlem.* New York: Bloomsbury, 2003. Print.

Jones, Amelia. "Postfeminism, Feminist Pleasures, and Embodied Theories of Art." *New Feminist Criticism: Art, Identity, Action.* Eds. Joanna Frueh, Cassandra L. Langer, and Arlene Raven. New York: Icon Editions, 1994. 16–41. Print.

Jones, Jacquie. "The New Ghetto Aesthetic." In *Mediated Messages and African-American Culture*. Eds. Venise T. Berry and Carmen L. Manning-Miller. Thousand Oaks, CA: Sage, 1996. 40–51. Print.

Jones, Joni L. "Performance Ethnography: The Role of Embodiment in Cultural Authenticity." *Theatre Topics* 12.1 (Mar. 2002): 1–15. Print.

Jones, Lisa. *Bulletproof Diva: Tales of Race, Sex and Hair*. New York: Anchor, 1994. Print.

Jordan, Jennifer. "Huey and Riley in the Boondocks: Sometimes I Feel like a Womanless Child." In *African American Humor, Irony, and Satire: Ishmael Reed, Satirically Speaking*. Ed. Dana A. Williams. Newcastle upon Tyne, UK: Cambridge Scholars, 2007. Print.

———. "The New Literary Blackface." *Black Issues Book Review* 4.2 (Mar.–Apr. 2002): 26–28. *Academic OneFile*. Web. 21 Dec. 2012.

Juvenal. *Satires* 1.30.

Kaiser, Ernest. "A Critical Look at Ellison's Fiction and at Social and Literary Criticism by and about the Author." *Black World* 20 (Dec. 1970): 53–59, 81–97. Print.

Kang, Stephanie. "Down in the *Boondocks*: Cartoonist Aaron McGruder." In *All the Rage: The Boondocks Past and Present*. By Aaron McGruder. New York: Three Rivers Press, 2007. 138–139. Print.

Kayser, Brian. "9th Wonder and Little Brother Part Ways; Rapper Pooh Clears Up Little Brother Rumors." *HipHopGame*. 27 Jan. 2007. Web. 21 Dec. 2012. http://hiphopgame .ihiphop.com/news.php3?id=1510.

Kelleher, Terry. "Picks and Pans Review: *Chappelle's Show*." *People* 24 Feb. 2003: 29. Print.

Kernan, Alvin P. "A Theory of Satire." In *Satire: Modern Essay in Criticism*. Ed. Ronald Paulson. Englewood Cliffs, NJ: Prentice-Hall, 1971. 249–277. Print.

Kierkegaard, Søren. *Concluding Unscientific Postscript to Philosophical Fragments*. Trans. David F. Swenson. Princeton, NJ: Princeton University Press, 1941. Print.

Kiley, Frederick, and J. M. Shuttleworth. *Satire from Aesop to Buckwald*. New York: Odyssey, 1971. Print.

Killens, John Oliver. *The Cotillion, or, One Good Bull Is Half the Herd*. 1971. Minneapolis: Coffee House Press. 2002. Print.

King, Geoff. *Film Comedy*. London: Wallflower Press, 2002. Print.

Klavan, Andrew. "A Man Alone: Jesse Lee Peterson versus the 'Black Experience.'" *City Journal* 20.1 (Winter 2010): n. pag. Web. 21 Dec. 2012. http://www.city-journal .org/2010/20_1_jesse-lee-peterson.html.

Knight, Charles A. *The Literature of Satire*. Cambridge: Cambridge UP, 2004. Print.

Kolin, Philip. "'You One of Uh Mines?': Dis(re)membering in Suzan-Lori Parks's *Imperceptible Mutabilities in the Third Kingdom*." In *Suzan-Lori Parks: Essays on the Plays and Other Works*. Ed. Philip C. Kolin. Jefferson, NC: McFarland, 2010. 45–55. Print.

Kreuz, Roger J., and Richard M. Roberts. "On Satire and Parody: The Importance of Being Ironic." *Metaphor and Symbolic Activity* 8.2 (1993): 97–109. Print.

Lait, Matt. "This One's for You, KBIG." *Los Angeles Times*, 10 Feb. 1994: n. pag. Web. 21 Dec. 2012. http://articles.latimes.com/1994-02-10/local/me-21215_1_barry-manilow.

Lanser, Susan. "Are We There Yet? The Intersectional Future of Feminist Narratology." *Foreign Languages Studies* 32.4 (2010): 32–41. Print.

Lanser, Susan S. "Toward a Feminist Narratology." In *Essentials of the Theory of Fiction*. Ed. Michael J. Hoffman and Patrick D. Murphy. Durham, NC: Duke UP, 1988. 453–472. Print.

Larson, Jennifer. *Understanding Suzan-Lori Parks*. Columbia: U of South Carolina P, 2012. Print.

Lee, Chris. "Donald Glover, Renaissance Man of Comedy and Rap." *Los Angeles Times*, 19 Jul. 2010: n. pag. Web. 21 Dec. 2012. http://articles.latimes.com/2010/jul/19/entertainment/la-et-glover-20100719.

Lee, Felicia R. "Arts, Briefly; Sharpton Protests Cartoon." *New York Times*, 25 Jan. 2006: n. pag. *Newspaper Source Plus*. Web. 21 Dec. 2012.

"Let's Nab Oprah." *The Boondocks: The Complete First Season*. Dir. Seung Eun Kim. Writ. Aaron McGruder, Rodney Barnes et al. Sony, 2006. DVD.

Lewis, Theophilus. "Magic Hours in the Theatre." *Pittsburgh Courier* 26 Feb. 1927, sec.2:1. Print.

———. "Survey of Negro Theatre, Part III." *The Messenger* 8.10 (Oct. 1926): 301–302. Print.

Little Brother. *The Listening*. ABB Records, 2003. CD.

———. *The Minstrel Show*. Atlantic/ABB Records, 2005. CD.

Locke, Alain. Foreword. In *The New Negro: An Interpretation*. New York: Albert and Charles Boni, 1925. ix–xi. Print.

———. "Self-Criticism: The Third Dimension in Culture." *Phylon* 11.4 (1950): 391–394. Print.

Lott, Eric. "Response to Trey Ellis's 'The New Black Aesthetic.'" *Callaloo* 38 (Winter 1989): 244–246. Print.

Lottery Ticket. Dir. Erik White. Perf. Bow Wow, Brandon T. Jackson, Naturi Naughton. Warner Home Video, 2010. DVD.

Lubiano, Wahneema. "Black Ladies, Welfare Queens, and State Minstrels: Ideological War by Narrative Means." In *Race-ing Justice, En-gendering Power: Essays on Anita Hill, Clarence Thomas and the Construction of Social Reality*. Ed. Toni Morrison. New York: Pantheon Books, 1992. Print.

Lupack, Barbara Tepa. "The Black Family on Film: From Mammy to Madea." *Separatecinema.com*, n.d. Web. 21 Dec. 2012. http://www.separatecinema.com.

"The Making of *Bamboozled*" (supplemental film on special edition DVD release of *Bamboozled*). Dir. Spike Lee and Samuel D. Pollard. New Line Cinema, 2001. DVD

Mansbach, Adam. *Angry Black White Boy, or The Miscegenation of Macon Detournay*. New York: Three Rivers Press, 2005. Print.

———. "The Audacity of Post-Racism." In *The Speech: Race and Barack Obama's "A More Perfect Union."* Ed. T. Denean Sharpley-Whitley. New York: Bloomsbury USA, 2009. 69–84. Print.

———. Telephone Interview. 28 Feb. 2012.

Marc, David. Foreword. In *Satire TV: Politics and Comedy in the Post-Network Era*. New York: New York UP, 2009. ix–xiv. Print.

Martin, Reginald. "An Interview with Ishmael Reed." *The Review of Contemporary Fiction* 4.2 (Summer 1984): 176–187. Print.

Massood, Paula J. *Black City Cinema*. Philadelphia: Temple UP, 2003. Print.

McAllister, Marvin. *Whiting Up: Whiteface Minstrels and Stage Europeans in African American Performance*. Chapel Hill: U of North Carolina P, 2011. Print.

McDowell, Deborah E. "Foreword: Lines of Descent/Dissenting Lines." In *Moses, Man of the Mountain*. By Zora Neale Hurston. 1939. New York: HarperPerennial, 1991. vii–xxii. Print.

McGrath, Ben. "The Radical: Why Do Editors Keep Throwing 'The Boondocks' off the Funnies Page?" *The New Yorker*, 19 Apr. 2004: n. pag. Web. 3 July 2012. http://www.newyorker.com/archive/2004/04/19/040419fa_fact2.

McGruder, Aaron. *All the Rage: The Boondocks Past and Present*. New York: Three Rivers Press, 2007. Print.

———. *Public Enemy #2: An All-New Boondocks Collection*. New York: Three Rivers Press, 2005. Print.

———. *A Right to Be Hostile: The Boondocks Treasury*. New York: Three Rivers Press, 2003. Print.

McHale, Brian. "Weak Narrativity: The Case of Avant-Garde Narrative Poetry." *Contemporary Narratology* 9.2 (2001): 161–167. Print.

McNulty, Charles. "Culture Monster: Theater Review: 'By the Way, Meet Vera Stark' at Second Stage Theatre." *Los Angeles Times*, 9 May 2011: n. pag. Web. 21 Dec. 2012. http://latimesblogs.latimes.com/culturemonster/2011/05/theater-reviewby-the-way-meet-vera-stark-at-second-stage-theatre.html.

Menashe, Doron, and Mutal E. Shamash. "The Narrative Fallacy." *International Commentary on Evidence* 3.1 (2005): 1–47. Print.

Mercer, Kobena. "Black Art and Burden of Representation." In *Welcome to the Jungle: New Positions in Black Cultural Studies*. New York: Routledge, 1994. 223–258. Print.

———. "Keith Piper: To Unbury the Disremembered Body." In *New Histories*. Ed. Malena Kalinovska. Boston: Institute of Contemporary Arts, 1996. 161–166. Print.

———. "Tropes of the Grotesque in Black Avant-Garde." In *Cosmopolitan Modernisms*. Ed. Kobena Mercer. Cambridge, MA: Institute of International Visual Arts and MIT Press, 2007. 136–159. Print.

Mezei, Kathy. "Introduction: Contextualizing Feminist Narratology." In *Ambiguous Discourse: Feminist Narratology and British Women Writers*. Ed. Kathy Mezei. Chapel Hill: U of North Carolina P, 1996. 1–20. Print.

Mezei, Kathy, ed. *Ambiguous Discourse: Feminist Narratology and British Women Writers*. Chapel Hill: U of North Carolina P, 1996. Print.

Mighty Casey. *Original Rudebwoy*. Busted Lip Records, 2003. CD.

———. Personal Web page. "Bio." *MySpace*. Web. 21 Dec. 2012. http://www.myspace.com/mcmightycasey.

Mills, Charles W. *The Racial Contract*. New York: Cornell UP, 1997. Print.

Mohammed, Patricia. "'But most of all mi love me browning': The Emergence in Eighteenth and Nineteenth-Century Jamaica of the Mulatto Woman as the Desired." *Feminist Review* 65 (1 Jun. 2000): 22–48. Print.

Moore, Michael. Foreword. In *A Right to Be Hostile: The Boondocks Treasury*. New York: Three Rivers Press, 2003. 7–8. Print.

Morgan, Marcyliena. *The Real Hiphop: Battling for Knowledge, Power, and Respect in the LA Underground*. Durham, NC: Duke UP, 2009. Print.

Morris, Linda A. "American Satire: Beginnings through Mark Twain." In *A Companion to Satire: Ancient and Modern*. Ed. Ruben Quintero. Chichester, UK: Wiley-Blackwell, 2011. 377–399. Print.

Morrison, Toni. *Playing in the Dark: Whiteness and the Literary Imagination.* New York: Vintage Books, 1993. Print.

Moten, Fred. *In the Break: The Aesthetics of the Black Radical Tradition.* Minneapolis: University of Minnesota Press, 2003. Print.

Mueller, Kurt. "Double Issue: Dawolu Jabari Anderson." *Gulf Coast: A Journal of Literature and Fine Arts* 22.2 (Summer–Fall 2010): 181–182. Print.

Murray, Derek, and Soraya Murray. "On Art and Contamination: Performing Authenticity in Global Art Practices." *Nka: Journal of Contemporary African Art* 22–23 (Spring–Summer 2008): 88–93. Print.

———. "Uneasy Bedfellows: Canonical Art Theory and the Politics of Identity." *Art Journal* 65.1 (Spring 2006): 22–39. Print.

Murray, Soraya. "Glenn Ligon: Going There." *Nka: Journal of Contemporary African Art* 19 (Summer 2004): 88–89. Print.

Nama, Adilifu. *Super Black: American Pop Culture and Black Superheroes.* Austin: U of Texas P, 2011. Print.

"NBA Crock Out." *In the Flow with Affion Crockett.* Writ. Affion Crockett, Jamie Foxx et al. Fox. 28 Aug. 2011. Television.

Neal, Larry. "The Black Arts Movement." *Drama Review* 12 (Summer 1968): 29–39. Print.

Neal, Mark Anthony. "Bennu Unchained: The 'Black Moses Barbie' Series." *The Huffington Post.* 15 Jan. 2013. Web. 16 Oct. 2013. http://www.huffingtonpost.com/mark-anthony-neal/black-moses-barbie_b_2470914.html.

———. *Soul Babies: Black Popular Culture and the Post-Soul Aesthetic.* New York: Routledge, 2002. Print.

Nelson, Alondra. "Introduction: Future Texts." *Social Text* 20.2 (2002): 1–15. Print.

Ngai, Sianne. *Ugly Feelings.* Cambridge, MA: Harvard UP, 2005. Print.

Norman, Larry F. *The Public Mirror: Molière and the Social Commerce of Depiction.* Chicago: U of Chicago P, 1999. Print.

Norris, Christopher. *Derrida.* Cambridge, MA: Harvard UP, 1987. Print.

Nottage, Lynn. *Intimate Apparel* and *Fabulation.* New York: Theatre Communications Group, 2006. Print.

———. *By the Way, Meet Vera Stark.* Second Stage Theatre. The Theatre at 43rd Street, New York. 14 May 2011. Performance.

———. *By the Way, Meet Vera Stark.* Unpublished play script.

Nussbaum, Felicity. *The Brink of All We Hate: English Satires on Women, 1660–1750.* Lexington: U of Kentucky P, 1984. Print.

Obama, Barack. Interview by Jimmy Fallon. *Late Night with Jimmy Fallon.* NBC. 24 Apr. 2012. Television.

———. "Remarks by the President at Congressional Black Caucus Foundation Annual Phoenix Awards Dinner." *Whitehouse.gov.* 24 Sep. 2011. Web. 21 Dec. 2012. http://www.whitehouse.gov/the-press-office/2011/09/24/remarks-president-congressional-black-caucus-foundation-annual-phoenix-a.

Ogunnaike, Lola. "The Long-Awaited, Albeit Brief, Return of Dave Chappelle." *New York Times,* 6 Jul. 2006: n. pag. *Newspaper Source Plus.* Web. 25 Dec. 2012.

O'Hagan, Sean. "Colour Bind," *The Guardian* 15 Mar. 2003. Web. 21 Dec. 2012. http://www .guardian.co.uk/books/2003/mar/16/fiction.features.

Osucha, Eden. "The Whiteness of Privacy: Race, Media, Law." *Camera Obscura* 24.1 (2009): 67–107. Print.

Packer, ZZ. *Drinking Coffee Elsewhere*. New York: Riverhead, 2003. Print.

Padgett, J. Michael. "Horse Men: Centaurs and Satyrs in Early Greek Art." *The Centaur's Smile: The Human Animal in Early Greek Art*. Ed. J. Michael Padgett. New Haven, CT: Yale UP, 2003: 3–46. Print.

Page, Ruth E. "Feminist Narratology? Literary and Linguistic Perspectives on Gender and Narrativity." *Language and Literature* 12.1 (2003): 43–56. Print.

Palmeri, Frank. *Satire in Narrative: Petronius, Swift, Gibbon, Melville, & Pynchon*. Austin: U of Texas P, 1990. Print.

Parks, Suzan-Lori. "The Death of the Last Black Man in the Whole Entire World." In *The America Play and Other Works*. New York: Theatre Communications Group, 1995. 99–131. Print.

———. "An Equation for Black People Onstage." In *The America Play and Other Works*. New York: Theatre Communications Group, 1995. 19–22. Print.

———. "from Elements of Style." In *The America Play and Other Works*. New York: Theatre Communications Group, 1995. 6–18. Print.

———. "New black math." *Theatre Journal* 57.4 (2005): 576–583. Print.

———. "Possession." In *The America Play and Other Works*. New York: Theatre Communications Group, 1995. 3–5. Print.

"Pass the Torch." *In the Flow with Affion Crockett*. Writ. Affion Crockett, Jamie Foxx et al. Fox. 14 Aug. 2011. Television.

"The Passion of Reverend Ruckus." *The Boondocks: The Complete First Season*. Dir. Sean Song. Writ. Aaron McGruder, Rodney Barnes et al. Sony, 2006. DVD.

Pate, Alexs D. Foreword. In *The Cotillion, or, One Good Bull Is Half the Herd*. By John Killens. Minneapolis: Coffee House Press, 2002. ix–xxi. Print.

Patterson, Orlando. "The Post-Black Condition." *New York Times*, 22 Sep. 2011: n. pag. Web. 21 Dec. 2012. http://www.nytimes.com/2011/09/25/books/review/whos-afraid-of-post -blackness-by-toure-book-review.html.

———. *Slavery and Social Death: A Comparative Study*. Cambridge, MA: Harvard UP, 1982. Print.

The Perfect Holiday. Dir. Lance Rivera. Perf. Morris Chestnut, Gabrielle Union. Sony, 2008. DVD.

Petry, Ann. *The Street*. 1946. Boston: Houghton Mifflin, 1991. Print.

Phiddian, Robert. *Swift's Parody*. Cambridge: Cambridge UP, 1995. Print.

Piersen, William D. *Black Legacy: America's Hidden Heritage*. Amherst: U of Massachusetts P, 1993. Print.

"Pilot." *Key & Peele*. Writ. Keegan-Michael Key, Jordan Peele et al. Comedy Central. 31 Jan. 2012. Television.

Pootie Tang. Dir. Louis C. K. Perf. Lance Crouther, Wanda Sykes, Chris Rock. Paramount, 2001. DVD.

Post Brothers. "History Decays into Images, Not Stories: On the Work of Travis Somerville." In *Shift: Three Projects Constructing a New Dialogue about Race in America*. San Francisco: San Francisco Arts Commission Gallery, 2011. 60. Exhibition catalogue. Print.

Powell, Kevin. "Heaven Hell Dave Chappelle." *Esquire*, 30 Apr. 2006: n. pag. Web. 21 Dec. 2012. http://www.esquire.com/features/ESQ0506CHAPPELLE_92.

Prashad, Vijay. "Bruce Lee and the Anti-imperialism of Kung Fu: A Polycultural Adventure." *positions: east asia cultures critique* 11.1 (Spring 2003): 51–90. Print.

Proschan, Frank. "The Semiotic Study of Puppets, Masks, and Performing Objects." *Semiotica* 47 (1983): 3–44. Print.

Pryor, Richard. "Super Nigger—Richard Pryor." *Youtube.com*. 24 Jul. 2010. Web. 21 Dec. 2012. http://www.youtube.com/watch?v=coHWOdN7OTQ.

Queen Ifrica. "Mek mi Grow." *elyrics.net*. n.d. Web. 21 Dec. 2012. http://www.elyrics.net/read/q/queen-ifrica-lyrics/mek-mi-grow-lyrics.html.

Rambsy, Howard. "Shine 2.0: Huey Freeman as Contemporary Folk Hero." In *The Funk Era and Beyond: New Perspectives on Black Popular Culture*. Ed. Tony Bolden. New York: Palgrave Macmillan, 2008: 143–158. Print.

Reed, Ishmael. *Reckless Eyeballing*. New York: St. Martin's Press, 1986. Print.

Reichardt, Ulfried. "Time and the African-American Experience: The Problem of Chronocentrism." *Amerikastudien/American Studies* 45.4 (2000): 465–484. Print.

Reid, Mark A. *Black Lenses, Black Voices: African American Film Now*. Lanham, MD: Rowman & Littlefield, 2005. Print.

Reising, Russell. *Loose Ends: Closure and Crisis in the American Social Text*. Durham, NC: Duke UP, 1996. Print.

"The Return of the King." *The Boondocks: The Complete First Season*. Dir. Kalvin Lee. Writ. Aaron McGruder, Rodney Barnes et al. Sony, 2006. DVD.

Richards, David. "Seeking Bits of Identity in History's Vast Abyss." *New York Times*, 11 Mar. 1994: C3. Print.

Rock, Chris. *Bring the Pain*. Dir. Keith Truesdell. Dreamworks, 2002. DVD.

Rock, Michael. "The Battle for Blue." *Wired* 11.6 June (2003): 157. Print.

Rohlehr, Gordon. *Calypso and Society in Pre-Independence Trinidad*. Port of Spain, Trinidad and Tobago: Gordon Rohlehr, 1989. Print.

Rose, Tricia. *The Hip Hop Wars: What We Talk about When We Talk about Hip Hop—and Why It Matters*. New York: BasicCivitas, 2008. Print.

Rosenblatt, Roger. "Black Autobiography: Life as the Death Weapon." In *Autobiography: Essays Theoretical and Critical*. Ed. James Olney. Princeton, NJ: Princeton UP, 1980. 169–180. Print.

Ross, Fran. *Oreo*. Boston: Northeastern UP, 2000. Print.

Round, Julia. "Impersonating Hollywood: The Conflicting Identity Discourses of Charlie Murphy's 'True Hollywood Stories.'" In *The Comedy of Dave Chappelle: Critical Essays*. Ed. K. A. Wisniewski. Jefferson, NC: McFarland, 2009. 86–101. Print.

Rowell, Charles H. "'I Just Want to Keep Telling Stories': An Interview with George C. Wolfe." *Callaloo* 16 (1993): 602–623. Print.

Rubell Family. "Inside Our Process." In *30 Americans*. Ed. Juan Roselione-Valadez et al. Miami, FL: Rubell Family Collection, 2011. 6–7. Print.

Russell, Kathy, Midge Wilson, and Ronald Hall. *The Color Complex: The Politics of Skin Color among African Americans*. New York: Harcourt Brace Jovanovich, 1992. Print.

Russett, Margaret. "Race under *Erasure*: for Percival Everett, 'a piece of fiction.'" *Callaloo* 28 (2005): 358–368. Print.

Santo, Avi. "Of Niggas and Citizens: The Boondocks Fans and Differentiated Black American Politics." In *Satire TV: Politics and Comedy in the Post-Network Era*. Ed. Jonathan Gray, Jeffrey P. Jones, and Ethan Thompson. New York: New York UP, 2009: 252–273. Print.

Schuyler, George S. *Black No More: Being an Account of the Strange and Wonderful Workings of Science in the Land of the Free, A.D. 1933–1940*. 1931. Boston: Northeastern UP, 1989. Print.

Sekora, John. "Black Message/White Envelope: Genre, Authenticity, and Authority in the Antebellum Slave Narrative." *Callaloo* 10.3 (1987): 482–515. Print.

"SFR Live Concerts: De La Soul." *YouTube*. 19 Mar. 2012. Web. 21 Dec. 2012. http://www.youtube.com/watch?v=yHlC8SpvMi4.

Sharpe, Christina A. *Monstrous Intimacies: Making Post-Slavery Subjects*. Durham, NC: Duke UP, 2010. Print.

Sharpley-Whiting, T. Denean. *Pimps Up, Ho's Down: Hip Hop's Hold on Young Black Women*. New York: New York UP, 2007. Print.

"Sharpton Criticizes 'Boondocks' for Showing King Saying the N-Word." *USA Today*, 26 Jan. 2010: n. pag. Web. 21 Dec. 2012. http://usatoday30.usatoday.com/life/television/news/2006-01-25-sharpton-boondocks_x.htm.

Shavers, Rone. "Percival Everett." *Bomb* 88 (Summer 2004): 46–51. Print.

Sienkiewics, Matt, and Nick Marx. "Beyond a Cutout World: Ethnic Humor and Discursive Integration in South Park." *Journal of Film and Video* 61.2 (Summer 2009): 5–18. Print.

Silverstein, Marc. "'Any Baggage You Don't Claim, We Trash': Living With(in) History in *The Colored Museum*." *American Drama* 8 (1998): 95–121. Print.

Sirmans, Franklin. "Art Chronicle." In *30 Americans*. Ed. Juan Roselione-Valadez et al. Miami, FL: Rubell Family Collection, 2011. 40–45. Print.

Smith, Jeanne Rosier. *Writing Tricksters: Mythic Gambols in American Ethnic Literature*. Berkeley: U of California P, 1997. Print.

Smith, Moira. "Humor, Unlaughter, and Boundary Maintenance." *Journal of American Folklore* 122.484 (2009): 148–171. Print.

Smith, Robert C. *We Have No Leaders: African Americans in the Post–Civil Rights Era*. Albany: State U of New York P, 1996. Print.

Somerville, Travis. *Well Division*. Catherine Clark Gallery. Web. 21 Dec. 2012. http://cclarkgallery.com/artists/works/travis-somerville#slide4.

———. "Re: Question." Message to Michael Gillespie. 13 August 2012. E-mail.

Sragow. Michael. "Black Like Spike." In *Spike Lee Interviews*. Ed. Cynthia Fuchs. Jackson: UP of Mississippi, 2002. 189–198. Print.

Stallings, L. H. "Punked for Life: Paul Beatty's The White Boy Shuffle and Radical Masculinities." *African American Review* 43.1 (2009): 99–116. Print.

Staples, Brent. "Nicki Minaj Crashes Hip-Hop's Boys Club." *New York Times*, 8 July 2012: SR10. Print.

Stepto, Robert B. *From Behind the Veil: A Study of Afro-American Narrative.* Urbana: U of Illinois P, 1979. Print.

———. *A Home Elsewhere: Reading African American Classics in the Age of Obama.* Cambridge: Harvard UP, 2010. Print.

Strachan, Ian. *Paradise and Plantation: Tourism and Culture in the Anglophone Caribbean.* Charlottesville and London: U Virginia P, 2002. Print.

Stromberg, Fredrik. *Black Images in the Comics: A Visual History.* Seattle: Fantagraphics Books, 2003. Print.

Swerdlick, David. "*Boondocks*: Cosby's Younger, Hipper Son." *AlterNet,* Independent Media Institute. 27 Jul. 2006. Web. 21 Dec. 2012. http://www.alternet.org/story/39571/boondocks%3A_cosby%27s_younger%2C_hipper_son.

Tate, Greg. *Flyboy in the Buttermilk: Essays on Contemporary America.* New York: Simon and Schuster, 1992. Print.

———. "Introduction: Nigs R us, or Now Blackfolk Became Fetish Objects." In *Everything But the Burden: What White People Are Taking from Black Culture.* Ed. Greg Tate. New York: Broadway Books, 2003. 1–14. Print.

———. "Wherein Lies the Wealth of the World?" In *Passing/Posing: Paintings and Faux Chapel.* By Kehinde Wiley et al. New York: Distributed Art Publishers, 2005. n. pag. Print.

Taylor, Paul C. "Post Black, Old Black." *African American Review* 41.4 (Winter 2007): 625–640. Print.

Thomas, Mickalene. "Do you have your I.D.?: Conversation Between Artists Mickalene Thomas and Travis Somerville." *Travis Somerville: Dedicated to the Proposition . . .* Los Angeles: OTIS Ben Maltz Gallery, 2009. n. pag. Exhibition catalogue. Print.

Tillet, Salamishah. *Sites of Slavery: Citizenship and Racial Democracy in the Post–Civil Rights Imagination.* Durham, NC: Duke UP, 2012. Print.

Touré. "I Live in the Hiphop Nation." In *Never Drank the Kool-Aid.* By Touré. New York: Picador, 2006. 333–338. Print.

———. "It Was a Wonderful World." In *Never Drank the Kool-Aid.* By Touré. New York: Picador, 2006. 15–17. Print.

———. *Never Drank the Kool-Aid.* New York: Picador, 2006. Print.

———. *The Portable Promised Land.* Boston: Little, Brown, 2002. Print.

———. *Soul City.* New York: Picador, 2004. Print.

———. *Who's Afraid of Post-Blackness?: What It Means to Be Black Now.* New York: Free Press, 2011. Print.

———. "Why I Miss the Monoculture." *Salon.com.* 28 Sep. 2011. Web. 21 Dec. 2012. http://www.salon.com/2011/09/29/how_niches_killed_culture.

"The Trial of Robert Kelly." *The Boondocks: The Complete First Season.* Dir. Anthony Bell. Writ. Aaron McGruder, Rodney Barnes et al. Sony, 2006. DVD.

"The Uncle Ruckus Reality Show." *The Boondocks: The Complete Second Season.* Dir. Seung Eun Kim and Bob Hathcock. Writ. Aaron McGruder, Rodney Barnes et al. Sony, 2008. DVD.

Villalongo, William. "The Centaur's Kiss." Web. 21 Dec. 2012. http://williamvillalongo.com/artwork/436756_The_Centaur_s_Kiss.html.

———. "Re: Question." Message to Michael Gillespie. 18 June 2012. E-mail.

Walker, Alice. "From an Interview." In *In Search of Our Mothers' Gardens: Womanist Prose*. By Alice Walker. New York: Harcourt Brace, 1983. 244–272. Print.

———. "Saving the Life That Is Your Own: The Importance of Models in the Artist's Life." In *In Search of Our Mothers' Gardens: Womanist Prose*. By Alice Walker. New York: Harcourt Brace, 1983. 3–14. Print.

Walker, Verbal. "Little Brother 'Too Intelligent' for BET?" *HipHopDX*. 7 Sep. 2005. Web. 21 Dec. 2012. http://www.hiphopdx.com/index/news/id.3516/title. little-brother-too-intelligent-for-bet.

Wallace, Maurice O. *Constructing the Black Masculine: Identity and Ideality in African American Men's Literature and Culture, 1775–1995*. Durham, NC: Duke UP, 2002. Print.

Walters, Ronald W., and Robert C. Smith. *African American Leadership*. Albany: State U of New York P, 1999. Print.

Wang, Oliver. "Reading *The Boondocks*." *Peacework* (Summer 2001): n. pag. Web. 21 Dec. 2012. http://www.peaceworkmagazine.org/pwork/0107/010720.htm.

Warhol, Robyn R. *Gendered Interventions: Narrative Discourse in the Victorian Novel*. Columbus: Ohio State UP, 1989. Print.

Warren, Kenneth W. *What Was African American Literature?* Cambridge, MA: Harvard UP, 2011. Print.

Watkins, Mel, ed. *African American Humor: The Best Black Comedy from Slavery to Today*. Chicago: Lawrence Hill Books, 2002. Print.

Wattstax. Dir. Mel Stuart. Columbia Pictures, 1973. DVD.

Weisenberger, Steven. *Fables of Subversion: Satire and the American Novel, 1930–1980*. Athens: U of Georgia P, 1995. Print.

West, Cornel. *Race Matters*. New York: Beacon, 1993. Print.

White, Michelle-Lee et al. "Afrotech and Outer Spaces." *Art Journal* 60.3 (2001): 91–104. Print.

Whitehead, Colson. *Sag Harbor*. New York: Doubleday, 2009. Print.

Wiegman, Robyn. *American Anatomies: Theorizing Race and Gender*. Durham, NC: Duke UP, 1995. Print.

Williams, Dana A. "'I Love Myself When I'm Laughing and Then Again When I'm Looking Mean and Impressive': Humor, Irony, and Satire in African American Literature and Popular Culture." In *African American Humor, Irony, and Satire: Ishmael Reed, Satirically Speaking*. Ed. Dana A. Williams. Newcastle upon Tyne, UK: Cambridge Scholars, 2007. 1–6. Print.

Willis, Hank Thomas. "Basketball and Chain." 2003. Web. 21 Dec. 2012. http://hankwillistho mas.com/2011/Branded/4.

———. "Cotton Bowl." 2011. Web. 21 Dec. 2012. http://hankwillisthomas.com/2011/Strange -Fruit/2/.

———. "NBA Trade." 2004. Web. 21 Dec. 2012. http://hankwillisthomas.com/2011/Branded /15/.

Wilson, August. "The Ground on Which I Stand." *Callaloo* 20 (1998): 493–503. Print.

Wilson, Scott. *Great Satan's Rage: American Negativity and Rap/Metal in the Age of Supercapitalism*. Manchester, UK: Manchester UP, 2008. Print.

Witt, Doris. *Black Hunger: Food and Politics of U.S. Identity*. Oxford: Oxford UP, 1999. Print.

Wolfe, George C. *The Colored Museum*. New York: Broadway Play Publishing, 1987. Print.

Wright, Richard. *Black Boy: A Record of Childhood and Youth*. 1945. New York: Harper Perennial, 1998. Print.

———. *Native Son*. New York: HarperCollins, 1940. Print.

Yearwood, Gladstone Lloyd. *Black Film as a Signifying Practice: Cinema, Narration and the African American Aesthetic Tradition*. Trenton, NJ: Africa World Press, 2000. Print.

Zeinbau, Irene D. "Blackface: An Esthetic Appreciation of *Bamboozled*." *Cineasté* 26.2 (2001): 16–17. Print.

Contributors

Bertram D. Ashe is Associate Professor of English and American Studies at the University of Richmond in Virginia. He has published *From within the Frame: Storytelling in African-American Fiction* (Routledge, 2002) as well as essays on black hair, jazz, the black vernacular tradition, and post–Civil Rights Movement black culture ("post-blackness") in the collections *Signifyin(g), Sanctifyin' and Slam Dunking: A Reader in African American Expressive Culture* (University of Massachusetts Press, 1999); *Thriving on a Riff: Jazz and Blues Influences in African American Literature and Film* (Oxford University Press, 2009); *The Obama Effect: Multidisciplinary Renderings of the 2008 Campaign* (SUNY Press, 2010); and *Blackberries and Redbones: Critical Articulations of Black Hair/Body Politics in Africana Communities* (Hampton Press, 2010), respectively. He has also published in such journals as *Columbia*, *African American Review*, and *Race, Gender and Class*. He recently co-edited a special issue on the post-soul aesthetic for the *African American Review* and is at work on a memoir titled "Twisted: The Dreadlock Chronicles" as well as a scholarly book on post-blackness.

Thomas R. Britt is Assistant Professor in the Film and Video Studies program at George Mason University in Fairfax, Virginia. His primary areas of teaching and research include media ethics, genre studies, documentary filmmaking, and screenwriting. He is the director of the documentaries *Lost in Winesburg*, *Stewart Summer*, and *Unpredictable*. His essays have appeared in the journals *Bright Lights Film Journal*, *Americana*, and *Cinephile*, as well as edited book collections, such as *Southerners on Film: Essays on Hollywood Portrayals since the 1970s* (McFarland, 2011) and *Habitus of the Hood* (Intellect, 2012). He is also a staff writer, columnist, and interviewer for PopMatters, an international online magazine of cultural criticism.

Darryl Dickson-Carr is Associate Professor of English at Southern Methodist University, where he teaches courses in twentieth-century American literature, African American literature, and satire. His researches focus primarily upon the New Negro and the Harlem Renaissance, as well as African American satirical works in the twentieth and twenty-first centuries. He has published essays in such recent collections as *Contemporary African American Literature: The Living Canon* (Indiana University Press, 2013), *Literary Expressions of African Spirituality* (Lexington Books, 2013), *The Cambridge History of African American Literature* (Cambridge University Press, 2011), and *Ebony Rising: Short Fiction from the Greater Harlem Renaissance* (Indiana University Press, 2004). He has also published articles in *American Literary History*, *Nineteenth Century Prose*, *Studies in Contemporary Satire*, and *CLA Journal*. He has authored *The Columbia Guide to Contemporary African American*

Fiction (Columbia University Press, 2005), which won an American Book Award in 2006, and *African American Satire: The Sacredly Profane Novel* (University of Missouri Press, 2001). He recently completed the manuscript for his next book, titled "Spoofing the Modern: The Role of Satire in the Harlem Renaissance."

James J. Donahue is Associate Professor of English and Communication at SUNY Potsdam, where he teaches courses in twentieth-century and ethnic American literatures. His work has appeared or is forthcoming in *The Journal of Narrative Theory*, *Studies in American Indian Literatures*, and *The Midwest Quarterly*. His current research interests include ethnic literary studies and narrative theory.

Michael B. Gillespie is Assistant Professor of Film in the School of Interdisciplinary Arts, School of Film and Department of African American Studies at Ohio University. His teaching and research focus on film theory, black visual and expressive culture, historiography, global cinema, film adaptation, and genre theory. His recent publications include "Reckless Eyeballing: *Coonskin*, Film Blackness, and the Racial Grotesque" in *Black American Cinema Reconsidered* (Routledge, 2012) and "Smiling Faces: *Chameleon Street*, Racial Performativity, and Film Blackness" in "The Politics of Appearance: Racial Passing in U.S. Fiction, Memoir, Television, and Film, 1990–2010" (SUNY Press, forthcoming). He is completing a book titled "Film Blackness: American Cinema and the Idea of Black Film" and co-editing two volumes, "Black Cinema Aesthetics Revisited," with Akil Houston, and "New Chester Himes Criticism," with Gary Holcomb.

Gillian Johns is Associate Professor of English and Africana Studies at Oberlin College, where she has developed and teaches courses in such areas as the textualization of orality and literacy in contemporary African American fiction (primarily works by Ernest Gaines, Toni Morrison, and John Edgar Wideman), black detective fiction, modernist Chicago urban writers and sociological theory, the August Wilson century cycle, humor and irony in twentieth-century African American fiction, black women writers and the autotext, and critical race theory as a lens into classical American fiction. She has published critical articles on tall humor, irony, and the comic in Richard Wright's *Lawd Today* and Ralph Ellison's *Invisible Man*, as well as a book chapter on William Wells Brown's negotiations of audience in re-published versions of *Clotel and Clotelle*; she is currently working on articles examining essays and fiction by Zora Neale Hurston and John Edgar Wideman. She is also working on a monograph that uses cognitive linguistics to examine African American authors' study and deployment of contemporaneous rhetorical, linguistic, and speech act theories of language in their efforts to transform spoken black English into a literary language.

Luvena Kopp is a doctoral candidate in American Studies at the Goethe University in Frankfurt, Germany. Her main research interests include African American culture, with a particular focus on African American film and the concepts of figurational sociology, especially the works of Pierre Bourdieu and Norbert Elias. Her dissertation utilizes the concepts of figurational sociology to uncover invisible mechanisms of power in the films of Spike Lee.

In 2012 she spent a year on a Fulbright grant to New York University's Department of Social and Cultural Analysis and Tisch School of the Arts.

Jennifer Larson teaches literature, writing, and film at the University of North Carolina at Chapel Hill. She is the author of *Understanding Suzan-Lori Parks* (University of South Carolina Press, 2012) and the assistant editor of *Reading Contemporary African-American Drama: Fragments of History, Fragments of Self* (Peter Lang, 2007). Her work has also appeared in *Women's Studies* and the *South Carolina Review*.

Cameron Leader-Picone is Assistant Professor of English at Kansas State University, where he teaches classes in African American literature, cultural studies, and American literature. He received his PhD in African and African American Studies at Harvard University in 2009, served as a Sheila Biddle Ford Fellow at the W. E. B. Du Bois Institute at Harvard University, and taught in the English Department at Ithaca College before coming to Kansas State. He is currently working on a book project that analyzes twenty-first-century African American literature and literary movements. Drawing on scholarship across disciplines such as political science, philosophy, sociology, and law in addition to literary criticism, the book examines how contemporary aesthetics such as post-soul and post-blackness attempt to imagine new definitions of blackness while maintaining racial identity as a central category. The book argues that recent scholarship questioning the very category of African American literature illustrates a tension in contemporary African American literature between an emphasis on the continuity of a racialized history and tradition and the desire to explore and represent new ways of being black. His current research also focuses on President Barack Obama as a major symbolic and representational figure in African American literature and culture. In addition to contemporary African American literature and culture, Cameron has published research on popular fiction, including the gangster fiction of Donald Goines. His research interests include the interdisciplinary study of race and politics, hip-hop culture, African American satire, and popular culture representations of blackness.

Brandon Manning is a doctoral candidate in the Department of English at Ohio State University, where his research focuses on twentieth- and twenty-first-century African American literature and specifically the construction of alternative black masculinities in satirical narratives. He received his MA in English from Ohio State University and his BA in English from Jackson State University. He is currently a Bell Doctoral Fellow for The Todd A. Bell National Resource Center on the African American Male and participated in the National Endowment for the Humanities summer institute on African American Literature and Pedagogy. His dissertation, titled, "Laughing at My Manhood: Transgressive Black Masculinities in African American Satire," interrogates the claim that African American satire is a gendered form focusing on the experiences and perspectives of black men. He is interested in visual and literary satirical narratives at the turn of the millennium and their ability to undermine and dismantle the patriarchal/nationalistic black male iconography that the Civil Rights and Black Power Movements popularized and that the 1990s resurrected. He currently teaches classes on race, gender, and sexuality and their intersections in African

American literature and pop culture. His other research interests are black feminism, queer theory, and hip-hop.

Derek C. Maus is entering his third decade of scholarly inquiry into his strong suspicion that satire is among the sanest responses to a largely insane world. In addition to his interest in African American satire from the Harlem Renaissance through the present, he has also written extensively on the nature of humanistic, anti-ideological satire during the Cold War, most extensively in a study titled *Unvarnishing Reality: Subversive Russian and American Cold War Satire* (University of South Carolina Press, 2011). He has also published scholarly articles on the satirical aspect of fiction by a motley crew of writers that includes J. M. Coetzee, Nikolai Gogol, Walter Mosley, Flannery O'Connor, Thomas Pynchon, Leo Tolstoy, and Colson Whitehead and has no plans whatsoever to become tied down to any period, nationality, language, political orientation, or ethnicity in surveying the ways in which people laugh in the face of absurd and corrupt authority.

Marvin McAllister is Assistant Professor of English and African American Studies at the University of South Carolina at Columbia, specializing in African American and American theatre, drama, and performance. He has taught at Cleveland State University, Howard University, Hunter College, the City University of New York's Graduate Center, the College of William and Mary, the Catholic University of America, the University of California-Berkeley, and the University of California-Davis. Professionally, he has worked as a dramaturg or literary manager for theatre companies in New York; the Washington, D.C., area; Chicago; Cleveland; and Seattle. He has published two books on African American theatre and performance, both with the University of North Carolina Press: "*White People Do Not Know How To Behave at Entertainments Designed for Ladies and Gentlemen of Colour*": *William Brown's African and American Theater* (2003) and *Whiting Up: Whiteface Minstrels and Stage Europeans in African American Performance* (2011). He is currently researching and developing a visual history of theatrical production at Howard University from the early 1900s to the present.

Danielle Fuentes Morgan is a doctoral candidate in English literature at Cornell University. She received her BA in English with a minor in African American Studies from the University of North Carolina at Chapel Hill, her MA in Teaching from Duke University, and her MA in English from North Carolina State University. Her academic interests are twentieth- and twenty-first-century African American literature, nationalism, gender and sexuality, and popular culture. More specifically, she is concerned with issues surrounding the ways in which popular culture, satire, and the satirical function in shaping a gendered understanding of blackness in the twenty-first century. She has presented her work at the International Society for the Study of Narrative, the American Comparative Literature Association, and the South Atlantic Modern Language Association. Her recent essay, "Feeling is Believing: Why Obama's Hair Matters," was published online at *Racialicious*. She is obsessed with *The Twilight Zone* and reads most episodes as having clear racial commentary both despite and because of the physical lack of black people in the series. Currently, she is working on papers examining the mainstream infatuation with black bodies, particularly the commodification of black masculinity as demonstrated in the creation of the Tupac Shakur hologram, and the emergence of the exceptional woman of color in post-1960s Broadway musicals. She tweets sporadically—and almost entirely about popular culture—at @mos_daf and hails from Durham, North Carolina. She lives in Ithaca, New York, with her husband, Matt, and her daughter (and muse) Calliope Angela.

Derek Conrad Murray is an interdisciplinary theorist specializing in the history, theory, and criticism of contemporary art, particularly African American / African diasporic art and culture, post-black aesthetics, theoretical approaches to identity and representation, and the methodologies and ethics of art history and visual studies. Murray received a PhD in the History of Art from Cornell University in 2005 and is currently Assistant Professor in the History of Art and Visual Culture program at the University of California-Santa Cruz. He has contributed to such leading magazines and journals of contemporary art as *Art in America; Parachute; Art Journal; Exit EXPRESS;* the *Documenta 12 Magazine Project; Public Art Review, Third Text;* and *Nka: Journal of Contemporary African Art,* for which he currently serves as associate editor. He is currently completing his first book, titled "Regarding Difference: Contemporary African-American Art and the Politics of Recognition," which is forthcoming as part of Manchester University Press's Rethinking Art's Histories series.

Kinohi Nishikawa is Assistant Professor of English at the University of Notre Dame, where he specializes in African American literary and popular culture. His recently completed book manuscript traces the rise of black-authored pulp fiction by the likes of Iceberg Slim and Donald Goines from its material roots in postwar men's literature to its cultural influence on contemporary hip-hop. His next research project will examine the historic but overlooked contributions of black-owned bookshops to African American social and political life. His writing has appeared in the journals *PMLA, American Literature,* and *Book History.*

Keenan Norris is the author of the novel *Brother and the Dancer,* which won the 2012 James D. Houston Award and was published by Heyday Books in 2013. He holds an MFA from Mills College and a PhD from the University of California-Riverside. His research interests include urban literature and the publishing industry. He teaches English, African American Literature, and Basic Skills at Evergreen Valley College in San Jose, California. His work, both fiction and nonfiction, has appeared in numerous forums, including *Santa Monica Review; Green Mountains Review;* and *Evansville Review; Connotation Press; Inlandia: A Literary Journey through California's Inland Empire* (2006), an edited collection; and *BOOM: A Journal of California.* He is also the editor of Scarecrow Press's upcoming collection of critical essays, "Street Lit: Popularity, Controversy and Analysis." He lives in the San Francisco Bay area.

Christian Schmidt is Lecturer in American and Intercultural Anglophone Studies at the University of Bayreuth in Germany. After specializing in American Literature, Cultural Studies, and Political Science at the University of Erlangen-Nuremberg and at Harvard University, he was a doctoral fellow in the Research Training Group, "Cultural Hermeneutics: Perspectives on Difference and Transdifference," funded by the German Research

Foundation. Currently, he is finishing his PhD project, which analyzes contemporary African American fiction by Charles Johnson, Paul Beatty, Trey Ellis, Percival Everett, and others. The central argument of this project is that these authors contribute to formulating a post-black aesthetics that crucially reformulates the role of race in contemporary literature. His further research interests include contemporary music (especially jazz and country), narratology, and ethical theory. The central focus of his current research is the role of authenticity and the question of the "real thing" in contemporary black literature and country music.

Linda Furgerson Selzer is an Associate Professor of English at Pennsylvania State University at University Park. She is the author of *Charles Johnson in Context* (University of Massachusetts Press, 2009) and co-editor of *New Essays on the African American Novel* (Palgrave, 2008). Her work on African American literature and culture has appeared in a number of scholarly collections and in journals such as *African American Review, Callaloo, MELUS, Massachusetts Review*, and *Rhetoric Review*. In 2003 she received the Darwin Turner Award for the year's best essay in *African American Review*.

Terrence T. Tucker is currently Assistant Professor of English at the University of Memphis. His general study of African American literature focuses on post–civil rights African American literature and black popular culture, which he pursues in his book manuscript, "Furiously Funny: Comic Rage in Late Twentieth-Century African American Literature." His second book project traces the representation of the African American elite in African American literature from Frank J. Webb's *The Garies and Their Friends* (1857) to recent works like Stephen L. Carter's *The Emperor of Ocean Park* (2002) and Erica Kennedy's *Bling* (2004). He considers the unique position occupied by the African American middle and upper classes in a literary tradition that has focused primarily on the African American underclass. He has published work in journals including *Pedagogy* and *Southern Literary Journal* on such authors as Walter Mosley, Richard Wright, and Ernest Gaines. His work on black popular culture has led to book chapters on African American superheroes that examine the presence of blacks in the conventionally white area of comics, graphic novels, and comic strips. His interest in black popular literature resulted in a book chapter on Donald Goines's Kenyatta series, which anticipates the emergence of popular literary forms like "street lit." His interest in race and pedagogy, part of a broader concern with how we critically engage controversial issues in the classroom, has led to multiple articles on both the African American professor and African American literature in the predominantly white classroom.

Sam Vásquez is Associate Professor of English at Dartmouth College. Her research focuses on Caribbean, African American, and other African diasporic literatures. She is the author of *Humor in the Caribbean Literary Canon* (Palgrave Macmillan, 2012). She is also a published poet, and her critical work has appeared or is forthcoming in journals such as *Caribbean Quarterly, Meridians, Journal of West Indian Literature*, and *Small Axe*.

Aimee Zygmonski is an independent scholar writing and publishing from Santa Cruz, California. Her scholarly interests lie at the intersections of African American theatre and historical iconography with a focus on playwrights Kia Corthron and Lynn Nottage. Her published essays and reviews appear in the anthology *The Cambridge Companion to African American Theatre* (Cambridge University Press, 2013) and the periodicals *Theatre Journal* and *Theatre Research International*. She is the co-editor of the collection *Lynn Nottage: A Casebook*, forthcoming in 2014. Her new research theorizes on the performance of celebrity chefs and food bloggers. She is an active member of both of the theatre higher education professional organizations, the Association for Theatre in Higher Education (ATHE) and the American Society for Theatre Research (ASTR), and has served on the board of the ATHE's Black Theatre Association focus group and as an Associate Editor for ASTR Online. As a dramaturg, she has worked with directors Kyle Donnelly (*Joe Turner's Come and Gone*), playwright directors Robert O'Hara (*Good Breeding*), and Chay Yew (*Gum*), among others, and has directed students at University of California-San Diego, Virginia Commonwealth University, and various off-off Broadway venues in New York. She also worked for many New York and regional theatres in publicity and marketing. She holds a PhD from the University of California-San Diego, an MFA from Virginia Commonwealth University, and a BFA from Emerson College.

Index

Abel, Elizabeth, 79–80
Abrahams, Roger, 255, 266
Adams, Nick, 274
 Work: *Making Friends with Black People*, 274
Afrocentrism, xxii, 12
Afrofuturism, 80–83
Ahmed, Sara, 132
Alexander, Michelle, 214–15
Alex-Assensoh, Yvette, 138
Ali, Layla, 5
All in the Family (television program), 257
Amos and Andy (radio/television program), 164
Anderson, Benedict, 117
Anderson, Jabari, 69, 80–82, 84n15
 Work: *The Gullah Sci-Fi Mysteries*, 69–70, 80–83
Appiah, Kwame Anthony, 3–4, 12–13, 18
Armstrong, Louis, 102–3, 105–7
Ashe, Bertram D., xviii, 101, 102, 107–8, 108n2, 190, 193, 200n2, 233
Assensoh, Akwasi, 138
ayo, damali, 272, 276–77, 278
 Work: *How to Rent a Negro*, 272, 276–77

Baartman, Sarah, 262
Baker, Houston, 77, 145, 167
Bakhtin, Mikhail, 68–69, 83n2, 108, 129, 264–66, 268n12
Bal, Mieke, 153
Baldwin, James, xiv, 130, 225, 273
Baraka, Amiri (Le Roi Jones), xv
Barthes, Roland, 85, 88–91, 93, 97n7–8, 154
Basquiat, Jean-Michel, xiv, 9

Baucom, Ian, 69–70
Beatty, Paul, xii, xvii–xviii, xx–xxi, xxiiin2, 101, 109n3, 137–40, 143–49, 149n6, 151–53, 156–58, 160, 161n10, 174n5, 272, 278–79
 Works: *Hokum*, xii, xvii–xviii, xxiiin2; *Slumberland*, xxi, xxiiin2, 151–53, 156–58, 160, 161n10, 272, 278–79; *The White Boy Shuffle*, xxi, 101, 109n3, 138–40, 143–49, 149n6, 174n5, 272
Bell, Sean, 227n13
Bell, W. Kamau, 253
Bennett, Louise, 268n9
Bennu, Pierre, 69, 73–76, 84n8
 Work: *Black Moses Barbie*, 69–70, 73–76, 82–83
Bernstein, Robin, 71–72, 73
Bhabha, Homi, 219
Birth of a Nation (film), 262
Black Arts Movement (BAM), xv, xvi, 137, 175–76, 178–79, 188, 269
Black Entertainment Television (BET), 33, 40, 43
blackness: and authenticity, xiv, 4–5, 23, 24, 26–31, 38–41, 42–44, 47–52, 57, 58, 79–80, 93, 98–101, 102–8, 112–14, 115, 132, 154–56, 157, 159–60, 162, 164–65, 172–74, 176–77, 202–3, 207, 212n5, 217–24, 228, 232–33, 240, 243, 249, 258–62; and the Caribbean, xxiii, 255–57, 260–67, 267n2, 267n7; changing definition of, xii–xix, xx, xxiii, 4–21, 103–6, 111, 112–13, 154–60, 162–64, 172–73, 182, 184–88, 191–92, 211–12, 232–33, 234, 241, 269–71,

273–75; and class, 91, 92, 95, 162,
167–69, 178, 202–3, 204–6, 249–50;
and commercialization, xx, 3–7, 12,
16–18, 56–60, 61–66, 70–73, 89, 91,
110–11, 164–65, 216–17, 219–20, 256–
57, 259–60, 261–64; and community,
xxi, 125–26, 131–32, 133–36, 175–85,
255–56; consumption of, xxi, 6–7, 12,
16–18, 111–16, 117–22, 215–16, 224, 241,
258–59, 262; and embodiment, xxii,
69–73, 240–53, 275–77; and femininity, 13–17, 70–74, 176–77, 179–80, 193,
197–98, 202, 204–6, 207–8, 209–10,
238n8, 240, 242–43, 262–63, 268n11;
and feminism, xxi, 13–17, 125–28, 131,
148, 200n5, 279n3; and folklore, xxii,
70–75, 202–3, 207–8, 222, 236–37;
generational views on, xii, xv, xviii,
4–6, 7, 28–30, 34–37, 102, 106–8, 163–
64, 240–42, 269–71, 274–75; and history, 140–42, 143; and homophobia,
20–21, 37, 50, 228–29, 231–32, 263–64;
and leadership, xxi, 137–49, 175, 181–
88, 246–47, 252–53; and masculinity,
5, 17–18, 19–20, 40–41, 45–46, 50, 162,
164–71, 173, 174n2, 228, 230–33, 238n8,
240–41, 243, 250, 279n3; queering of,
6, 14–15, 17, 19–21, 148; and reading,
85–90, 91–96, 151–53, 165–68, 170,
175–77; representations of, xiv, xxi,
23–27, 29–33, 34–37, 56–58, 60–67,
70–78, 80–83, 84n18, 89–91, 98–101,
102–5, 112, 113–22, 129–30, 131–32,
138–39, 140–41, 142–46, 152–60,
162–68, 176–85, 190–91, 192–99,
202–12, 216–20, 224–25, 229–30,
231–33, 234–35, 237, 240, 242–44,
246–47, 249–50, 258, 260–61, 262–65,
269–70, 272, 276; and stereotypes,
xx, xxii, 10–11, 12–15, 26–27, 28, 31–33,
40–41, 45–46, 47–48, 52, 54, 70–75,
116, 117–18, 120, 123n6, 129, 146, 162,
164–65, 168–70, 190, 193–94, 197, 199,
202–6, 207, 209–12, 212n7, 214–19,

221–22, 224–25, 240, 244, 254, 258–60,
267n6; whiteness, in relation to, xviii,
12, 30, 35–37, 49–50, 75, 76–80, 117–18,
132–33, 162–64, 168–70, 171–72, 174n6,
176–78, 179–88, 189–92, 194–95, 203,
206, 216, 217, 218–20, 224, 240, 241,
242–43, 249–50, 258, 262
Black Power, 4, 5, 15, 32, 175–76, 178, 181–83,
186, 188
blaxploitation films, 13–14, 16, 58, 60, 231
"blaxploration" (Ashe), xix–xx, 101–8, 193,
233
Bogle, Donald, 225–26n1
Boondocks, The (comic strip), xx, 23–27, 30,
33–34, 36–37, 137–38
Boondocks, The (television program), xi,
xvi, xx, xxi, 23–37, 137–43, 145, 146–
49, 149n3–5, 238n6, 257, 278
    Episodes: "A Date with the Health
    Inspector," 27; "A Huey Freeman
    Christmas," 27; "The Itis," 28; "It's
    a Black President, Huey Freeman,"
    148–49; "Let's Nab Oprah," 35–36;
    "The Passion of Reverend Ruckus,"
    31–33; "The Return of the King,"
    34–35, 140–43, 147–48, 149n4–5;
    "The Trial of R. Kelly," 29; "The
    Uncle Ruckus Reality Show," 33
Bourdieu, Pierre, 215–16, 217–21, 224–25,
226n4–5, 226–27n9
Bow Wow (Shad Gregory Moss), 58
Bradford, Mark, 9
Brisco, Connie, 272
    Work: P. G. County, 272
Brooks, Daphne, xiii
Brown, Bill, 72
Brown, Iona Rozeal, 5, 9
Brown, Kimberly Nichele, 125, 129, 130
Brown, Sterling, 87, 89
Butler, Octavia, xiv

Cain, Herman, 184
Carpio, Glenda, xii–xiii, 68, 147, 196–97,
206, 214, 223, 240, 245, 255, 260

Cassuto, Leonard, 69

Catanese, Brandi Wilkins, 190–91

Chappelle, Dave, xvii, xxii–xxiii, 25, 29, 57, 64, 174n4, 228–38, 238n2, 238n7, 239n13–16, 241–44, 245–46, 247–50, 251, 253, 254–55, 256–62, 265, 266–67, 267n7–8, 275–76, 280n7; anxiety about success of *Chappelle's Show*, xvii, xxii, 57, 174n4, 245–46, 254–55, 275–76; as portrayed by Affion Crockett, 246

Chappelle's Show (television program), xvii, xxii–xxiii, 36, 57, 174n4, 228–38, 238n5–7, 238n10, 239n11, 239n13–16, 241–44, 248–50, 251, 254–55, 256–62, 265, 266–67, 267n6–8, 268n12, 275–76, 278, 280n7

    Skits: "*Chappelle's Show* Trading Spouses," 236, 242–43, 258–60, 262, 265, 267n6; "Charlie Murphy's True Hollywood Stories," 228–38, 238n7, 239n16, 275–76; "Frontline: Clayton Bigsby," 236, 239n11; "I Know Black People," 249–50, 251; "Inside *Chappelle's Show* Studio," 234; "The Mad Real World," 236; "Making the Band," 260–61, 266, 267n7, 268n12; "A Moment in the Life of Lil' Jon," 234; "The Niggar Family," 236, 238n10, 239n11; "The Playa Haters," 268n12; "Pretty White Girl Sings Dave's Thoughts," 239n15; "The Racial Draft," 239n11, 280n7; "Reparations 2003," 243; "R. Kelly's 'Piss on You' Videos," 234; "The World Series of Dice," 236; "Wu Tang Financial," 234

Charles, Michael Ray, 11–13

    Work: *(Forever Free) Tommy Hilnigguh*, 12

Cheney, Charise L., 54n3

Childish Gambino (Donald Glover), 39, 47–51, 52, 54

    Albums: *Camp*, 47; *Culdesac*, 47–50

    Songs: "The Last," 48–50; "Put It in My Video," 47–48

Christian, Barbara, 127

Civil Rights Movement, xvi, 5, 23, 28, 29, 32, 33, 35, 78–80, 102, 138–49, 175, 214, 269

C.K., Louis, 57

    Film: *Pootie Tang*, 57–59, 60–61, 62–64

Clinton, George, xiv–xv, xviii–xix, xxiii. *See also* Funkadelic

Colbert Report, The (television program), 22

Coleman, Ornette, xiv

Colescott, Robert, 6, 9, 10

Combahee River Collective, 127–28, 131

Community (television program), 50–51

Cosby, Bill, 25, 35–36

Crockett, Affion, xxii, 241–42, 244–46, 247–48, 250–51, 253

"cultural mulatto" (Ellis), xiv, xix, 28–29, 161n8, 185–86, 269–70, 271

Daily Show with Jon Stewart, The (television program), 22, 257, 278

Dance, Daryl Cumber, 255

Davis, Miles, xiv, 102

De La Soul, 51–53, 54, 55n8–9

    Albums: *De La Soul Is Dead*, 52; *First Serve*, 52; *3 Feet High and Rising*, 51–52

    Songs: "Me Myself and I," 51; "Move 'Em In, Move 'Em Out," 53; "Must B the Music," 52–53; "Pop Life," 53; "Pushing Aside, Pushing Along," 52

Delcita and Shebada, 261

Delue, Rachael, 218, 219, 220–22

Derrida, Jacques, 161n5

Diallo, Amadou, 227n13

Dickson-Carr, Darryl, xii, xiv, xv–xvi, 12, 15, 21, 59, 108n2, 116, 125–26, 139, 152, 198, 201, 216–17, 228–29, 230–31, 235, 254–55

Doonesbury (comic strip), 25

Du Bois, W. E. B., 6, 7, 29, 76, 96n1, 137, 146, 149n6, 214, 219; and double consciousness, 6, 76, 219

duCille, Anne, 74, 276

Dyson, Michael Eric, xiv, 100

Ebert, Roger, 217

Edwards, Erica, 140, 143, 145

Elam, Harry J., 195, 197-98

Elliott, Missy, 101

Ellis, Ian "Ity," 261-67

Ellis, Trey, xii-xv, xviii, xxi, xxii, 28-29, 101, 108n2, 125, 129, 130, 131, 133, 161n8, 185-86, 190, 200n2, 229-30, 269-71, 273, 274-75, 277-79

Works: "The New Black Aesthetic," xii-xv, 28-29, 108n2, 161n8, 185-86, 190, 200n2, 229-30, 269-71, 273, 274-75, 277-78; Platitudes, xxi, 101, 125, 130, 278

Ellison, Ralph, xiv, 37, 54, 68, 89, 95, 106-7, 119-20, 153, 155, 157-58, 165, 169, 186, 215, 218, 222, 224, 225-26n1, 227n14-15, 272-73, 277, 279n2

Works: "Change the Joke and Slip the Yoke," 222; "An Extravagance of Laughter," 215, 219; Invisible Man, 54, 89, 106-7, 119-20, 155, 157-58, 165, 169, 186, 215, 218, 219, 227n14-15, 277

Eshun, Kodwo, 82

Evans, Patrice, xi-xii, xiii-xiv, xvi, xvii, xxii, xxiii

Everett, Percival, xii, xx-xxi, xxiiin1, 85-97, 101, 129-30, 131, 133, 151-56, 157, 158-60, 160n1, 161n2-3, 161n9, 161n11, 162-70, 172, 173-74, 236, 271-72, 273, 274, 278

Works: Erasure, xxi, xxiiin1, 85-86, 88-97, 101, 129-30, 151-56, 157, 158, 160, 161n9, 162-70, 172, 173-74, 271, 273, 274, 278; Glyph, 236; God's Country, 236; A History of the African-American People [Proposed] by Strom Thurmond. As Told to Percival

Everett and James Kincaid, xxi, 151-53, 158-60, 160n1, 161n3, 161n11, 271; I Am Not Sidney Poitier, 161n2, 271; "Signing to the Blind," 85, 89

Farrakhan, Louis, 20, 41, 54n3

Favor, J. Martin, 26, 28-30

Fey, Tina, 49-50

Foxx, Jamie, 244

Foxx, Redd, 257

Freestyle (art exhibition), xx, 4, 6-7, 8-9, 13

Frye, Northrop, 116

Fuller, Hoyt, 180

Funkadelic, xviii-xix

Album: One Nation Under a Groove, xix

Song: "Mommy, What's a Funkadelic?," xviii-xix

Garvey, Marcus, 137

Gates, Henry Louis, Jr., 87, 96n5, 106, 203

George, Nelson, xv, xviii, xxii, 108n2

Gilroy, Paul, 38, 54n1, 212n5

Golden, Thelma, xx, xxii, 4, 6, 8, 13, 100, 108n2, 161n4

Green, Renée, 9

Gregory, Dick, 25, 249, 257

Griffin, Dustin, 150

Griffith, D. W., 262

Gubar, Susan, 216-17

Guerrero, Ed, 222

Haggins, Bambi, xii-xiii, 56-57, 210, 239n12, 241, 243, 245

Hammons, David, xv, 6

Hannaham, James, 69, 70-73

Work: "Napkin Ring," 69-73, 76, 82-83

Hansberry, Lorraine, 193, 197

Work: Raisin in the Sun, 193, 197

Hardware, Alton "Fancy Cat," 261-67

Harlem Renaissance, xiv, xv, xvi, 89, 269-70

Harris, Michael D., 13

Harris, Trudier, 134

Harrison, Anthony Kwame, 54n2

Hartman, Saidiya, 222
Heading South (film), 267n5
Heller, Joseph, 186
    Work: *Catch-22*, 186
Help, The (film), 226n1
Hendricks, Barkley L., 9
Hendrix, Jimi, xiv, 120–21
Highet, Gilbert, 222–23
hip-hop, xx, xxi, 17, 25, 27, 38–54, 57, 58,
    61–63, 111–14, 156, 163–64, 168–69,
    172–73, 221, 227n12, 250–51
Hopkinson, Natalie, xvi
Howe, Irving, 272–73, 279n2
How Stella Got Her Groove Back (film),
    267n5
Hughes, Langston, xii, xiv, 270, 276
    Works: "The Negro Artist and the
    Racial Mountain," 270; "Simple" sto-
    ries, xiv
Hume, Kathryn, 125, 129
Hunter, Tera, 274
Hurricane Katrina, 192
Hurston, Zora Neale, xiv, 86, 88, 96n6, 162,
    165
    Works: *Moses, Man of the Mountain*,
    86, 96n6; "What White Publishers
    Won't Print," 162
Hyde, Lewis, 206–7

Ice Cube (O'Shea Jackson), 54n3, 58
In Living Color (television program), 244,
    275
In the Flow (television program), 241,
    244–46, 250–51
Ity and Fancy Cat (television program),
    xxiii, 257, 261–67, 267n2, 268n12,
    268n14
    Skits: "The After Life," 263–64; "The
    Bigga Shopping Show," 262–63,
    264–65, 266; "2 Fortune Cookie to
    Go," 264

Jackson, Jesse, xvii, 32
Jackson, Samuel L., 36, 59

James, Darius, 101, 109n3, 272
    Work: *Negrophobia: An Urban Parable*,
    101, 109n3, 272
James, Rick, xxii, 36, 228–35, 237, 238n7,
    275; as depicted by Dave Chappelle,
    228–35, 237, 238n7, 275
Jay-Z (Shawn Corey Carter), 42, 49–50, 61,
    63, 234
Jeffersons, The (television program), 257
Johnson, Charles, 24
Johnson, E. Patrick, 212n5
Johnson, Mat, xxii, 101, 175, 182–88, 272–73,
    278
    Works: *Hunting in Harlem*, xxii, 101,
    175, 182–88, 272–73; *Pym*, 272
Johnson, Rashid, 9
Johnson, William H., 14
Jones, Jacquie, 66
Jones, Joni L. (Omi Osun Olomo), 242
Jones, Lisa, 108n2, 274
Jordan, Jennifer, 137, 139, 148
Juvenal, 277

Kaiser, Ernest, 188
Kelley, William Melvin, xvi
Kennedy, Adrienne, 198, 200n5
Kernan, Alvin P., 222
Key, Keegan-Michael, xxii, 241–42, 246–48,
    251–53
Key & Peele (television program), xxii,
    241–42, 246–48, 251–53, 278
Killens, John Oliver, xvi, xxii, 175–83, 185,
    186, 187–88
    Work: *The Cotillion*, xxii, 175–83, 185,
    186, 187–88
Kincaid, James, 158–60, 160n1, 161n3
King, Geoff, 61
King, Martin Luther, Jr., xxi, 34–35, 138,
    139–40, 175, 246–47; as fictional
    character, 34–35, 138, 139–49, 149n6
Knight, Charles, 131, 150

Lanser, Susan, 126–28, 131
Lee, Robert E., 76; as fictional character, 76

Lee, Spike, xxii, 12–13, 44, 59, 72, 216–25, 226n2, 226n5–8, 226–27n9, 227n10–15, 272, 274
   Films: *Bamboozled*, xxii, 12–13, 44, 72, 216–25, 226n2, 226n5–8, 226–27n9, 227n10–15, 272; *Do the Right Thing*, 59; *Joe's Bed-Stuy Barbershop: We Cut Heads*, 226n7

Levine, Lawrence W., 255

Lewis, Theophilus, 240–42, 243–44, 246, 248, 251, 253

Lichtenstein, Roy, 80

Ligon, Glenn, xiii, xx, xxii, 4, 9, 18–21, 100
   Works: *Hands*, 19–21; *Untitled (Malcolm X)*, 18–19

Lil' Kim (Kimberly Denise Jones), 101

Lincoln, Abraham, 78

Linzy, Kalup, 5, 9

Little Brother, 39, 43–46, 51, 54, 55n5
   Albums: *The Listening*, 43–44; *The Minstrel Show*, 43–46, 52
   Songs: "Cheatin'," 55n5; "Not Enough," 45; "Say It Again," 45–46

Locke, Alain, xvi, 87, 269

Lott, Eric, 274

Lubiano, Wahneema, 204

Mabley, Jackie "Moms," 243

Major, Clarence, xv

Malcolm X, 18–19, 168, 246–47

Manet, Edouard, 16

Mansbach, Adam, xvii, xxi, 162–64, 168–74
   Works: *Angry Black White Boy*, xvii, xxi, 162–64, 168–74; "The Audacity of Racism," 169

Marc, David, 257, 261

Marsalis, Wynton, 274

Marshall, Kerry James, 9, 14

Marx, Nick, 256, 267n3

Massood, Paula, 222

McAllister, Marvin, 242, 243

McGruder, Aaron, xi, xvi, xx, 23–37, 137–43, 145, 146–49, 149n4

McMillan, Terry, 273
   Work: *Waiting to Exhale*, 273

Mercer, Kobena, 6–7, 82, 83n2

Mezei, Kathy, 126

Mighty Casey (Casey Gane-McGalla), 39–43, 51, 52, 54, 54n4
   Songs: "Black Rapping School," 40, 42–43; "White Girls," 40–42

Mills, Charles W., 215

minstrelsy, xxii, 12, 31, 36, 43–46, 57, 79, 193–94, 215–16, 220–21, 222–24, 226n2, 227n10, 235, 240–47; and blackface, 31, 36, 43–46, 56, 79, 194, 215–16, 220–21, 222–24, 240–41, 262; satirical inversion of, through whiteface, 222, 242–44, 258, 262

Mohammed, Patricia, 268n11

Molière (Jean-Baptiste Poquelin), 247–48

Monk, Thelonious, xiv

Mooney, Paul, 25, 226n8

Morgan, Marcyliena, 54n2

Morris, Linda A., 229

Morrison, Toni, xv, 83n2, 128, 163, 173, 186
   Work: *Playing in the Dark*, 83n2, 128, 163, 173

Moten, Fred, 75–76

MTV (television network), 43, 110–14, 260

Murphy, Charlie, xx, 36, 58, 61, 228–38, 238n8, 239n16

Murphy, Eddie, 25, 257, 274

Nama, Adilifu, 82, 84n18

Neal, Larry, xvi, 178–79

Neal, Mark Anthony, xv, xxiii, 84n8, 108n2, 139, 145–46

"New Black Aesthetic" (Ellis), xii–xv, xxii, 28–29, 161n8, 185–86, 190, 200n2, 269–71, 273, 274, 279; "cultural mulatto" as component of, xiv, xix, 28–29, 161n8, 185–86, 200n2, 269–70, 271, 273, 279

New Jack City (film), 174n1

Newkirk, Kori, 5

Newsome, Rashad, 5

Ngai, Sianne, 70
Nicki Minaj (Onika Tanya Maraj), 101
Norman, Larry, 247–48
Notorious B.I.G., The (Christopher Wallace), 57, 112–13, 123n4, 174n1
Nottage, Lynn, xxii, 201–12, 212n2
    Works: *By the Way, Meet Vera Stark*, xxii, 201, 207–12; *Fabulation*, xxii, 201–7, 208, 211–12, 212n2
Nussbaum, Felicity, 130–31

Obama, Barack, xvi, 23, 28, 34, 78, 80, 96n1, 148–49, 175, 184, 252–53, 270, 274, 278–79
O'Neill, Eugene, 114
Osucha, Eden, 72

Packer, ZZ, xxi, 126, 131–36
    Works: "Brownies," xxi, 126, 131–36; *Drinking Coffee Elsewhere*, 131–32
Parks, Suzan-Lori, xxii, 189–200, 200n1, 200n3–4
    Essays: "An Equation for Black People on Stage," 191–93; "from Elements of Style," 195–96, 198–99; "New black math," 192, 196; "Possession," 200n1
    Plays: *The America Play*, 189; *The Death of the Last Black Man in the Whole Entire World*, 189, 193–200; *Getting Mother's Body*, 189; *Imperceptible Mutabilities in the Third Kingdom*, 189, 200n4; *Topdog/Underdog*, 189; *Venus*, 189
parody, 22–24, 25–27, 29–36, 42–43, 44–46, 48–54, 55n5, 61–62, 70–72, 73–74, 76–77, 80–83, 85, 89–94, 140–41, 142–43, 146, 150–52, 153–56, 158–60, 164–67, 168–73, 190, 193–95, 196–98, 199, 207–12, 216, 218, 220–22, 224–25, 230–37, 242–43, 244–45, 246–47, 249–50, 252–53, 258–61, 262–63, 264, 271–72, 276–77
Pate, Alexs D., 175–76, 272
    Work: *The Multicultiboho Sideshow*, 272

Patterson, Orlando, 220
P. Diddy (Sean Combs), 61, 62–63, 234, 260
Peele, Jordan, xxii, 241–42, 246–48, 251–53
Perry, Tyler, xi
Piersen, William, 248
Pope.L, William, xvii, 9
"post-blackness" (Golden and Ligon), xii, xx, 4–21, 100, 108n2, 111, 121, 161n4, 233, 245–46
"post-soul": as aesthetic, xv, xvii, xviii, 100–108, 108n2, 162–64, 167, 170–72, 190, 193, 200n2, 228, 233, 238, 241, 270–72; and "blaxploration," xix–xx, 101–8, 193, 233; as generational discourse, xii, xv, xviii, 56–57, 113, 121–22, 163, 238, 241, 270–72
Prince, xiv, xxii, 36, 228–29, 231–35, 237, 238n8–9, 239n14; as depicted by Dave Chappelle, 228–29, 231–35, 237
Pryor, Richard, xiv–xv, 23, 25, 36–37, 57, 75, 102, 119, 219, 226n8, 240, 243, 245, 257

Queen Latifah (Dana Elaine Owens), 58, 59, 101

Rabelais, François, 69
Rae, Issa, 174n5
    Work: *The Mis-Adventures of Awkward Black Girl*, 174n5
race: and commodifcation, xx, xxii, 5, 7, 10–15, 17–18, 38–42, 44–45, 46–48, 51–53, 66–67, 70–73, 165, 174n1, 227n12, 240–43, 249–50, 258–59, 272–73, 275–79; and history, 69–83, 127, 138–49, 156–59, 174n6, 175–76, 180–81, 182, 184–85, 186–88, 200n1, 225–26n1, 246–47; and representation, xxi, xxiii, 5–7, 10–21, 35–37, 70–83, 129–30, 131–36, 163–72, 242–43, 244–46, 249–53, 258–61, 262, 264–65; and transnationalism, 255–57, 260–63, 264–65, 266–67, 267n1, 268n10

Rambsy, Howard, 147

Reagan, Ronald, as fictional character, 31–33

Reed, Ishmael, xii, xv, xvi, 23, 119–20, 125, 128, 129, 131, 137, 174n5, 272, 274, 279n3

Works: *Mumbo Jumbo*, 174n5; *Reckless Eyeballing*, 125, 128, 272

Reichardt, Ulfried, 223

Rivera, Lance, 57

Film: *The Perfect Holiday*, 57–60, 61–63, 64–65, 66–67

R. Kelly (Robert Kelly), 29, 55n5, 234

Rock, Chris, 23, 25, 36–37, 43, 54n4, 58, 60, 257

Rohlehr, Gordon, 264, 268n13

Rose, Tricia, 39

Rosenblatt, Roger, 172

Russell, Kathy, 238n8

Saar, Bettye, 6, 10–11

Work: *The Liberation of Aunt Jemima*, 10–11

Samuels, Oliver, 261

Santo, Avi, 141–42, 147–48, 259

satire: and "comic rage," xx, 22–24, 25, 27, 29, 32, 34–37; in comics, 24, 80–82, 137–38; degenerative mode of, 139, 148, 150–60; and distinctive characteristics of post-soul variety, xiii–xix, 100–108, 190, 193, 200n2, 241, 270–72, 274, 277–78; in drama, xxii, 189–213, 240–41, 247–48; in fiction, xx–xxii, 85–86, 89–97, 98–99, 101–8, 110–24, 125–26, 129–36, 137–38, 139, 143–49, 151–60, 162–74, 175–85, 186–88, 271–72, 273–74, 278–79; in film, xx, xxii, 56–67, 73–76, 216–25; Horatian mode, xiii, 228, 230, 233, 247; Juvenalian mode, xiv, 228, 233, 242, 246; and music, xx, 38–55, 114–16, 120–22, 156–58; need for, in African American community, xi–xii, xvi, xvii, xxiii, 23, 85, 88, 100–101, 128–29, 151–52, 166, 172, 175–76, 188, 242, 248,

253, 263–64; and new media, 73–76, 276–77; and "racial grotesque," xx, 68–83, 265; resistance to, within African American community, xi, xvi–xviii, 9–15, 18; slavery as theme in, xx, 10–11, 13, 65–66, 70–79, 81–82, 89, 205, 209–10, 212n7, 220, 222, 229, 234–36; in television, xxi, xxii–xxiii, 137–38, 139–43, 148, 228–38, 241–47, 249–53, 254, 256–67, 275–76, 278; in visual art, xiii, xx, 4–21, 70–73, 76–80; and women, xxi, 13–17, 70–76, 125, 131, 176–78, 179–80, 189–90, 191–95, 196–200, 202–12, 268n14, 272

Saturday Night Live (television program), 257

Schuyler, George, xii, xiv, 86, 88, 119, 137, 174n5, 212n3

Work: *Black No More*, xiv, 86, 119, 137, 174n5, 212n3

Sekora, John, 87, 93

Shakur, Tupac, 57, 123n4, 174n1

Shange, Ntozake, 193, 197, 198, 200n5

Work: *For Colored Girls who Have Considered Suicide When the Rainbow is Enuf*, 193, 197

Sharpton, Al, 35, 140, 149n3

Shepherd, Eli G., xi

Sienkiewics, Matt, 256, 267n3

Silverstein, Marc, 191, 197

Simone, Nina, xiv

Simpson, Lorna, 9

Simpsons, The (television program), 257

Sirmans, Franklin, 6

slavery, as satirical theme, xx, 10–11, 13, 65–66, 70–79, 81–82, 89, 205, 209–10, 212n7, 220, 222, 229, 234–36

Smith, Jeanne Rosier, 201

Smith, Moira, 132–33, 203–4

Smith, Robert C., 138, 139

Snoop Dogg (Calvin Broadus, Jr.), 174n1

Somerville, Travis, 69, 78–80, 84n14

Work: *Well Division*, 69–70, 78–80, 82–83

South Park (television program), 257,
     267n3, 278
Stallings, L. H., 145, 148
Starsky and Hutch (television program/
     film), 174n1
Stepto, Robert, 85, 86, 96n1
Stetson, Jeff, 246
Stone, Sly, xiv
Strachan, Ian, 258–59, 267n6
Swerdlick, David, 34–36
Swift, Jonathan, 185, 212n1
Sykes, Wanda, 60, 253

Tate, Greg, xii, 7–8, 17–18, 108n2, 227n12
Taylor, Paul C., xii
30 Americans (art exhibition), 6, 9, 15, 17, 18
Thomas, Hank Willis, xiii, 280n7
Thomas, Mickalene, 5, 13–17
     Works: *Hotter Than July,* 13–15; *Sista Sista
     Lady Blue, From Odalisque,* 16–17
Thurman, Wallace, xii, xiv, 137
     Works: *The Blacker the Berry,* xiv; *The
     Infants of Spring,* xiv, 137
Thurston, Baratunde, 100, 212n3
     Work: *How to Be Black,* 100, 212n3
Tillet, Salamishah, 72–73
Totally Biased (television program), 253
Touré, xiv–xv, xx, 4, 21n1, 98–124, 224, 233,
     239n11, 245–46
     Works: *Never Drank the Kool-Aid,*
     112–15, 122, 123n2–3; *The Portable
     Promised Land,* xxi, 98–109, 110,
     123n7; *Soul City,* xxi, 109n4, 110–24;
     Who's Afraid of Post-Blackness?, xiv–
     xv, xxi, 4, 21n1, 98–101, 104, 106–8,
     108n1, 110, 111, 121, 224, 233, 239n11,
     245–46; "Why I Miss the Monocul-
     ture," 110–11, 112, 113–14, 121
Townsend, Robert, 29, 42
     Film: *Hollywood Shuffle,* 42
T-Pain (Faheem Rasheed Najm), 58
trickster figures, xviii, xxii, xxiiin2, 201–12
Trudeau, Garry, 25

Tubman, Harriet, 73–76; as fictional char-
     acter, 73–76
Tyree, Omar, 273, 274

Villalongo, William, 69, 76–78
     Work: *The Centaur's Kiss,* 69–70, 76–78,
     82–83

Walker, Alice, 164, 274, 277, 278, 279n3
     Work: *The Color Purple,* 164, 279n3
Walker, Kara, xiii, 9, 10–11, 13
Wallace, Maurice O., 165, 169
Ward, Douglas Turner, xvi
Warhol, Robyn R., 128–29
Warren, Kenneth, 273–75
Watkins, Mel, 210, 255
Wayans, Damon, 218, 244
Wayans, Keenan Ivory, 29, 244
Weems, Carrie Mae, 9
Weisenburger, Steven, 139, 146, 148, 150–53,
     159
West, Cornel, 144, 149n5
White, Erik, 57
     Film: *Lottery Ticket,* 57–61, 62–63,
     65–67
Whitehead, Colson, xix, 236, 278
     Works: *John Henry Days,* 236; *Sag Har-
     bor,* xix
whiteness, xviii, 12, 30, 35–37, 49–50, 75,
     76–80, 117–18, 132–33, 162–64, 168–70,
     171–72, 174n6, 176–78, 179–88, 189–92,
     194–95, 203, 206, 216, 217, 218–20, 224,
     240, 241, 242–43, 249–50, 258, 262
Whitman, Walt, 212n2
Wideman, John Edgar, xv
Wiegman, Robyn, 230
Wiley, Kehinde, 5, 9, 17–18
     Work: *Passing/Posing, Three Graces,* 17
Williams, Dana, xii–xiii, 198
Wilson, August, 28, 192
Wilson, Scott, 57
Wolfe, George C., xiii, xxii, 189–98, 200,
     200n2, 272, 274

Work: *The Colored Museum*, 189–98,
200, 272
Wright, Richard, 89, 96n2, 153, 154, 164,
169–70, 193, 197, 199, 272–73
Work: *Native Son*, 89, 91, 96n2, 154, 164,
169–70, 193, 197, 199

Yearwood, Gladstone, 60–61

CPSIA information can be obtained
at www.ICGtesting.com
Printed in the USA
BVHW070406220120
570129BV00001B/138